# Richard Henry Dana, Jr.

# TWO YEARS BEFORE THE MAST
## A PERSONAL NARRATIVE

"Housed on the wild sea, with wild usages"

### With an Afterword by
# WRIGHT MORRIS

A SIGNET CLASSIC

SIGNET CLASSIC
Published by the Penguin Group
Penguin Books USA Inc., 375 Hudson Street,
New York, New York 10014, U.S.A.
Penguin Books Ltd, 27 Wrights Lane,
London W8 5TZ, England
Penguin Books Australia Ltd, Ringwood,
Victoria, Australia
Penguin Books Canada Ltd, 10 Alcorn Avenue,
Toronto, Ontario, Canada M4V 3B2
Penguin Books (N.Z.) Ltd, 182–190 Wairau Road,
Auckland 10, New Zealand

Penguin Books Ltd, Registered Offices:
Harmondsworth, Middlesex, England

Published by Signet Classic, an imprint of Dutton Signet,
a division of Penguin Books USA Inc.

First Signet Classic Printing, May, 1964
18  17  16  15  14  13  12

Afterword copyright © 1964 by New American Library,
a division of Penguin Books USA Inc.
All rights reserved

Illustrations on pp. 372-375 courtesy of Houghton, Mifflin Company.

Ⓒ REGISTERED TRADEMARK—MARCA REGISTRADA

Printed in the United States of America

## PREFACE TO NEW EDITION

After twenty-eight years, the copyright of this book has reverted to me. In presenting the first "author's edition" to the public, I have been encouraged to add an account of a visit to the old scenes, made twenty-four years after, together with notices of the subsequent story and fate of the vessels, and of some of the persons with whom the reader is made acquainted.

R. H. D., JR.

BOSTON, May 6, 1869

# CONTENTS

# CHAPTER I

The fourteenth of August was the day fixed upon for the sailing of the brig *Pilgrim*, on her voyage from Boston, round Cape Horn, to the western coast of North America. As she was to get under way early in the afternoon, I made my appearance on board at twelve o'clock, in full sea rig, with my chest, containing an outfit for a two or three years' voyage, which I had undertaken from a determination to cure, if possible, by an entire change of life, and by a long absence from books, with a plenty of hard work, plain food, and open air, a weakness of the eyes, which had obliged me to give up my studies, and which no medical aid seemed likely to remedy.

The change from the tight frock coat, silk cap, and kid gloves of an undergraduate at Harvard, to the loose duck trousers, checked shirt, and tarpaulin hat of a sailor, though somewhat of a transformation, was soon made; and I supposed that I should pass very well for a jack-tar. But it is impossible to deceive the practiced eye in these matters; and while I thought myself to be looking as salt as Neptune himself, I was, no doubt, known for a landsman by everyone on board as soon as I hove in sight. A sailor has a peculiar cut to his clothes, and a way of wearing them, which a green hand can never get. The trousers, tight round the hips and thence hanging long and loose round the feet, a superabundance of checked shirt, a low-crowned, well-varnished black hat, worn on the back of the head, with half a fathom of black ribbon hanging over the left eye, and a slip tie to the black silk neckerchief, with sundry other minutiae, are signs the want of which betrays the beginner at once. Besides the points in my dress which were out of the way, doubtless my complexion and hands were quite enough to distinguish me from the reg-

9

ular "salt," who, with a sunburned cheek, wide step, and rolling gait, swings his bronzed and toughened hands athwartships, half opened, as though just ready to grasp a rope.

"With all my imperfections on my head," I joined the crew, and we hauled out into the stream, and came to anchor for the night. The next day we were employed in preparation for sea, reeving studding-sail gear, crossing royal yards, putting on chafing gear, and taking on board our powder. On the following night, I stood my first watch. I remained awake nearly all the first part of the night from fear that I might not hear when I was called; and when I went on deck, so great were my ideas of the importance of my trust that I walked regularly fore and aft the whole length of the vessel, looking out over the bows and taffrail at each turn, and was not a little surprised at the coolness of the old seaman whom I called to take my place, in stowing himself snugly away under the longboat for a nap. That was a sufficient lookout, he thought, for a fine night, at anchor in a safe harbor.

The next morning was Saturday, and, a breeze having sprung up from the southward, we took a pilot on board, hove up our anchor, and began beating down the bay. I took leave of those of my friends who came to see me off, and had barely opportunity for a last look at the city and well-known objects, as no time is allowed on board ship for sentiment. As we drew down into the lower harbor, we found the wind ahead in the bay, and were obliged to come to anchor in the roads. We remained there through the day and a part of the night. My watch began at eleven o'clock at night, and I received orders to call the captain if the wind came out from the westward. About midnight the wind became fair, and, having summoned the captain, I was ordered to call all hands. How I accomplished this I do not know, but I am quite sure that I did not give the true hoarse boatswain call of "A-a-ll ha-a-a-nds! Up anchor, a-ho-oy!" In a short time everyone was in motion, the sails loosed, the yards braced, and we began to heave up the anchor, which was our last hold upon Yankee land. I could take but small part in these preparations. My little knowledge of a vessel was all at fault. Unintelligible orders were so rapidly given, and so immediately executed; there was such a hurrying about, and such an intermingling of strange cries and stranger actions, that I was completely bewildered. There is not so helpless and pitiable an object in the world as a landsman beginning a sailor's life. At length those peculiar, long-drawn sounds which denote that the crew are heaving at the windlass began, and in a few minutes we were under way. The noise of the water thrown from the bows was heard, the vessel leaned over from the damp night breeze, and rolled with the heavy ground swell, and we had actually begun our long, long journey. This was literally bidding good night to my native land.

# CHAPTER  II

The first day we passed at sea was Sunday. As we were just from port, and there was a great deal to be done on board, we were kept at work all day, and at night the watches were set, and everything was put into sea order. When we were called aft to be divided into watches, I had a good specimen of the manner of a sea captain. After the division had been made, he gave a short characteristic speech, walking the quarterdeck with a cigar in his mouth, and dropping the words out between the puffs.

"Now, my men, we have begun a long voyage. If we get along well together, we shall have a comfortable time; if we don't, we shall have hell afloat. All you have got to do is to obey your orders, and do your duty like men—then you will fare well enough; if you don't, you will fare hard enough, I can tell you. If we pull together, you will find me a clever fellow; if we don't, you will find me a bloody rascal. That's all I've got to say. Go below, the larboard * watch!"

* Of late years, the British and American marine, naval and mercantile, have adopted the word "port" instead of "larboard," in all cases on board ship, to avoid mistake from similarity of sound. At this time "port" was used only at the helm.

I, being in the starboard or second mate's watch, had the opportunity of keeping the first watch at sea. Stimson, a young man making, like myself, his first voyage, was in the same watch, and as he was the son of a professional man, and had been in a merchant's counting room in Boston, we found that we had some acquaintances and topics in common. We talked these matters over—Boston, what our friends were probably doing, our voyage, &c.—until he went to take his turn at the lookout, and left me to myself. I had now a good opportunity for reflection. I felt for the first time the perfect silence of the sea. The officer was walking the quarterdeck, where I had no right to go, one or two men were talking on the forecastle, whom I had little inclination to join, so that I was left open to the full impression of everything about me. However much I was affected by the beauty of the sea, the bright stars, and the clouds driven swiftly over them, I could not but remember that I was separating myself from all the social and intellectual enjoyments of life. Yet, strange as it may seem, I did then and afterward take pleasure in these reflections, hoping by them to prevent my becoming insensible to the value of what I was losing.

But all my dreams were soon put to flight by an order from the officer to trim the yards, as the wind was getting ahead; and I could plainly see by the looks the sailors occasionally cast to windward, and by the dark clouds that were fast coming up, that we had bad weather to prepare for, and I had heard the captain say that he expected to be in the Gulf Stream by twelve o'clock. In a few minutes eight bells were struck, the watch called, and we went below. I now began to feel the first discomforts of a sailor's life. The steerage, in which I lived, was filled with coils of rigging, spare sails, old junk, and ship stores, which had not been stowed away. Moreover, there had been no berths put up for us to sleep in, and we were not allowed to drive nails to hang our clothes upon. The sea, too, had risen, the vessel was rolling heavily, and everything was pitched about in grand confusion. There was a complete "hurrah's nest," as the sailors say, "everything on top and nothing at hand." A large hawser had been coiled away on my chest; my hats, boots, mattress, and blankets had all fetched away and gone over to leeward, and were jammed and broken under the boxes and coils of rigging. To crown all, we were allowed no light to find anything with, and I was just beginning to feel strong symptoms of seasickness, and that listlessness and inactivity which accompany it. Giving up all attempts to collect my things together, I lay down on the sails, expecting every moment to hear the cry, "All hands ahoy!" which the approaching storm would make necessary. I shortly heard the raindrops falling on deck thick and fast, and the watch evidently had their hands full of work, for I could hear the loud and repeated orders of the mate, trampling of feet, creaking of the blocks, and all the accompaniments of a coming storm. In a few minutes the slide of the hatch was thrown back, which let down the noise and tumult of the deck still louder, the cry of "All hands ahoy! Tumble up here and take in sail," saluted our ears, and the hatch was quickly shut again. When I got upon deck, a new scene and a new experience was before me.

The little brig was close-hauled upon the wind, and lying over, as it then seemed to me, nearly upon her beam ends. The heavy head sea was beating against her bows with the noise and force almost of a sledgehammer, and flying over the deck, drenching us completely through. The topsail halyards had been let go, and the great sails were filling out and backing against the masts with a noise like thunder; the wind was whistling through the rigging; loose ropes were flying about; loud and, to me, unintelligible orders constantly given, and rapidly executed; and the sailors "singing out" at the ropes in their hoarse and peculiar strains.

In addition to all this, I had not got my "sea legs on," was dreadfully seasick, with hardly strength enough to hold on to anything, and it was "pitch dark." This was my condition when I was ordered aloft, for the first time, to reef topsails.

How I got along, I cannot now remember. I "laid out" on the yards and held on with all my strength. I could not have been of much service, for I remember having been sick several times before I left the topsail yard, making wild vomits into the black night, to leeward. Soon all was snug aloft, and we were again allowed to go below. This I did not consider much of a favor, for the confusion of everything below, and that inexpressible sickening smell caused by the shaking up of bilge water in the hold, made the steerage but an indifferent refuge from the cold, wet decks. I had often read of the nautical experiences of others, but I felt as though there could be none worse than mine; for, in addition to every other evil,

I could not but remember that this was only the first night of a two years' voyage. When we were on deck, we were not much better off, for we were continually ordered about by the officer, who said that it was good for us to be in motion. Yet anything was better than the horrible state of things below. I remember very well going to the hatchway and putting my head down, when I was oppressed by nausea, and always being relieved immediately. It was an effectual emetic.

This state of things continued for two days.

*Wednesday, August 20th.* We had the watch on deck from four till eight this morning. When we came on deck at four o'clock, we found things much changed for the better. The sea and wind had gone down, and the stars were out bright. I experienced a corresponding change in my feelings, yet continued extremely weak from my sickness. I stood in the waist on the weather side, watching the gradual breaking of the day, and the first streaks of the early light. Much has been said of the sunrise at sea; but it will not compare with the sunrise on shore. It lacks the accompaniments of the songs of birds, the awakening hum of humanity, and the glancing of the first beams upon trees, hills, spires, and housetops, to give it life and spirit. There is no scenery. But, although the actual rise of the sun at sea is not so beautiful, yet nothing will compare for melancholy and dreariness with the early breaking of day upon "Old Ocean's gray and melancholy waste."

There is something in the first gray streaks stretching along the eastern horizon and throwing an indistinct light upon the face of the deep, which combines with the boundlessness and unknown depth of the sea around, and gives one a feeling of loneliness, of dread, and of melancholy foreboding, which nothing else in nature can. This gradually passes away as the light grows brighter, and when the sun comes up, the ordinary monotonous sea day begins.

From such reflections as these, I was aroused by the order from the officer: "Forward there! Rig the head pump!" I found that no time was allowed for daydreaming, but that we must "turn to" at the first light. Having called up the "idlers," namely, carpenter, cook, and steward, and rigged the pump, we began washing down the decks. This operation, which is performed every morning at sea, takes nearly two hours; and I had hardly strength enough to get through it. After we had

finished, swabbed down decks, and coiled up the rigging, I
sat on the spars, waiting for seven bells, which was the signal
for breakfast. The officer, seeing my lazy posture, ordered me
to slush the mainmast, from the royal masthead down. The
vessel was then rolling a little, and I had taken no food for
three days, so that I felt tempted to tell him that I had rather
wait till after breakfast; but I knew that I must "take the
bull by the horns," and that if I showed any sign of want of
spirit or backwardness, I should be ruined at once. So I took
my bucket of grease and climbed up to the royal masthead.
Here the rocking of the vessel, which increases the higher
you go from the foot of the mast, which is the fulcrum of the
lever, and the smell of the grease, which offended my fastidious senses, upset my stomach again, and I was not a little
rejoiced when I had finished my job and got upon the comparative *terra firma* of the deck. In a few minutes seven bells
were struck, the log hove, the watch called, and we went to
breakfast. Here I cannot but remember the advice of the
cook, a simplehearted African. "Now," says he, "my lad,
you are well cleaned out; you haven't got a drop of your
longshore 'swash' aboard of you. You must begin on a new
tack—pitch all your sweetmeats overboard, and turn to upon
good hearty salt beef and ship bread, and I'll promise you,
you'll have your ribs well sheathed, and be as hearty as any
of 'em, afore you are up to the Horn." This would be good
advice to give to passengers, when they set their hearts on the
little niceties which they have laid in, in case of seasickness.

I cannot describe the change which half a pound of cold
salt beef and a biscuit or two produced in me. I was a new
being. Having a watch below until noon, so that I had some
time to myself, I got a huge piece of strong, cold salt beef
from the cook, and kept gnawing upon it until twelve o'clock.
When we went on deck, I felt somewhat like a man, and
could begin to learn my sea duty with considerable spirit.
At about two o'clock, we heard the loud cry of "Sail ho!" from
aloft, and soon saw two sails to windward, going directly
athwart our hawse. This was the first time that I had seen a
sail at sea. I thought then, and have always since, that no
sight exceeds it in interest, and few in beauty. They passed
to leeward of us, and out of hailing distance; but the captain
could read the names on their sterns with the glass. They were

the ship *Helen Mar*, of New York, and the brig *Mermaid*, of Boston. They were both steering westward, and were bound in for our "dear native land."

*Thursday, August 21st.* This day the sun rose clear; we had a fine wind, and everything was bright and cheerful. I had now got my sea legs on, and was beginning to enter upon the regular duties of a sea life. About six bells, that is, three o'clock P.M., we saw a sail on our larboard bow. I was very desirous, like every new sailor, to speak her. She came down to us, backed her main topsail, and the two vessels stood "head on," bowing and curveting at each other like a couple of war horses reined in by their riders. It was the first vessel that I had seen near, and I was surprised to find how much she rolled and pitched in so quiet a sea. She plunged her head into the sea, and then, her stern settling gradually down, her huge bows rose up, showing the bright copper, and her stem and breasthooks dripping, like old Neptune's locks, with the brine. Her decks were filled with passengers, who had come up at the cry of "Sail ho!" and who, by their dress and features, appeared to be Swiss and French emigrants. She hailed us at first in French, but receiving no answer, she tried us in English. She was the ship *La Carolina*, from Havre, for New York. We desired her to report the brig *Pilgrim*, from Boston, for the northwest coast of America, five days out. She then filled away and left us to plow on through our waste of waters.

There is a settled routine for hailing ships at sea: "Ship a-hoy!" Answer: "Hulloa!" "What ship is that, pray?" "The ship *Carolina*, from Havre, bound to New York. Where are you from?" "The brig *Pilgrim*, from Boston, bound to the coast of California, five days out." Unless there is leisure, or something special to say, this form is not much varied from.

This day ended pleasantly; we had got into regular and comfortable weather, and into that routine of sea life which is only broken by a storm, a sail, or the sight of land.

# CHAPTER III

As we have now had a long "spell" of fine weather, without any incident to break the monotony of our lives, I may have no better place for a description of the duties, regulations, and customs of an American merchantman, of which ours was a fair specimen.

The captain, in the first place, is lord paramount. He stands no watch, comes and goes when he pleases, is accountable to no one, and must be obeyed in everything, without a question even from his chief officer. He has the power to turn his officers off duty, and even to break them and make them do duty as sailors in the forecastle.* Where there are no passengers and no supercargo, as in our vessel, he has no companion but his own dignity, and few pleasures, unless he differs from most of his kind, beyond the consciousness of possessing supreme power, and, occasionally, the exercise of it.

The prime minister, the official organ, and the active and superintending officer is the chief mate. He is first lieutenant, boatswain, sailing master, and quartermaster. The captain tells him what he wishes to have done, and leaves to him the care of overseeing, of allotting the work, and also the responsibility of its being well done. *The* mate (as he is always called, *par excellence*) also keeps the logbook, for which he is responsible to the owners and insurers, and has the charge of the stowage, safekeeping, and delivery of the cargo. He is also, *ex officio*, the wit of the crew; for the captain does not condescend to joke with the men, and the second mate no one cares for; so that when "the mate" thinks fit to entertain "the people" with a coarse joke or a little practical wit, everyone feels bound to laugh.

The second mate's is proverbially a dog's berth. He is neither officer nor man. He is obliged to go aloft to reef and furl the topsails, and to put his hands into the tar and slush, with the rest, and the men do not much respect him as an officer. The crew call him the "sailor's waiter," as he has to furnish them with spun yarn, marline, and all other stuffs that they need in their work, and has charge of the boatswain's locker, which includes serving boards, marlinespikes, &c., &c.

* There is a doubt of his power to do the latter.

17

He is expected by the captain to maintain his dignity and to enforce obedience, and still is kept at a great distance from the mate, and obliged to work with the crew. He is one to whom little is given and of whom much is required. His wages are usually double those of a common sailor, and he eats and sleeps in the cabin; but he is obliged to be on deck nearly all his time, and eats at the second table, that is, makes a meal out of what the captain and chief mate leave.

The steward is the captain's servant, and has charge of the pantry, from which everyone, even the mate himself, is excluded. These distinctions usually find him an enemy in the mate, who does not like to have anyone on board who is not entirely under his control; the crew do not consider him as one of their number, so he is left to the mercy of the captain.

The cook, whose title is "Doctor," is the patron of the crew, and those who are in his favor can get their wet mittens and stockings dried, or light their pipes at the galley in the night watch. These two worthies, together with the carpenter (and sailmaker, if there be one), stand no watch, but, being employed all day, are allowed to "sleep in" at night, unless all hands are called.

The crew are divided into two divisions, as equally as may be, called the watches. Of these, the chief mate commands the larboard, and the second mate the starboard. They divide the time between them, being on and off duty, or, as it is called, on deck and below, every other four hours. The three night watches are called the first, the middle, and the morning watch. If, for instance, the chief mate with the larboard watch have the first night watch from eight to twelve, at that hour the starboard watch and the second mate take the deck, while the larboard watch and the first mate go below until four in the morning, when they come on deck again and remain until eight. As the larboard watch will have been on deck eight hours out of twelve, while the starboard watch will have been up only four hours, the former have what is called a "forenoon watch below," that is, from 8 A.M. till 12 noon. In a man-of-war, and in some merchantmen, this alternation of watches is kept up throughout the twenty-four hours, which is called having "watch and watch"; but our ship, like most merchantmen, had "all hands" from twelve o'clock till dark, except in very bad weather, when we were allowed "watch and watch."

An explanation of the "dog watches" may perhaps be necessary to one who has never been at sea. Their purpose is to shift the watches each night, so that the same watch shall not be on deck at the same hours throughout a voyage. In order to effect this, the watch from 4 to 8 P.M. is divided into two half watches, one from 4 to 6, and the other from 6 to 8. By this means they divide the twenty-four hours into seven watches instead of six, and thus shift the hours every night. As the dog watches come during twilight, after the day's work is done, and before the night watch is set, they are the watches in which everybody is on deck. The captain is up, walking on the weather side of the quarterdeck, the chief mate on the lee side, and the second mate about the weather gangway. The steward has finished his work in the cabin, and has come up to smoke his pipe with the cook in the galley. The crew are sitting on the windlass or lying on the forecastle, smoking, singing, or telling long yarns. At eight o'clock eight bells are struck, the log is hove, the watch set, the wheel relieved, the galley shut up, and the watch off duty goes below.

The morning begins with the watch on deck's "turning to" at daybreak and washing down, scrubbing, and swabbing the decks. This, together with filling the "scuttle butt" with fresh water, and coiling up the rigging, usually occupies the time until seven bells (half after seven), when all hands get breakfast. At eight the day's work begins, and lasts until sundown, with the exception of an hour for dinner.

Before I end my explanations, it may be well to define a "day's work," and to correct a mistake prevalent among landsmen about a sailor's life. Nothing is more common than to hear people say, "Are not sailors very idle at sea? What can they find to do?" This is a natural mistake, and, being frequently made, is one which every sailor feels interested in having corrected. In the first place, then, the discipline of the ship requires every man to be at work upon *something* when he is on deck, except at night and on Sundays. At all other times you will never see a man, on board a well-ordered vessel, standing idle on deck, sitting down, or leaning over the side. It is the officers' duty to keep everyone at work, even if there is nothing to be done but to scrape the rust from the chain cables. In no state prison are the convicts more regularly set to work, and more closely watched. No conversation is allowed among the crew at their duty, and though they frequently do talk when aloft, or when near one another, yet they stop when an officer is nigh.

With regard to the work upon which the men are put, it is a matter which probably would not be understood by one who has not been at sea. When I first left port, and found that we were kept regularly employed for a week or two, I supposed that we were getting the vessel into sea trim, and that it would soon be over, and we should have nothing to do but to sail the ship; but I found that it continued so for two years, and at the end of the two years there was as much to be done as ever. As has often been said, a ship is like a lady's watch, always out of repair. When first leaving port, studding-sail gear is to be rove, all the running rigging to be examined, that which is unfit for use to be got down, and new rigging rove in its place; then the standing rigging is to be overhauled, replaced, and repaired in a thousand different ways; and wherever any of the numberless ropes or the yards are chafing or wearing upon it, there "chafing gear," as it is called, must be put on. This chafing gear consists of worming, parceling, roundings, battens, and service of all kinds—rope yarns, spun yarn, marline, and seizing stuffs. Taking off, putting on, and mending the chafing gear alone, upon a vessel, would find constant employment for a man or two men, during working hours, for a whole voyage.

The next point to be considered is that all the "small stuffs" which are used on board a ship—such as spun yarn, marline, seizing stuff, &c., &c.—are made on board. The owners of a vessel buy up incredible quantities of "old junk," which the sailors unlay, and, after drawing out the yarns, knot them together, and roll them up in balls. These "rope yarns" are constantly used for various purposes, but the greater part is manufactured into spun yarn. For this purpose, every vessel is furnished with a "spun-yarn winch," which is very simple, consisting of a wheel and spindle. This may be heard constantly going on deck in pleasant weather; and we had employment, during a great part of the time, for three hands, in drawing and knotting yarns, and making spun yarn.

Another method of employing the crew is "setting up" rigging. Whenever any of the standing rigging becomes slack (which is continually happening), the seizings and coverings must be taken off, tackles got up, and, after the rigging is boused well taut, the seizings and coverings be replaced, which is a very nice piece of work. There is also such a connection between different parts of a vessel, that one rope can seldom be touched without requiring a change in another. You cannot stay a mast aft by the back stays, without slacking up the head stays, &c., &c. If we add to this all the tarring, greasing, oiling, varnishing, painting, scraping, and scrubbing which is required in the course of a long voyage, and also remember this is all to be done in *addition to* watching at night, steering, reefing, furling, bracing, making and setting sail, and pulling, hauling, and climbing in every direction, one will hardly ask, "What can a sailor find to do at sea?"

If, after all this labor—after exposing their lives and limbs in storms, wet and cold,

> "Wherein the cub-drawn bear would couch,
> The lion and the belly-pinched wolf
> Keep their furs dry"—

the merchants and captains think that the sailors have not earned their twelve dollars a month (out of which they clothe themselves), and their salt beef and hard bread; they keep them picking oakum—*ad infinitum.* This is the usual resource upon a rainy day, for then it will not do to work upon rigging; and when it is pouring down in floods, instead of letting the sailors stand about in sheltered places, and talk, and keep themselves comfortable, they are separated to different parts of the ship and kept at work picking oakum. I have seen oakum stuff placed about in different parts of the ship, so that the sailors might not be idle in the snatches between the frequent squalls upon crossing the equator. Some officers have been so driven to find work for the crew in a ship ready for sea, that they have set them to pounding the anchors (often done) and scraping the chain cables. The "Philadelphia Catechism" is:

> "Six days shalt thou labor and do all thou art able,
> And on the seventh, holystone the decks and scrape the cable."

This kind of work, of course, is not kept up off Cape Horn, Cape of Good Hope, and in extreme north and south latitudes; but I have seen the decks washed down and scrubbed when the water would have frozen if it had been fresh, and all hands kept at work upon the rigging, when we had on our pea jackets, and our hands so numb that we could hardly hold our marlinespikes.

I have here gone out of my narrative course in order that any who read this may, at the start, form as correct an idea of a sailor's life and duty as possible. I have done it in this place because, for some time, our life was nothing but the unvarying repetition of these duties, which can be better described together. Before leaving this description, however, I would state, in order to show landsmen how little they know of the nature of a ship, that a ship carpenter is kept constantly employed, during good weather, on board vessels which are in what is called perfect sea order.

# CHAPTER IV

After speaking the *Carolina*, on the twenty-first of August, nothing occurred to break the monotony of our life until—

*Friday, September 5th*, when we saw a sail on our weather (starboard) beam. She proved to be a brig under English colors, and, passing under our stern, reported herself as forty-nine days from Buenos Aires, bound to Liverpool. Before she had passed us, "Sail ho!" was cried again, and we made another sail, broad on our weather bow, and steering athwart our hawse. She passed out of hail, but we made her out to be a hermaphrodite brig, with Brazilian colors in her main rigging. By her course, she must have been bound from Brazil to the south of Europe, probably Portugal.

*Sunday, September 7th.* Fell in with the northeast trade winds. This morning we caught our first dolphin, which I was very eager to see. I was disappointed in the colors of this fish when dying. They were certainly very beautiful, but not equal to what has been said of them. They are too indistinct. To do the fish justice, there is nothing more beautiful than the dolphin when swimming a few feet below the surface, on a bright day. It is the most elegantly formed, and also the quickest, fish in salt water; and the rays of the sun striking upon it, in its rapid and changing motions, reflected from the water, make it look like a stray beam from a rainbow.

This day was spent like all pleasant Sundays at sea. The decks are washed down, the rigging coiled up, and everything put in order; and, throughout the day, only one watch is kept on deck at a time. The men are all dressed in their best white duck trousers, and red or checked shirts, and have nothing to do but to make the necessary changes in the sails. They employ themselves in reading, talking, smoking, and mending their clothes. If the weather is pleasant, they bring their work and their books upon deck, and sit down upon the forecastle and windlass. This is the only day on which these privileges are allowed them. When Monday comes, they put on their tarry trousers again, and prepare for six days of labor.

To enhance the value of Sunday to the crew, they are allowed on that day a pudding, or, as it is called, a "duff." This is nothing more than flour boiled with water, and eaten with molasses. It is very heavy, dark, and clammy, yet it is looked upon as a luxury, and really forms an agreeable variety with salt beef and pork. Many a rascally captain has made up with his crew for hard usage by allowing them duff twice a week on the passage home.

On board some vessels Sunday is made a day of instruction and of religious exercises; but we had a crew of swearers, from the captain to the smallest boy; and a day of rest, and of something like quiet, social enjoyment, was all that we could expect.

We continued running large before the northeast trade winds for several days, until—

*Monday, September 22nd,* when, upon coming on deck at seven bells in the morning, we found the other watch aloft throwing water upon the sails; and, looking astern, we saw a small clipper-built brig with a black hull heading directly after us. We went to work immediately, and put all the canvas upon the brig which we could get upon her, rigging out oars for extra studding-sail yards, and continued wetting down the sails by buckets of water whipped up to the masthead, until about nine o'clock, when there came on a drizzling rain. The vessel continued in pursuit, changing her course as we changed ours, to keep before the wind. The captain, who watched her with his glass, said that she was armed, and full of men, and showed no colors. We continued running dead before the wind, knowing that we sailed better so, and that clippers are fastest on the wind. We had also another advantage. The wind was light, and we spread more canvas than she did, having royals and skysails fore and aft, and ten studding sails; while she, being a hermaphrodite brig, had only a gaff topsail aft. Early in the morning she was overhauling us a little, but after the rain came on and the wind grew lighter, we began to leave her astern. All hands remained on deck throughout the day, and we got our firearms in order; but we were too few to have done anything with her, if she had proved to be what we feared. Fortunately there was no moon, and the night which followed was exceedingly dark, so that, by putting out all the lights on board and altering our course four points, we hoped to get out of her reach. We removed the light in the binnacle, and steered by the stars, and kept perfect silence through the night. At daybreak there was no sign of anything in the horizon, and we kept the vessel off to her course.

*Wednesday, October 1st.* Crossed the equator in lon. 24° 24' W. I now, for the first time, felt at liberty, according to the old usage, to call myself a son of Neptune, and was very glad to be able to claim the title without the disagreeable initiation which so many have to go through. After once crossing the line, you can never be subjected to the process, but are considered as a son of Neptune, with full powers to play tricks upon others. This ancient custom is now seldom allowed, unless there are passengers on board, in which case there is always a good deal of sport.

It had been obvious to all hands for some time that the second mate, whose name was Foster, was an idle, careless fellow, and not much of a sailor, and that the captain was exceedingly dissatisfied with him. The power of the captain in these cases was well known, and we all anticipated a difficulty. Foster (called "Mister" by virtue of his office) was but half a sailor, having always been on short voyages, and remained at home a long time between them. His father was a man of some property, and intended to have given his son a liberal education; but he, being idle and worthless, was sent off to sea, and succeeded no better there; for, unlike many scamps, he had none of the qualities of a sailor—he was "not of the stuff that they make sailors of." He used to hold long yarns with the crew, and talk against the captain, and play with the boys, and relax discipline in every way. This kind of conduct always makes the captain suspicious, and is never pleasant, in the end, to the men, they preferring to have an officer active, vigilant, and distant as may be with kindness. Among other bad practices, he frequently slept on his watch, and, having been discovered asleep by the captain, he was told that he would be turned off duty if he did it again. To prevent his sleeping on deck, the hencoops were ordered to be knocked up, for the captain never sat down on deck himself, and never permitted an officer to do so.

The second night after crossing the equator, we had the watch from eight till twelve, and it was "my helm" for the last two hours. There had been light squalls through the night, and the captain told Mr. Foster, who commanded our watch, to keep a bright lookout. Soon after I came to the helm, I found that he was quite drowsy, and at last he stretched himself on the companion and went fast asleep. Soon afterward the captain came softly on deck, and stood by me for some time, looking at the compass. The officer at length became aware of the captain's presence, but, pretending not to know it, began humming and whistling to himself, to show that he was not asleep, and went forward, without looking behind him, and ordered the main royal to be loosed. On turning round to come aft, he pretended surprise at seeing the master on deck. This would not do. The captain was too "wide awake" for him, and, beginning upon him at once, gave him a grand blowup, in true nautical style: "You're a lazy, good-for-nothing rascal; you're neither man, boy, 'soger,' nor sailor! You're no more than a *thing* aboard a vessel! You don't earn your salt! You're worse than a 'Mahon soger'!" and other still more choice extracts from the sailor's vocabulary. After the poor fellow had taken this harangue, he was sent into his stateroom, and the captain stood the rest of the watch himself.

At seven bells in the morning, all hands were called aft,

and told that Foster was no longer an officer on board, and
that we might choose one of our own number for second
mate. It is not uncommon for the captain to make this offer,
and it is good policy, for the crew think themselves the
choosers, and are flattered by it, but have to obey, neverthe-
less. Our crew, as is usual, refused to take the responsibility
of choosing a man of whom we would never be able to complain, and left it to the captain. He picked out an active and
intelligent young sailor, born on the banks of the Kennebec,
who had been several Canton voyages, and proclaimed him in
the following manner: "I choose Jim Hall; he's your second
mate. All you've got to do is to obey him as you would me;
and remember that he is *Mr.* Hall." Foster went forward into
the forecastle as a common sailor, and lost the "handle to his
name," while young foremast Jim became Mr. Hall, and took
up his quarters in the land of knives and forks and teacups.

*Sunday, October 5th.* It was our morning watch, when,
soon after the day began to break, a man on the forecastle
called out, "Land ho!" I had never heard the cry before, and
did not know what it meant (and few would suspect what the
words were, when hearing the strange sound for the first
time); but I soon found, by the direction of all eyes, that
there was land stretching along on our weather beam. We
immediately took in studding sails and hauled our wind,
running in for the land. This was done to determine our
longitude; for by the captain's chronometer we were in
25° W., but by his observations we were much farther; and he
had been for some time in doubt whether it was his chronometer or his sextant which was out of order. This landfall
settled the matter, and the former instrument was condemned, and, becoming still worse, was never afterward used.

As we ran in toward the coast, we found that we were directly off the port of Pernambuco, and could see with the telescope the roofs of the houses, and one large church, and the
town of Olinda. We ran along by the mouth of the harbor,
and saw a full-rigged brig going in. At 2 P.M. we again stood
out to sea, leaving the land on our quarter, and at sundown
it was out of sight. It was here that I first saw one of those
singular things called catamarans. They are composed of
logs lashed together upon the water, the men sitting with their
feet in the water; have one large sail, are quite fast, and,

strange as it may seem, are trusted as good sea boats. We saw several, with from one to three men in each, boldly putting out to sea, after it had become almost dark. The Indians go out in them after fish, and as the weather is regular in certain seasons, they have no fear. After taking a new departure from Olinda, we kept off on our way to Cape Horn.

We met with nothing remarkable until we were in the latitude of the river La Plata. Here there are violent gales from the southwest, called pamperos, which are very destructive to the shipping in the river, and are felt for many leagues at sea. They are usually preceded by lightning. The captain told the mates to keep a bright lookout, and if they saw lightning at the southwest, to take in sail at once. We got the first touch of one during my watch on deck. I was walking in the lee gangway, and thought that I saw lightning on the lee bow. I told the second mate, who came over and looked out for some time. It was very black in the southwest, and in about ten minutes we saw a distinct flash. The wind, which had been southeast, had now left us, and it was dead calm. We sprang aloft immediately and furled the royals and topgallant sails, and took in the flying jib, hauled up the mainsail and trysail, squared the after yards, and awaited the attack. A huge mist capped with black clouds came driving toward us, extending over that portion of the horizon, and covering the stars, which shone brightly in the other part of the heavens. It came upon us at once with a blast, and a shower of hail and rain, which almost took our breath from us. The hardiest was obliged to turn his back. We let the halyards run, and fortunately were not taken aback. The little vessel "paid off" from the wind, and ran on for some time directly before it, tearing through the water with everything flying. Having called all hands, we close-reefed the topsails and trysail, furled the courses and jib, set the fore-topmast staysail, and brought her up nearly to her course, with the weather braces hauled in a little, to ease her.

This was the first blow I had met which could really be called a gale. We had reefed our topsails in the Gulf Stream, and I thought it something serious, but an older sailor would have thought nothing of it. As I had now become used to the vessel and to my duty, I was of some service on a yard, and could knot my reef point as well as anybody. I obeyed the order to lay * aloft with the rest, and found the reefing a very exciting scene; for one watch reefed the fore-topsail, and the other the main, and everyone did his utmost to get his topsail hoisted first. We had a great advantage over the larboard watch, because the chief mate never goes aloft, while our new second mate used to jump into the rigging as soon as we began to haul out the reef tackle, and have the weather earing passed before there was a man upon the yard. In this way we were almost always able to raise the cry of "Haul out to leeward" before them; and, having knotted our points, would slide down the shrouds and backstays, and sing out at the topsail halyards, to let it be known that we were ahead of them. Reefing is the most exciting part of a sailor's duty. All hands are engaged upon it, and after the halyards are let go, there is no time to be lost—no "sogering," or hanging back, then. If one is not quick enough, another runs over him. The first on the yard goes to the weather earing, the second to the lee, and the next two to the "dog's ears"; while the others lay along into the bunt, just giving each other elbow room. In reefing, the yardarms (the extremes of the yards) are the posts of honor; but in furling, the strongest and most experienced stand in the slings (or middle of the yard) to make up the bunt. If the second mate is a smart fellow, he will never let anyone take either of these posts from him; but if he is wanting either in seamanship, strength, or activity, some better man will get the bunt and earings from him, which immediately brings him into disrepute.

We remained for the rest of the night, and throughout the next day, under the same close sail, for it continued to blow very fresh; and though we had no more hail, yet there was a soaking rain, and it was quite cold and uncomfortable; the more so, because we were not prepared for cold weather, but had on our thin clothes. We were glad to get a watch below, and put on our thick clothing, boots, and southwesters. Toward sundown the gale moderated a little, and it began to clear off in the southwest. We shook our reefs out, one by one, and before midnight had topgallant sails upon her.

* This word "lay," which is in such general use on board ship, being used in giving orders instead of "go," as "Lay forward!" "Lay aft!" "Lay aloft!" &c., I do not understand to be the neuter verb "lie," mispronounced, but to be the active verb "lay," with the objective case understood; as, "Lay (yourselves) forward!" "Lay (yourselves) aft!" &c. At all events, "lay" is an active verb at sea, and means "go."

We had now made up our minds for Cape Horn and cold weather, and entered upon the necessary preparations.

*Tuesday, November 4th.* At daybreak, saw land upon our larboard quarter. There were two islands, of different size, but of the same shape; rather high, beginning low at the water's edge, and running with a curved ascent to the middle. They were so far off as to be of a deep blue color, and in a few hours we sank them in the northeast. These were the Falkland Islands. We had run between them and the mainland of Patagonia. At sunset, the second mate, who was at the masthead, said that he saw land on the starboard bow. This must have been the island of Staten Land; and we were now in the region of Cape Horn, with a fine breeze from the northward, topmast and topgallant studding sails set, and every prospect of a speedy and pleasant passage round.

# CHAPTER V

*Wednesday, November 5th.* The weather was fine during the previous night, and we had a clear view of the Magellan Clouds and of the Southern Cross. The Magellan Clouds consist of three small nebulae in the southern part of the heavens—two bright, like the Milky Way, and one dark. They are first seen just above the horizon, soon after crossing the southern tropic. The Southern Cross begins to be seen at 18° N., and, when off Cape Horn, is nearly overhead. It is composed of four stars in that form, and is one of the brightest constellations in the heavens.

During the first part of this day (Wednesday) the wind was light, but after noon it came on fresh, and we furled the royals. We still kept the studding sails out, and the captain said he should go round with them if he could. Just before eight o'clock (then about sundown, in that latitude) the cry of "All hands ahoy!" was sounded down the fore scuttle and the after hatchway, and, hurrying upon deck, we found a large black cloud rolling on toward us from the southwest, and darkening the whole heavens. "Here comes Cape Horn!" said the chief mate; and we had hardly time to haul down and clew up before it was upon us. In a few minutes a heavier sea was raised than I had ever seen, and as it was directly ahead, the little brig, which was no better than a bathing machine, plunged into it, and all the forward part of her was under water; the sea pouring in through the bow ports and hawseholes and over the knightheads, threatening to wash everything overboard. In the lee scuppers it was up to a man's waist. We sprang aloft and double-reefed the topsails, and furled the other sails, and made all snug. But this would not do; the brig was laboring and straining against the head sea, and the gale was growing worse and worse. At the same time sleet and hail were driving with all fury against us. We clewed down, and hauled out the reef tackles again, and close-reefed the fore-topsail, and furled the main, and hove her to, on the starboard tack. Here was an end to our fine prospects. We made up our minds to head winds and cold weather; sent down the royal yards, and unrove the gear; but all the rest of the top hamper remained aloft, even to the skysail masts and studding-sail booms.

Throughout the night it stormed violently, rain, hail, snow, and sleet beating upon the vessel, the wind continuing ahead, and the sea running high. At daybreak (about 3 A.M.) the deck was covered with snow. The captain sent up the steward with a glass of grog to each of the watch; and all the time that we were off the Cape, grog was given to the morning watch, and to all hands whenever we reefed topsails. The clouds cleared away at sunrise, and, the wind becoming more fair, we again made sail and stood nearly up to our course.

*Thursday, November 6th.* It continued more pleasant through the first part of the day, but at night we had the same scene over again. This time we did not heave to, as on the night before, but endeavored to beat to windward under close-reefed topsails, balance-reefed trysail, and fore-topmast staysail. This night it was my turn to steer, or, as the sailors say, my "trick" at the helm, for two hours. Inexperienced as I was, I made out to steer to the satisfaction of the officer, and neither Stimson nor I gave up our tricks, all the time that we were off the Cape. This was something to boast of, for it requires a good deal of skill and watchfulness to steer a vessel close-hauled, in a gale of wind, against a heavy head sea. "Ease her when she pitches" is the word; and a little carelessness in letting her ship a heavy sea might sweep the decks, or take a mast out of her.

*Friday, November 7th.* Toward morning the wind went down, and during the whole forenoon we lay tossing about in a dead calm, and in the midst of a thick fog. The calms here are unlike those in most parts of the world, for here there is generally so high a sea running, with periods of calm so short that it has no time to go down; and vessels, being under no command of sails or rudder, lie like logs upon the water. We were obliged to steady the booms and yards by guys and braces, and to lash everything well below. We now found our top hamper of some use, for though it is liable to be carried away or sprung by the sudden "bringing up" of a vessel when pitching in a chopping sea, yet it is a great help in steadying a vessel when rolling in a long swell, giving more slowness, ease, and regularity to the motion.

The calm of the morning reminds me of a scene which I forgot to describe at the time of its occurrence, but which I remember from its being the first time that I had heard the near breathing of whales. It was on the night that we passed between the Falkland Islands and Staten Land. We had the watch from twelve to four, and, coming upon deck, found the little brig lying perfectly still, enclosed in a thick fog, and the sea as smooth as though oil had been poured upon it; yet now and then a long, low swell rolling under its surface, slightly lifting the vessel, but without breaking the glassy smoothness of the water. We were surrounded far and near by shoals of sluggish whales and grampuses, which the fog prevented our seeing, rising slowly to the surface, or perhaps lying out at length, heaving out those lazy, deep, and long-drawn breathings which give such an impression of supineness and strength. Some of the watch were asleep, and the others were quiet, so that there was nothing to break the illusion, and I stood leaning over the bulwarks, listening to the slow breathings of the mighty creatures—now one breaking the water just alongside, whose black body I almost fancied that I could see through the fog; and again another, which I could just hear in the distance—until the low and regular swell seemed like the heaving of the ocean's mighty bosom to the sound of its own heavy and long-drawn respirations.

Toward the evening of this day (Friday, seventh) the fog cleared off, and we had every appearance of a cold blow; and soon after sundown it came on. Again it was clew up and haul down, reef and furl, until we had got her down to close-reefed topsails, double-reefed trysail, and reefed fore spencer. Snow, hail, and sleet were driving upon us most of the night, and the sea was breaking over the bows and covering the forward part of the little vessel; but, as she would lay her course, the captain refused to heave her to.

*Saturday, November 8th.* This day began with calm and thick fog, and ended with hail, snow, a violent wind, and close-reefed topsails.

*Sunday, November 9th.* Today the sun rose clear and continued so until twelve o'clock, when the captain got an observation. This was very well for Cape Horn, and we thought it a little remarkable that, as we had not had one unpleasant Sunday during the whole voyage, the only tolerable day here should be a Sunday. We got time to clear up the steerage and forecastle, and set things to rights, and to overhaul our wet clothes a little. But this did not last very long. Between five and six—the sun was then nearly three hours high—the cry of "All Starbowlines * ahoy!" summoned our watch on deck, and immediately all hands were called. A true specimen of Cape Horn was coming upon us. A great cloud of a dark slate color was driving on us from the southwest; and we did our best to take in sail (for the light sails had been set during the first part of the day) before we were in the midst of it. We had got the light sails furled, the courses hauled up, and the topsail reef tackles hauled out, and were just mounting the forerigging when the storm struck us. In an instant the sea, which had been comparatively quiet, was running higher and higher; and it became almost as dark as night. The hail and sleet were harder than I had

_____

* It is the fashion to call the respective watches Starbowlines and Larbowlines.

yet felt them; seeming almost to pin us down to the rigging. We were longer taking in sail than ever before; for the sails were stiff and wet, the ropes and rigging covered with snow and sleet, and we ourselves cold and nearly blinded with the violence of the storm. By the time we had got down upon deck again, the little brig was plunging madly into a tremendous head sea, which at every drive rushed in through the bow ports and over the bows, and buried all the forward part of the vessel. At this instant the chief mate, who was standing on the top of the windlass, at the foot of the spencer mast, called out, "Lay out there and furl the jib!" This was no agreeable or safe duty, yet it must be done. John, a Swede (the best sailor on board), who belonged on the forecastle, sprang out upon the bowsprit. Another one must go. It was a clear case of holding back. I was near the mate, but sprang past several, threw the downhaul over the windlass, and jumped between the knightheads out upon the bowsprit. The crew stood abaft the windlass and hauled the jib down, while John and I got out upon the weather side of the jib boom, our feet on the foot ropes, holding on by the spar, the great jib flying off to leeward and "slatting" so as almost to throw us off the boom. For some time we could do nothing but hold on, and the vessel, diving into two huge seas, one after the other, plunged us twice into the water up to our chins. We hardly knew whether we were on or off when, the boom lifting us up dripping from the water, we were raised high into the air and then plunged below again. John thought the boom would go every moment, and called out to the mate to keep the vessel off, and haul down the staysail; but the fury of the wind and the breaking of the seas against the bows defied every attempt to make ourselves heard, and we were obliged to do the best we could in our situation. Fortunately no other seas so heavy struck her, and we succeeded in furling the jib "after a fashion"; and, coming in over the staysail nettings, were not a little pleased to find that all was snug, and the watch gone below; for we were soaked through, and it was very cold. John admitted that it had been a post of danger, which good sailors seldom do when the thing is over. The weather continued nearly the same through the night.

*Monday, November 10th.* During a part of this day we were hove to, but the rest of the time were driving on, under

close-reefed sails, with a heavy sea, a strong gale, and frequent
squalls of hail and snow.

*Tuesday, November 11th.* The same.

*Wednesday.* The same.

*Thursday.* The same.

We had now got hardened to Cape weather, the vessel
was under reduced sail, and everything secured on deck
and below, so that we had little to do but to steer and to
stand our watch. Our clothes were all wet through, and
the only change was from wet to more wet. There is no
fire in the forecastle, and we cannot dry clothes at the galley.
It was in vain to think of reading or working below, for
we were too tired, the hatchways were closed down, and
everything was wet and uncomfortable, black and dirty,
heaving and pitching. We had only to come below when the
watch was out, wring our wet clothes, hang them up to
chafe against the bulkheads, and turn in and sleep as soundly
as we could, until our watch was called again. A sailor can
sleep anywhere—no sound of wind, water, canvas, rope,
wood, or iron can keep him awake—and we were always
fast asleep when three blows on the hatchway, and the un-
welcome cry of "All Starbowlines ahoy! Eight bells there
below! Do you hear the news?" (the usual formula of calling
the watch) roused us up from our berths upon the cold,
wet decks. The only time when we could be said to take any
pleasure was at night and morning, when we were allowed
a tin pot full of hot tea (or, as the sailors significantly call it,
"water bewitched") sweetened with molasses. This, bad as it
was, was still warm and comforting, and, together with our
sea biscuit and cold salt beef, made a meal. Yet even this
meal was attended with some uncertainty. We had to go
ourselves to the galley and take our kid of beef and tin pots of
tea, and run the risk of losing them before we could get
below. Many a kid of beef have I seen rolling in the scuppers,
and the bearer lying at his length on the decks. I remember
an English lad who was the life of the crew—whom we
afterward lost overboard—standing for nearly ten minutes
at the galley, with his pot of tea in his hand, waiting for a
chance to get down into the forecastle, and, seeing what he
thought was a "smooth spell," started to go forward. He had
just got to the end of the windlass when a great sea broke
over the bows, and for a moment I saw nothing of him

but his head and shoulders; and at the next instant, being taken off his legs, he was carried aft with the sea, until, her stern lifting up, and sending the water forward, he was left high and dry at the side of the longboat, still holding on to his tin pot, which had now nothing in it but salt water. But nothing could ever daunt him, or overcome, for a moment, his habitual good humor. Regaining his legs, and shaking his fist at the man at the wheel, he rolled below, saying, as he passed, "A man's no sailor if he can't take a joke." The ducking was not the worst of such an affair, for, as there was an allowance of tea, you could get no more from the galley; and though the others would never suffer a man to go without, but would always turn in a little from their own pots to fill up his, yet this was at best but dividing the loss among all hands.

Something of the same kind befell me a few days after. The cook had just made for us a mess of hot "scouse"— that is, biscuit pounded fine, salt beef cut into small pieces, and a few potatoes, boiled up together and seasoned with pepper. This was a rare treat, and I, being the last at the galley, had it put in my charge to carry down for the mess. I got along very well as far as the hatchway, and was just going down the steps, when a heavy sea, lifting the stern out of water, and, passing forward, dropping it again, threw the steps from their place, and I came down into the steerage a little faster than I meant to, with the kid on top of me, and the whole precious mess scattered over the floor. Whatever your feelings may be, you must make a joke of everything at sea; and if you were to fall from aloft and be caught in the belly of a sail, and thus saved from instant death, it would not do to look at all disturbed, or to treat it as a serious matter.

*Friday, November 14th.* We were now well to the westward of the Cape, and were changing our course to northward as much as we dared, since the strong southwest winds, which prevailed then, carried us in toward Patagonia. At 2 P.M. we saw a sail on our larboard beam, and at four we made it out to be a large ship, steering our course, under single-reefed topsails. We at that time had shaken the reefs out of our topsails, as the wind was lighter, and set the main topgallant sail. As soon as our captain saw what sail she was under, he set the fore-topgallant sail and flying jib; and the

old whaler—for such his boats and short sail showed him to
be—felt a little ashamed, and shook the reefs out of his
topsails, but could do no more, for he had sent down his
topgallant masts off the Cape. He ran down for us, and
answered our hail as the whaleship *New England*, of Pough-
keepsie, one hundred and twenty days from New York. Our
captain gave our name, and added, ninety-two days from
Boston. They then had a little conversation about longitude,
in which they found that they could not agree. The ship
fell astern, and continued in sight during the night. Toward
morning, the wind having become light, we crossed our
royal and skysail yards, and at daylight we were seen under a
cloud of sail, having royals and skysails fore and aft. The
"spouter," as the sailors call a whaleman, had sent up his
main-topgallant mast and set the sail, and made signal for us to
heave to. About half-past seven their whaleboat came alongside, and Captain Job Terry sprang on board, a man known in
every port and by every vessel in the Pacific Ocean. "Don't you
know Job Terry? I thought everybody knew Job Terry," said
a green hand, who came in the boat, to me, when I asked
him about his captain. He was indeed a singular man. He
was six feet high, wore thick cowhide boots, and brown coat
and trousers, and, except a sunburned complexion, had not
the slightest appearance of a sailor; yet he had been forty
years in the whale trade, and, as he said himself, had owned
ships, built ships, and sailed ships. His boat's crew were a
pretty raw set, just out of the bush, and, as the sailor's phrase
is, "hadn't got the hayseed out of their hair." Captain Terry
convinced our captain that our reckoning was a little out,
and, having spent the day on board, put off in his boat at sunset for his ship, which was now six or eight miles astern. He
began a "yarn" when he came aboard, which lasted, with
but little intermission, for four hours. It was all about himself, and the Peruvian government, and the Dublin frigate,
and her captain, Lord James Townshend, and President Jackson, and the ship *Ann McKim*, of Baltimore. It would
probably never have come to an end, had not a good breeze
sprung up, which sent him off to his own vessel. One of the
lads who came in his boat, a thoroughly countrified-looking
fellow, seemed to care very little about the vessel, rigging,
or anything else, but went round looking at the livestock, and

leaned over the pigsty, and said he wished he was back again tending his father's pigs.

A curious case of dignity occurred here. It seems that in a whaleship there is an intermediate class, called boat steerers. One of them came in Captain Terry's boat, but we thought he was cockswain of the boat, and a cockswain is only a sailor. In the whaler, the boat steerers are between the officers and crew, a sort of petty officers; keep by themselves in the waist, sleep amidships, and eat by themselves, either at a separate table, or at the cabin table, after the captain and mates are done. Of all this hierarchy we were entirely ignorant, so the poor boat steerer was left to himself. The second mate would not notice him, and seemed surprised at his keeping amidships, but his pride of office would not allow him to go forward. With dinnertime came the *experimentum crucis*. What would he do? The second mate went to the second table without asking him. There was nothing for him but famine or humiliation. We asked him into the forecastle, but he faintly declined. The whaleboat's crew explained it to us, and we asked him again. Hunger got the victory over pride of rank, and his boat-steering majesty had to take his grub out of our kid, and eat with his jackknife. Yet the man was ill at ease all the time, was sparing of his conversation, and kept up the notion of a condescension under stress of circumstances. One would say that, instead of a tendency to equality in human beings, the tendency is to make the most of inequalities, natural or artificial.

At eight o'clock we altered our course to the northward, bound for Juan Fernández.

This day we saw the last of the albatrosses, which had been our companions a great part of the time off the Cape. I had been interested in the bird from descriptions, and Coleridge's poem, and was not at all disappointed. We caught one or two with a baited hook which we floated astern upon a shingle. Their long, flapping wings, long legs, and large, staring eyes give them a very peculiar appearance. They look well on the wing; but one of the finest sights that I have ever seen was an albatross asleep upon the water, during a calm, off Cape Horn, when a heavy sea was running. There being no breeze, the surface of the water was unbroken, but a long, heavy swell was rolling, and we saw the fellow,

all white, directly ahead of us, asleep upon the waves, with
his head under his wing; now rising on the top of one of
the big billows, and then falling slowly until he was lost
in the hollow between. He was undisturbed for some time,
until the noise of our bows, gradually approaching, roused
him, when, lifting his head, he stared upon us for a moment,
and then spread his wide wings and took his flight.

# CHAPTER VI

*Monday, November 19th.* This was a black day in our calendar. At seven o'clock in the morning, it being our watch
below, we were aroused from a sound sleep by the cry of
"All hands ahoy! A man overboard!" This unwonted cry sent
a thrill through the heart of everyone, and, hurrying on deck,
we found the vessel hove flat aback, with all her studding sails
set; for, the boy who was at the helm leaving it to throw
something overboard, the carpenter, who was an old sailor,
knowing that the wind was light, put the helm down and
hove her aback. The watch on deck were lowering away the
quarter boat, and I got on deck just in time to fling myself into
her as she was leaving the side; but it was not until out
upon the wide Pacific, in our little boat, that I knew whom
we had lost. It was George Ballmer, the young English sailor,
whom I have before spoken of as the life of the crew. He
was prized by the officers as an active and willing seaman,
and by the men as a lively, hearty fellow, and a good shipmate. He was going aloft to fit a strap round the maintop
masthead, for ringtail halyards, and had the strap and
block, a coil of halyards, and a marlinespike about his neck.
He fell from the starboard futtock shrouds, and, not knowing

how to swim, and being heavily dressed, with all those things round his neck, he probably sank immediately. We pulled astern, in the direction in which he fell, and though we knew that there was no hope of saving him, yet no one wished to speak of returning, and we rowed about for nearly an hour, without an idea of doing anything, but unwilling to acknowledge to ourselves that we must give him up. At length we turned the boat's head and made toward the brig.

Death is at all times solemn, but never so much so as at sea. A man dies on shore; his body remains with his friends, and "the mourners go about the streets"; but when a man falls overboard at sea and is lost, there is a suddenness in the event, and a difficulty in realizing it, which give to it an air of awful mystery. A man dies on shore—you follow his body to the grave, and a stone marks the spot. You are often prepared for the event. There is always something which helps you to realize it when it happens, and to recall it when it has passed. A man is shot down by your side in battle, and the mangled body remains an object, and a real evidence; but at sea, the man is near you—at your side—you hear his voice, and in an instant he is gone, and nothing but a vacancy shows his loss. Then, too, at sea—to use a homely but expressive phrase—you *miss* a man so much. A dozen men are shut up together in a little bark upon the wide, wide sea, and for months and months see no forms and hear no voices but their own, and one is taken suddenly from among them, and they miss him at every turn. It is like losing a limb. There are no new faces or new scenes to fill up the gap. There is always an empty berth in the forecastle, and one man wanting when the small night watch is mustered. There is one less to take the wheel, and one less to lay out with you upon the yard. You miss his form, and the sound of his voice, for habit had made them almost necessary to you, and each of your senses feels the loss.

All these things make such a death peculiarly solemn, and the effect of it remains upon the crew for some time. There is more kindness shown by the officers to the crew, and by the crew to one another. There is more quietness and seriousness. The oath and the loud laugh are gone. The officers are more watchful, and the crew go more carefully aloft. The lost man is seldom mentioned, or is dismissed with a sailor's rude eulogy—"Well, poor George is gone! His cruise is up

soon! He knew his work, and did his duty, and was a good
shipmate." Then usually follows some allusion to another
world, for sailors are almost all believers, in their way,
though their notions and opinions are unfixed and at loose
ends. They say, "God won't be hard upon the poor fellow,"
and seldom get beyond the common phrase which seems
to imply that their sufferings and hard treatment here will
be passed to their credit in the books of the Great Captain
hereafter—"*To work hard, live hard, die hard, and go to hell
after all would be hard indeed!*" Our cook, a simplehearted
old African, who had been through a good deal in his day,
and was rather seriously inclined, always going to church
twice a day when on shore, and reading his Bible on a
Sunday in the galley, talked to the crew about spending the
Lord's Days badly, and told them that they might go as
suddenly as George had, and be as little prepared.

Yet a sailor's life is at best but a mixture of a little good
with much evil, and a little pleasure with much pain. The
beautiful is linked with the revolting, the sublime with the
commonplace, and the solemn with the ludicrous.

Not long after we had returned on board with our sad
report, an auction was held of the poor man's effects. The
captain had first, however, called all hands aft and asked them
if they were satisfied that everything had been done to save
the man, and if they thought there was any use in remaining
there longer. The crew all said that it was in vain, for the
man did not know how to swim, and was very heavily
dressed. So we then filled away and kept the brig off to her
course.

The laws regulating navigation make the captain answerable
for the effects of a sailor who dies during the voyage, and
it is either a law or a custom, established for convenience,
that the captain should soon hold an auction of his things, in
which they are bid off by the sailors, and the sums which
they give are deducted from their wages at the end of the
voyage. In this way the trouble and risk of keeping his things
through the voyage are avoided, and the clothes are usually
sold for more than they would be worth on shore. Accordingly, we had no sooner got the ship before the wind, than
his chest was brought up upon the forecastle, and the sale
began. The jackets and trousers in which we had seen him
dressed so lately were exposed and bid off while the life

was hardly out of his body, and his chest was taken aft and used as a store chest, so that there was nothing left which could be called *his*. Sailors have an unwillingness to wear a dead man's clothes during the same voyage, and they seldom do so, unless they are in absolute want.

As is usual after a death, many stories were told about George. Some had heard him say that he repented never having learned to swim, and that he knew that he should meet his death by drowning. Another said that he never knew any good to come of a voyage made against the will, and the deceased man shipped and spent his advance, and was afterward very unwilling to go, but, not being able to refund, was obliged to sail with us. A boy, too, who had become quite attached to him, said that George talked to him, during most of the watch on the night before, about his mother and family at home, and this was the first time that he had mentioned the subject during the voyage.

The night after this event, when I went to the galley to get a light, I found the cook inclined to be talkative, so I sat down on the spars, and gave him an opportunity to hold a yarn. I was the more inclined to do so, as I found that he was full of the superstitions once more common among seamen, and which the recent death had waked up in his mind. He talked about George's having spoken of his friends, and said he believed few men died without having a warning of it, which he supported by a great many stories of dreams, and of unusual behavior of men before death. From this he went on to other superstitions, the Flying Dutchman, &c., and talked rather mysteriously, having something evidently on his mind. At length he put his head out of the galley and looked carefully about to see if anyone was within hearing, and, being satisfied on that point, asked me in a low tone:

"I say! You know what countryman 'e carpenter be?"

"Yes," said I, "he's a German."

"What kind of a German!" said the cook.

"He belongs to Bremen," said I.

"Are you sure o' dat?" said he.

I satisfied him on that point by saying that he could speak no language but the German and English.

"I'm plaguy glad o' dat," said the cook. "I was mighty 'fraid he was a Finn. I tell you what, I been plaguy civil to that man all the voyage."

I asked him the reason of this, and found that he was fully possessed with the notion that Finns are wizards, and especially have power over winds and storms. I tried to reason with him about it, but he had the best of all arguments, that from experience, at hand, and was not to be moved. He had been to the Sandwich Islands in a vessel in which the sailmaker was a Finn, and could do anything he was of a mind to. This sailmaker kept a junk bottle in his berth, which was always just half full of rum, though he got drunk upon it nearly every day. He had seen him sit for hours together, talking to this bottle, which he stood up before him on the table. The same man cut his throat in his berth, and everybody said he was possessed.

He had heard of ships, too, beating up the Gulf of Finland against a head wind, and having a ship heave in sight astern, overhaul and pass them, with as fair a wind as could blow, and all studding sails out, and find she was from Finland.

"Oh, no!" said he. "I've seen too much o' dem men to want to see 'em 'board a ship. If dey can't have dare own way, they'll play the d——l with you."

As I still doubted, he said he would leave it to John, who was the oldest seaman aboard, and would know, if anybody did. John, to be sure, was the oldest, and at the same time the most ignorant, man in the ship; but I consented to have him called. The cook stated the matter to him, and John, as I anticipated, sided with the cook, and said that he himself had been in a ship where they had a head wind for a fortnight, and the captain found out at last that one of the men, with whom he had had some hard words a short time before, was a Finn, and immediately told him if he didn't stop the head wind he would shut him down in the forepeak. The Finn would not give in, and the captain shut him down in the forepeak, and would not give him anything to eat. The Finn held out for a day and a half, when he could not stand it any longer, and did something or other which brought the wind round again, and they let him up.

"Dar," said the cook, "what you tink o' dat?"

I told him I had no doubt it was true, and that it would have been odd if the wind had not changed in fifteen days, Finn or no Finn.

"Oh," says he, "go 'way! You tink, 'cause you been to

college, you know better dan anybody. You know better dan dem as 'as seen it wid der own eyes. You wait till you've been to sea as long as I have, and den you'll know."

# CHAPTER VII

We continued sailing along with a fair wind and fine weather until—

*Tuesday, November 25th,* when at daylight we saw the island of Juan Fernández directly ahead, rising like a deep-blue cloud out of the sea. We were then probably nearly seventy miles from it; and so high and so blue did it appear that I mistook it for a cloud resting over the island, and looked for the island under it, until it gradually turned to a deader and greener color, and I could mark the inequalities upon its surface. At length we could distinguish trees and rocks; and by the afternoon this beautiful island lay fairly before us, and we directed our course to the only harbor. Arriving at the entrance soon after sundown, we found a Chilean man-of-war brig, the only vessel, coming out. She hailed us; and an officer on board, whom we supposed to be an American, advised us to run in before night, and said that they were bound to Valparaiso. We ran immediately for the anchorage, but, owing to the winds which drew about the mountains and came to us in flaws from different points of the compass, we did not come to an anchor until nearly midnight. We had a boat ahead all the time that we were working in, and those aboard ship were continually bracing the yards about for every puff that struck us, until about twelve o'clock, when we came to in forty fathoms water, and our anchor struck bottom for the first time since we left Boston—one hundred and three days. We were then divided into three watches, and thus stood out the remainder of the night.

I was called on deck to stand my watch at about three in the morning, and I shall never forget the peculiar sensation which I experienced on finding myself once more surrounded by land, feeling the night breeze coming from off shore, and hearing the frogs and crickets. The mountains seemed almost to hang over us, and apparently from the very heart of them there came out, at regular intervals, a loud echoing sound, which affected me as hardly human. We saw no lights, and could hardly account for the sound until the mate, who had been there before, told us that it was the *alerta* of the Chilean soldiers, who were stationed over some convicts confined in caves nearly halfway up the mountain. At the expiration of my watch, I went below, feeling not a little anxious for the day, that I might see more nearly, and perhaps tread upon, this romantic, I may almost say classic, island.

When all hands were called it was nearly sunrise, and between that time and breakfast, although quite busy on board in getting up water casks, &c., I had a good view of the objects about me. The harbor was nearly landlocked, and at the head of it was a landing, protected by a small breakwater of stones, upon which two large boats were hauled up, with a sentry standing over them. Near this was a variety of huts or cottages, nearly a hundred in number, the best of them built of mud or unburned clay, and whitewashed, but the greater part *Robinson Crusoe*-like—only of posts and branches of trees. The governor's house, as it is called, was the most conspicuous, being large, with grated windows, plastered walls, and roof of red tiles; yet, like all the rest, only of one story. Near it was a small chapel, distinguished by a cross; and a long, low, brown-looking building, surrounded by something like a palisade, from which an old and dingy-looking Chilean flag was flying. This, of course, was dignified by the title of presidio. A sentinel was stationed at the chapel, another at the governor's house, and a few soldiers, armed with bayonets, looking rather ragged, with shoes out at the toes, were strolling about among the houses, or waiting at the landing place for our boat to come ashore.

The mountains were high, but not so overhanging as they appeared to be by starlight. They seemed to bear off toward the center of the island, and were green and well wooded, with some large and, I am told, exceedingly fertile valleys, with mule tracks leading to different parts of the island.

I cannot here forget how Stimson and I got the laugh of the crew upon us by our eagerness to get on shore. The captain having ordered the quarter boat to be lowered, we both, thinking it was going ashore, sprang down into the forecastle, filled our jacket pockets with tobacco to barter with the people ashore, and, when the officer called for "four hands in the boat," nearly broke our necks in our haste to be first over the side, and had the pleasure of pulling ahead of the brig with a towline for half an hour, and coming on board again to be laughed at by the crew, who had seen our maneuver.

After breakfast, the second mate was ordered ashore with five hands to fill the water casks, and, to my joy, I was among the number. We pulled ashore with empty casks; and here again fortune favored me, for the water was too thick and muddy to be put into the casks, and the governor had sent men up to the head of the stream to clear it out for us, which gave us nearly two hours of leisure. This leisure we employed in wandering about among the houses, and eating a little fruit which was offered to us. Ground apples, melons, grapes, strawberries of an enormous size, and cherries abound here. The latter are said to have been planted by Lord Anson. The soldiers were miserably clad, and asked with some interest whether we had shoes to sell on board. I doubt very much if they had the means of buying them. They were very eager to get tobacco, for which they gave shells, fruit, &c. Knives were also in demand, but we were forbidden by the governor to let anyone have them, as he told us that all the people there, except the soldiers and a few officers, were convicts sent from Valparaiso, and that it was necessary to keep all weapons from their hands. The island, it seems, belongs to Chile, and had been used by the government as a penal colony for nearly two years; and the governor—an Englishman who had entered the Chilean navy—with a priest, half a dozen taskmasters, and a body of soldiers, were stationed there to keep them in order. This was no easy task; and, only a few months before our arrival, a few of them had stolen a boat at night, boarded a brig lying in the harbor, sent the captain and crew ashore in their boat, and gone off to sea. We were informed of this, and loaded our arms and kept strict watch on board through the night, and were careful not to let the convicts get our knives from us when on shore. The worst part of the convicts, I found, were locked up under sentry, in caves dug into the side of the mountain, nearly halfway up, with mule tracks leading to them, whence they were taken by day and set to work under taskmasters upon building an aqueduct, a wharf, and other public works; while the rest lived in the houses which they put up for themselves, had their families with them, and seemed to me to be the laziest people on the face of the earth. They did nothing but take a *paseo* into the woods, a *paseo* among the houses, a *paseo* at the landing place, looking at us and our vessel, and too lazy to speak fast; while the others were driven about, at a rapid trot, in single file, with burdens on their shoulders, and followed up by their taskmasters, with long rods in their hands, and broad-brimmed straw hats upon their heads. Upon what precise grounds this great distinction was made, I do not know, and I could not very well know, for the governor was the only man who spoke English upon the island, and he was out of my walk, for I was a sailor ashore as well as on board.

Having filled our casks, we returned on board, and soon after, the governor, dressed in a uniform like that of an American militia officer, the *Padre*, in the dress of the gray friars, with hood and all complete, and the *capitán*, with big whiskers and dirty regimentals, came on board to dine. While at dinner a large ship appeared in the offing, and soon afterward we saw a light whaleboat pulling into the harbor. The ship lay off and on, and a boat came alongside of us, and put on board the captain, a plain young Quaker, dressed all in brown. The ship was the *Cortes*, whaleman, of New Bedford, and had put in to see if there were any vessels from round the Horn, and to hear the latest news from America. They remained aboard a short time, and had a little talk with the crew, when they left us and pulled off to their ship, which, having filled away, was soon out of sight.

A small boat which came from the shore to take away

the governor and suite—as they styled themselves—brought, as a present to the crew, a large pail of milk, a few shells, and a block of sandalwood. The milk, which was the first we had tasted since leaving Boston, we soon dispatched; a piece of the sandalwood I obtained, and learned that it grew on the hills in the center of the island. I regretted that I did not bring away other specimens; but what I had— the piece of sandalwood, and a small flower which I plucked and brought on board in the crown of my tarpaulin, and carefully pressed between the leaves of a volume of Cowper's *Letters*—were lost, with my chest and its contents, by another's negligence, on our arrival home.

About an hour before sundown, having stowed our water casks, we began getting under way, and were not a little while about it; for we were in thirty fathoms water, and in one of the gusts which came from off shore had let go our other bow anchor; and as the southerly wind draws round the mountains and comes off in uncertain flaws, we were continually swinging round, and had thus got a very foul hawse. We hove in upon our chain, and after stoppering and unshackling it again and again, and hoisting and hauling down sail, we at length tripped our anchor and stood out to sea. It was bright starlight when we were clear of the bay, and the lofty island lay behind us in its still beauty, and I gave a parting look and bade farewell to the most romantic spot of earth that my eyes had ever seen. I did then, and have ever since felt an attachment for that island altogether peculiar. It was partly, no doubt, from its having been the first land that I had seen since leaving home, and still more from the associations which everyone has connected with it in his childhood from reading *Robinson Crusoe*. To this I may add the height and romantic outline of its mountains, the beauty and freshness of its verdure and the extreme fertility of its soil, and its solitary position in the midst of the wide expanse of the South Pacific, as all concurring to give it its charm.

When thoughts of this place have occurred to me at different times, I have endeavored to recall more particulars with regard to it. It is situated in about 33° 30′ S., and is distant a little more than three hundred miles from Valparaiso, on the coast of Chile, which is in the same latitude. It is about fifteen miles in length and five in breadth. The harbor in which we anchored (called by Lord Anson Cum-

berland Bay) is the only one in the island, two small "bights"
of land on each side of the main bay (sometimes dignified
by the name of bays) being little more than landing places
for boats. The best anchorage is at the western side of the
harbor, where we lay at about three cables' lengths from
the shore, in a little more than thirty fathoms water. This
harbor is open to the NNE., and in fact nearly from N. to E.;
but the only dangerous winds being the southwest, on which
side are the highest mountains, it is considered safe. The
most remarkable thing, perhaps, about it is the fish with which
it abounds. Two of our crew, who remained on board, caught
in a short time enough to last us for several days, and one
of the men, who was a Marblehead man, said that he never
saw or heard of such an abundance. There were cod, bream,
silverfish, and other kinds, whose names they did not know,
or which I have forgotten.

There is an abundance of the best of water upon the
island, small streams running through every valley, and
leaping down from the sides of the hills. One stream of considerable size flows through the center of the lawn upon which
the houses are built, and furnishes an easy and abundant
supply to the inhabitants. This, by means of a short wooden
aqueduct, was brought quite down to our boats. The convicts
had also built something in the way of a breakwater, and were
to build a landing place for boats and goods, after which the
Chilean government intended to lay port charges.

Of the wood, I can only say that it appeared to be
abundant; the island in the month of November, when we
were there, being in all the freshness and beauty of spring,
appeared covered with trees. These were chiefly aromatic,
and the largest was the myrtle. The soil is very loose and
rich, and wherever it is broken up there spring up radishes,
turnips, ground apples, and other garden fruits. Goats, we
were told, were not abundant, and we saw none, though it
was said we might, if we had gone into the interior. We saw
a few bullocks winding about in the narrow tracks upon the
sides of the mountains, and the settlement was completely
overrun with dogs of every nation, kindred, and degree.
Hens and chickens were also abundant, and seemed to be
taken good care of by the women. The men appeared to be
the laziest of mortals; and indeed, as far as my observation
goes, there are no people to whom the newly invented Yankee

word of "loafer" is more applicable than to the Spanish Americans. These men stood about doing nothing, with their cloaks, little better in texture than an Indian's blanket, but of rich colors, thrown over their shoulders with an air which it is said that a Spanish beggar can always give to his rags, and with politeness and courtesy in their address, though with holes in their shoes, and without a sou in their pockets. The only interruption to the monotony of their day seemed to be when a gust of wind drew round between the mountains and blew off the boughs which they had placed for roofs to their houses, and gave them a few minutes' occupation in running about after them. One of these gusts occurred while we were ashore, and afforded us no little amusement in seeing the men look round, and, if they found that their roofs had stood, conclude that they might stand, too, while those who saw theirs blown off, after uttering a few Spanish oaths, gathered their cloaks over their shoulders, and started off after them. However, they were not gone long, but soon returned to their habitual "occupation" of doing nothing.

It is perhaps needless to say that we saw nothing of the interior; but all who have seen it give favorable accounts of it. Our captain went with the governor and a few servants upon mules over the mountains, and, upon their return, I heard the governor request him to stop at the island on his passage home, and offer him a handsome sum to bring a few deer with him from California, for he said that there were none upon the island, and he was very desirous of having it stocked.

A steady though light southwesterly wind carried us well off from the island, and when I came on deck for the middle watch I could just distinguish it from its hiding a few low stars in the southern horizon, though my unpracticed eyes would hardly have known it for land. At the close of the watch a few trade-wind clouds which had arisen, though we were hardly yet in their latitude, shut it out from our view, and the next day—

*Thursday, November 27th,* upon coming on deck in the morning, we were again upon the wide Pacific, and saw no more land until we arrived upon the western coast of the great continent of America.

# CHAPTER VIII

As we saw neither land nor sail from the time of leaving Juan Fernández until our arrival in California, nothing of interest occurred except our own doings on board. We caught the southeast trades, and ran before them for nearly three weeks, without so much as altering a sail or bracing a yard. The captain took advantage of this fine weather to get the vessel in order for coming upon the coast. The carpenter was employed in fitting up a part of the steerage into a trade room; for our cargo, we now learned, was not to be landed, but to be sold by retail on board; and this trade room was built for the samples and the lighter goods to be kept in, and as a place for the general business. In the meantime we were employed in working upon the rigging. Everything was set up taut, the lower rigging rattled down, or rather rattled *up* (according to the modern fashion), an abundance of spun yarn and seizing stuff made, and finally the whole standing rigging, fore and aft, was tarred down. It was my first essay at the latter business, and I had enough of it; for nearly all of it came upon my friend Stimson and myself. The men were needed at the other work, and Henry Mellus, the other young man who came out with us before the mast, was laid up with the rheumatism in his feet, and the boy Sam was rather too young and small for the business; and as the winds were light and regular, he was kept during most of the daytime at the helm, so that we had quite as much as we wished of it. We put on short duck frocks, and, taking a small bucket of tar and a bunch of oakum in our hands, went aloft, one at the main-royal masthead, and the other at the fore, and began tarring down. This is an important operation, and is usually done about once in six months in vessels upon a long voyage. It was done in our vessel several times afterward, but by the whole crew at once, and finished off in a day; but at this time, as most of it, as I have said, came upon two of us, and we were new at the business, it took several days. In this operation they always begin at the masthead, and work down, tarring the shrouds, backstays, standing parts of the lifts, the ties, runners, &c., and go out to the yardarms, and come in, tarring, as they come, the lifts and foot ropes. Tarring the

50

stays is more difficult, and is done by an operation which the sailors call "riding down." A long piece of rope—topgallant-studding-sail halyards, or something of the kind—is taken up to the masthead from which the stay leads, and rove through a block for a girtline, or, as the sailors usually call it, a gant-line; with the end of this, a bowline is taken round the stay, into which the man gets with his bucket of tar and bunch of oakum; and the other end being fast on deck, with someone to tend it, he is lowered down gradually, and tars the stay carefully as he goes. There he "swings aloft 'twixt heaven and earth," and if the rope slips, breaks, or is let go, or if the bowline slips, he falls overboard or breaks his neck. This, however, is a thing which never enters into a sailor's calculation. He only thinks of leaving no "holidays" (places not tarred)—for, in case he should, he would have to go over the whole again—or of dropping no tar upon deck, for then there would be a soft word in his ear from the mate. In this manner I tarred down all the head stays, but found the rigging about the jib booms, martingale, and spritsail yard, upon which I was afterward put, the hardest. Here you have to "hang on with your eyelids" and tar with your hands.

This dirty work could not last forever; and on Saturday night we finished it, scraped all the spots from the deck and rails, and, what was of more importance to us, cleaned our-selves thoroughly, rolled up our tarry frocks and trousers and laid them away for the next occasion, and put on our clean duck clothes, and had a good comfortable sailor's Saturday night. The next day was pleasant, and indeed we had but one unpleasant Sunday during the whole voyage, and that was off Cape Horn, where we could expect nothing better. On Mon-day we began painting, and getting the vessel ready for port. This work, too, is done by the crew, and every sailor who has been long voyages is a little of a painter, in addition to his other accomplishments. We painted her, both inside and out, from the truck to the water's edge. The outside is painted by lowering stages over the side by ropes, and on those we sat, with our brushes and paint pots by us, and our feet half the time in the water. This must be done, of course, on a smooth day, when the vessel does not roll much. I remember very well being over the side, painting in this way, one fine afternoon, our vessel going quietly along at the rate of four or five knots, and a pilot fish, the sure precursor of a shark,

swimming alongside of us. The captain was leaning over the
rail watching him, and we went quietly on with our work. In
the midst of our painting, on—

*Friday, December 19th,* we crossed the equator for the
second time. I had the sense of incongruity which all have
when, for the first time, they find themselves living under an
entire change of seasons, as crossing the line under a burning
sun in the midst of December.

*Thursday, December 25th.* This day was Christmas, but
it brought us no holiday. The only change was that we had a
"plum duff" for dinner, and the crew quarreled with the steward because he did not give us our usual allowance of molasses
to eat with it. He thought the plums would be a substitute for
the molasses, but we were not to be cheated out of our rights
in that way.

Such are the trifles which produce quarrels on shipboard.
In fact, we had been too long from port. We were getting
tired of one another, and were in an irritable state, both forward and aft. Our fresh provisions were, of course, gone, and
the captain had stopped our rice, so that we had nothing but
salt beef and salt pork throughout the week, with the exception
of a very small duff on Sunday. This added to the discontent;
and many little things, daily and almost hourly occurring,
which no one who has not himself been on a long and tedious
voyage can conceive of or properly appreciate—little wars
and rumors of wars, reports of things said in the cabin, misunderstanding of words and looks, apparent abuses—brought
us into a condition in which everything seemed to go wrong.
Every encroachment upon the time allowed for rest appeared
unnecessary. Every shifting of the studding sails was only to
"haze" * the crew.

In the midst of this state of things, my messmate Stimson
and I petitioned the captain for leave to shift our berths from
the steerage, where we had previously lived, into the forecastle.
This, to our delight, was granted, and we turned in to "bunk"
and mess with the crew forward. We now began to feel like
sailors, which we never fully did when we were in the steerage.
While there, however useful and active you may be, you are

---

* "Haze" is a word of frequent use on board ship. It is very expressive to a sailor, and means to punish by hard work. Let an officer once
say, "I'll haze you," and your fate is fixed. You will be "worked up,"
if you are not a better man than he is.

but a mongrel—a sort of afterguard and "ship's cousin." You
are immediately under the eye of the officers, cannot dance,
sing, play, smoke, make a noise, or "growl," or take any other
sailor's pleasure; and you live with the steward, who is usually
a go-between; and the crew never feel as though you were
"one of them." But if you live in the forecastle, you are "as
independent as a wood sawyer's clerk" (*nauticé*), and are a
*sailor*. You hear sailors' talk, learn their ways, their peculiarities of feeling as well as speaking and acting; and, moreover,
pick up a great deal of curious and useful information in seamanship, ship's customs, foreign countries, &c., from their long
yarns and equally long disputes. No man can be a sailor, or
know what sailors are, unless he has lived in the forecastle
with them—turned in and out with them, and eaten from the
common kid. After I had been a week there, nothing would
have tempted me to go back to my old berth, and never afterward, even in the worst of weather, when in a close and leaking forecastle off Cape Horn, did I for a moment wish myself
in the steerage. Another thing which you learn better in the
forecastle than you can anywhere else is to make and mend
clothes, and this is indispensable to sailors. A large part of
their watches below they spend at this work, and here I
learned the art myself, which stood me in so good stead afterward.

But to return to the state of the crew. Upon our coming
into the forecastle, there was some difficulty about the uniting
of the allowances of bread, by which we thought we were to
lose a few pounds. This set us into a ferment. The captain
would not condescend to explain, and we went aft in a body,
with John, the Swede, the oldest and best sailor of the crew,
for spokesman. The recollection of the scene that followed
always brings up a smile, especially the quarterdeck dignity
and elocution of the captain. He was walking the weather side
of the quarterdeck, and, seeing us coming aft, stopped short
in his walk, and with a voice and look intended to annihilate
us, called out, "Well, what the d——l do you want now?"
Whereupon we stated our grievances as respectfully as we
could, but he broke in upon us, saying that we were getting
fat and lazy, didn't have enough to do, and it was that which
made us find fault. This provoked us, and we began to give
word for word. This would never answer. He clenched his fist,
stamped and swore, and ordered us all forward, saying, with

oaths enough interspersed to send the words home, "Away with you! Go forward every one of you! I'll *haze* you! I'll work you up! You don't have enough to do! If you a'n't careful I'll make a hell of heaven! . . . You've mistaken your man! I'm Frank Thompson, all the way from 'down east.' I've been through the mill, ground and bolted, and come out a 'regular-built down-east johnnycake'—when it's hot, d——d good, but when it's cold, d——d sour and indigestible; and you'll find me so!" The latter part of this harangue made a strong impression, and the "down-east johnnycake" became a byword for the rest of the voyage, and on the coast of California, after our arrival. One of his nicknames in all the ports was the "Down-East Johnnycake." So much for our petition for the redress of grievances. The matter was, however, set right, for the mate, after allowing the captain due time to cool off, explained it to him, and at night we were all called aft to hear another harangue, in which, of course, the whole blame of the misunderstanding was thrown upon us. We ventured to hint that he would not give us time to explain; but it wouldn't do. We were driven back discomfited. Thus the affair blew over, but the irritation caused by it remained; and we never had peace or a good understanding again so long as the captain and crew remained together.

We continued sailing along in the beautiful temperate climate of the Pacific. The Pacific well deserves its name, for except in the southern part, at Cape Horn, and in the western parts, near the China and Indian oceans, it has few storms, and is never either extremely hot or cold. Between the tropics there is a slight haziness, like a thin gauze, drawn over the sun, which, without obstructing or obscuring the light, tempers the heat which comes down with perpendicular fierceness in the Atlantic and Indian tropics. We sailed well to the westward to have the full advantage of the northeast trades, and when we had reached the latitude of Point Conception, where it is usual to make the land, we were several hundred miles to the westward of it. We immediately changed our course due east, and sailed in that direction for a number of days. At length we began to heave to after dark, for fear of making the land at night, on a coast where there are no lighthouses and but indifferent charts, and at daybreak on the morning of—

*Tuesday, January 13th, 1835,* we made the land at Point

Conception, lat. 34° 32′ N., lon. 120° 06′ W. The port of
Santa Barbara, to which we were bound, lying about fifty miles
to the southward of this point, we continued sailing down the
coast during the day and following night, and on the next
morning—

*January 14th,* we came to anchor in the spacious bay of
Santa Barbara, after a voyage of one hundred and fifty days
from Boston.

# CHAPTER IX

California extends along nearly the whole of the western coast
of Mexico, between the Gulf of California in the south and
the Bay of San Francisco on the north, or between the 22nd
and 38th degrees of north latitude. It is subdivided into two
provinces—Lower or Old California, lying between the gulf
and the 32nd degree of latitude, or near it (the division line
running, I believe, between the bay of Todos Santos and the
port of San Diego); and New or Upper California, the south-
ernmost port of which is San Diego, in lat. 32° 39′, and the
northernmost, San Francisco, situated in the large bay discovered by Sir Francis Drake, in lat. 37° 58′, and now known
as the bay of San Francisco, so named, I suppose, by Fran-
ciscan missionaries. Upper California has the seat of its government at Monterey, where is also the customhouse, the only
one on the coast, and at which every vessel intending to trade
on the coast must enter its cargo before it can begin its traffic.
We were to trade upon this coast exclusively, and therefore
expected to go first to Monterey, but the captain's orders from
home were to put in at Santa Barbara, which is the central

port of the coast, and wait there for the agent who transacts all the business for the firm to which our vessel belonged.

The bay, or, as it was commonly called, the canal of Santa Barbara, is very large, being formed by the mainland on one side (between Point Conception on the north and Point Santa Buenaventura on the south), which here bends in like a crescent, and by three large islands opposite to it and at the distance of some twenty miles. These points are just sufficient to give it the name of a bay, while at the same time it is so large and so much exposed to the southeast and northwest winds that it is little better than an open roadstead; and the whole swell of the Pacific Ocean rolls in here before a south-easter, and breaks with so heavy a surf in the shallow waters that it is highly dangerous to lie near in to the shore during the southeaster season, that is, between the months of November and April.

This wind (the southeaster) is the bane of the coast of California. Between the months of November and April (including a part of each), which is the rainy season in this latitude, you are never safe from it; and accordingly, in the ports which are open to it, vessels are obliged, during these months, to lie at anchor at a distance of three miles from the shore, with slip ropes on their cables, ready to slip and go to sea at a moment's warning. The only ports which are safe from this wind are San Francisco and Monterey in the north, and San Diego in the south.

As it was January when we arrived, and the middle of the southeaster season, we came to anchor at the distance of three miles from the shore, in eleven fathoms water, and bent a slip rope and buoys to our cables, cast off the yardarm gaskets from the sails, and stopped them all with rope yarns. After we had done this, the boat went ashore with the captain, and returned with orders to the mate to send a boat ashore for him at sundown. I did not go in the first boat, and was glad to find that there was another going before night; for after so long a voyage as ours had been, a few hours seem a long time to be in sight and out of reach of land. We spent the day on board in the usual duties; but as this was the first time we had been without the captain, we felt a little more freedom, and looked about us to see what sort of a country we had got into, and were to pass a year or two of our lives in.

It was a beautiful day, and so warm that we wore straw

hats, duck trousers, and all the summer gear. As this was midwinter, it spoke well for the climate; and we afterward found that the thermometer never fell to the freezing point throughout the winter, and that there was very little difference between the seasons, except that during a long period of rainy and southeasterly weather, thick clothes were not uncomfortable.

The large bay lay about us, nearly smooth, as there was hardly a breath of wind stirring, though the boat's crew who went ashore told us that the long ground swell broke into a heavy surf on the beach. There was only one vessel in the port —a long, sharp brig of about three hundred tons, with raking masts, and very square yards, and English colors at her peak. We afterward learned that she was built at Guayaquil, and named the *Ayacucho*, after the place where the battle was fought that gave Peru her independence, and was now owned by a Scotchman named Wilson, who commanded her, and was engaged in the trade between Callao and other parts of South America and California. She was a fast sailer, as we frequently afterward saw, and had a crew of Sandwich Islanders on board. Beside this vessel, there was no object to break the surface of the bay. Two points ran out as the horns of the crescent, one of which—the one to the westward—was low and sandy, and is that to which vessels are obliged to give a wide berth when running out for a southeaster; the other is high, bold, and well wooded, and has a mission upon it, called Santa Buenaventura, from which the point is named. In the middle of this crescent, directly opposite the anchoring ground, lie the mission and town of Santa Barbara, on a low plain, but little above the level of the sea, covered with grass, though entirely without trees, and surrounded on three sides by an amphitheater of mountains, which slant off to the distance of fifteen or twenty miles. The mission stands a little back of the town, and is a large building, or rather collection of buildings, in the center of which is a high tower, with a belfry of five bells. The whole, being plastered, makes quite a show at a distance, and is the mark by which vessels come to anchor. The town lies a little nearer to the beach—about half a mile from it—and is composed of one-story houses built of sun-baked clay, or adobe, some of them whitewashed, with red tiles on the roofs. I should judge that there were about a hundred of them; and in the midst of them stands the presidio, or fort, built of the same materials, and apparently but little stronger. The town is finely situated, with a bay in front, and an amphitheater of hills behind. The only thing which diminishes its beauty is that the hills have no large trees upon them, they having been all burned by a great fire which swept them off about a dozen years ago, and they had not yet grown again. The fire was described to me by an inhabitant as having been a very terrible and magnificent sight. The air of the whole valley was so heated that the people were obliged to leave the town and take up their quarters for several days upon the beach.

Just before sundown, the mate ordered a boat's crew ashore, and I went as one of the number. We passed under the stern of the English brig, and had a long pull ashore. I shall never forget the impression which our first landing on the beach of California made upon me. The sun had just gone down; it was getting dusky; the damp night wind was beginning to blow, and the heavy swell of the Pacific was setting in, and breaking in loud and high "combers" upon the beach. We lay on our oars in the swell, just outside of the surf, waiting for a good chance to run in, when a boat, which had put off from the *Ayacucho*, came alongside of us, with a crew of dusky Sandwich Islanders, talking and hallooing in their outlandish tongue. They knew that we were novices in this kind of boating, and waited to see us go in. The second mate, however, who steered our boat, determined to have the advantage of their experience, and would not go in first. Finding, at length, how matters stood, they gave a shout, and taking advantage of a great comber which came swelling in, rearing its head, and lifting up the sterns of our boats nearly perpendicular, and again dropping them in the trough, they gave three or four long and strong pulls, and went in on top of the great wave, throwing their oars overboard, and as far from the boat as they could throw them, and, jumping out the instant the boat touched the beach, they seized hold of her by the gunwale, on each side, and ran her up high and dry upon the sand. We saw, at once, how the thing was to be done, and also the necessity of keeping the boat stern out to the sea; for the instant the sea should strike upon her broadside or quarter, she would be driven up broadside on, and capsized. We pulled strongly in, and as soon as we felt that the sea had got hold of us, and was carrying us in with the speed of a race horse,

we threw the oars as far from the boat as we could, and took
hold of the gunwales, ready to spring out and seize her when
she struck, the officer using his utmost strength, with his
steering oar, to keep her stern out. We were shot up upon the
beach, and, seizing the boat, ran her up high and dry, and,
picking up our oars, stood by her, ready for the captain to
come down.

Finding that the captain did not come immediately, we put
our oars in the boat, and, leaving one to watch it, walked
about the beach to see what we could of the place. The beach
is nearly a mile in length between the two points, and of
smooth sand. We had taken the only good landing place,
which is in the middle, it being more stony toward the ends.
It is about twenty yards in width from high-water mark to a
slight bank at which the soil begins, and so hard that it is a
favorite place for running horses. It was growing dark, so
that we could just distinguish the dim outlines of the two
vessels in the offing; and the great seas were rolling in in regular lines, growing larger and larger as they approached the
shore, and hanging over the beach upon which they were to
break, when their tops would curl over and turn white with
foam, and, beginning at one extreme of the line, break rapidly
to the other, as a child's long card house falls when a card is
knocked down at one end. The Sandwich Islanders, in the
meantime, had turned their boat round, and ran her down
into the water, and were loading her with hides and tallow.
As this was the work in which we were soon to be engaged,
we looked on with some curiosity. They ran the boat so far
into the water that every large sea might float her, and two
of them, with their trousers rolled up, stood by the bows,
one on each side, keeping her in her right position. This was
hard work; for beside the force they had to use upon the boat,
the large seas nearly took them off their legs. The others were
running from the boat to the bank, upon which, out of the
reach of the water, was a pile of dry bullocks' hides, doubled
lengthwise in the middle, and nearly as stiff as boards. These
they took upon their heads, one or two at a time, and carried
down to the boat, in which one of their number stowed them
away. They were obliged to carry them on their heads to
keep them out of the water, and we observed that they had
on thick woolen caps. "Look here, Bill, and see what you're
coming to!" said one of our men to another who stood by

the boat. "Well, Dana," said the second mate to me, "this does not look much like Harvard College, does it? But it is what I call 'head work.'" To tell the truth, it did not look very encouraging.

After they had got through with the hides, the Kanakas laid hold of the bags of tallow (the bags are made of hide, and are about the size of a common meal bag), and lifted each upon the shoulders of two men, one at each end, who walked off with them to the boat, when all prepared to go aboard. Here, too, was something for us to learn. The man who steered shipped his oar and stood up in the stern, and those that pulled the two after oars sat upon their benches, with their oars shipped, ready to strike out as soon as she was afloat. The two men remained standing at the bows; and when, at length, a large sea came in and floated her, seized hold of the gunwales, and ran out with her till they were up to their armpits, and then tumbled over the gunwales into the bows, dripping with water. The men at the oars struck out, but it wouldn't do; the sea swept back and left them nearly high and dry. The two fellows jumped out again; and the next time they succeeded better, and, with the help of a deal of outlandish hallooing and bawling, got her well off. We watched them till they were out of the breakers, and saw them steering for their vessel, which was now hidden in the darkness.

The sand of the beach began to be cold to our bare feet; the frogs set up their croaking in the marshes, and one solitary owl, from the end of the distant point, gave out his melancholy note, mellowed by the distance, and we began to think that it was high time for "the old man," as a shipmaster is commonly called, to come down. In a few minutes we heard something coming toward us. It was a man on horseback. He came on the full gallop, reined up near us, addressed a few words to us, and, receiving no answer, wheeled round and galloped off again. He was nearly as dark as an Indian, with a large Spanish hat, blanket cloak or serape, and leather leggings, with a long knife stuck in them. "This is the seventh city that ever I was in, and no Christian one neither," said Bill Brown. "Stand by!" said John. "You haven't seen the worst of it yet." In the midst of this conversation the captain appeared; and we winded the boat round, shoved her down, and prepared to go off. The captain, who had been on the coast before, and "knew the ropes," took the steering oar, and we went off in the same way as the other boat. I, being the youngest, had the pleasure of standing at the bow, and getting wet through. We went off well, though the seas were high. Some of them lifted us up, and, sliding from under us, seemed to let us drop through the air like a flat plank upon the body of the water. In a few minutes we were in the low, regular swell, and pulled for a light, which, as we neared it, we found had been run up to our trysail gaff.

Coming aboard, we hoisted up all the boats, and, diving down into the forecastle, changed our wet clothes, and got our supper. After supper the sailors lighted their pipes (cigars, those of us who had them), and we had to tell all we had seen ashore. Then followed conjectures about the people ashore, the length of the voyage, carrying hides, &c., &c., until eight bells, when all hands were called aft, and the "anchor watch" set. We were to stand two in a watch, and, as the nights were pretty long, two hours were to make a watch. The second mate was to keep the deck until eight o'clock, all hands were to be called at daybreak, and the word was passed to keep a bright lookout, and to call the mate if it should come on to blow from the southeast. We had, also, orders to strike the bells every half hour through the night, as at sea. My watchmate was John, the Swedish sailor, and we stood from twelve to two, he walking the larboard side and I the starboard. At daylight all hands were called, and we went through the usual process of washing down, swabbing, &c., and got breakfast at eight o'clock. In the course of the forenoon, a boat went aboard of the *Ayacucho* and brought off a quarter of beef, which made us a fresh bite for dinner. This we were glad enough to have, and the mate told us that we should live upon fresh beef while we were on the coast, as it was cheaper here than the salt. While at dinner, the cook called, "Sail ho!" and, coming on deck, we saw two sails bearing round the point. One was a large ship under topgallant sails, and the other a small hermaphrodite brig. They both backed their topsails and sent boats aboard of us. The ship's colors had puzzled us, and we found that she was from Genoa, with an assorted cargo, and was trading on the coast. She filled away again, and stood out, being bound up the coast to San Francisco. The crew of the brig's boat were Sandwich Islanders, but one of them, who spoke a little English, told us that she was the *Loriotte*, Captain Nye, from Oahu, and was engaged in the hide-and-tallow trade. She was a lump of a thing, what the sailors call a butterbox. This vessel, as well as the *Ayacucho*, and others which we afterward saw engaged in the same trade, have English or Americans for officers, and two or three before the mast to do the work upon the rigging, and to be relied upon for seamanship, while the rest of the crew are Sandwich Islanders, who are active and very useful in boating.

The three captains went ashore after dinner, and came off again at night. When in port, everything is attended to by the chief mate; the captain, unless he is also supercargo, has little to do, and is usually ashore much of his time. This we thought would be pleasanter for us, as the mate was a good-natured man, and not very strict. So it was for a time, but we were worse off in the end; for wherever the captain is a severe, energetic man, and the mate has neither of these qualities, there will always be trouble. And trouble we had already begun to anticipate. The captain had several times found fault with the mate, in presence of the crew; and hints had been dropped that all was not right between them. When this is the case, and the captain suspects that his chief officer is too easy and familiar with the crew, he begins to interfere in all the duties, and to draw the reins more taut, and the crew have to suffer.

# CHAPTER X

This night, after sundown, it looked black at the southward and eastward, and we were told to keep a bright lookout. Expecting to be called, we turned in early. Waking up about midnight, I found a man who had just come down from his watch striking a light. He said that it was beginning to puff from the southeast, that the sea was rolling in, and he had called the captain; and as he threw himself down on his chest with all his clothes on, I knew that he expected to be called. I felt the vessel pitching at her anchor, and the chain surging and snapping, and lay awake, prepared for an instant summons. In a few minutes it came—three knocks on the scuttle, and "All hands ahoy! Bear-a-hand * up and make sail." We sprang for our clothes, and were about half dressed, when the mate called out, down the scuttle, "Tumble up here, men, tumble up, before she drags her anchor!" We were on deck in an instant. "Lay aloft and loose the topsails!" shouted the captain, as soon as the first man showed himself. Springing into the rigging, I saw that the *Ayacucho's* topsails were loosed, and heard her crew singing out at the sheets as they were hauling them home. This had probably started our captain, as Old Wilson (the captain of the *Ayacucho*) had been many years on the coast, and knew the signs of the weather. We soon had the topsails loosed; and one hand remaining, as usual, in each top, to overhaul the rigging and light the sail out, the rest of us came down to man the sheets. While sheeting home, we saw the *Ayacucho* standing athwart our hawse, sharp upon the wind, cutting through the head seas like a knife, with her raking masts, and her sharp bows running up like the head of a greyhound. It was a beautiful sight. She was like a bird which had been frightened and had spread her wings in flight. After our topsails had been sheeted home, the head yards braced aback, the fore-topmast staysail hoisted, and the buoys streamed, and all ready forward for slipping, we went aft and manned the slip rope which came through the stern port with a turn round the timberheads. "All ready forward?" asked the captain. "Aye, aye, sir; all ready," answered the mate. "Let go!" "All gone, sir"; and the chain cable grated over the windlass and through the hawsehole, and the little vessel's head swinging off from the wind under the force of her backed head sails brought the strain upon the slip rope. "Let go aft!" Instantly all was gone, and we were under way. As soon as she was well off from the wind, we filled away the head yards, braced all up sharp, set the foresail and trysail, and left our anchorage well astern, giving the point a good

* "Bear-a-hand" is to make haste.

berth. "Nye's off, too," said the captain to the mate; and, looking astern, we could just see the little hermaphrodite brig under sail, standing after us.

It now began to blow fresh; the rain fell fast, and it grew black; but the captain would not take in sail until we were well clear of the point. As soon as we left this on our quarter, and were standing out to sea, the order was given, and we went aloft, double-reefed each topsail, furled the foresail, and double-reefed the trysail, and were soon under easy sail. In these cases of slipping for southeasters there is nothing to be done, after you have got clear of the coast, but to lie to under easy sail, and wait for the gale to be over, which seldom lasts more than two days, and is sometimes over in twelve hours; but the wind never comes back to the southward until there has a good deal of rain fallen. "Go below, the watch," said the mate; but here was a dispute which watch it should be. The mate soon settled it by sending his watch below, saying that we should have our turn the next time we got under way. We remained on deck till the expiration of the watch, the wind blowing very fresh and the rain coming down in torrents. When the watch came up, we wore ship, and stood on the other tack, in toward land. When we came up again, which was at four in the morning, it was very dark, and there was not much wind, but it was raining as I thought I had never seen it rain before. We had on oilcloth suits and southwester caps, and had nothing to do but to stand bolt upright and let it pour down upon us. There are no umbrellas, and no sheds to go under, at sea.

While we were standing about on deck, we saw the little brig drifting by us, hove to under her fore-topsail double-reefed; and she glided by like a phantom. Not a word was spoken, and we saw no one on deck but the man at the wheel. Toward morning the captain put his head out of the companionway and told the second mate, who commanded our watch, to look out for a change of wind, which usually followed a calm, with heavy rain. It was well that he did; for in a few minutes it fell dead calm, the vessel lost her steerageway, the rain ceased, we hauled up the trysail and courses, squared the afteryards, and waited for the change, which came in a few minutes, with a vengeance, from the northwest, the opposite point of the compass. Owing to our precautions, we were not taken aback, but ran before the wind with square yards. The captain coming on deck, we braced up a little and stood back for our anchorage. With the change of wind came a change of weather, and in two hours the wind moderated into the light steady breeze which blows down the coast the greater part of the year, and, from its regularity, might be called a trade wind. The sun came up bright, and we set royals, skysails, and studding sails, and were under fair way for Santa Barbara. The little *Loriotte* was astern of us, nearly out of sight; but we saw nothing of the *Ayacucho*. In a short time she appeared, standing out from Santa Rosa island, under the lee of which she had been hove to all night. Our captain was eager to get in before her, for it would be a great credit to us, on the coast, to beat the *Ayacucho*, which had been called the best sailer in the North Pacific, in which she had been known as a trader for six years or more. We had an advantage over her in light winds, from our royals and sky-sails which we carried both at the fore and main, and also from our studding sails; for Captain Wilson carried nothing above topgallant sails, and always unbent his studding sails when on the coast. As the wind was light and fair, we held our own, for some time, when we were both obliged to brace up and come upon a taut bowline, after rounding the point; and here he had us on his own ground, and walked away from us, as you would haul in a line. He afterward said that we sailed well enough with the wind free, but that give him a taut bowline, and he would beat us, if we had all the canvas of the *Royal George*.

The *Ayacucho* got to the anchoring ground about half an hour before us, and was furling her sails when we came to it. This picking up your cables is a nice piece of work. It requires some seamanship to do it, and to come to at your former moorings, without letting go another anchor. Captain Wilson was remarkable, among the sailors on the coast, for his skill in doing this; and our captain never let go a second anchor during all the time that I was with him. Coming a little to windward of our buoy, we clewed up the light sails, backed our main topsail, and lowered a boat, which pulled off, and made fast a spare hawser to the buoy on the end of the slip rope. We brought the other end to the capstan, and hove in upon it until we came to the slip rope, which we took to the windlass, and walked her up to her chain, occasionally helping her by backing and filling the sails. The chain is then passed through the hawsehole and round the windlass, and bitted, the slip rope taken round outside and brought into the stern port, and she is safe in her old berth. After we had got through, the mate told us that this was a small touch of California, the like of which we must expect to have through the winter.

After we had furled the sails and got dinner, we saw the *Loriotte* nearing, and she had her anchor before night. At sundown we went ashore again, and found the *Loriotte's* boat waiting on the beach. The Sandwich Islander who could speak English told us that he had been up to the town; that our agent, Mr. Robinson, and some other passengers were going to Monterey with us, and that we were to sail the same night. In a few minutes Captain Thompson, with two gentlemen and a lady, came down, and we got ready to go off. They had a good deal of baggage, which we put into the bows of the boat, and then two of us took the *señora* in our arms, and waded with her through the water, and put her down safely in the stern. She appeared much amused with the transaction, and her husband was perfectly satisfied, thinking any arrangement good which saved his wetting his feet. I pulled the after oar, so that I heard the conversation, and learned that one of the men, who, as well as I could see in the darkness, was a young-looking man, in the European dress, and covered up in a large cloak, was the agent of the firm to which our vessel belonged; and the other, who was dressed in the Spanish dress of the country, was a brother of our captain, who had been many years a trader on the coast, and that the lady was his wife. She was a delicate, dark-complexioned young woman, of one of the respectable families of California. I also found that we were to sail the same night.

As soon as we got on board, the boats were hoisted up, the sails loosed, the windlass manned, the slip ropes and gear cast off; and after about twenty minutes of heaving at the windlass, making sail, and bracing yards, we were well under way, and going with a fair wind up the coast to Monterey. The *Loriotte* got under way at the same time, and was also bound up to Monterey, but as she took a different course from us, keeping the land aboard, while we kept well out to sea, we soon lost sight of her. We had a fair wind, which is something unusual when going up, as the prevailing wind is the north, which blows directly down the coast; whence the northern are called the windward, and the southern the leeward ports.

## CHAPTER XI

We got clear of the islands before sunrise the next morning, and by twelve o'clock were out of the canal, and off Point Conception, the place where we first made the land upon our arrival. This is the largest point on the coast, and is an uninhabited headland, stretching out into the Pacific, and has the reputation of being very windy. Any vessel does well which gets by it without a gale, especially in the winter season. We were going along with studding sails set on both sides, when, as we came round the point, we had to haul our wind, and take in the lee studding sails. As the brig came more upon the wind, she felt it more, and we doused the skysails, but kept the weather studding sails on her, bracing the yards forward, so that the swinging boom nearly touched the spritsail yard. She now lay over to it, the wind was freshening, and the captain was evidently "dragging on to her." His brother and Mr. Robinson, looking a little disturbed, said something to him, but he only answered that he knew the vessel and what she would carry. He was evidently "showing off," and letting them know he could carry sail. He stood up to windward, holding on by the backstays, and looking up at the sticks to see how much they would bear, when a puff came which settled the matter. Then it was "haul down" and "clew up" royals, flying jib, and studding sails, all at once. There was what the sailors call a "mess"—everything let go, nothing hauled in, and everything flying. The poor Mexican woman came to the companionway, looking as pale as a ghost, and nearly frightened to death. The mate and some men forward were trying to haul in the lower studding sail, which had blown over the spritsail yardarm and round the guys, while the topmast-studding-sail boom, after buckling up and springing out again like a piece of whalebone, broke off at the boom iron. I jumped aloft to take in the main-topgallant studding sail, but before I got into the top the tack parted, and away went the sail, swinging forward of the topgallant sail, and tearing and slatting itself to pieces. The halyards were at this moment let go by the run, and such a piece of work I never had before in taking in a sail. After great exertions I got it, or the remains of it, into the top, and was making it fast, when the captain, looking up, called out to me, "Lay aloft there, Dana, and furl that main royal." Leaving the studding sail, I went up to the crosstrees; and here it looked rather squally. The foot of the topgallant mast was working between the cross and trestle trees, and the mast lay over at a fearful angle with the topmast below, while everything was working and cracking, strained to the utmost.

There's nothing for Jack to do but to obey orders, and I went up upon the yard; and there was a worse mess, if possible, than I had left below. The braces had been let go, and the yard was swinging about like a turnpike gate, and the whole sail having blown out to leeward, the lee leach was over the yardarm, and the skysail was all adrift and flying about my head. I looked down, but it was in vain to attempt to make myself heard, for everyone was busy below, and the wind roared, and sails were flapping in all directions. Fortunately, it was noon and broad daylight, and the man at the wheel, who had his eyes aloft, soon saw my difficulty, and after numberless signs and gestures, got someone to haul the necessary ropes taut. During this interval I took a look below. Everything was in confusion on deck; the little vessel was tearing through the water as if she had lost her wits, the seas flying over her, and the masts leaning over at a wide angle from the vertical. At the other royal masthead was Stimson, working away at the sail, which was blowing from him as fast as he could gather it in. The topgallant sail below me was soon clewed up, which relieved the mast, and in a short time I got my sail furled, and went below; but I lost overboard a new tarpaulin hat, which troubled me more than anything else. We worked for about half an hour with might and main; and in an hour from the time the squall struck us, from having all our flying kites abroad, we came down to double-reefed topsails and the storm sails.

The wind had hauled ahead during the squall, and we were standing directly in for the point. So, as soon as we had got all snug, we wore round and stood off again, and had the pleasant prospect of beating up to Monterey, a distance of a hundred miles, against a violent head wind. Before night it began to rain; and we had five days of rainy, stormy weather, under close sail all the time, and were blown several hundred miles off the coast. In the midst of this, we discovered that our fore-topmast was sprung (which no doubt happened in the squall), and were obliged to send down the fore-topgallant mast and carry as little sail as possible forward. Our four passengers were dreadfully seasick, so that we saw little or nothing of them during the five days. On the sixth day it cleared off, and the sun came out bright, but the wind and sea were still very high. It was quite like being in midocean again; no land for hundreds of miles, and the captain taking the sun every day at noon. Our passengers now made their appearance, and I had for the first time the opportunity of seeing what a miserable and forlorn creature a seasick passenger is. Since I had got over my own sickness, the third day from Boston, I had seen nothing but hale, hearty men, with their sea legs on, and able to go anywhere (for we had no passengers on our voyage out); and I will own there was a pleasant feeling of superiority in being able to walk the deck, and eat, and go aloft, and compare one's self with two poor, miserable, pale creatures, staggering and shuffling about decks, or holding on and looking up with giddy heads, to see us climbing to the mastheads, or sitting quietly at work on the ends of the lofty yards. A well man at sea has little sympathy with one who is seasick; he is apt to be too conscious of a comparison which seems favorable to his own manhood.

After a few days we made the land at Point Pinos, which is the headland at the entrance of the bay of Monterey. As we drew in and ran down the shore, we could distinguish well the face of the country, and found it better wooded than that to the southward of Point Conception. In fact, as I afterward discovered, Point Conception may be made the dividing line

between two different faces of the country. As you go to the
northward of the point, the country becomes more wooded,
has a richer appearance, and is better supplied with water.
This is the case with Monterey, and still more so with San
Francisco; while to the southward of the point, as at Santa
Barbara, San Pedro, and particularly San Diego, there is
very little wood, and the country has a naked, level appearance, though it is still fertile.

The bay of Monterey is wide at the entrance, being about
twenty-four miles between the two points, Año Nuevo at the
north, and Pinos at the south, but narrows gradually as you
approach the town, which is situated in a bend, or large cove,
at the southeastern extremity, and from the points about
eighteen miles, which is the whole depth of the bay. The shores
are extremely well wooded (the pine abounding upon them),
and as it was now the rainy season, everything was as green
as nature could make it—the grass, the leaves, and all; the
birds were singing in the woods, and great numbers of wild
fowl were flying over our heads. Here we could lie safe from
the southeasters. We came to anchor within two cable lengths
of the shore, and the town lay directly before us, making a
very pretty appearance; its houses being of whitewashed
adobe, which gives a much better effect than those of Santa
Barbara, which are mostly left of a mud color. The red tiles,
too, on the roofs, contrasted well with the white sides, and
with the extreme greenness of the lawn upon which the houses
—about a hundred in number—were dotted about, here and
there, irregularly. There are in this place, and in every other
town which I saw in California, no streets nor fences (except
that here and there a small patch might be fenced in for a
garden), so that the houses are placed at random upon the
green. This, as they are of one story, and of the cottage form,
gives them a pretty effect when seen from a little distance.

It was a fine Saturday afternoon that we came to anchor,
the sun about an hour high, and everything looking pleasantly.
The Mexican flag was flying from the little square presidio,
and the drums and trumpets of the soldiers, who were out on
parade, sounded over the water, and gave great life to the
scene. Everyone was delighted with the appearance of things.
We felt as though we had got into a Christian (which in the
sailor's vocabulary means civilized) country. The first impression which California had made upon us was very disagree-

able—the open roadstead of Santa Barbara; anchoring three miles from the shore; running out to sea before every southeaster; landing in a high surf; with a little dark-looking town, a mile from the beach; and not a sound to be heard, nor anything to be seen, but Kanakas, hides, and tallow bags. Add to this the gale off Point Conception, and no one can be at a loss to account for our agreeable disappointment in Monterey. Besides, we soon learned, which was of no small importance to us, that there was little or no surf here, and this afternoon the beach was as smooth as a pond.

We landed the agent and passengers, and found several persons waiting for them on the beach, among whom were some who, though dressed in the costume of the country, spoke English, and who, we afterward learned were English and Americans who had married and settled here.

I also connected with our arrival here another circumstance which more nearly concerns myself; viz., my first act of what the sailors will allow to be seamanship—sending down a royal yard. I had seen it done once or twice at sea; and an old sailor, whose favor I had taken some pains to gain, had taught me carefully everything which was necessary to be done, and in its proper order, and advised me to take the first opportunity when we were in port, and try it. I told the second mate, with whom I had been pretty "thick" when he was before the mast, that I could do it, and got him to ask the mate to send me up the first time the royal yards were struck. Accordingly, I was called upon, and went aloft, repeating the operations over in my mind, taking care to get each thing in its order, for the slightest mistake spoils the whole. Fortunately, I got through without any word from the officer, and heard the "well done" of the mate, when the yard reached the deck, with as much satisfaction as I ever felt at Cambridge on seeing a *"Bene"* at the foot of a Latin exercise.

# CHAPTER XII

The next day being Sunday, which is the liberty day among merchantmen, when it is usual to let a part of the crew go ashore, the sailors had depended upon a holiday, and were already disputing who should ask to go, when, upon being called in the morning, we were turned to upon the rigging, and found that the topmast, which had been sprung, was to come down, and a new one to go up, with topgallant and royal masts, and the rigging to be set. This was too bad. If there is anything that irritates sailors, and makes them feel hardly used, it is being deprived of their Sunday. Not that they would always, or indeed generally, spend it improvingly, but it is their only day of rest. Then, too, they are so often necessarily deprived of it by storms, and unavoidable duties of all kinds, that to take it from them when lying quietly and safely in port, without any urgent reason, bears the more hardly. The only reason in this case was that the captain had determined to have the customhouse officers on board on Monday, and wished to have his brig in order. Jack is a slave aboard ship; but still he has many opportunities of thwarting and balking his master. When there is danger or necessity, or when he is well used, no one can work faster than he; but the instant he feels that he is kept at work for nothing, or, as the nautical phrase is, "humbugged," no sloth could make less headway. He must not refuse his duty, or be in any way disobedient, but all the work that an officer gets out of him, he may be welcome to. Every man who has been three months at sea knows how to "work Tom Cox's traverse"—"three turns round the longboat, and a pull at the scuttle butt." This morning everything went in this way. "Sogering" was the order of the day. Send a man below to get a block, and he would capsize everything before finding it, then not bring it up till an officer had called him twice, and take as much time to put things in order again. Marlinespikes were not to be found; knives wanted a prodigious deal of sharpening, and, generally, three or four were waiting round the grindstone at a time. When a man got to the masthead, he would come slowly down again for something he had left; and after the tackles were got up, six men would pull less than three who pulled "with a will."

When the mate was out of sight, nothing was done. It was all uphill work; and at eight o'clock, when we went to breakfast, things were nearly where they were when we began.

During our short meal the matter was discussed. One proposed refusing to work; but that was mutiny, and of course was rejected at once. I remember, too, that one of the men quoted Father Taylor (as they call the seamen's preacher at Boston), who told them that, if they were ordered to work on Sunday, they must not refuse their duty, and the blame would not come upon them. After breakfast, it leaked out, through the officers, that, if we would get through work soon, we might have a boat in the afternoon and go a-fishing. This bait was well thrown, and took with several who were fond of fishing; and all began to find that as we had one thing to do, and were not to be kept at work for the day, the sooner we did it the better. Accordingly, things took a new aspect; and before two o'clock, this work, which was in a fair way to last two days, was done; and five of us went a-fishing in the jolly boat, in the direction of Point Pinos; but leave to go ashore was refused. Here we saw the *Loriotte*, which sailed with us from Santa Barbara, coming slowly in with a light sea breeze, which sets in toward afternoon, having been becalmed off the point all the first part of the day. We took several fish of various kinds, among which cod and perch abounded, and Foster (the *ci-devant* second mate), who was of our number, brought up with his hook a large and beautiful pearl-oyster shell. We afterward learned that this place was celebrated for shells, and that a small schooner had made a good voyage by carrying a cargo of them to the United States.

We returned by sundown, and found the *Loriotte* at anchor within a cable's length of the *Pilgrim*. The next day we were "turned to" early, and began taking off the hatches, overhauling the cargo, and getting everything ready for inspection. At eight, the officers of the customs, five in number, came on board, and began examining the cargo, manifest, &c. The Mexican revenue laws are very strict, and require the whole cargo to be landed, examined, and taken on board again; but our agent had succeeded in compounding for the last two vessels, and saving the trouble of taking the cargo ashore. The officers were dressed in the costume which we found prevailed through the country—broad-brimmed hat, usually of a black or dark-brown color, with a gilt or figured band round

the crown, and lined under the rim with silk; a short jacket
of silk, or figured calico (the European skirted body coat is
never worn); the shirt open in the neck; rich waistcoat, if
any; pantaloons open at the sides below the knee, laced with
gilt, usually of velveteen or broadcloth; or else short breeches
and white stockings. They wear the deerskin shoe, which is
of a dark-brown color, and (being made by Indians) usually
a good deal ornamented. They have no suspenders, but always
wear a sash round the waist, which is generally red, and varying in quality with the means of the wearer. Add to this the
never-failing poncho, or the serape, and you have the dress
of the Californian. This last garment is always a mark of the
rank and wealth of the owner. The *gente de razón*, or better
sort of people, wear cloaks of black or dark-blue broadcloth,
with as much velvet and trimmings as may be; and from this
they go down to the blanket of the Indian, the middle classes
wearing a poncho, something like a large square cloth, with a
hole in the middle for the head to go through. This is often
as coarse as a blanket, but being beautifully woven with various colors, is quite showy at a distance. Among the Mexicans
there is no working class (the Indians being practically serfs,
and doing all the hard work); and every rich man looks like
a grandee, and every poor scamp like a broken-down gentleman. I have often seen a man with a fine figure and courteous
manners, dressed in broadcloth and velvet, with a noble horse
completely covered with trappings, without a real in his pockets, and absolutely suffering for something to eat.

# CHAPTER XIII

The next day, the cargo having been entered in due form, we
began trading. The trade room was fitted up in the steerage,

and furnished out with the lighter goods, and with specimens
of the rest of the cargo; and Mellus, a young man who came
out from Boston with us before the mast, was taken out of
the forecastle, and made supercargo's clerk. He was well qualified for this business, having been clerk in a countinghouse in
Boston; but he had been troubled for some time with rheumatism, which unfitted him for the wet and exposed duty of a
sailor on the coast. For a week or ten days all was life on
board. The people came off to look and to buy—men, women,
and children; and we were continually going in the boats,
carrying goods and passengers, for they have no boats of their
own. Everything must dress itself and come aboard and see
the new vessel, if it were only to buy a paper of pins. The
agent and his clerk managed the sales, while we were busy in
the hold or in the boats. Our cargo was an assorted one; that
is, it consisted of everything under the sun. We had spirits of
all kinds (sold by the cask), teas, coffee, sugars, spices, raisins,
molasses, hardware, crockeryware, tinware, cutlery, clothing
of all kinds, boots and shoes from Lynn, calicoes and cottons
from Lowell, crapes, silks; also, shawls, scarfs, necklaces,
jewelry, and combs for the women; furniture; and, in fact,
everything that can be imagined, from Chinese fireworks to
English cart wheels—of which we had a dozen pairs with their
iron tires on.

The Californians are an idle, thriftless people, and can
make nothing for themselves. The country abounds in grapes,
yet they buy, at a great price, bad wine made in Boston and
brought round by us, and retail it among themselves at a real
(twelve and a half cents) by the small wineglass. Their hides,
too, which they value at two dollars in money, they barter for
something which costs seventy-five cents in Boston; and buy
shoes (as like as not made of their own hides, which have
been carried twice round Cape Horn) at three and four
dollars, and "chicken-skin boots" at fifteen dollars a pair.
Things sell, on an average, at an advance of nearly 300 per
cent upon the Boston prices. This is partly owing to the heavy
duties which the government, in their wisdom, with an idea,
no doubt, of keeping the silver in the country, has laid upon
imports. These duties, and the enormous expenses of so long
a voyage, keep all merchants but those of heavy capital from
engaging in the trade. Nearly two-thirds of all the articles
imported into the country from round Cape Horn, for the last

six years, have been by the single house of Bryant, Sturgis & Co., to whom our vessel belonged.

This kind of business was new to us, and we liked it very well for a few days, though we were hard at work every minute from daylight to dark, and sometimes even later.

By being thus continually engaged in transporting passengers, with their goods, to and fro, we gained considerable knowledge of the character, dress, and language of the people. The dress of the men was as I have before described it. The women wore gowns of various texture—silks, crape, calicoes, &c.—made after the European style, except that the sleeves were short, leaving the arm bare, and that they were loose about the waist, corsets not being in use. They wore shoes of kid or satin, sashes or belts of bright colors, and almost always a necklace and earrings. Bonnets they had none. I only saw one on the coast, and that belonged to the wife of an American sea captain who had settled in San Diego, and had imported the chaotic mass of straw and ribbon as a choice present to his new wife. They wear their hair (which is almost invariably black, or a very dark brown) long in their necks, sometimes loose, and sometimes in long braids; though the married women often do it up on a high comb. Their only protection against the sun and weather is a large mantle which they put over their heads, drawing it close round their faces, when they go out of doors, which is generally only in pleasant weather. When in the house, or sitting out in front of it, which they often do in fine weather, they usually wear a small scarf or neckerchief of a rich pattern. A band, also, about the top of the head, with a cross, star, or other ornament in front, is common. Their complexions are various, depending—as well as their dress and manner—upon the amount of Spanish blood they can lay claim to, which also settles their social rank. Those who are of pure Spanish blood, having never intermarried with the aborigines, have clear brunette complexions, and sometimes even as fair as those of English women. There are but few of these families in California, being mostly those in official stations, or who, on the expiration of their terms of office, have settled here upon property they have acquired; and others who have been banished for state offenses. These form the upper class, intermarrying, and keeping up an exclusive system in every respect. They can be distinguished, not only by their complexion, dress, and manners, but also by their speech; for, calling themselves Castilians, they are very ambitious of speaking the pure Castilian, while all Spanish is spoken in a somewhat corrupted dialect by the lower classes. From this upper class, they go down by regular shades, growing more and more dark and muddy, until you come to the pure Indian, who runs about with nothing upon him but a small piece of cloth, kept up by a wide leather strap drawn round his waist. Generally speaking, each person's caste is decided by the quality of the blood, which shows itself, too plainly to be concealed, at first sight. Yet the least drop of Spanish blood, if it be only of a quadroon or octoroon, is sufficient to raise one from the position of a serf, and entitle him to wear a suit of clothes—boots, hat, cloak, spurs, long knife, all complete, though coarse and dirty as may be—and to call himself *Español,* and to hold property, if he can get any.

The fondness for dress among the women is excessive, and is sometimes their ruin. A present of a fine mantle, or of a necklace or pair of earrings, gains the favor of the greater part. Nothing is more common than to see a woman living in a house of only two rooms, with the ground for a floor, dressed in spangled satin shoes, silk gown, high comb, and gilt, if not gold, earrings and necklace. If their husbands do not dress them well enough, they will soon receive presents from others. They used to spend whole days on board our vessel, examining the fine clothes and ornaments, and frequently making purchases at a rate which would have made a seamstress or waiting maid in Boston open her eyes.

Next to the love of dress, I was most struck with the fineness of the voices and beauty of the intonations of both sexes. Every common ruffian-looking fellow, with a slouched hat, blanket cloak, dirty underdress, and soiled leather leggings, appeared to me to be speaking elegant Spanish. It was a pleasure simply to listen to the sound of the language, before I could attach any meaning to it. They have a good deal of the Creole drawl, but it is varied by an occasional extreme rapidity of utterance, in which they seem to skip from consonant to consonant, until, lighting upon a broad, open vowel, they rest upon that to restore the balance of sound. The women carry this peculiarity of speaking to a much greater extreme than the men, who have more evenness and stateliness of utterance. A common bullock driver, on horseback, delivering a message, seemed to speak like an ambassador at a royal audience. In fact, they sometimes appeared to me to be a people on whom a curse had fallen, and stripped them of everything but their pride, their manners, and their voices.

Another thing that surprised me was the quantity of silver in circulation. I never, in my life, saw so much silver at one time, as during the week that we were at Monterey. The truth is, they have no credit system, no banks, and no way of investing money but in cattle. Besides silver, they have no circulating medium but hides, which the sailors call "California banknotes." Everything that they buy they must pay for by one or the other of these means. The hides they bring down dried and doubled, in clumsy oxcarts, or upon mules' backs, and the money they carry tied up in a handkerchief, fifty or a hundred dollars and half dollars.

I had not studied Spanish at college, and could not speak a word when at Juan Fernández; but, during the latter part of the passage out, I borrowed a grammar and dictionary from the cabin, and by a continual use of these, and a careful attention to every word that I heard spoken, I soon got a vocabulary together, and began talking for myself. As I soon knew more Spanish than any of the crew (who, indeed, knew none at all), and had studied Latin and French, I got the name of a great linguist, and was always sent by the captain and officers for provisions, or to take letters and messages to different parts of the town. I was often sent for something which I could not tell the name of to save my life; but I liked the business, and accordingly never pleaded ignorance. Sometimes I managed to jump below and take a look at my dictionary before going ashore; or else I overhauled some English resident on my way, and learned the word from him; and then, by signs, and by giving a Latin or French word a twist at the end, contrived to get along. This was a good exercise for me, and no doubt taught me more than I should have learned by months of study and reading; it also gave me opportunities of seeing the customs, characters, and domestic arrangements of the people, besides being a great relief from the monotony of a day spent on board ship.

Monterey, as far as my observation goes, is decidedly the pleasantest and most civilized-looking place in California. In the center of it is an open square, surrounded by four lines of one-story buildings, with half a dozen cannon in the cen-

ter, some mounted, and others not. This is the presidio, or
fort. Every town has a presidio in its center; or rather every
presidio has a town built around it; for the forts were first
built by the Mexican government, and then the people built
near them, for protection. The presidio here was entirely open
and unfortified. There were several officers with long titles, and
about eighty soldiers, but they were poorly paid, fed, clothed,
and disciplined. The governor general, or, as he is commonly
called, the general, lives here, which makes it the seat of
government. He is appointed by the central government at
Mexico, and is the chief civil and military officer. In addition to him, each town has a commandant who is its chief
officer, and has charge of the fort, and of all transactions
with foreigners and foreign vessels; while two or three alcaldes and corregidores, elected by the inhabitants, are the
civil officers. Courts strictly of law, with a system of jurisprudence, they have not. Small municipal matters are regu-
lated by the alcaldes and corregidores, and everything
relating to the general government, to the military, and to
foreigners, by the commandants, acting under the governor
general. Capital cases are decided by the latter, upon personal
inspection, if near; or upon minutes sent him by the proper
officers, if the offender is at a distant place. No Protestant has
any political rights, nor can he hold property, or, indeed, remain more than a few weeks on shore, unless he belong to a
foreign vessel. Consequently, Americans and English who in-
tend to reside here become Papists, the current phrase among
them being: "A man must leave his conscience at Cape Horn."

But, to return to Monterey. The houses here, as everywhere else in California, are of one story, built of adobes,
that is, clay made into large bricks, about a foot and a half
square, and three or four inches thick, and hardened in the
sun. These are joined together by a cement of the same material, and the whole are a common dirt color. The floors are
generally of earth, the windows grated and without glass;
and the doors, which are seldom shut, open directly into the
common room, there being no entries. Some of the more
wealthy inhabitants have glass to their windows and board
floors; and in Monterey nearly all the houses are whitewashed on the outside. The better houses, too, have red tiles
upon the roofs. The common ones have two or three rooms
which open into each other, and are furnished with a bed or

two, a few chairs and tables, a looking glass, a crucifix, and
small daubs of paintings enclosed in glass, representing some
miracle or martyrdom. They have no chimneys or fireplaces
in the houses, the climate being such as to make a fire unnecessary; and all their cooking is done in a small kitchen,
separated from the house. The Indians, as I have said before,
do all the hard work, two or three being attached to the better house; and the poorest persons are able to keep one, at
least, for they have only to feed them, and give them a small
piece of coarse cloth and a belt for the men, and a coarse
gown, without shoes or stockings, for the women.

In Monterey there are a number of English and Americans
(English or *Inglés* all are called who speak the English
language) who have married Californians, become united
to the Roman Church, and acquired considerable property.
Having more industry, frugality, and enterprise than the
natives, they soon get nearly all the trade into their hands.
They usually keep shops, in which they retail the goods purchased in larger quantities from our vessels, and also send a
good deal into the interior, taking hides in pay, which they
again barter with our ships. In every town on the coast there
are foreigners engaged in this kind of trade, while I recollect
but two shops kept by natives. The people are naturally suspicious of foreigners, and they would not be allowed to remain, were it not that they conform to the Church, and by
marrying natives, and bringing up their children as Roman
Catholics and Mexicans, and not teaching them the English
language, they quiet suspicion, and even become popular and
leading men. The chief alcaldes in Monterey and Santa Barbara were Yankees by birth.

The men in Monterey appeared to me to be always on
horseback. Horses are as abundant here as dogs and chickens
were in Juan Fernández. There are no stables to keep them
in, but they are allowed to run wild and graze wherever they
please, being branded, and having long leather ropes, called
lassos, attached to their necks and dragging along behind
them, by which they can be easily taken. The men usually
catch one in the morning, throw a saddle and bridle upon
him, and use him for the day, and let him go at night, catching another the next day. When they go on long journeys, they
ride one horse down, and catch another, throw the saddle and
bridle upon him, and, after riding him down, take a third, and

so on to the end of the journey. There are probably no better riders in the world. They are put upon a horse when only four or five years old, their little legs not long enough to come halfway over his sides, and may almost be said to keep on him until they have grown to him. The stirrups are covered or boxed up in front, to prevent their catching when riding through the woods; and the saddles are large and heavy, strapped very tight upon the horse, and have large pommels, or loggerheads, in front, round which the lasso is coiled when not in use. They can hardly go from one house to another without mounting a horse, there being generally several standing tied to the doorposts of the little cottages. When they wish to show their activity, they make no use of their stirrups in mounting, but, striking the horse, spring into the saddle as he starts, and, sticking their long spurs into him, go off on the full run. Their spurs are cruel things, having four or five rowels, each an inch in length, dull and rusty. The flanks of the horses are often sore from them, and I have seen men come in from chasing bullocks, with their horses' hind legs and quarters covered with blood. They frequently give exhibitions of their horsemanship in races, bull-baitings, &c., but as we were not ashore during any holiday, we saw nothing of it. Monterey is also a great place for cockfighting, gambling of all sorts, fandangos, and various kinds of amusement and knavery. Trappers and hunters, who occasionally arrive here from over the Rocky Mountains, with their valuable skins and furs, are often entertained with amusements and dissipation, until they have wasted their opportunities and their money, and then go back, stripped of everything.

Nothing but the character of the people prevents Monterey from becoming a large town. The soil is as rich as man could wish, climate as good as any in the world, water abundant, and situation extremely beautiful. The harbor, too, is a good one, being subject only to one bad wind, the north; and though the holding ground is not the best, yet I heard of but one vessel's being driven ashore here. That was a Mexican brig, which went ashore a few months before our arrival, and was a total wreck, all the crew but one being drowned. Yet this was owing to the carelessness or ignorance of the captain, who paid out all his small cable before he let go his other anchor. The ship *Lagoda*, of Boston, was there at the time, and rode out the gale in safety, without dragging at all, or finding it necessary to strike her topgallant masts.

The only vessel in port with us was the little *Loriotte*. I frequently went on board her, and became well acquainted with her Sandwich Island crew. One of them could speak a little English, and from him I learned a good deal about them. They were well formed and active, with black eyes, intelligent countenances, dark olive, or, I should rather say, copper complexions, and coarse black hair, but not woolly like the Negroes. They appeared to be talking continually. In the forecastle there was a complete Babel. Their language is extremely guttural, and not pleasant at first, but improves as you hear it more; and it is said to have considerable capacity. They use a good deal of gesticulation, and are exceedingly animated, saying with their might what their tongues find to say. They are complete waterdogs, and therefore very good in boating. It is for this reason that there are so many of them on the coast of California, they being very good hands in the surf. They are also ready and active in the rigging, and good hands in warm weather; but those who have been with them round Cape Horn, and in high latitudes, say that they are of little use in cold weather. In their dress, they are precisely like our sailors. In addition to these Islanders, the *Loriotte* had two English sailors, who acted as boatswains over the Islanders, and took care of the rigging. One of them I shall always remember as the best specimen of the thoroughbred English sailor that I ever saw. He had been to sea from a boy, having served a regular apprenticeship of seven years, as English sailors are obliged to do, and was then about four or five and twenty. He was tall; but you only perceived it when he was standing by the side of others, for the great breadth of his shoulders and chest made him appear but little above the middle height. His chest was as deep as it was wide, his arm like that of Hercules, and his hand "the fist of a tar— every hair a rope yarn." With all this, he had one of the pleasantest smiles I ever saw. His cheeks were of a handsome brown, his teeth brilliantly white, and his hair, of a raven black, waved in loose curls over his head and fine, open forehead; and his eyes he might have sold to a duchess at the price of diamonds, for their brilliancy. As for their color, every change of position and light seemed to give them a new hue; but their prevailing color was black, or nearly so. Take him with his well-varnished black tarpaulin, stuck upon the back of his head, his long locks coming down almost into his eyes, his white duck trousers and shirt, blue jacket, and black kerchief, tied loosely round his neck, and he was a fine specimen of manly beauty. On his broad chest was stamped with India ink "Parting moments"—a ship ready to sail, a boat on the beach, and a girl and her sailor lover taking their farewell. Underneath were printed the initials of his own name, and two other letters, standing for some name which he knew better than I. The printing was very well done, having been executed by a man who made it his business to print with India ink, for sailors, at Havre. On one of his broad arms he had a crucifix, and on the other, the sign of the "foul anchor."

He was fond of reading, and we lent him most of the books which we had in the forecastle, which he read and returned to us the next time we fell in with him. He had a good deal of information, and his captain said he was a perfect seaman, and worth his weight in gold on board a vessel, in fair weather and in foul. His strength must have been great, and he had the sight of a vulture. It is strange that one should be so minute in the description of an unknown, outcast sailor, whom one may never see again, and whom no one may care to hear about; yet so it is. Some persons we see under no remarkable circumstances, but whom, for some reason or other, we never forget. He called himself Bill Jackson; and I know no one of all my accidental acquaintances to whom I would more gladly give a shake of the hand than to him. Whoever falls in with him will find a handsome, hearty fellow, and a good shipmate.

Sunday came again while we were at Monterey; but, as before, it brought us no holiday. The people on shore dressed and came off in greater numbers than ever, and we were employed all day in boating and breaking out cargo, so that we had hardly time to eat. Our former second mate, who was determined to get liberty if it was to be had, dressed himself in a long coat and black hat, and polished his shoes, and went aft, and asked to go ashore. He could not have done a more imprudent thing; for he knew that no liberty would be given; and besides, sailors, however sure they may be of having liberty granted them, always go aft in their working clothes, to appear as though they had no reason to expect anything, and then wash, dress, and shave after the matter is settled. But this poor fellow was always getting into hot water, and if there was a wrong way of doing a thing, was sure to hit upon it. We looked to see him go aft, knowing pretty well what his reception would be. The captain was walking the quarterdeck, smoking his morning cigar, and Foster went as far as the break of the deck, and there waited for him to notice him. The captain took two or three turns, and then, walking directly up to him, surveyed him from head to foot, and, lifting up his forefinger, said a word or two, in a tone too low for us to hear, but which had a magical effect upon poor Foster. He walked forward, jumped down into the forecastle, and in a moment more made his appearance in his common clothes, and went quietly to work again. What the captain said to him, we never could get him to tell, but it certainly changed him outwardly and inwardly in a surprising manner.

# CHAPTER XIV

After a few days, finding the trade beginning to slacken, we hove our anchor up, set our topsails, ran the stars and stripes up to the peak, fired a gun, which was returned from the presidio, and left the little town astern, standing out of the bay, and bearing down the coast again for Santa Barbara. As we were now going to leeward, we had a fair wind, and aplenty of it. After doubling Point Pinos, we bore up, set studding sails alow and aloft, and were walking off at the rate of eight or nine knots, promising to traverse in twenty-four hours the distance which we were nearly three weeks in traversing on the passage up. We passed Point Conception at a flying rate, the wind blowing so that it would have seemed half a gale to us if we had been going the other way and close-hauled. As we drew near the islands of Santa Barbara, it died away a little, but we came to at our old anchoring ground in less than thirty hours from the time of leaving Monterey.

Here everything was pretty much as we left it—the large bay without a vesssel in it, the surf roaring and rolling in upon the beach, the white mission, the dark town, and the high, treeless mountains. Here, too, we had our southeaster tacks aboard again—slip ropes, buoy ropes, sails furled with reefs in them, and rope yarns for gaskets. We lay at this place about a fortnight, employed in landing goods and taking off hides, occasionally, when the surf was not high; but there did not appear to be one-half the business doing here that there was in Monterey. In fact, so far as we were concerned, the town might almost as well have been in the middle of the Cordilleras. We lay at a distance of three miles from the beach, and the town was nearly a mile farther, so that we saw little or nothing of it. Occasionally we landed a few goods, which were taken away by Indians in large, clumsy oxcarts, with the bow of the yoke on the ox's neck instead of under it, and with small solid wheels. A few hides were brought down, which we carried off in the California style. This we had now got pretty well accustomed to, and hardened to also; for it does require a little hardening, even to the toughest.

The hides are brought down dry, or they will not be received. When they are taken from the animal, they have holes cut in the ends, and are staked out, and thus dried in the sun without shrinking. They are then doubled once, lengthwise, with the hair side usually in, and sent down upon mules or in carts, and piled above high-water mark; and then we take them upon our heads, one at a time, or two, if they are small, and wade out with them and throw them into the boat, which, as there are no wharves, we usually kept anchored by a small kedge, or keelek, just outside of the surf. We all provided ourselves with thick Scotch caps, which would be soft to the head, and at the same time protect it; for we soon learned that, however it might look or feel at first, the "head work" was the only system for California. For besides that the seas, breaking high, often obliged us to carry the hides so, in order to keep them dry, we found that, as they were very large and heavy, and nearly as stiff as boards, it was the only way that we could carry them with any convenience to ourselves. Some of the crew tried other expedients, saying that that looked too much like West India Negroes; but they all came to it at last. The great art is in getting them on the head. We had to take them from the ground, and as they were often very heavy, and as wide as the arms could stretch, and were easily taken by the wind, we used to have some trouble with them. I have often been laughed at myself, and joined in laughing at others, pitching ourselves down in the sand, in trying to swing a large hide upon our heads, or nearly blown over with one in a little gust of wind. The captain made it harder for us, by telling us that it was "California fashion" to carry two on the head at a time; and as he insisted upon it, and we did not wish to be outdone by other vessels, we carried two for the first few months; but after falling in with a few other "hide droghers," and finding that they carried only one at a time, we "knocked off" the extra one, and thus made our duty somewhat easier.

After our heads had become used to the weight, and we had learned the true California style of "tossing a hide," we could carry off two or three hundred in a short time, without much trouble; but it was always wet work, and, if the beach was stony, bad for our feet; for we, of course, went barefooted on this duty, as no shoes could stand such constant wetting with salt water. And after this, we had a pull of three miles, with a loaded boat, which often took a couple of hours.

We had now got well settled down into our harbor duties, which, as they are a good deal different from those at sea, it may be well enough to describe. In the first place, all hands are called at daylight, or rather—especially if the days are short—before daylight, as soon as the first gray of the morning. The cook makes his fire in the galley; the steward goes about his work in the cabin; and the crew rig the head pump, and wash down the decks. The chief mate is always on deck, but takes no active part, all the duty coming upon the second mate, who has to roll up his trousers and paddle about decks barefooted, like the rest of the crew. The washing, swabbing, squilgeeing, &c., lasts, or is made to last, until eight o'clock, when breakfast is ordered, fore and aft. After breakfast, for which half an hour is allowed, the boats are lowered down, and made fast astern, or out to the swinging booms by guess-warps, and the crew are turned to upon their day's work. This is various, and its character depends upon circumstances. There is always more or less of boating, in small boats; and if heavy goods are to be taken ashore, or hides are brought down to the beach for us, then all hands are sent ashore with an officer in the longboat. Then there is a good deal to be done in the hold—goods to be broken out, and cargo to be shifted, to make room for hides, or to keep the trim of the vessel. In addition to this, the usual work upon the rigging must be going on. There is much of the latter kind of work, which can only be done when the vessel is in port. Everything, too, must be kept taut and in good order—spun yarn made, chafing gear repaired, and all the other ordinary work. The great difference between sea and harbor duty is in the division of time. Instead of having a watch on deck and a watch below, as at sea, all hands are at work together, except at mealtimes, from daylight till dark; and at night an "anchor watch" is kept, which, with us, consisted of only two at a time, all the crew taking turns. An hour is allowed for dinner, and at dark the decks are cleared up, the boats hoisted, supper ordered; and at eight the lights are put out, except in the binnacle, where the glass stands; and the anchor watch is set. Thus, when at anchor, the crew have more time at night (standing watch only about two hours), but have no time to themselves in the day; so that reading, mending clothes, &c., has to be put off until Sunday, which is usually given. Some religious captains give their crews Saturday afternoons to do their washing and mending in, so that they may have their Sundays free. This is a good arrangement, and goes far to account for the preference sailors usually show for vessels under such command. We were well satisfied if we got even Sunday to ourselves; for, if any hides came down on that day, as was often the case when they were brought from a distance, we were obliged to take them off, which usually occupied half a day; besides, as we now lived on fresh beef, and ate one bullock a week, the animal was almost always brought down on Sunday, and we had to go ashore, kill it, dress it, and bring it aboard, which was another interruption. Then, too, our common day's work was protracted and made more fatiguing by hides coming down late in the afternoon, which sometimes kept us at work in the surf by starlight, with the prospect of pulling on board, and stowing them all away, before supper.

But all these little vexations and labors would have been nothing—they would have been passed by as the common evils of a sea life, which every sailor who is a man will go through without complaint—were it not for the uncertainty, or worse than uncertainty, which hung over the nature and length of our voyage. Here we were, in a little vessel, with a small crew, on a half-civilized coast, at the ends of the earth, and with a prospect of remaining an indefinite period—two or three years at the least. When we left Boston, we supposed that ours was to be a voyage of eighteen months, or two years, at most; but, upon arriving on the coast, we learned something more of the trade, and found that, in the scarcity of hides, which was yearly greater and greater, it would take us a year, at least, to collect our own cargo, besides the passage out and home; and that we were also to collect a cargo for a large ship belonging to the same firm, which was soon to come on the coast, and to which we were to act as tender. We had heard rumors of such a ship to follow us, which had leaked out from the captain and mate, but we passed them by as mere "yarns," till our arrival, when they were confirmed by the letters which we brought from the owners to their agent. The ship *California*, belonging to the same firm, had been nearly two years on the coast getting a full cargo, and was now at San Diego, from which port she was expected to sail in a few weeks for Boston; and we were to collect all the hides we could, and deposit them at San Diego, when the new ship, which would carry forty thousand, was to be filled and sent home; and then we were to begin anew upon our own cargo. Here was a gloomy prospect indeed. The *Lagoda*, a smaller ship than the *California*, carrying only thirty-one or thirty-two thousand, had been two years getting her cargo; and we were to collect a cargo of forty thousand besides our own, which would be twelve or fifteen thousand; and hides were said to be growing scarcer. Then, too, this ship, which had been to us a worse phantom than any Flying Dutchman, was no phantom, or ideal thing, but had been reduced to a certainty; so much so that a name was given her, and it was said that she was to be the *Alert*, a well-known Indiaman, which was expected in Boston in a few months, when we sailed. There could be no doubt, and all looked black enough. Hints were thrown out about three years and four years; the older sailors said they never should see Boston again, but should lay their bones in California; and a cloud seemed to hang over the whole voyage. Besides, we were not provided for so long a voyage, and clothes, and all sailors' necessaries, were excessively dear—300 or 400 per cent advance upon the Boston prices. This was bad enough for the crew; but still worse was it for me, who did not mean to be a sailor for life, having intended only to be gone eighteen months or two years. Three or four years might make me a sailor in every respect, mind and habits, as well as body, *nolens volens*, and would put all my companions so far ahead of me that a college degree and a profession would be in vain to think of; and I made up my mind that, feel as I might, a sailor I might have to be, and to command a merchant vessel might be the limit of my ambition.

Besides the length of the voyage, and the hard and exposed life, we were in the remote parts of the earth, on an almost desert coast, in a country where there is neither law nor gospel, and where sailors are at their captain's mercy, there being no American consul, or anyone to whom a complaint could be made. We lost all interest in the voyage, cared nothing about the cargo, which we were only collecting for others, began to patch our clothes, and felt as though our fate was fixed beyond all hope of change.

In addition to, and perhaps partly as a consequence of, this state of things, there was trouble brewing on board the vessel. Our "mate" (as the first mate is always called, *par excellence*) was a worthy man—a more honest, upright, and kindhearted man I never saw—but he was too easy and amiable for the mate of a merchantman. He was not the man to call a sailor a "son of a bitch," and knock him down with a handspike. Perhaps he really lacked the energy and spirit for such a voyage as ours, and for such a captain. Captain Thompson was a vigorous, energetic fellow. As sailors say, "He hadn't a lazy bone in him." He was made of steel and whalebone. He was a man to "toe the mark," and to make everyone else step up to it. During all the time that I was with him, I never saw him sit down on deck. He was always active and driving, severe in his discipline, and expected the same of his officers. The mate not being enough of a "driver" for him, he was dissatisfied with him, became suspicious that discipline was getting relaxed, and began to interfere in everything. He drew the reins tighter; and as, in all quarrels between officers, the sailors side with the one who treats them best, he became suspicious of the crew. He saw that things went wrong, that nothing was done "with a will"; and in his attempt to remedy the difficulty by severity he made everything worse. We were in all respects unfortunately situated —captain, officers, and crew entirely unfitted for one another; and every circumstance and event was like a two-edged sword, and cut both ways. The length of the voyage, which made us dissatisfied, made the captain, at the same time, see the necessity of order and strict discipline; and the nature of the country, which caused us to feel that we had nowhere to go for redress, but were at the mercy of a hard master, made the captain understand, on the other hand, that he must depend entirely upon his own resources. Severity created discontent, and signs of discontent provoked severity. Then, too, ill-treatment and dissatisfaction are no *linimenta laborum;* and many a time have I heard the sailors say that they should not mind the length of the voyage, and the hardships, if they were only kindly treated, and if they could feel that something was done to make work lighter and life easier. We felt as though our situation was a call upon our superiors to give us occasional relaxations, and to make our yoke easier. But the opposite policy was pursued. We were kept at work all day when in port; which, together with a watch at night, made us glad to turn in as soon as we got below. Thus we had no time for reading, or—which was of more importance to us—for washing and mending our clothes. And then, when we were at sea, sailing from port to port, instead of giving us "watch and watch," as was the custom on board every other vessel on the coast, we were all kept on deck and at work, rain or shine, making spun yarn and rope, and at other work in good weather, and picking oakum when it was too wet for anything else. All hands were called to "come up and see it rain," and kept on deck hour after hour in a drenching rain, standing round the deck so far apart so as to prevent our talking with one another, with our tarpaulins and oilcloth jackets on, picking old rope to pieces, or laying up gaskets and robands. This was often done, too, when we were lying in port with two anchors down, and no necessity for more than one man on deck as a lookout. This is what is called "hazing" a crew, and "working their old iron up."

While lying at Santa Barbara, we encountered another southeaster; and, like the first, it came on in the night; the great black clouds moving round from the southward, covering the mountain, and hanging down over the town, appearing almost to rest upon the roofs of the houses. We made sail, slipped our cable, cleared the point, and beat about for four days in the offing, under close sail, with continual rain and high seas and winds. No wonder, thought we, they have no rain in the other seasons, for enough seemed to have fallen in those four days to last through a common summer. On the fifth day it cleared up, after a few hours, as is usual, of rain coming down like a four hours' showerbath, and we found ourselves drifted nearly ten leagues from the anchorage; and, having light head winds, we did not return until the sixth day. Having recovered our anchor, we made preparations for getting under way to go down to leeward. We had hoped to go directly to San Diego, and thus fall in with the *California* before she sailed for Boston; but our orders were to stop at an intermediate port called San Pedro; and, as we were to lie there a week or two, and the *California* was to sail in a few days, we lost the opportunity. Just before sailing, the captain took on board a short, red-haired, round-shouldered, vulgar-looking fellow, who had lost one eye and squinted with the other, and, introducing him as *Mr.* Russell, told us that he was an officer on board. This was too bad. We had lost overboard, on the passage, one of the best of our number, another had been taken from us and appointed clerk; and thus weakened and reduced, instead of shipping some hands to make our work easier, he had put another officer over us, to watch and drive us. We had now four officers, and only six in the forecastle. This was bringing her too much down by the stern for our comfort.

Leaving Santa Barbara, we coasted along down, the country appearing level or moderately uneven, and, for the most part, sandy and treeless; until, doubling a high sandy point, we let go our anchor at a distance of three or three and a half miles from shore. It was like a vessel bound to St. John's, Newfoundland, coming to anchor on the Grand Banks; for the shore, being low, appeared to be at a greater distance

than it actually was, and we thought we might as well have
stayed at Santa Barbara, and sent our boat down for the
hides. The land was of a clayey quality, and, as far as the eye
could reach, entirely bare of trees and even shrubs; and there
was no sign of a town—not even a house to be seen. What
brought us into such a place, we could not conceive. No
sooner had we come to anchor, than the slip rope, and the
other preparations for southeasters, were got ready; and
there was reason enough for it, for we lay exposed to every
wind that could blow, except the northerly winds, and they
came over a flat country with a rake of more than a league
of water. As soon as everything was snug on board, the boat
was lowered, and we pulled ashore, our new officer, who had
been several times in the port before, taking the place of
steersman. As we drew in, we found the tide low, and the
rocks and stones, covered with kelp and seaweed, lying bare
for the distance of nearly an eighth of a mile. Leaving the
boat, and picking our way barefooted over these, we came
to what is called the landing place, at high-water mark. The
soil was, as it appeared at first, loose and clayey, and, except
the stalks of the mustard plant, there was no vegetation. Just
in front of the landing, and immediately over it, was a small
hill, which, from its being not more than thirty or forty feet
high, we had not perceived from our anchorage. Over this hill
we saw three men coming down, dressed partly like sailors
and partly like Californians, one of them having on a pair of
untanned leather trousers and a red baize shirt. When they
reached us, we found that they were Englishmen. They told
us that they had belonged to a small Mexican brig which had
been driven ashore here in a southeaster, and now lived in a
small house just over the hill. Going up this hill with them,
we saw, close behind it, a small, low building, with one room,
containing a fireplace, cooking apparatus, &c., and the rest
of it unfinished, and used as a place to store hides and goods.
This, they told us, was built by some traders in the Pueblo (a
town about thirty miles in the interior, to which this was the
port), and used by them as a storehouse, and also as a lodg-
ing place when they came down to trade with the vessels.
These three men were employed by them to keep the house
in order, and to look out for the things stored in it. They said
that they had been there nearly a year; had nothing to do
most of the time, living upon beef, hard bread, and frijoles,

a peculiar kind of bean, very abundant in California. The nearest house, they told us, was a rancho, or cattle farm, about three miles off; and one of them went there, at the request of our officer, to order a horse to be sent down, with which the agent, who was on board, might go up to the Pueblo. From one of them, who was an intelligent English sailor, I learned a good deal, in a few minutes' conversation, about the place, its trade, and the news from the southern ports. San Diego, he said, was about eighty miles to the leeward of San Pedro; that they had heard from there, by a Mexican who came up on horseback, that the *California* had sailed for Boston, and that the *Lagoda*, which had been in San Pedro only a few weeks before, was taking in her cargo for Boston. The *Ayacucho* was also there, loading for Callao, and the little *Loriotte*, which had run directly down from Monterey, where we left her. San Diego, he told me, was a small, snug place, having very little trade, but decidedly the best harbor on the coast, being completely landlocked, and the water as smooth as a duck pond. This was the depot for all the vessels engaged in the trade; each one having a large house there, built of rough boards, in which they stowed their hides as fast as they collected them in their trips up and down the coast, and when they had procured a full cargo, spent a few weeks there taking it in, smoking ship, laying in wood and water, and making other preparations for the voyage home. The *Lagoda* was now about this business. When we should be about it was more than I could tell—two years, at least, I thought to myself.

I also learned, to my surprise, that the desolate-looking place we were in furnished more hides than any port on the coast. It was the only port for a distance of eighty miles, and about thirty miles in the interior was a fine plane country, filled with herds of cattle, in the center of which was the Pueblo de los Angeles—the largest town in California—and several of the wealthiest missions; to all of which San Pedro was the seaport.

Having made arrangements for a horse to take the agent to the Pueblo the next day, we picked our way again over the green, slippery rocks, and pulled toward the brig, which was so far off that we could hardly see her, in the increasing darkness; and when we got on board, the boats were hoisted up, and the crew at supper. Going down into the forecastle, eating our supper, and lighting our cigars and pipes, we had, as usual, to tell what we had seen or heard ashore. We all agreed that it was the worst place we had seen yet, especially for getting off hides, and our lying off at so great a distance looked as though it was bad for southeasters. After a few disputes as to whether we should have to carry our goods up the hill, or not, we talked of San Diego, the probability of seeing the *Lagoda* before she sailed, &c., &c.

The next day we pulled the agent ashore, and he went up to visit the Pueblo and the neighboring missions; and in a few days, as the result of his labors, large oxcarts, and droves of mules, loaded with hides, were seen coming over the flat country. We loaded our longboat with goods of all kinds, light and heavy, and pulled ashore. After landing and rolling them over the stones upon the beach, we stopped, waiting for the carts to come down the hill and take them; but the captain soon settled the matter by ordering us to carry them all up to the top, saying that that was "California fashion." So what the oxen would not do, we were obliged to do. The hill was low, but steep, and the earth, being clayey and wet with the recent rains, was but bad holding ground for our feet. The heavy barrels and casks we rolled up with some difficulty, getting behind and putting our shoulders to them; now and then our feet, slipping, added to the danger of the casks rolling back upon us. But the greatest trouble was with the large boxes of sugar. These we had to place upon oars, and, lifting them up, rest the oars upon our shoulders, and creep slowly up the hill with the gait of a funeral procession. After an hour or two of hard work, we got them all up, and found the carts standing full of hides, which we had to unload, and to load the carts again with our own goods, the lazy Indians who came down with them squatting on their hams, looking on, doing nothing, and when we asked them to help us, only shaking their heads, or drawling out, "*No quiero.*"

Having loaded the carts, we started up the Indians, who went off, one on each side of the oxen, with long sticks, sharpened at the end, to punch them with. This is one of the means of saving labor in California—two Indians to two oxen. Now the hides were to be got down; and for this purpose we brought the boat round to a place where the hill was steeper, and threw them off, letting them slide over the slope. Many of them lodged, and we had to let ourselves down and set them a-going again, and in this way became covered with dust, and our clothes torn. After we had the hides all down, we were obliged to take them on our heads, and walk over the stones, and through the water, to the boat. The water and the stones together would wear out a pair of shoes a day, and as shoes were very scarce and very dear, we were compelled to go barefooted. At night we went on board, having had the hardest and most disagreeable day's work that we had yet experienced. For several days we were employed in this manner, until we had landed forty or fifty tons of goods, and brought on board about two thousand hides, when the trade began to slacken, and we were kept at work on board during the latter part of the week, either in the hold or upon the rigging. On Thursday night there was a violent blow from the northward; but as this was offshore, we had only to let go our other anchor and hold on. We were called up at night to send down the royal yards. It was as dark as a pocket, and the vessel pitching at her anchors. I went up to the fore, and Stimson to the main, and we soon had them down "shipshape and Bristol fashion"; for, as we had now become used to our duty aloft, everything above the crosstrees was left to us, who were the youngest of the crew, except one boy.

# CHAPTER XV

For several days the captain seemed very much out of humor. Nothing went right, or fast enough for him. He quarreled with the cook, and threatened to flog him for throwing wood on deck, and had a dispute with the mate about reeving a Spanish burton; the mate saying that he was right, and had been taught how to do it by a man *who was a sailor!* This the captain took in dudgeon, and they were at swords' points at once. But his displeasure was chiefly turned against a large, heavy-molded fellow from the Middle States, who was called Sam. This man hesitated in his speech, was rather slow in his motions, and was only a tolerably good sailor, but usually seemed to do his best; yet the captain took a dislike to him, thought he was surly and lazy, and "if you once give a dog a bad name," as the sailor phrase is, "he may as well jump overboard." The captain found fault with everything this man did, and hazed him for dropping a marlinespike from the main yard, where he was at work. This, of course, was an accident, but it was set down against him. The captain was on board all day Friday, and everything went on hard and disagreeably. "The more you drive a man, the less he will do" was as true with us as with any other people. We worked late Friday night, and were turned to early Saturday morning. About ten o'clock the captain ordered our new officer, Russell, who by this time had become thoroughly disliked by all the crew, to get the gig ready to take him ashore. John, the Swede, was sitting in the boat alongside, and Mr. Russell and I were standing by the main hatchway, waiting for the captain, who was down in the hold, where the crew were at work, when we heard his voice raised in violent dispute with somebody, whether it was with the mate or one of the crew I could not tell, and then came blows and scuffling. I ran to the side and beckoned to John, who came aboard, and we leaned down the hatchway, and though we could see no one, yet we knew that the captain had the advantage, for his voice was loud and clear:

"You see your condition! You see your condition! Will you ever give me any more of your 'jaw'?" No answer; and then came wrestling and heaving, as though the man was trying to turn him. "You may as well keep still, for I have got you," said the captain. Then came the question, "Will you ever give me any more of your jaw?"

"I never gave you any, sir," said Sam; for it was his voice that we heard, though low and half choked.

"That's not what I ask you. Will you ever be impudent to me again?"

"I never have been, sir," said Sam.

"Answer my question, or I'll make a spread eagle of you! I'll flog you, by G—d."

"I'm no Negro slave," said Sam.

"Then I'll make you one," said the captain; and he came to the hatchway, and sprang on deck, threw off his coat, and, rolling up his sleeves, called out to the mate, "Seize that man up, Mr. Amerzene! Seize him up! Make a spread eagle of him! I'll teach you all who is master aboard!"

The crew and officers followed the captain up the hatchway; but it was not until after repeated orders that the mate laid hold of Sam, who made no resistance, and carried him to the gangway.

"What are you going to flog that man for, sir?" said John, the Swede, to the captain.

Upon hearing this, the captain turned upon John; but, knowing him to be quick and resolute, he ordered the steward to bring the irons, and, calling upon Russell to help him, went up to John.

"Let me alone," said John. "I'm willing to be put in irons. You need not use any force"; and, putting out his hands, the captain slipped the irons on, and sent him aft to the quarterdeck. Sam, by this time, was "seized up," as it is called, that is, placed against the shrouds, with his wrists made fast to them, his jacket off, and his back exposed. The captain stood on the break of the deck, a few feet from him, and a little raised, so as to have a good swing at him, and held in his hand the end of a thick, strong rope. The officers stood round, and the crew grouped together in the waist. All these preparations made me feel sick and almost faint, angry and excited as I was. A man—a human being, made in God's likeness—fastened up and flogged like a beast! A man, too, whom I had lived with, eaten with, and stood watch with for months, and knew so well! If a thought of resistance crossed the minds of any of the men, what was to be done? Their time for it had gone by. Two men were fast, and there were left only two men besides Stimson and myself, and a small boy of ten or twelve years of age; and Stimson and I would not have joined the men in a mutiny, as they knew. And then, on the other side, there were (beside the captain) three officers, steward, agent, and clerk, and the cabin supplied with weapons. But beside the numbers, what is there for sailors to do? If they resist, it is mutiny; and if they succeed, and take the vessel, it is piracy. If they ever yield again, their punishment must come; and if they do not yield, what are they to be for the rest of their lives? If a sailor resist his commander, he resists the law, and piracy or submission is his only alternative. Bad as it was, they saw it must be borne. It is what a sailor ships for. Swinging the rope over his head, and bending his body so as to give it full force, the captain brought it down upon the poor fellow's back. Once, twice—six times. "Will you ever give me any more of your jaw?" The man writhed with pain, but said not a word. Three times more. This was too much, and he muttered something which I could not hear; this brought as many more as the man could stand, when the captain ordered him to be cut down, and to go forward.

"Now for you," said the captain, making up to John, and taking his irons off. As soon as John was loose, he ran forward to the forecastle. "Bring that man aft!" shouted the captain. The second mate, who had been in the forecastle with these men the early part of the voyage, stood still in the waist, and the mate walked slowly forward; but our third officer, anxious to show his zeal, sprang forward over the windlass, and laid hold of John; but John soon threw him from him. The captain stood on the quarterdeck, bareheaded, his eyes flashing with rage, and his face as red as blood, swinging the rope, and calling out to his officers, "Drag him aft! Lay hold of him! I'll 'sweeten' him!" &c., &c. The mate now went forward, and told John quietly to go aft; and he, seeing resistance vain, threw the blackguard third mate from him, said he would go aft of himself, that they should not drag him, and went up to the gangway and held out his hands; but as soon as the captain began to make him fast, the indignity was too much, and he struggled; but, the mate and Russell holding him, he was soon seized up. When he was made fast, he turned to the captain, who stood rolling up his sleeves and getting ready for the blow, and asked him what he was to be flogged for. "Have I ever refused my duty, sir? Have you ever known me to hang back, or to be insolent, or not to know my work?"

"No," said the captain, "it is not that that I flog you for; I flog you for your interference, for asking questions."

"Can't a man ask a question here without being flogged?"

"No," shouted the captain. "Nobody shall open his mouth aboard this vessel but myself," and began laying the blows upon his back, swinging half round between each blow, to give it full effect. As he went on, his passion increased, and he danced about the deck, calling out, as he swung the rope, "If you want to know what I flog you for, I'll tell you. It's because I like to do it—because I like to do it! It suits me! That's what I do it for!"

The man writhed under the pain until he could endure it no longer, when he called out, with an exclamation more common among foreigners than with us: "O Jesus Christ! O Jesus Christ!"

"Don't call on Jesus Christ," shouted the captain. "*He can't help you. Call on Frank Thompson!* He's the man! He can help you! Jesus Christ can't help you now!"

At these words, which I never shall forget, my blood ran cold. I could look on no longer. Disgusted, sick, I turned away, and leaned over the rail, and looked down into the water. A few rapid thoughts, I don't know what—our situation, a resolution to see the captain punished when we got home—crossed my mind; but the falling of the blows and the cries of the man called me back once more. At length they ceased, and, turning round, I found that the mate, at a signal from the captain, had cast him loose. Almost doubled up with pain, the man walked slowly forward, and went down into the forecastle. Everyone else stood still at his post, while the captain, swelling with rage, and with the importance of his achievement, walked the quarterdeck, and at each turn, as he came forward, calling out to us: "You see your condition! You see where I've got you all, and you know what to expect! . . . You've been mistaken in me; you didn't know what I was! Now you know what I am! . . . I'll make you toe the mark, every soul of you, or I'll flog you all, fore and aft, from the boy up! . . . You've got a driver over you! Yes, a *slave driver—a nigger driver!* I'll see who'll tell me he isn't a nigger slave!" With this and the like matter, equally calculated to quiet us, and to allay any apprehensions of future trouble, he entertained us for about ten minutes, when he went below. Soon after, John came aft, with his bare back covered with stripes and wales in every direction, and dreadfully swollen, and asked the steward to ask the captain to let him have some salve, or balsam, to put upon it. "No," said the captain, who heard him from below. "Tell him to put his shirt on; that's the best thing for him, and pull me ashore in the boat. Nobody is going to lay up on board this vessel." He then called to Mr. Russell to take those two men and two others in the boat, and pull him ashore. I went for one. The two men could hardly bend their backs, and the captain called to them to "give way . . . give way!" but, finding they did their best, he let them alone. The agent was in the stern sheets, but during the whole pull—a league or more—not a word was spoken. We landed; the captain, agent, and officer went up to the house, and left us with the boat. I, and the man with me, stayed near the boat, while John and Sam walked slowly away, and sat down on the rocks. They talked some time together, but at length separated, each sitting alone. I had some fears of John. He was a foreigner, and violently tempered, and under suffering; and he had his knife with him, and the captain was to come down alone to the boat. But nothing happened; and we went quietly on board. The captain was probably armed, and if either of them had lifted a hand against him, they would have had nothing before them but flight, and starvation in the woods of California, or capture by the soldiers and Indians, whom the offer of twenty dollars would have set upon them.

After the day's work was done, we went down into the forecastle, and ate our plain supper; but not a word was spoken. It was Saturday night; but there was no song, no "sweethearts and wives." A gloom was over everything. The two men lay in their berths, groaning with pain, and we all turned in, but, for myself, not to sleep. A sound coming now and then from the berths of the two men showed that they were awake, as awake they must have been, for they could hardly lie in one posture long; the dim, swinging lamp shed its light over the dark hole in which we lived, and many and various reflections and purposes coursed through my mind. I had no apprehension that the captain would try to lay a hand on me; but I thought of our situation, living under a tyranny, with an ungoverned, swaggering fellow administering it; of the character of the country we were in; the length of the voyage; the uncertainty attending our return to America; and then, if we should return, the prospect of obtaining justice and satisfaction for these poor men; and I vowed that, if God should ever give me the means, I would do something to redress the grievances and relieve the sufferings of that class of beings with whom my lot had so long been cast.

The next day was Sunday. We worked, as usual, washing decks, &c., until breakfast time. After breakfast we pulled the captain ashore, and, finding some hides there which had been brought down the night before, he ordered me to stay ashore and watch them, saying that the boat would come again before night. They left me, and I spent a quiet day on the hill, eating dinner with the three men at the little house. Unfortunately they had no books; and, after talking with them, and walking about, I began to grow tired of doing nothing. The little brig, the home of so much hardship and suffering, lay in the offing, almost as far as one could see; and the only other thing which broke the surface of the great bay was a small, dreary-looking island, steep and conical, of a clayey soil, and without the sign of vegetable life upon it, yet which had a peculiar and melancholy interest, for on the top of it were buried the remains of an Englishman, the commander of a small merchant brig, who died while lying in this port. It was always a solemn and affecting spot to me. There it stood, desolate, and in the midst of desolation; and there were the remains of one who died and was buried alone and friendless. Had it been a common burying place, it would have been nothing. The single body corresponded well with the solitary character of everything around. It was the only spot in California that impressed me with anything like poetic interest. Then, too, the man died far from home, without a friend near him—by poison, it was suspected, and no one to inquire into it—and without proper funeral rites; the mate (as I was told), glad to have him out of the way, hurrying him up the hill and into the ground, without a word or a prayer.

I looked anxiously for a boat, during the latter part of the afternoon, but none came; until toward sundown, when I saw a speck on the water, and as it drew near I found it was the gig, with the captain. The hides, then, were not to go off. The captain came up the hill, with a man, bringing my monkey jacket and a blanket. He looked pretty black, but inquired whether I had enough to eat; told me to make a house out of the hides, and keep myself warm, as I should have to sleep there among them, and to keep good watch over them. I got a moment to speak to the man who brought my jacket.

"How do things go aboard?" said I.

"Bad enough," said he. "Hard work and not a kind word spoken."

"What!" said I. "Have you been at work all day?"

"Yes! No more Sunday for us. Everything has been moved

in the hold, from stem to stern, and from the waterways to the keelson."

I went up to the house to supper. We had frijoles (the perpetual food of the Californians, but which, when well cooked, are the best bean in the world), coffee made of burned wheat, and hard bread. After our meal, the three men sat down by the light of a tallow candle, with a pack of greasy Spanish cards, to the favorite game of *Treinte Uno*, a sort of Spanish Everlasting. I left them and went out to take up my bivouac among the hides. It was now dark; the vessel was hidden from sight, and except the three men in the house there was not a living soul within a league. The coyotes (a wild animal of a nature and appearance between that of the fox and the wolf) set up their sharp, quick bark, and two owls, at the end of two distant points running out into the bay, on different sides of the hill where I lay, kept up their alternate dismal notes. I had heard the sound before at night, but did not know what it was, until one of the men, who came down to look at my quarters, told me it was the owl. Mellowed by the distance, and heard alone, at night, it was a most melancholy and boding sound. Through nearly all the night they kept it up, answering one another slowly at regular intervals. This was relieved by the noisy coyotes, some of which came quite near to my quarters, and were not very pleasant neighbors. The next morning, before sunrise, the longboat came ashore, and the hides were taken off.

We lay at San Pedro about a week, engaged in taking off hides and in other labors which had now become our regular duties. I spent one more day on the hill, watching a quantity of hides and goods, and this time succeeded in finding a part of a volume of Scott's *Pirate*, in a corner of the house; but it failed me at a most interesting moment, and I betook myself to my acquaintances on shore, and from them learned a good deal about the customs of the country, the harbors, &c. This, they told me, was a worse harbor than Santa Barbara for southeasters, the bearing of the headland being a point and a half more to windward, and it being so shallow that the sea broke often as far out as where we lay at anchor. The gale for which we slipped at Santa Barbara had been so bad a one here, that the whole bay, for a league out, was filled with the foam of the breakers, and seas actually broke over the *endlessness of voyage*

Dead Man's Island. The *Lagoda* was lying there, and slipped at the first alarm, and in such haste that she was obliged to leave her launch behind her at anchor. The little boat rode it out for several hours, pitching at her anchor, and standing with her stern up almost perpendicularly. The men told me that they watched her till toward night, when she snapped her cable and drove up over the breakers high and dry upon the beach.

On board the *Pilgrim* everything went on regularly, each one trying to get along as smoothly as possible; but the comfort of the voyage was evidently at an end. "That is a long lane which has no turning," "Every dog must have his day, and mine will come by and by," and the like proverbs were occasionally quoted; but no one spoke of any probable end to the voyage, or of Boston, or anything of the kind; or, if he did, it was only to draw out the perpetual surly reply from his shipmate: "Boston, is it? You may thank your stars if you ever see that place. You had better have your back sheathed, and your head coppered, and your feet shod, and make out your log for California for life!" or else something of this kind: "Before you get to Boston, the hides will wear all the hair off your head, and you'll take up all your wages in clothes, and won't have enough left to buy a wig with!"

The flogging was seldom, if ever, alluded to by us in the forecastle. If anyone was inclined to talk about it, the others, with a delicacy which I hardly expected to find among them, always stopped him, or turned the subject. But the behavior of the two men who were flogged toward one another showed a consideration which would have been worthy of admiration in the highest walks of life. Sam knew John had suffered solely on his account; and in all his complaints he said that, if he alone had been flogged, it would have been nothing; but he never could see him without thinking that he had been the means of bringing this disgrace upon him; and John never, by word or deed, let anything escape him to remind the other that it was by interfering to save his shipmate that he had suffered. Neither made it a secret that they thought the Dutchman Bill and Foster might have helped them; but they did not expect it of Stimson or me. While we showed our sympathy for their suffering, and our indignation at the captain's violence, we did not feel sure that there was only one side to the beginning of the difficulty, and we kept clear of any engagement with them, except our promise to help them when they got home.*

Having got all our spare room filled with hides, we hove up our anchor, and made sail for San Diego. In no operation can the disposition of a crew be better discovered than in getting under way. Where things are done "with a will," everyone is like a cat aloft; sails are loosed in an instant; each one lays out his strength on his handspike, and the windlass goes briskly round with the loud cry of "Yo heave ho! Heave and pawl! Heave hearty, ho!" and the chorus of "Cheerly, men!" cats the anchor. But with us, at this time, it was all dragging work. No one went aloft beyond his ordinary gait, and the chain came slowly in over the windlass. The mate, between the knightheads, exhausted all his official rhetoric in calls of "Heave with a will!" "Heave hearty, men! Heave hearty!" "Heave, and raise the dead!" "Heave, and away!" &c., &c.; but it would not do. Nobody broke his back or his handspike by his efforts. And when the cat-tackle-fall was strung along, and all hands—cook, steward, and all— laid hold, to cat the anchor, instead of the lively song of

---

*Owing to the change of vessels that afterward took place, Captain Thompson arrived in Boston nearly a year before the *Pilgrim*, and was off on another voyage, and beyond the reach of these men. Soon after the publication of the first edition of this book, in 1841, I received a letter from Stimson, dated at Detroit, Michigan, where he had re-entered mercantile life, from which I make this extract: "As to your account of the flogging scene, I think you have given a fair history of it, and, if anything, been too lenient toward Captain Thompson for his brutal, cowardly treatment of those men. As I was in the hold at the time the affray commenced, I will give you a short history of it as near as I can recollect. We were breaking out goods in the fore hold, and, in order to get at them, we had to shift our hides from forward to aft. After having removed part of them, we came to the boxes, and attempted to get them out without moving any more of the hides. While doing so, Sam accidentally hurt his hand, and, as usual, began swearing about it, and was not sparing of his oaths, although I think he was not aware that Captain Thompson was so near him at the time. Captain Thompson asked him in a moderate way, what was the matter with him. Sam, on account of the impediment in his speech, could not answer immediately, although he endeavored to, but as soon as possible answered in a manner that almost anyone would, under the like circumstances, yet, I believe, not with the intention of giving a short answer; but being provoked, and suffering pain from the injured hand, he perhaps answered rather short, or sullenly. Thus commenced the scene you have so vividly described, and which seems to me exactly the history of the whole affair without any exaggeration."

"Cheerly, men!" in which all hands join in the chorus, we pulled a long, heavy, silent pull, and, as sailors say a song is as good as ten men, the anchor came to the cathead pretty slowly. "Give us 'Cheerly!'" said the mate; but there was no "Cheerly" for us, and we did without it. The captain walked the quarterdeck, and said not a word. He must have seen the change, but there was nothing which he could notice officially.

We sailed leisurely down the coast before a light, fair wind, keeping the land well aboard, and saw two other missions, looking like blocks of white plaster, shining in the distance; one of which, situated on the top of a high hill, was San Juan Capistrano, under which vessels sometimes come to anchor, in the summer season, and take off hides. At sunset on the second day we had a large and well-wooded headland directly before us, behind which lay the little harbor of San Diego. We were becalmed off this point all night, but the next morning, which was Saturday, the fourteenth of March, having a good breeze, we stood round the point, and, hauling our wind, brought the little harbor, which is rather the outlet of a small river, right before us. Everyone was desirous to get a view of the new place. A chain of high hills, beginning at the point (which was on our larboard hand coming in), protected the harbor on the north and west, and ran off into the interior, as far as the eye could reach. On the other sides the land was low and green, but without trees. The entrance is so narrow as to admit but one vessel at a time, the current swift, and the channel runs so near to a low, stony point that the ship's sides appeared almost to touch it. There was no town in sight, but on the smooth sand beach, abreast, and within a cable's length of which three vessels lay moored, were four large houses, built of rough boards, and looking like the great barns in which ice is stored on the borders of the large ponds near Boston, with piles of hides standing round them, and men in red shirts and large straw hats walking in and out of the doors. These were the hide houses. Of the vessels: one, a short, clumsy little hermaphrodite brig, we recognized as our old acquaintance the *Loriotte;* another, with sharp bows and raking masts, newly painted and tarred, and glittering in the morning sun, with the blood-red banner and cross of St. George at her peak, was the handsome *Ayacucho.* The third was a large ship, with topgallant masts housed and sails unbent, and looking as rusty and worn as two years' hide

droghing could make her. This was the *Lagoda.* As we drew
near, carried rapidly along by the current, we overhauled our
chain, and clewed up the topsails. "Let go the anchor!" said
the captain; but either there was not chain enough forward
of the windlass, or the anchor went down foul, or we had too
much headway on, for it did not bring us up. "Pay out chain!"
shouted the captain; and we gave it to her; but it would not
do. Before the other anchor could be let go, we drifted down,
broadside on, and went smash into the *Lagoda.* Her crew were
at breakfast in the forecastle, and her cook, seeing us coming,
rushed out of his galley, and called up the officers and men.

Fortunately, no great harm was done. Her jib boom passed
between our fore- and mainmasts, carrying away some of our
rigging, and breaking down the rail. She lost her martingale.
This brought us up, and, as they paid out chain, we swung
clear of them, and let go the other anchor; but this had as bad
luck as the first, for, before anyone perceived it, we were
drifting down upon the *Loriotte.* The captain now gave out his
orders rapidly and fiercely, sheeting home the topsails, and
backing and filling the sails, in hope of starting or clearing the
anchors; but it was all in vain, and he sat down on the rail,
taking it very leisurely, and calling out to Captain Nye that
he was coming to pay him a visit. We drifted fairly into the
*Loriotte,* her larboard bow into our starboard quarter, carrying away a part of our starboard-quarter railing, and breaking
off her larboard bumpkin, and one or two stanchions above
the deck. We saw our handsome sailor, Jackson, on the forecastle, with the Sandwich Islanders, working away to get us
clear. After paying out chain, we swung clear, but our anchors
were, no doubt, afoul of hers. We manned the windlass, and
hove, and hove away, but to no purpose. Sometimes we got
a little upon the cable, but a good surge would take it all
back again. We now began to drift down toward the *Ayacucho;* when her boat put off, and brought her commander,
Captain Wilson, on board. He was a short, active, well-built
man, about fifty years of age; and being some twenty years
older than our captain, and a thorough seaman, he did not
hesitate to give his advice, and, from giving advice, he gradually came to taking the command; ordering us when to heave
and when to pawl, and backing and filling the topsails, setting
and taking in jib and trysail, whenever he thought best. Our
captain gave a few orders, but as Wilson generally counter-

manded them, saying, in an easy, fatherly kind of way, "Oh, no, Captain Thompson, you don't want the jib on her," or "It isn't time yet to heave!" he soon gave it up. We had no objections to this state of things, for Wilson was a kind man, and had an encouraging and pleasant way of speaking to us, which made everything go easily. After two or three hours of constant labor at the windlass, heaving and yo-ho-ing with all our might, we brought up an anchor, with the *Loriotte*'s small bower fast to it. Having cleared this, and let it go, and cleared our hawse, we got our other anchor, which had dragged half over the harbor. "Now," said Wilson, "I'll find you a good berth"; and, setting both the topsails, he carried us down, and brought us to anchor, in handsome style, directly abreast of the hide house which we were to use. Having done this, he took his leave, while we furled the sails and got our breakfast, which was welcome to us, for we had worked hard, and eaten nothing since yesterday afternoon, and it was nearly twelve o'clock. After breakfast, and until night, we were employed in getting out the boats and mooring ship.

After supper, two of us took the captain on board the *Lagoda*. As he came alongside, he gave his name, and the mate, in the gangway, called out to Captain Bradshaw, down the companionway, "Captain Thompson has come aboard, sir!" "Has he brought his brig with him?" asked the rough old fellow, in a tone which made itself heard fore and aft. This mortified our captain not a little, and it became a standing joke among us, and, indeed, over the coast, for the rest of the voyage. The captain went down into the cabin, and we walked forward and put our heads down the forecastle, where we found the men at supper. "Come down, shipmates,* come down!" said they, as soon as they saw us; and we went down, and found a large, high forecastle, well lighted, and a crew of twelve or fourteen men eating out of their kids and pans, and drinking their tea, and talking and laughing, all as independent and easy as so many "woodsawyer's clerks." This looked like comfort and enjoyment, compared with the dark little forecastle, and scanty, discontented crew of the brig. It was Saturday night; they had got through their work for the week, and, being snugly moored, had nothing to do until Monday again. After two years' hard service, they had seen

* "Shipmate" is the term by which sailors address one another when not acquainted.

the worst, and all, of California; had got their cargo nearly stowed, and expected to sail, in a week or two, for Boston.

We spent an hour or more with them, talking over California matters, until the word was passed: "Pilgrims, away!" and we went back to our brig. The Lagodas were a hardy, intelligent set, a little roughened, and their clothes patched and old, from California wear; all able seamen, and between the ages of twenty and thirty-five or forty. They inquired about our vessel, the usage on board, &c., and were not a little surprised at the story of the flogging. They said there were often difficulties in vessels on the coast, and sometimes knockdowns and fightings, but they had never heard before of a regular seizing-up and flogging. "Spread eagles" were a new kind of bird in California.

Sunday, they said, was always given in San Diego, both at the hide houses and on board the vessels, a large number usually going up to the town, on liberty. We learned a good deal from them about the curing and stowing of hides, &c., and they were desirous to have the latest news (seven months old) from Boston. One of their first inquiries was for Father Taylor, the seamen's preacher in Boston. Then followed the usual strain of conversation, inquiries, stories, and jokes, which one must always hear in a ship's forecastle, but which are, perhaps, after all, no worse, though more gross and coarse, than those one may chance to hear from some well-dressed gentlemen around their tables.

# CHAPTER XVI

The next day being Sunday, after washing and clearing decks, and getting breakfast, the mate came forward with leave for one watch to go ashore, on liberty. We drew lots, and it fell to the larboard, which I was in. Instantly all was preparation. Buckets of fresh water (which we were allowed in port) and soap were put in use; go-ashore jackets and trousers got out and brushed; pumps, neckerchiefs, and hats overhauled, one lending to another; so that among the whole each got a good fitout. A boat was called to pull the "liberty men" ashore, and we sat down in the stern sheets, "as big as pay passengers," and, jumping ashore, set out on our walk for the town, which was nearly three miles off.

It is a pity that some other arrangement is not made in merchant vessels with regard to the liberty day. When in port, the crews are kept at work all the week, and the only day they are allowed for rest or pleasure is Sunday; and unless they go ashore on that day, they cannot go at all. I have heard of a religious captain who gave his crew liberty on Saturdays, after twelve o'clock. This would be a good plan, if shipmasters would bring themselves to give their crews so much time. For young sailors especially, many of whom have been brought up with a regard for the sacredness of the day, this strong temptation to break it is exceedingly injurious. As it is, it can hardly be expected that a crew, on a long and hard voyage, will refuse a few hours of freedom from toil and the restraints of a vessel, and an opportunity to tread the ground and see the sights of society and humanity, because it is a Sunday. They feel no objection to being drawn out of a pit on the Sabbath day.

I shall never forget the delightful sensation of being in the open air, with the birds singing around me, and escaped from the confinement, labor, and strict rule of a vessel—of being once more in my life, though only for a day, my own master. A sailor's liberty is but for a day; yet while it lasts it is entire. He is under no one's eye, and can do whatever, and go wherever, he pleases. This day, for the first time, I may truly say, in my whole life, I felt the meaning of a term which I had often heard—the sweets of liberty. Stimson was with me, and, turning our backs upon the vessels, we walked slowly along, talking of the pleasure of being our own masters, of the times past, when we were free and in the midst of friends, in America, and of the prospect of our return; and planning where we would go and what we would do, when we reached home. It was wonderful how the prospect brightened, and how short and tolerable the voyage appeared, when viewed in this new

light. Things looked differently from what they did when we
talked them over in the little dark forecastle, the night after
the flogging, at San Pedro. It is not the least of the advantages of allowing sailors occasionally a day of liberty, that it
gives them a spring, and makes them feel cheerful and independent, and leads them insensibly to look on the bright side
of everything for some time after.

Stimson and I determined to keep as much together as possible, though we knew that it would not do to "cut" our shipmates; for, knowing our birth and education, they were a little
suspicious that we would try to put on the gentleman when we
got ashore, and would be ashamed of their company; and this
won't do with Jack. When the voyage is at an end, you do as
you please; but so long as you belong to the same vessel, you
must be a shipmate to him on shore, or he will not be a
shipmate to you on board. Being forewarned of this before
I went to sea, I took no "long togs" with me; and being
dressed like the rest, in white duck trousers, blue jacket, and
straw hat, which would prevent my going into better company, and showing no disposition to avoid them, I set all suspicion at rest. Our crew fell in with some who belonged to
the other vessels, and, sailor-like, steered for the first grogshop. This was a small adobe building, of only one room, in
which were liquors, "drygoods," West India goods, shoes,
bread, fruits, and everything which is vendible in California.
It was kept by a Yankee, a one-eyed man, who belonged formerly to Fall River, came out to the Pacific in a whaleship,
left her at the Sandwich Islands, and came to California and
set up a *pulpería*. Stimson and I followed in our shipmates'
wake, knowing that to refuse to drink with them would be
the highest affront, but determining to slip away at the first
opportunity. It is the universal custom with sailors for each
one, in his turn, to treat the whole, calling for a glass all
round, and obliging everyone who is present, even to the
keeper of the shop, to take a glass with him. When we first
came in, there was some dispute between our crew and the
others, whether the newcomers or the old California rangers
should treat first; but it being settled in favor of the latter,
each of the crews of the other vessels treated all round in their
turn, and as there were a good many present (including some
"loafers" who had dropped in, knowing what was going on,
to take advantage of Jack's hospitality), and the liquor was

a real (twelve and a half cents) a glass, it made somewhat
of a hole in their lockers. It was now our ship's turn, and
Stimson and I, desirous to get away, stepped up to call for
glasses; but we soon found that we must go in order, the oldest
first, for the old sailors did not choose to be preceded by
a couple of youngsters; and *bon gré, mal gré,* we had to wait
our turn, with the twofold apprehension of being too late for
our horses, and of getting too much; for drink you must,
every time; and if you drink with one, and not with another,
it is always taken as an insult.

Having at length gone through our turns and acquitted ourselves of all obligations, we slipped out, and went about
among the houses, endeavoring to find horses for the day,
so that we might ride round and see the country. At first we
had but little success, all that we could get out of the lazy
fellows, in reply to our questions, being the eternal drawling
*"Quién sabe?"* ("Who knows?") which is an answer to all
questions. After several efforts, we at length fell in with a little
Sandwich Island boy, who belonged to Captain Wilson, of the
*Ayacucho,* and was well acquainted in the place; and he,
knowing where to go, soon procured us two horses, ready
saddled and bridled, each with a lasso coiled over the pommel.
These we were to have all day, with the privilege of riding
them down to the beach at night, for a dollar, which we had
to pay in advance. Horses are the cheapest thing in California;
very fair ones not being worth more than ten dollars apiece,
and the poorer being often sold for three and four. In taking
a day's ride, you pay for the use of the saddle, and for the
labor and trouble of catching the horses. If you bring the saddle back safe, they care but little what becomes of the horse.
Mounted on our horses, which were spirited beasts (and
which, by the way, in this country, are always steered in the
cavalry fashion, by pressing the contrary rein against the neck,
and not by pulling on the bit), we started off on a fine run
over the country. The first place we went to was the old
ruinous presidio, which stands on a rising ground near the
village, which it overlooks. It is built in the form of an open
square, like all the other presidios, and was in a most ruinous
state, with the exception of one side, in which the commandant lived, with his family. There were only two guns, one of
which was spiked, and the other had no carriage. Twelve
half-clothed and half-starved-looking fellows composed the

garrison; and they, it was said, had not a musket apiece. The
small settlement lay directly below the fort, composed of
about forty dark-brown-looking huts, or houses, and three or
four larger ones, whitewashed, which belonged to the *gente
de razón*. This town is not more than half as large as Monterey, or Santa Barbara, and has little or no business. From
the presidio, we rode off in the direction of the mission,
which we were told was three miles distant. The country was
rather sandy, and there was nothing for miles which could be
called a tree, but the grass grew green and rank, there were
many bushes and thickets, and the soil is said to be good.
After a pleasant ride of a couple of miles, we saw the white
walls of the mission, and, fording a small stream, we came
directly before it. The mission is built of adobe and plastered.
There was something decidedly striking in its appearance: a
number of irregular buildings, connected with one another,
and disposed in the form of a hollow square, with a church
at one end, rising above the rest, with a tower containing five
belfries, in each of which hung a large bell, and with very
large rusty iron crosses at the tops. Just outside of the buildings, and under the walls, stood twenty or thirty small huts,
built of straw and of the branches of trees, grouped together,
in which a few Indians lived, under the protection and in the
service of the mission.

Entering a gateway, we drove into the open square, in
which the stillness of death reigned. On one side was the
church; on another, a range of high buildings with grated
windows; a third was a range of smaller buildings, or offices,
and the fourth seemed to be little more than a high connecting
wall. Not a living creature could we see. We rode twice round
the square, in the hope of waking up someone; and in one
circuit saw a tall monk, with shaven head, sandals, and the
dress of the Gray Friars, pass rapidly through a gallery, but
he disappeared without noticing us. After two circuits, we
stopped our horses, and at last a man showed himself in
front of one of the small buildings. We rode up to him, and
found him dressed in the common dress of the country, with
a silver chain round his neck, supporting a large bunch of
keys. From this, we took him to be the steward of the mission, and, addressing him as *"Mayordomo,"* received a low
bow and an invitation to walk into his room. Making our
horses fast, we went in. It was a plain room, containing a

table, three or four chairs, a small picture or two of some saint, or miracle, or martyrdom, and a few dishes and glasses. *"Hay alguna cosa de comer?"* said I, from my grammar. *"Sí, Señor!"* said he. *"Qué gusta usted?"* Mentioning frijoles, which I knew they must have if they had nothing else, and beef and bread, with a hint for wine, if they had any, he went off to another building across the court, and returned in a few minutes with a couple of Indian boys bearing dishes and a decanter of wine. The dishes contained baked meats, frijoles stewed with peppers and onions, boiled eggs, and California flour baked into a kind of macaroni. These, together with the wine, made the most sumptuous meal we had eaten since we left Boston; and, compared with the fare we had lived upon for seven months, it was a regal banquet. After dispatching it, we took out some money and asked him how much we were to pay. He shook his head, and crossed himself, saying that it was charity—that the Lord gave it to us. Knowing the amount of this to be that he did not sell, but was willing to receive a present, we gave him ten or twelve reals, which he pocketed with admirable nonchalance, saying, *"Diós se lo pague."* Taking leave of him, we rode out to the Indians' huts. The little children were running about among the huts, stark naked, and the men wore not much more; but the women had generally coarse gowns of a sort of tow cloth. The men are employed, most of the time, in tending the cattle of the mission, and in working in the garden, which is a very large one, including several acres, and filled, it is said, with the best fruits of the climate. The language of these people, which is spoken by all the Indians of California, is the most brutish, without any exception, that I ever heard, or that could well be conceived of. It is a complete "slabber." The words fall off of the ends of their tongues, and a continual slabbering sound is made in the cheeks, outside of the teeth. It cannot have been the language of Montezuma and the independent Mexicans.

Here, among the huts, we saw the oldest man that I had ever met with; and, indeed, I never supposed that a person could retain life and exhibit such marks of age. He was sitting out in the sun, leaning against the side of a hut; and his legs and arms, which were bare, were of a dark-red color, the skin withered and shrunk up like burned leather, and the limbs not larger round than those of a boy of five years. He had a few gray hairs, which were tied together at the back of his head, and he was so feeble that, when we came up to him, he raised his hands slowly to his face, and, taking hold of his lids with his fingers, lifted them up to look at us; and, being satisfied, let them drop again. All command over the lid seemed to have gone. I asked his age, but could get no answer but *"Quién sabe?"* and they probably did not know it.

Leaving the mission, we returned to the village, going nearly all the way on a full run. The California horses have no medium gait, which is pleasant, between walking and running; for as there are no streets and parades, they have no need of the genteel trot, and their riders usually keep them at the top of their speed until they are tired, and then let them rest themselves by walking. The fine air of the afternoon, the rapid gait of the animals, who seemed almost to fly over the ground, and the excitement and novelty of the motion to us, who had been so long confined on shipboard, were exhilarating beyond expression, and we felt willing to ride all day long. Coming into the village, we found things looking very lively. The Indians, who always have a holiday on Sunday, were engaged at playing a kind of running game of ball, on a level piece of ground, near the houses. The old ones sat down in a ring, looking on, while the young ones—men, boys, and girls—were chasing the ball, and throwing it with all their might. Some of the girls ran like greyhounds. At every accident, or remarkable feat, the old people set up a deafening screaming and clapping of hands. Several bluejackets were reeling about among the houses, which showed that the *pulperías* had been well patronized. One or two of the sailors had got on horseback, but being rather indifferent horsemen, and the Mexicans having given them vicious beasts, they were soon thrown, much to the amusement of the people. A half-dozen Sandwich Islanders, from the hide houses and the two brigs, bold riders, were dashing about on the full gallop, hallooing and laughing like so many wild men.

It was now nearly sundown, and Stimson and I went into a house and sat quietly down to rest ourselves before going to the beach. Several people soon collected to see *los marineros ingleses*, and one of them, a young woman, took a great fancy to my pocket handkerchief, which was a large silk one that I had before going to sea, and a handsomer one than they had been in the habit of seeing. Of course, I gave it to her, which brought me into high favor; and we had a present of some pears and other fruits, which we took down to the beach with us. When we came to leave the house, we found that our horses, which we had tied at the door, were both gone. We had paid for them to ride down to the beach, but they were not to be found. We went to the man of whom we hired them, but he only shrugged his shoulders, and to our question, "Where are the horses?" only answered, *"Quién sabe?"* but as he was very easy, and made no inquiries for the saddles, we saw that he knew very well where they were. After a little trouble, determined not to walk to the beach—a distance of three miles—we procured two, at four reals more apiece, with two Indian boys to run behind and bring them back. Determined to have "the go" out of the horses, for our trouble, we went down at full speed, and were on the beach in a few minutes. Wishing to make our liberty last as long as possible, we rode up and down among the hide houses, amusing ourselves with seeing the men as they arrived (it was now dusk), some on horseback and others on foot. The Sandwich Islanders rode down, and were in "high snuff." We inquired for our shipmates, and were told that two of them had started on horseback, and been thrown, or had fallen off, and were seen heading for the beach, but steering pretty wild, and, by the looks of things, would not be down much before midnight.

The Indian boys having arrived, we gave them our horses, and, having seen them safely off, hailed for a boat, and went aboard. Thus ended our first liberty day on shore. We were well tired, but had had a good time, and were more willing to go back to our old duties. About midnight we were waked up by our two watchmates, who had come aboard in high dispute. It seems they had started to come down on the same horse, double-backed; and each was accusing the other of being the cause of his fall. They soon, however, turned in and fell asleep, and probably forgot all about it, for the next morning the dispute was not renewed.

# CHAPTER XVII

The next sound that we heard was "All hands ahoy!" and, looking up the scuttle, saw that it was just daylight. Our liberty had now truly taken flight, and with it we laid away our pumps, stockings, blue jackets, neckerchiefs, and other go-ashore paraphernalia, and putting on old duck trousers, red shirts, and Scotch caps, began taking out and landing our hides. For three days we were hard at work in this duty, from the gray of the morning until starlight, with the exception of a short time allowed for meals. For landing and taking on board hides, San Diego is decidedly the best place in California. The harbor is small and landlocked; there is no surf; the vessels lie within a cable's length of the beach, and the beach itself is smooth, hard sand, without rocks or stones. For these reasons, it is used by all the vessels in the trade as a depot; and, indeed, it would be impossible, when loading with the cured hides for the passage home, to take them on board at any of the open ports, without getting them wet in the surf, which would spoil them. We took possession of one of the hide houses, which belonged to our firm, and had been used by the *California*. It was built to hold forty thousand hides, and we had the pleasing prospect of filling it before we could leave the coast; and toward this our thirty-five hundred, which we brought down with us, would do but little. There was scarce a man on board who did not go often into the house, looking round, reflecting, and making some calculation of the time it would require.

The hides, as they come rough and uncured from the vessels, are piled up outside of the houses, whence they are taken and carried through a regular process of pickling, drying, and cleaning, and stowed away in the house, ready to be put on board. This process is necessary in order that they may keep during a long voyage and in warm latitudes. For the purpose of curing and taking care of them, an officer and a part of the crew of each vessel are usually left ashore; and it was for this business, we found, that our new officer had joined us. As soon as the hides were landed, he took charge of the house, and the captain intended to leave two or three

116

of us with him, hiring Sandwich Islanders in our places on board; but he could not get any Sandwich Islanders to go, although he offered them fifteen dollars a month; for the report of the flogging had got among them, and he was called *aole maikai* ("no good"); and that was an end of the business. They were, however, willing to work on shore, and four of them were hired and put with *Mr.* Russell to cure the hides.

After landing our hides, we next sent ashore our spare spars and rigging, all the stores which we did not need in the course of one trip to windward, and, in fact, everything which we could spare, so as to make room on board for hides; among other things, the pigsty, and with it "Old Bess." This was an old sow that we had brought from Boston, and who lived to get round Cape Horn, where all the other pigs died from cold and wet. Report said that she had been a Canton voyage before. She had been the pet of the cook during the whole passage, and he had fed her with the best of everything, and taught her to know his voice, and to do a number of strange tricks for his amusement. Tom Cringle says that no one can fathom a Negro's affection for a pig; and I believe he is right, for it almost broke our poor darky's heart when he heard that Bess was to be taken ashore, and that he was to have the care of her no more. He had depended upon her as a solace, during the long trips up and down the coast. "Obey orders, if you break owners!" said he—"break *hearts*," he might have said—and lent a hand to get her over the side, trying to make it as easy for her as possible. We got a whip on the main yard, and, hooking it to a strap round her body, swayed away, and, giving a wink to one another, ran her chock up to the yardarm. " 'Vast there! 'Vast!" said the mate. "None of your skylarking! Lower away!" But he evidently enjoyed the joke. The pig squealed like the "crack of doom," and tears stood in the poor darky's eyes; and he muttered something about having no pity on a dumb beast. "*Dumb* beast!" said Jack. "If she's what you call a dumb beast, then my eyes a'n't mates." This produced a laugh from all but the cook. He was too intent upon seeing her safe in the boat. He watched her all the way ashore, where, upon her landing, she was received by a whole troop of her kind, who had been set ashore from the other vessels, and had multiplied and formed a large commonwealth. From the door of his galley the cook used to watch them in their maneuvers, setting up a shout and clapping his hands whenever Bess came off victorious in the struggles for pieces of rawhide and half-picked bones which were lying about the beach. During the day, he saved all the nice things, and made a bucket of swill, and asked us to take it ashore in the gig, and looked quite disconcerted when the mate told him that he would pitch the swill overboard, and him after it, if he saw any of it go into the boats. We told him that he thought more about the pig than he did about his wife, who lived down in Robinson's Alley; and, indeed, he could hardly have been more attentive, for he actually, on several nights after dark, when he thought he would not be seen, sculled himself ashore in a boat, with a bucket of nice swill, and returned like Leander from crossing the Hellespont.

The next Sunday the other half of our crew went ashore on liberty, and left us on board, to enjoy the first quiet Sunday we had had upon the coast. Here were no hides to come off, and no southeasters to fear. We washed and mended our clothes in the morning, and spent the rest of the day in reading and writing. Several of us wrote letters to send home by the *Lagoda*. At twelve o'clock, the *Ayacucho* dropped her fore-topsail, which was a signal for her sailing. She unmoored and warped down into the bight, from which she got under way. During this operation her crew were a long time heaving at the windlass, and I listened to the musical notes of a Sandwich Islander named Mahanna, who "sang out" for them. Sailors, when heaving at a windlass, in order that they may heave together, always have one to sing out, which is done in high and long-drawn notes, varying with the motion of the windlass. This requires a clear voice, strong lungs, and much practice, to be done well. This fellow had a very peculiar, wild sort of note, breaking occasionally into a falsetto. The sailors thought that it was too high, and not enough of the boatswain hoarseness about it; but to me it had a great charm. The harbor was perfectly still, and his voice rang among the hills as though it could have been heard for miles. Toward sundown, a good breeze having sprung up, the *Ayacucho* got under way, and with her long, sharp head cutting elegantly through the water on a taut bowline, she stood directly out of the harbor, and bore away to the southward. She was bound to Callao, and thence to the Sandwich Islands, and expected to be on the coast again in eight or ten months.

At the close of the week we were ready to sail, but were delayed a day or two by the running away of Foster, the man who had been our second mate and was turned forward. From the time that he was "broken," he had had a dog's berth on board the vessel, and determined to run away at the first opportunity. Having shipped for an officer when he was not half a seaman, he found little pity with the crew, and was not man enough to hold his ground among them. The captain called him a "soger," * and promised to "ride him down as he would the main tack"; and when officers are once determined to "ride a man down," it is a gone case with him. He had had several difficulties with the captain, and asked leave to go home in the *Lagoda;* but this was refused him. One night he was insolent to an officer on the beach, and refused to come aboard in the boat. He was reported to the captain; and, as he came aboard—it being past the proper hour—he was called aft, and told that he was to have a flogging. Immediately he fell down on deck, calling out, "Don't flog me, Captain Thompson, don't flog me!" and the captain, angry and disgusted with him, gave him a few blows over the back with a rope's end, and sent him forward. He was not much hurt, but a good deal frightened, and made up his mind to run away that night. This was managed better than anything he ever did in his life, and seemed really to show some spirit and forethought. He gave his bedding and mattress to one of the *Lagoda's* crew, who promised to keep it for him, and took it aboard his ship as something which he had bought. He then unpacked his chest, putting all his valuable clothes into a large canvas bag, and told one of us who had the watch to call him at midnight. Coming on deck at midnight, and finding no officer on deck, and all still aft,

---

* "Soger" ("soldier") is the worst term of reproach that can be applied to a sailor. It signifies a skulk, a shirk—one who is always trying to get clear of work, and is out of the way, or hanging back, when duty is to be done. "Marine" is the term applied more particularly to a man who is ignorant and clumsy about seaman's work—a greenhorn, a land-lubber. To make a sailor shoulder a handspike, and walk fore and aft the deck, like a sentry, is as ignominious a punishment as can be put upon him. Such a punishment inflicted upon an able seaman in a vessel of war might break down his spirit more than a flogging.

he lowered his bag into a boat, got softly down into it, cast off the painter, and let it drop silently with the tide until he was out of hearing, when he sculled ashore.

The next morning, when all hands were mustered, there was a great stir to find Foster. Of course, we would tell nothing, and all they could discover was that he had left an empty chest behind him, and that he went off in a boat; for they saw the boat lying high and dry on the beach. After breakfast, the captain went up to the town, and offered a reward of twenty dollars for him; and for a couple of days the soldiers, Indians, and all others who had nothing to do were scouring the country for him, on horseback, but without effect; for he was safely concealed, all the time, within fifty rods of the hide houses. As soon as he had landed, he went directly to the *Lagoda*'s hide house, and a part of her crew, who were living there on shore, promised to conceal him and his "traps" until the *Pilgrim* should sail, and then to intercede with Captain Bradshaw to take him on board his ship. Just behind the hide houses, among the thickets and underwood, was a small cave, the entrance to which was known only to two men on the beach, and which was so well concealed that though, when I afterward came to live on shore, it was shown to me two or three times, I was never able to find it alone. To this cave he was carried before daybreak in the morning, and supplied with bread and water, and there remained until he saw us under way and well round the point.

*Friday, March 27th.* The captain having given up all hope of finding Foster, and being unwilling to delay any longer, gave orders for unmooring ship, and we made sail, dropping slowly down with the tide and light wind. We left letters with Captain Bradshaw to take to Boston, and were made miserable by hearing him say that he should be back again before we left the coast. The wind, which was very light, died away soon after we doubled the point, and we lay becalmed for two days, not moving three miles the whole time, and a part of the second day were almost within sight of the vessels. On the third day, about noon, a cool sea breeze came rippling and darkening the surface of the water, and by sundown we were off San Juan, which is about forty miles from San Diego, and is called halfway to San Pedro, where we were bound. Our crew was now considerably weakened. One man we had lost overboard, another had been taken aft as clerk, and a third had run away; so that, besides Stimson and myself, there were only three able seamen and one boy of twelve years of age. With this diminished and discontented crew, and in a small vessel, we were now to battle the watch through a couple of years of hard service; yet there was not one who was not glad that Foster had escaped; for, shiftless and good for nothing as he was, no one could wish to see him dragging on a miserable life, cowed down and disheartened; and we were all rejoiced to hear, upon our return to San Diego, about two months afterward, that he had been immediately taken aboard the *Lagoda*, and had gone home in her, on regular seaman's wages.

After a slow passage of five days, we arrived on Wednesday, the first of April, at our old anchoring ground at San Pedro. The bay was as deserted and looked as dreary as before, and formed no pleasing contrast with the security and snugness of San Diego, and the activity and interest which the loading and unloading of four vessels gave to that scene. In a few days the hides began to come slowly down, and we got into the old business of rolling goods up the hill, pitching hides down, and pulling our long league off and on. Nothing of note occurred while we were lying here, except that an attempt was made to repair the small Mexican brig which had been cast away in a southeaster, and which now lay up, high and dry, over one reef of rocks and two sandbanks. Our carpenter surveyed her, and pronounced her capable of being refitted, and in a few days the owners came down from the Pueblo, and having waited for the high spring tides, with the help of our cables, kedges, and crew, hauled her off after several trials. The three men at the house on shore, who had formerly been a part of her crew, now joined her, and seemed glad enough at the prospect of getting off the coast.

On board our own vessel, things went on in the common monotonous way. The excitement which immediately followed the flogging scene had passed off, but the effect of it upon the crew, and especially upon the two men themselves, remained. The different manner in which these men were affected, corresponding to their different characters, was not a little remarkable. John was a foreigner and high-tempered, and though mortified, as anyone would be at having had the worst of an encounter, yet his chief feeling seemed to be anger; and he talked much of satisfaction and revenge, if he ever got back to Boston. But with the other it was very different. He was an American, and had had some education; and this thing coming upon him seemed completely to break him down. He had a feeling of the degradation that had been inflicted upon him, which the other man was incapable of. Before that, he had a good deal of fun in him, and amused us often with queer Negro stories (he was from a slave state); but afterward he seldom smiled, seemed to lose all life and elasticity, and appeared to have but one wish, and that was for the voyage to be at an end. I have often known him to draw a long sigh when he was alone, and he took but little part or interest in John's plans of satisfaction and retaliation.

After a stay of about a fortnight, during which we slipped for one southeaster, and were at sea two days, we got under way for Santa Barbara. It was now the middle of April, the southeaster season was nearly over, and the light, regular winds, which blow down the coast, began to set steadily in, during the latter part of each day. Against these we beat slowly up to Santa Barbara—a distance of about ninety miles —in three days. There we found, lying at anchor, the large Genoese ship which we saw in the same place on the first day of our coming upon the coast. She had been up to San Francisco, or, as it is called, "chock up to windward," had stopped at Monterey on her way down, and was shortly to proceed to San Pedro and San Diego, and thence, taking in her cargo, to sail for Valparaiso and Cádiz. She was a large, clumsy ship, and, with her topmasts stayed forward, and high poopdeck, looked like an old woman with a crippled back. It was now the close of Lent, and on Good Friday she had all her yards acockbill, which is customary among Catholic vessels. Some also have an effigy of Judas, which the crew amuse themselves with keelhauling and hanging by the neck from the yardarms.

# CHAPTER XVIII

The next Sunday was Easter, and as there had been no liberty at San Pedro, it was our turn to go ashore and misspend another Sunday. Soon after breakfast, a large boat, filled with men in blue jackets, scarlet caps, and various-colored under-clothes, bound ashore on liberty, left the Italian ship, and passed under our stern, the men singing beautiful Italian boat songs all the way, in fine, full chorus. Among the songs I recognized the favorite *"O Pescator dell' Onda."* It brought back to my mind pianofortes, drawing rooms, young ladies singing, and a thousand other things which as little befitted me, in my situation, to be thinking upon. Supposing that the whole day would be too long a time to spend ashore, as there was no place to which we could take a ride, we remained quietly on board until after dinner. We were then pulled ashore in the stern of the boat—for it is a point with liberty men to be pulled off and back as passengers by their ship-mates—and, with orders to be on the beach at sundown, we took our way for the town. There, everything wore the appearance of a holiday. The people were dressed in their best, the men riding about among the houses, and the women sitting on carpets before the doors. Under the piazza of a *pul-pería* two men were seated, decked out with knots of ribbons and bouquets, and playing the violin and the Spanish guitar. These are the only instruments, with the exception of the drums and trumpets at Monterey, that I ever heard in California; and I suspect they play upon no others, for at a great fandango at which I was afterward present, and where they mustered all the music they could find, there were three violins and two guitars, and no other instruments. As it was now too near the middle of the day to see any dancing, and hearing that a bull was expected down from the country, to be baited in the presidio square, in the course of an hour or two, we took a stroll among the houses. Inquiring for an American who, we had been told, had married in the place, and kept a shop, we were directed to a long, low building, at the end of which was a door, with a sign over it, in Spanish. Entering the shop, we found no one in it, and the whole had an empty, deserted air. In a few minutes the man made his appearance, and apologized for having nothing to entertain us with, saying that he had had a fandango at his house the night before, and the people had eaten and drunk up everything.

"Oh, yes!" said I. "Easter holidays!"

"No!" said he, with a singular expression on his face. "I had a little daughter die the other day, and that's the custom of the country."

At this I felt somewhat awkwardly, not knowing what to say, and whether to offer consolation or not, and was beginning to retire, when he opened a side door and told us to walk in. Here I was no less astonished; for I found a large room, filled with young girls, from three or four years of age up to fifteen and sixteen, dressed all in white, with wreaths of flowers on their heads, and bouquets in their hands. Following our conductor among these girls, who were playing about in high spirits, we came to a table, at the end of the room, covered with a white cloth, on which lay a coffin, about three feet long, with the body of his child. The coffin was covered with white cloth, and lined with white satin, and was strewn with flowers. Through an open door, we saw, in another room, a few elderly people in common dresses; while the benches and tables thrown up in a corner, and the stained walls, gave evident signs of the last night's "high go." Feeling, like Garrick, between Tragedy and Comedy, an uncertainty of purpose, I asked the man when the funeral would take place, and being told that it would move toward the mission in about an hour, took my leave.

To pass away the time, we hired horses and rode to the beach and there saw three or four Italian sailors, mounted, and riding up and down on the hard sand at a furious rate. We joined them, and found it fine sport. The beach gave us a stretch of a mile or more, and the horses flew over the smooth, hard sand, apparently invigorated and excited by the salt sea breeze, and by the continual roar and dashing of the breakers. From the beach we returned to the town, and, finding that the funeral procession had moved, rode on and overtook it, about halfway to the mission. Here was as peculiar a sight as we had seen before in the house, the one looking as much like a funeral procession as the other did like a house of mourning. The little coffin was borne by eight girls, who were continually relieved by others running forward from the procession and taking their places. Behind it came a straggling company of girls, dressed, as before, in white and flowers, and including, I should suppose by their numbers, nearly all the girls between five and fifteen in the place. They played along on the way, frequently stopping and running all together to talk to someone, or to pick up a flower, and then running on again to overtake the coffin. There were a few elderly women in common colors; and a herd of young men and boys, some on foot and others mounted, followed them, or walked or rode by their side, frequently interrupting them by jokes and questions. But the most singular thing of all was that two men walked, one on each side of the coffin, carrying muskets in their hands, which they continually loaded, and fired into the air. Whether this was to keep off the evil spirits or not, I do not know. It was the only interpretation that I could put upon it.

As we drew near the mission, we saw the great gate thrown open, and the *padre* standing on the steps, with a crucifix in his hand. The mission is a large and deserted-looking place, the outbuildings going to ruin, and everything giving one the impression of decayed grandeur. A large stone fountain threw out pure water, from four mouths, into a basin, before the church door; and we were on the point of riding up to let our horses drink, when it occurred to us that it might be consecrated, and we forbore. Just at this moment, the bells set up their harsh, discordant clangor, and the procession moved into the court. I wished to follow, and see the ceremony, but the horse of one of my companions had become frightened, and was tearing off toward the town; and, having thrown his rider, and got one of his hoofs caught in the tackling of the saddle, which had slipped, was fast dragging and ripping it to pieces. Knowing that my shipmate could not speak a word of Spanish, and fearing that he would get into difficulty, I was obliged to leave the ceremony and ride after him. I soon overtook him, trudging along, swearing at the horse, and carrying the remains of the saddle, which he had picked up on the road. Going to the owner of the horse, we made a settlement with him, and found him surprisingly liberal. All parts of the saddle were brought back, and, being capable of repair, he was satisfied with six reals. We thought it would have been a few dollars. We pointed to the horse, which was now halfway up one of the mountains; but he shook his head, saying, "*No importa!*" and giving us to understand that he had plenty more.

Having returned to the town, we saw a crowd collected in the square before the principal *pulperia*, and, riding up, found that all these people—men, women, and children— had been drawn together by a couple of bantam cocks. The cocks were in full tilt, springing into one another, and the people were as eager, laughing and shouting, as though the combatants had been men. There had been a disappointment about the bull; he had broken his bail, and taken himself off, and it was too late to get another, so the people were obliged to put up with a cockfight. One of the bantams having been knocked in the head, and having an eye put out, gave in, and two monstrous prize cocks were brought on. These were the object of the whole affair; the bantams having been merely served up as a first course, to collect the people together. Two fellows came into the ring, holding the cocks in their arms, and stroking them, and running about on all fours, encouraging and setting them on. Bets ran high, and, like most other contests, it remained for some time undecided. Both cocks showed great pluck, and fought probably better and longer than their masters would have done. Whether, in the end, it was the white or the red that beat, I do not recollect, but whichever it was, he strutted off with the true *veni-vidi-vici* look, leaving the other lying panting on his beam ends.

This matter having been settled, we heard some talk about "*caballos*" and "*carrera*," and seeing the people streaming off in one direction, we followed, and came upon a level piece of ground, just out of the town, which was used as a race course. Here the crowd soon became thick again, the ground was marked off, the judges stationed, and the horses led up to one end. Two fine-looking old gentlemen—Don Carlos and Don Domingo, so called—held the stakes, and all was now ready. We waited some time, during which we could just see the horses twisting round and turning, until, at length, there was a shout along the lines, and on they came, heads stretched out and eyes starting—working all over, both man and beast. The steeds came by us like a couple of chain shot, neck and neck; and now we could see nothing but their backs and their hind hoofs flying in the air. As fast as the horses passed, the crowd broke up behind them,

and ran to the goal. When we got there, we found the horses
returning on a slow walk, having run far beyond the mark,
and heard that the long, bony one had come in head and
shoulders before the other. The riders were light-built men,
had handkerchiefs tied round their heads, and were bare-
armed and bare-legged. The horses were noble-looking beasts,
not so sleek and combed as our Boston stable horses, but
with fine limbs and spirited eyes. After this had been settled,
and fully talked over, the crowd scattered again, and flocked
back to the town.

Returning to the large *pulpería*, we heard the violin and
guitar screaming and twanging away under the piazza, where
they had been all day. As it was now sundown, there began
to be some dancing. The Italian sailors danced, and one of
our crew exhibited himself in a sort of West India shuffle,
much to the amusement of the bystanders, who cried out,
*"Bravo!"* *"Otra vez!"* and *"Vivan los marineros!"* but the
dancing did not become general, as the women and the
*gente de razón* had not yet made their appearance. We wished
very much to stay and see the style of dancing; but, although
we had had our own way during the day, yet we were,
after all, but foremast jacks; and, having been ordered to be
on the beach by sunset, did not venture to be more than an
hour behind the time, so we took our way down. We found
the boat just pulling ashore through the breakers, which
were running high, there having been a heavy fog outside,
which, from some cause or other, always brings on, or
precedes, a heavy sea. Liberty men are privileged from the
time they leave the vessel until they step on board again; so
we took our places in the stern sheets, and were congratulating ourselves upon getting off dry, when a great comber
broke fore and aft the boat, and wet us through and through,
filling the boat half full of water. Having lost her buoyancy
by the weight of the water, she dropped heavily into every
sea that struck her, and by the time we had pulled out of
the surf into deep water, she was but just afloat, and we were
up to our knees. By the help of a small bucket and our
hats, we bailed her out, got on board, hoisted the boats, ate
our supper, changed our clothes, gave (as is usual) the whole
history of our day's adventures to those who had stayed
on board, and, having taken a night smoke, turned in. Thus
ended our second day's liberty on shore.

On Monday morning, as an offset to our day's sport, we were all set to work "tarring down" the rigging. Some got girtlines up for riding down the stays and backstays, and others tarred the shrouds, lifts, &c., laying out on the yards, and coming down the rigging. We overhauled our bags, and took out our old tarry trousers and frocks, which we had used when we tarred down before, and were all at work in the rigging by sunrise. After breakfast, we had the satisfaction of seeing the Italian ship's boat go ashore, filled with men, gaily dressed, as on the day before, and singing their barcarolles. The Easter holidays are kept up on shore for three days; and, being a Catholic vessel, her crew had the advantage of them. For two successive days, while perched up in the rigging, covered with tar and engaged in our disagreeable work, we saw these fellows going ashore in the morning, and coming off again at night, in high spirits. So much for being Protestants. There's no danger of Catholicism's spreading in New England, unless the Church cuts down her holidays; Yankees can't afford the time. American shipmasters get nearly three weeks' more labor out of their crews, in the course of a year, than the masters of vessels from Catholic countries. As Yankees don't usually keep Christmas, and shipmasters at sea never know when Thanksgiving comes, Jack has no festival at all.

About noon, a man aloft called out, "Sail ho!" and, looking off, we saw the head sails of a vessel coming round the point. As she drew round, she showed the broadside of a full-rigged brig, with the Yankee ensign at her peak. We ran up our stars and stripes, and, knowing that there was no American brig on the coast but ours, expected to have news from home. She rounded to and let go her anchor; but the dark faces on her yards, when they furled the sails, and the Babel on deck, soon made known that she was from the Islands. Immediately afterward, a boat's crew came aboard, bringing her skipper, and from them we learned that she was from Oahu, and was engaged in the same trade with the *Ayacucho* and *Loriotte*, between the coast, the Sandwich Islands, and the leeward coast of Peru and Chile. Her captain and officers were Americans, and also a part of her crew; the rest were Islanders. She was called the *Catalina*, and, like the vessels in that trade, except the *Ayacucho*, her papers and colors were from Uncle Sam. They, of course, brought us no news, and we were doubly disappointed, for we had thought, at first, it might be the ship which we were expecting from Boston.

After lying here about a fortnight, and collecting all the hides the place afforded, we set sail again for San Pedro. There we found the brig which we had assisted in getting off lying at anchor, with a mixed crew of Americans, English, Sandwich Islanders, Spaniards, and Spanish Indians; and though much smaller than we, yet she had three times the number of men; and she needed them, for her officers were Californians. No vessels in the world go so sparingly manned as American and English; and none do so well. A Yankee brig of that size would have had a crew of four men, and would have worked round and round her. The Italian ship had a crew of thirty men, nearly three times as many as the *Alert*, which was afterward on the coast, and was of the same size; yet the *Alert* would get under way and come to in half the time, and get two anchors, while they were all talking at once, jabbering like a parcel of Yahoos, and running about decks to find their cat block.

There was only one point in which they had the advantage over us, and that was in lightening their labors in the boats by their songs. The Americans are a time- and money-saving people, but have not yet, as a nation, learned that music may be "turned to account." We pulled the long distances to and from the shore, with our loaded boats, without a word spoken, and with discontented looks, while they not only lightened the labor of rowing, but actually made it pleasant and cheerful, by their music. So true is it, that:

> "For the tired slave, song lifts the languid oar,
>    And bids it aptly fall, with chime
> That beautifies the fairest shore,
>    And mitigates the harshest clime."

After lying about a week in San Pedro, we got under way for San Diego, intending to stop at San Juan, as the southeaster season was nearly over, and there was little or no danger.

This being the spring season, San Pedro, as well as all the other open ports upon the coast, was filled with whales, that had come in to make their annual visit upon soundings.

For the first few days that we were here and at Santa Barbara, we watched them with great interest, calling out, "There she blows!" every time we saw the spout of one breaking the surface of the water; but they soon became so common that we took little notice of them. They often "broke" very near us, and one thick, foggy night, during a dead calm, while I was standing anchor watch, one of them rose so near that he struck our cable, and made all surge again. He did not seem to like the encounter much himself, for he sheered off, and spouted at a good distance. We once came very near running one down in the gig, and should probably have been knocked to pieces or thrown sky-high. We had been on board the little Spanish brig, and were returning, stretching out well at our oars, the little boat going like a swallow; our faces were turned aft (as is always the case in pulling), and the captain, who was steering, was not looking out, when, all at once, we heard the spout of a whale directly ahead. "Back water! Back water, for your lives!" shouted the captain; and we backed our blades in the water, and brought the boat to in a smother of foam. Turning our heads, we saw a great, rough, humpbacked whale slowly crossing our fore foot, within three or four yards of the boat's stem. Had we not backed water just as we did, we should inevitably have gone smash upon him, striking him with our stem just about amidships. He took no notice of us, but passed slowly on, and dived a few yards beyond us, throwing his tail high in the air. He was so near that we had a perfect view of him, and, as may be supposed, had no desire to see him nearer. He was a disgusting creature, with a skin rough, hairy, and of an iron-gray color. This kind differs much from the sperm, in color and skin, and is said to be fiercer. We saw a few sperm whales; but most of the whales that come upon the coast are finbacks and humpbacks, which are more difficult to take, and are said not to give oil enough to pay for the trouble. For this reason, whaleships do not come upon the coast after them. Our captain, together with Captain Nye of the *Loriotte*, who had been in a whaleship, thought of making an attempt upon one of them with two boats' crews; but as we had only two harpoons, and no proper lines, they gave it up.

During the months of March, April, and May, these whales appear in great numbers in the open ports of Santa Barbara, San Pedro, &c., and hover off the coast, while a few find their way into the close harbors of San Diego and Monterey. They are all off again before midsummer, and make their appearance on the "offshore ground." We saw some fine "schools" of sperm whales, which are easily distinguished by their spout, blowing away, a few miles to windward, on our passage to San Juan.

Coasting along on the quiet shore of the Pacific, we came to anchor in twenty fathoms water, almost out at sea, as it were, and directly abreast of a steep hill which overhung the water, and was twice as high as our royal masthead. We had heard much of this place from the *Lagoda*'s crew, who said it was the worst place in California. The shore is rocky, and directly exposed to the southeast, so that vessels are obliged to slip and run for their lives on the first sign of a gale; and late as it was in the season, we got up our slip rope and gear, though we meant to stay only twenty-four hours. We pulled the agent ashore, and were ordered to wait for him, while he took a circuitous way round the hill to the mission, which was hidden behind it. We were glad of the opportunity to examine this singular place, and hauling the boat up, and making her well fast, took different directions up and down the beach, to explore it.

San Juan is the only romantic spot on the coast. The country here for several miles is high tableland, running boldly to the shore, and breaking off in a steep cliff, at the foot of which the waters of the Pacific are constantly dashing. For several miles the water washes the very base of the hill, or breaks upon ledges and fragments of rocks which run out into the sea. Just where we landed was a small cove, or bight, which gave us, at high tide, a few square feet of sand beach between the sea and the bottom of the hill. This was the only landing place. Directly before us rose the perpendicular height of four or five hundred feet. How we were to get hides down, or goods up, upon the tableland on which the mission was situated was more than we could tell. The agent had taken a long circuit, and yet had frequently to jump over breaks, and climb steep places, in the ascent. No animal but a man or a monkey could get up it. However, that was not our lookout; and, knowing that the agent would be gone an hour or more, we strolled about, picking up shells, and following the sea where it tumbled in, roaring and spouting, among the crevices of the great rocks. What a

sight, thought I, must this be in a southeaster! The rocks were
as large as those of Nahant or Newport, but, to my eye,
more grand and broken. Beside, there was a grandeur in
everything around, which gave a solemnity to the scene, a
silence and solitariness which affected every part! Not a
human being but ourselves for miles, and no sound heard but
the pulsations of the great Pacific! And the great steep hill
rising like a wall, and cutting us off from all the world but the
"world of waters"! I separated myself from the rest, and sat
down on a rock, just where the sea ran in and formed a fine
spouting horn. Compared with the plain, dull sand beach of
the rest of the coast, this grandeur was as refreshing as a
great rock in a weary land. It was almost the first time that I
had been positively alone—free from the sense that human
beings were at my elbow, if not talking with me—since I had
left home. My better nature returned strong upon me. Everything was in accordance with my state of feeling, and I
experienced a glow of pleasure at finding that what of poetry
and romance I ever had in me had not been entirely deadened
by the laborious life, with its paltry, vulgar associations,
which I had been leading. Nearly an hour did I sit, almost
lost in the luxury of this entire new scene of the play in which
I had been so long acting, when I was aroused by the distant
shouts of my companions, and saw that they were collecting
together, as the agent had made his appearance, on his way
back to our boat.

We pulled aboard, and found the longboat hoisted out,
and nearly laden with goods; and, after dinner, we all went
on shore in the quarter boat, with the longboat in tow.
As we drew in, we descried an oxcart and a couple of men
standing directly on the brow of the hill; and having landed,
the captain took his way round the hill, ordering me and
one other to follow him. We followed, picking our way out,
and jumping and scrambling up, walking over briers and
prickly pears, until we came to the top. Here the country
stretched out for miles, as far as the eye could reach, on a
level, table surface, and the only habitation in sight was the
small white mission of San Juan Capistrano, with a few
Indian huts about it, standing in a small hollow, about a mile
from where we were. Reaching the brow of the hill, where
the cart stood, we found several piles of hides, and Indians
sitting round them. One or two other carts were coming slowly

on from the mission, and the captain told us to begin and
throw the hides down. This, then, was the way they were to
be got down—thrown down, one at a time, a distance of
four hundred feet! This was doing the business on a great
scale. Standing on the edge of the hill, and looking down
the perpendicular height, the sailors

> ". . . that walked upon the beach
> Appeared like mice; and *our* tall anchoring bark
> Diminished to her cock; her cock a buoy
> Almost too small for sight."

Down this height we pitched the hides, throwing them as
far out into the air as we could; and as they were all large,
stiff, and doubled, like the cover of a book, the wind took
them, and they swayed and eddied about, plunging and rising
in the air, like a kite when it has broken its string. As it was
now low tide, there was no danger of their falling into the
water; and, as fast as they came to ground, the men below
picked them up, and, taking them on their heads, walked
off with them to the boat. It was really a picturesque sight:
the great height, the scaling of the hides, and the continual
walking to and fro of the men, who looked like mites, on
the beach. This was the romance of hide droghing!

Some of the hides lodged in cavities under the bank and
out of our sight, being directly under us; but by pitching
other hides in the same direction, we succeeded in dislodging
them. Had they remained there, the captain said he should
have sent on board for a couple of pairs of long halyards,
and got someone to go down for them. It was said that one
of the crew of an English brig went down in the same way,
a few years before. We looked over, and thought it would
not be a welcome task, especially for a few paltry hides;
but no one knows what he will do until he is called upon; for,
six months afterward, I descended the same place by a pair
of topgallant-studding-sail halyards, to save half a dozen
hides which had lodged there.

Having thrown them all over, we took our way back again,
and found the boat loaded and ready to start. We pulled off,
took the hides all aboard, hoisted in the boats, hove up our
anchor, made sail, and before sundown were on our way
to San Diego.

*Friday, May 8th, 1835.* Arrived at San Diego. We found the little harbor deserted. The *Lagoda, Ayacucho, Loriotte,* all had sailed from the coast, and we were left alone. All the hide houses on the beach but ours were shut up, and the Sandwich Islanders, a dozen or twenty in number, who had worked for the other vessels, and been paid off when they sailed, were living on the beach, keeping up a grand carnival. There was a large oven on the beach, which, it seems, had been built by a Russian discovery ship that had been on the coast a few years ago, for baking her bread. This the Sandwich Islanders took possession of, and had kept ever since, undisturbed. It was big enough to hold eight or ten men, and had a door at the side, and a vent hole at top. They covered the floor with Oahu mats for a carpet, stopped up the vent hole in bad weather, and made it their headquarters. It was now inhabited by as many as a dozen or twenty men, crowded together, who lived there in complete idleness—drinking, playing cards, and carousing in every way. They bought a bullock once a week, which kept them in meat, and one of them went up to the town every day to get fruit, liquor, and provisions. Besides this, they had bought a cask of ship bread, and a barrel of flour from the *Lagoda,* before she sailed. There they lived, having a grand time, and caring for nobody. Captain Thompson wished to get three or four of them to come on board the *Pilgrim,* as we were so much diminished in numbers, and went up to the oven, and spent an hour or two trying to negotiate with them. One of them—a finely built, active, strong, and intelligent fellow, who was a sort of king among them—acted as spokesman. He was called Mannini—or rather, out of compliment to his known importance and influence, *Mr.* Mannini—and was known all over California. Through him, the captain offered them fifteen dollars a month, and one month's pay in advance; but it was like throwing pearls before swine, or, rather, carrying coals to Newcastle. So long as they had money, they would not work for fifty dollars a month, and when their money was gone, they would work for ten.

"What do you do here, Mr. Mannini?" * said the captain.

"Oh, we play cards, get drunk, smoke—do anything we're a mind to."

* The vowels in the Sandwich Island language have the sound of those in the languages of Continental Europe.

"Don't you want to come aboard and work?"

"*Aole! Aole make make makou i ka hana.* Now got plenty money; no good, work. *Mamule,* money *pau*—all gone. Ah! Very good, work! *Maikai, hana hana nui!*"

"But you'll spend all your money in this way," said the captain.

"Aye! Me know that. By-'em-by money *pau*—all gone; then Kanaka work plenty."

This was a hopeless case, and the captain left them, to wait patiently until their money was gone.

We discharged our hides and tallow, and in about a week were ready to set sail again for the windward. We unmoored, and got everything ready, when the captain made another attempt upon the oven. This time he had more regard to the *mollia tempora fandi,* and succeeded very well. He won over Mr. Mannini to his interest, and as the shot was getting low in the locker at the oven, prevailed upon him and three others to come on board with their chests and baggage, and sent a hasty summons to me and the boy to come ashore with our things, and join the gang at the hide house. This was unexpected to me; but anything in the way of variety I liked; so we made ready, and were pulled ashore. I stood on the beach while the brig got under way, and watched her until she rounded the point, and then went to the hide house to take up my quarters for a few months.

# CHAPTER XIX

Here was a change in my life as complete as it had been sudden. In the twinkling of an eye I was transformed from a sailor into a "beachcomber" and a hide curer; yet the

novelty and the comparative independence of the life were
not unpleasant. Our hide house was a large building, made
of rough boards, and intended to hold forty thousand hides.
In one corner of it a small room was parted off, in which
four berths were made, where we were to live, with mother
earth for our floor. It contained a table, a small locker for
pots, spoons, plates, &c., and a small hole cut to let in the
light. Here we put our chests, threw our bedding into the
berths, and took up our quarters. Over our heads was another
small room, in which *Mr.* Russell lived, who had charge of
the hide house, the same man who was for a time an officer of
the *Pilgrim*. There he lived in solitary grandeur, eating and
sleeping alone (and these were his principal occupations),
and communing with his own dignity. The boy, a Marblehead
hopeful, whose name was Sam, was to act as cook; while I,
a giant of a Frenchman named Nicholas, and four Sandwich
Islanders were to cure the hides. Sam, Nicholas, and I lived
together in the room, and the four Sandwich Islanders worked
and ate with us, but generally slept at the oven. My new
messmate, Nicholas, was the most immense man that I had
ever seen. He came on the coast in a vessel which was afterward wrecked, and now let himself out to the different
houses to cure hides. He was considerably over six feet, and
of a frame so large that he might have been shown for a
curiosity. But the most remarkable thing about him was
his feet. They were so large that he could not find a pair of
shoes in California to fit him, and was obliged to send to
Oahu for a pair; and when he got them, he was compelled
to wear them down at the heel. He told me once that he
was wrecked in an American brig on the Goodwin Sands,
and was sent up to London, to the charge of the American
consul, with scant clothing to his back and no shoes to his
feet, and was obliged to go about London streets in his
stocking feet three or four days, in the month of January,
until the consul could have a pair of shoes *made for him*.
His strength was in proportion to his size, and his ignorance
to his strength—"strong as an ox, and ignorant as strong."
He knew how neither to read nor to write. He had been to
sea from a boy, had seen all kinds of service, and been in
all sorts of vessels—merchantmen, men-of-war, privateers, and
slavers; and from what I could gather from his accounts of
himself, and from what he once told me, in confidence,

after we had become better acquainted, he had been in even worse business than slave-trading. He was once tried for his life in Charleston, South Carolina, and, though acquitted, was so frightened that he never would show himself in the United States again. I was not able to persuade him that he could not be tried a second time for the same offense. He said he had got safe off from the breakers, and was too good a sailor to risk his timbers again.

Though I knew what his life had been, yet I never had the slightest fear of him. We always got along very well together, and, though so much older, stronger, and larger than I, he showed a marked respect for me, on account of my education, and of what he had heard of my situation before coming to sea, such as may be expected from a European of the humble class. "I'll be good friends with you," he used to say, "for by and by you'll come out here captain, and then you'll haze me well!" By holding together, we kept the officer in good order, for he was evidently afraid of Nicholas, and never interfered with us, except when employed upon the hides. My other companions, the Sandwich Islanders, deserve particular notice.

A considerable trade has been carried on for several years between California and the Sandwich Islands, and most of the vessels are manned with Islanders, who, as they for the most part sign no articles, leave whenever they choose, and let themselves out to cure hides at San Diego, and to supply the places of the men left ashore from the American vessels while on the coast. In this way a little colony of them had become settled at San Diego, as their headquarters. Some of these had recently gone off in the *Ayacucho* and *Loriotte*, and the *Pilgrim* had taken Mr. Mannini and three others, so that there were not more than twenty left. Of these, four were on pay at the *Ayacucho*'s house, four more working with us, and the rest were living at the oven in a quiet way; for their money was nearly gone, and they must make it last until some other vessel came down to employ them.

During the four months that I lived here, I got well acquainted with all of them, and took the greatest pains to become familiar with their language, habits, and characters. Their language I could only learn orally, for they had not any books among them, though many of them had been taught to read and write by the missionaries at home. They spoke a little English, and, by a sort of compromise, a mixed language was used on the beach, which could be understood by all. The long name of "Sandwich Islanders" is dropped, and they are called by the whites, all over the Pacific Ocean, "Kanakas," from a word in their own language—signifying, I believe, man, human being—which they apply to themselves, and to all South Sea Islanders, in distinction from whites, whom they call "Haole." This name, Kanaka, they answer to, both collectively and individually. Their proper names in their own language being difficult to pronounce and remember, they are called by any names which the captains or crews may choose to give them. Some are called after the vessel they are in; others by our proper names, as Jack, Tom, Bill; and some have fancy names, as Banyan, Foretop, Rope Yarn, Pelican, &c., &c. Of the four who worked at our house, one was named "Mr. Bingham," after the missionary at Oahu; another, Hope, after a vessel that he had been in; a third, Tom Davis, the name of his first captain; and the fourth, Pelican, from his fancied resemblance to that bird. Then there was Lagoda Jack, California Bill, &c., &c. But by whatever names they might be called, they were the most interesting, intelligent, and kindhearted people that I ever fell in with. I felt a positive attachment for almost all of them; and many of them I have, to this day, a feeling for, which would lead me to go a great way for the pleasure of seeing them, and which will always make me feel a strong interest in the mere name of a Sandwich Islander.

Tom Davis knew how to read, write, and cipher in common arithmetic, had been to the United States, and spoke English quite well. His education was as good as that of three-quarters of the Yankees in California, and his manners and principles a good deal better; and he was so quick of apprehension that he might have been taught navigation, and the elements of many of the sciences, with ease. Old "Mr. Bingham" spoke very little English, almost none, and could neither read nor write; but he was the besthearted old fellow in the world. He must have been over fifty years of age. He had two of his front teeth knocked out, which was done by his parents as a sign of grief at the death of Kamehameha, the great king of the Sandwich Islands. We used to tell him that he ate Captain Cook, and lost his teeth in that way. That was the only thing that ever made him angry. He would

always be quite excited at that, and say *"Aole!"* ("No.")
"Me no eatee Capnee Cook! Me pickaninny—small—so high
—no more! My fader see Capnee Cook! Me—no!" None of
them liked to have anything said about Captain Cook, for the
sailors all believe that he was eaten, and that they cannot
endure to be taunted with. "New Zealand Kanaka eatee white
man; Sandwich Island Kanaka—no. Sandwich Island Kanaka
*ua like pu na haole*—all 'e same a' you!"

Mr. Bingham was a sort of patriarch among them, and was
treated with great respect, though he had not the education
and energy which gave Mr. Mannini his power over them.
I have spent hours in talking with this old fellow about
Kamehameha, the Charlemagne of the Sandwich Islands; his
son and successor, Riho Riho, who died in England, and
was brought to Oahu in the frigate *Blonde*, Captain Lord
Byron, and whose funeral he remembered perfectly; and also
about the customs of his boyhood, and the changes which
had been made by the missionaries. He never would allow
that human beings had been eaten there; and, indeed, it always
seemed an insult to tell so affectionate, intelligent, and
civilized a class of men that such barbarities had been practiced in their own country within the recollection of many
of them. Certainly, the history of no people on the globe
can show anything like so rapid an advance from barbarism.
I would have trusted my life and all I had in the hands
of any one of these people; and certainly, had I wished for
a favor or act of sacrifice, I would have gone to them all,
in turn, before I should have applied to one of my own
countrymen on the coast, and should have expected to see
it done, before my own countrymen had got half through
counting the cost. Their customs, and manner of treating
one another, show a simple, primitive generosity which is truly
delightful, and which is often a reproach to our own people.
Whatever one has they all have. Money, food, clothes they
share with one another, even to the last piece of tobacco
to put in their pipes. I once heard old Mr. Bingham say,
with the highest indignation, to a Yankee trader who was
trying to persuade him to keep his money to himself, "No!
We no all 'e same a' you! . . . Suppose one got money, all
got money. You—suppose one got money—lock him up in
chest. . . . No good! . . . Kanaka all 'e same a' one!" This
principle they carry so far that none of them will eat any-

thing in sight of others without offering it all round. I have seen one of them break a biscuit, which had been given him, into five parts, at a time when I knew he was on a very short allowance, as there was but little to eat on the beach.

My favorite among all of them, and one who was liked by both officers and men, and by whomever he had anything to do with, was Hope. He was an intelligent, kindhearted little fellow, and I never saw him angry, though I knew him for more than a year, and have seen him imposed upon by white people, and abused by insolent mates of vessels. He was always civil, and always ready, and never forgot a benefit. I once took care of him when he was ill, getting medicines from the ship's chests, when no captain or officer would do anything for him, and he never forgot it. Every Kanaka has one particular friend, whom he considers himself bound to do everything for, and with whom he has a sort of contract— an alliance offensive and defensive—and for whom he will often make the greatest sacrifices. This friend they call *aikane;* and for such did Hope adopt me. I do not believe I could have wanted anything which he had, that he would not have given me. In return for this, I was his friend among the Americans, and used to teach him letters and numbers; for he left home before he had learned how to read. He was very curious respecting Boston (as they called the United States), asking many questions about the houses, the people, &c., and always wished to have the pictures in books explained to him. They were all astonishingly quick in catching at explanations, and many things which I had thought it utterly impossible to make them understand they often seized in an instant, and asked questions which showed that they knew enough to make them wish to go farther. The pictures of steamboats and railroad cars, in the columns of some newspapers which I had, gave me great difficulty to explain. The grading of the road, the rails, the construction of the carriages, they could easily understand, but the motion produced by steam was a little too refined for them. I attempted to show it to them once by an experiment upon the cook's coppers, but failed—probably as much from my own ignorance as from their want of apprehension—and, I have no doubt, left them with about as clear an idea of the principle as I had myself. This difficulty, of course, existed in the same force with respect to the steamboats; and all I could do was to give them some account of the results, in the shape of speed; for, failing in the reason, I had to fall back upon the fact. In my account of the speed, I was supported by Tom, who had been to Nantucket, and seen a little steamboat which ran over to New Bedford. And, by the way, it was strange to hear Tom speak of America, when the poor fellow had been all the way round Cape Horn and back, and had seen nothing but Nantucket.

A map of the world, which I once showed them, kept their attention for hours, those who knew how to read pointing out the places and referring to me for the distances. I remember being much amused with a question which Hope asked me. Pointing to the large, irregular place which is always left blank round the poles, to denote that it is undiscovered, he looked up and asked, *"Pau?"* ("Done—ended?")

The system of naming the streets and numbering the houses they easily understood, and the utility of it. They had a great desire to see America, but were afraid of doubling Cape Horn, for they suffer much in cold weather, and had heard dreadful accounts of the Cape from those of their number who had been round it.

They smoke a great deal, though not much at a time, using pipes with large bowls, and very short stems, or no stems at all. These they light, and, putting them to their mouths, take a long draught, getting their mouths as full as they can hold of smoke, and their cheeks distended, and then let it slowly out through their mouths and nostrils. The pipe is then passed to others, who draw in the same manner, one pipeful serving for half a dozen. They never take short, continuous draughts, like Europeans, but one of these "Oahu puffs," as the sailors call them, serves for an hour or two, until someone else lights his pipe, and it is passed round in the same manner. Each Kanaka on the beach had a pipe, flint, steel, tinder, a hand of tobacco, and a jackknife, which he always carried about with him.*

That which strikes a stranger most peculiarly is their style of singing. They run on, in a low, guttural, monotonous sort of chant, their lips and tongues seeming hardly to move, and the sounds apparently modulated solely in the throat. There is very little tune to it, and the words, so far as I could learn, are extempore. They sing about persons and things which are

---

* Matches had not come into use then. I think there were none on board any vessels on the coast. We used the tinderbox in our forecastle.

around them, and adopt this method when they do not wish
to be understood by any but themselves; and it is very effectual, for with the most careful attention I never could detect a
word that I knew. I have often heard Mr. Mannini, who was
the most noted *improvisatore* among them, sing for an hour
together, when at work in the midst of Americans and Englishmen; and, by the occasional shouts and laughter of the
Kanakas, who were at a distance, it was evident that he was
singing about the different men that he was at work with.
They have great powers of ridicule, and are excellent mimics,
many of them discovering and imitating the peculiarities of
our own people before we had observed them ourselves.

These were the people with whom I was to spend a few
months, and who, with the exception of the officer, Nicholas
the Frenchman, and the boy, made the whole population of
the beach. I ought, perhaps, to except the dogs, for they were
an important part of our settlement. Some of the first vessels
brought dogs out with them, who, for convenience, were left
ashore, and there multiplied, until they came to be a great
people. While I was on the beach, the average number was
about forty, and probably an equal, or greater, number are
drowned, or killed in some other way, every year. They are
very useful in guarding the beach, the Indians being afraid
to come down at night; for it was impossible for anyone to
get within half a mile of the hide houses without a general
alarm. The father of the colony, old Sachem, so called from
the ship in which he was brought out, died while I was there,
full of years, and was honorably buried. Hogs and a few
chickens were the rest of the animal tribe, and formed, like
the dogs, a common company, though they were all known,
and usually fed at the houses to which they belonged.

I had been but a few hours on the beach, and the *Pilgrim*
was hardly out of sight, when the cry of "Sail ho!" was raised,
and a small hermaphrodite brig rounded the point, bore up
into the harbor, and came to anchor. It was the Mexican
brig *Fazio*, which we had left at San Pedro, and which had
come down to land her tallow, try it all over, and make new
bags, and then take it in and leave the coast. They moored
ship, erected their tryworks on shore, put up a small tent, in
which they all lived, and commenced operations. This addition
gave a change and variety to our "society," and we spent many
evenings in their tent, where, amid the Babel of English, Span-

ish, French, Indian, and Kanaka, we found some words that we could understand in common.

The morning after my landing, I began the duties of hide curing. In order to understand these, it will be necessary to give the whole history of a hide, from the time it is taken from a bullock until it is put on board the vessel to be carried to Boston. When the hide is taken from the bullock, holes are cut round it, near the edge, by which it is staked out to dry. In this manner it dries without shrinking. After the hides are thus dried in the sun, and doubled with the skin out, they are received by the vessels at the different ports on the coast, and brought down to the depot at San Diego. The vessels land them, and leave them in large piles near the houses. Then begins the hide curer's duty.

The first thing is to put them in soak. This is done by carrying them down at low tide, and making them fast, in small piles, by ropes, and letting the tide come up and cover them. Every day we put in soak twenty-five for each man, which, with us, made a hundred and fifty. There they lie forty-eight hours, when they are taken out, and rolled up, in wheelbarrows, and thrown into the vats. These vats contain brine, made very strong, being sea water, with great quantities of salt thrown in. This pickles the hides, and in this they lie forty-eight hours; the use of the sea water, into which they are first put, being merely to soften and clean them. From these vats they are taken, and lie on a platform for twenty-four hours, and then are spread upon the ground, and carefully stretched and staked out, with the skin up, that they may dry smooth. After they had been staked, and while yet wet and soft, we used to go upon them with our knives, and carefully cut off all the bad parts—the pieces of meat and fat, which would corrupt and infect the whole if stowed away in a vessel for many months, the large "flippers," the ears, and all other parts which would prevent close stowage. This was the most difficult part of our duty, as it required much skill to take off everything that ought to come off, and not to cut or injure the hide. It was also a long process, as six of us had to clean a hundred and fifty, most of which required a great deal to be done to them, as the Spaniards are very careless in skinning their cattle. Then, too, as we cleaned them while they were staked out, we were obliged to kneel down upon them, which always gives beginners the backache. The first day I was so slow and awkward that I cleaned only eight; at the end of a few days I doubled my number; and, in a fortnight or three weeks, could keep up with the others, and clean my twenty-five.

This cleaning must be got through with before noon, for by that time the hides get too dry. After the sun has been upon them a few hours, they are carefully gone over with scrapers, to get off all the grease which the sun brings out. This being done, the stakes are pulled up, and the hides carefully doubled, with the hair side out, and left to dry. About the middle of the afternoon they are turned over, for the other side to dry, and at sundown piled up and covered over. The next day they are spread out and opened again, and at night, if fully dry, are thrown upon a long, horizontal pole, five at a time, and beaten with flails. This takes all the dust from them. Then, having been salted, scraped, cleaned, dried, and beaten, they are stowed away in the house. Here ends their history, except that they are taken out again when the vessel is ready to go home, beaten, stowed away on board, carried to Boston, tanned, made into shoes and other articles for which leather is used, and many of them, very probably, in the end, brought back again to California in the shape of shoes, and worn out in pursuit of other bullocks, or in the curing of other hides.

By putting a hundred and fifty in soak every day, we had the same number at each stage of curing on each day; so that we had, every day, the same work to do upon the same number—a hundred and fifty to put in soak, a hundred and fifty to wash out and put in the vat, the same number to haul from the vat and put on the platform to drain, the same number to spread, and stake out, and clean, and the same number to beat and stow away in the house. I ought to except Sunday; for, by a prescription which no captain or agent has yet ventured to break in upon, Sunday has been a day of leisure on the beach for years. On Saturday night, the hides, in every stage of progress, are carefully covered up, and not uncovered until Monday morning. On Sundays we had absolutely no work to do, unless it might be to kill a bullock, which was sent down for our use about once a week, and sometimes came on Sunday. Another advantage of the hide-curing life was that we had just so much work to do, and when that was through, the time was our own. Knowing this, we worked hard, and needed no driving. We "turned out" every morning with the first signs of daylight, and allowing a short time, at about eight o'clock, for breakfast, generally got through our labor between one and two o'clock, when we dined, and had the rest of the time to ourselves, until just before sundown, when we beat the dry hides and put them in the house, and covered over all the others. By this means we had about three hours to ourselves every afternoon, and at sundown we had our supper, and our work was done for the day. There was no watch to stand, and no topsails to reef. The evenings we generally spent at one another's houses, and I often went up and spent an hour or so at the oven, which was called the "Kanaka Hotel," and the "Oahu Coffeehouse." Immediately after dinner we usually took a short siesta, to make up for our early rising, and spent the rest of the afternoon according to our own fancies. I generally read, wrote, and made or mended clothes; for necessity, the mother of invention, had taught me these two latter arts. The Kanakas went up to the oven, and spent the time in sleeping, talking, and smoking, and my messmate, Nicholas, who neither knew how to read nor write, passed away the time by a long siesta, two or three smokes with his pipe, and a *paseo* to the other houses. This leisure time is never interfered with, for the captains know that the men earn it by working hard and fast, and that, if they interfered with it, the men could easily make their twenty-five hides apiece last through the day. We were pretty independent, too, for the master of the house—*capitán de la casa*—had nothing to say to us, except when we were at work on the hides; and although we could not go up to the town without his permission, this was seldom or never refused.

The great weight of the wet hides, which we were obliged to roll about in wheelbarrows; the continual stooping upon those which were pegged out to be cleaned; and the smell of the nasty vats, into which we were often obliged to wade, knee-deep, to press down the hides—all made the work disagreeable and fatiguing; but we soon became hardened to it, and the comparative independence of our life reconciled us to it, for there was nobody to haze us and find fault; and when we were through for the day, we had only to wash and change our clothes, and our time was our own. There was, however, one exception to the time's being our own, which was that on two afternoons of every week we were obliged to go off for

wood for the cook to use in the galley. Wood is very scarce
in the vicinity of San Diego, there being no trees of any size
for miles. In the town, the inhabitants burn the small wood
which grows in thickets, and for which they send out Indians,
in large numbers, every few days. Fortunately, the climate is
so fine that they have no need of a fire in their houses, and
only use it for cooking. With us, the getting of wood was a
great trouble; for all that in the vicinity of the houses had
been cut down, and we were obliged to go off a mile or two,
and to carry it some distance on our backs, as we could not
get the handcart up the hills and over the uneven places. Two
afternoons in the week, generally Monday and Thursday, as
soon as we were through dinner, we started off for the bush,
each of us furnished with a hatchet and a long piece of rope,
and dragging the handcart behind us, and followed by the
whole colony of dogs, who were always ready for the bush,
and were half mad whenever they saw our preparations. We
went with the handcart as far as we could conveniently drag
it, and, leaving it in an open, conspicuous place, separated
ourselves, each taking his own course, and looking about for
some good place to begin upon. Frequently, we had to go
nearly a mile from the handcart before we could find any fit
place. Having lighted upon a good thicket, the next thing was
to clear away the underbrush, and have fair play at the trees.
These trees are seldom more than five or six feet high, and the
highest that I ever saw in these expeditions could not have
been more than twelve, so that, with lopping off the branches
and clearing away the underwood, we had a good deal of
cutting to do for a very little wood. Having cut enough for a
"backload," the next thing was to make it well fast with the
rope, and heaving the bundle upon our backs, and taking the
hatchet in hand, to walk off, up hill and down dale, to the
handcart. Two good backloads apiece filled the handcart, and
that was each one's proportion. When each had brought
down his second load, we filled the handcart, and took our
way again slowly back to the beach. It was generally sundown
when we got back; and unloading, covering the hides for the
night, and getting our supper finished the day's work.

These wooding excursions had always a mixture of something rather pleasant in them. Roaming about in the woods
with hatchet in hand, like a backwoodsman, followed by a
troop of dogs, starting up birds, snakes, hares, and foxes, and

examining the various kinds of trees, flowers, and birds' nests was, at least, a change from the monotonous drag and pull on shipboard. Frequently, too, we had some amusement and adventure. The coyotes, of which I have before spoken—a sort of mixture of the fox and wolf breeds; fierce little animals, with bushy tails and large heads, and a quick, sharp bark—abound here, as in all other parts of California. These the dogs were very watchful for, and, whenever they saw them, started off in full run after them. We had many fine chases; yet, although our dogs ran fast, the rascals generally escaped. They are a match for the dog, one to one, but as the dogs generally went in squads, there was seldom a fair fight. A smaller dog, belonging to us, once attacked a coyote singly, and was considerably worsted, and might, perhaps, have been killed, had we not come to his assistance. We had, however, one dog which gave them a good deal of trouble and many hard runs. He was a fine, tall fellow, and united strength and agility better than any dog that I have ever seen. He was born at the Islands, his father being an English mastiff and his mother a greyhound. He had the high head, long legs, narrow body, and springing gait of the latter, and the heavy jaw, thick jowls, and strong forequarters of the mastiff. When he was brought to San Diego, an English sailor said that he looked, about the face, like the Duke of Wellington, whom he had once seen at the Tower; and, indeed, there was something about him which resembled the portraits of the Duke. From this time he was christened Welly, and became the favorite and bully of the beach. He always led the dogs by several yards in the chase, and had killed two coyotes at different times in single combats. We often had fine sport with these fellows. A quick, sharp bark from a coyote, and in an instant every dog was at the height of his speed. A few minutes made up for an unfair start, and gave each dog his right place. Welly, at the head, seemed almost to skim over the bushes, and after him came Fanny, Feliciana, Childers, and the other fleet ones—the spaniels and terriers; and then, behind, followed the heavy corps—bulldogs, &c., for we had every breed. Pursuit by us was in vain, and in about half an hour the dogs would begin to come panting and straggling back.

Beside the coyotes, the dogs sometimes made prizes of rabbits and hares, which are plentiful here, and numbers of

which we often shot for our dinners. Among the other animals
there was a reptile I was not so much disposed to find amusement from, the rattlesnake. These snakes are very abundant
here, especially during the spring of the year. The latter part
of the time that I was on shore, I did not meet with so many,
but for the first two months we seldom went into "the bush"
without one of our number starting some of them. I remember
perfectly well the first one that I ever saw. I had left my companions, and was beginning to clear away a fine clump of
trees, when, just in the midst of the thicket, but a few yards
from me, one of these fellows set up his hiss. It is a sharp,
continuous sound, and resembles very much the letting off
of the steam from the small pipe of a steamboat, except that
it is on a smaller scale. I knew, by the sound of an ax, that
one of my companions was near, and called out to him, to let
him know what I had fallen upon. He took it very lightly,
and as he seemed inclined to laugh at me for being afraid, I
determined to keep my place. I knew that so long as I could
hear the rattle I was safe, for these snakes never make a noise
when they are in motion. Accordingly I continued my work,
and the noise which I made with cutting and breaking the
trees kept him in alarm; so that I had the rattle to show me
his whereabouts. Once or twice the noise stopped for a short
time, which gave me a little uneasiness, and, retreating a few
steps, I threw something into the bush, at which he would set
his rattle a-going, and, finding that he had not moved from
his first place, I was easy again. In this way I continued at
my work until I had cut a full load, never suffering him to be
quiet for a moment. Having cut my load, I strapped it together, and got everything ready for starting. I felt that I
could now call the others without the imputation of being
afraid, and went in search of them. In a few minutes we were
all collected, and began an attack upon the bush. The big
Frenchman, who was the one that I had called to at first, I
found as little inclined to approach the snake as I had been.
The dogs, too, seemed afraid of the rattle, and kept up a
barking at a safe distance; but the Kanakas showed no fear,
and, getting long sticks, went into the bush, and, keeping a
bright lookout, stood within a few feet of him. One or two
blows struck near him, and a few stones thrown started him,
and we lost his track, and had the pleasant consciousness that
he might be directly under our feet. By throwing stones and

chips in different directions, we made him spring his rattle again, and began another attack. This time we drove him into the clear ground, and saw him gliding off, with head and tail erect, when a stone, well aimed, knocked him over the bank, down a declivity of fifteen or twenty feet, and stretched him at his length. Having made sure of him by a few more stones, we went down, and one of the Kanakas cut off his rattle. These rattles vary in number, it is said, according to the age of the snake; though the Indians think they indicate the number of creatures they have killed. We always preserved them as trophies, and at the end of the summer had a considerable collection. None of our people were bitten by them, but one of our dogs died of a bite, and another was supposed to have been bitten, but recovered. We had no remedy for the bite, though it was said that the Indians of the country had, and the Kanakas professed to have an herb which would cure it, but it was fortunately never brought to the test.

Hares and rabbits, as I said before, were abundant, and, during the winter months, the waters are covered with wild ducks and geese. Crows, too, abounded, and frequently alighted in great numbers upon our hides, picking at the pieces of dried meat and fat. Bears and wolves are numerous in the upper parts of the coast, and in the interior (and, indeed, a man was killed by a bear within a few miles of San Pedro, while we were there), but there were none in our immediate neighborhood. The only other animals were horses. More than a dozen of these were owned by men on the beach, and were allowed to run loose among the hills, with a long lasso attached to them, to pick up feed wherever they could find it. We were sure of seeing them once a day, for there was no water among the hills, and they were obliged to come down to the well which had been dug upon the beach. These horses were bought at from two to six and eight dollars apiece, and were held very much as common property. We generally kept one fast to one of the houses, so that we could mount him and catch any of the others. Some of them were really fine animals, and gave us many good runs up to the presidio and over the country.

# CHAPTER XX

After we had been a few weeks on shore, and had begun to feel broken into the regularity of our life, its monotony was interrupted by the arrival of two vessels from the windward. We were sitting at dinner in our little room, when we heard the cry of "Sail ho!" This, we had learned, did not always signify a vessel, but was raised whenever a woman was seen coming down from the town, or an oxcart, or anything unusual, hove in sight upon the road; so we took no notice of it. But it soon became so loud and general from all parts of the beach that we were led to go to the door; and there, sure enough, were two sails coming round the point, and leaning over from the strong northwest wind, which blows down the coast every afternoon. The headmost was a ship, and the other a brig. Everybody was alive on the beach, and all manner of conjectures were abroad. Some said it was the *Pilgrim*, with the Boston ship, which we were expecting; but we soon saw that the brig was not the *Pilgrim*, and the ship, with her stump topgallant masts and rusty sides, could not be a dandy Boston Indiaman. As they drew nearer, we discovered the high poop, and topgallant forecastle, and other marks of the Italian ship *Rosa*, and the brig proved to be the *Catalina*, which we saw at Santa Barbara, just arrived from Valparaiso. They came to anchor, moored ship, and began discharging hides and tallow. The *Rosa* had purchased the house occupied by the *Lagoda*, and the *Catalina* took the other spare one between ours and the *Ayacucho's*, so that now each house was occupied, and the beach, for several days, was all animation. The *Catalina* had several Kanakas on board, who were immediately laid hold of by the others, and carried up to the oven, where they had a long powwow and a smoke. Two Frenchmen, who belonged to the *Rosa's* crew, came in every evening to see Nicholas; and from them we learned that the *Pilgrim* was at San Pedro, and was the only vessel from the United States now on the coast. Several of the Italians slept on shore at their hide house; and there, and at the tent in which the *Fazio's* crew lived, we had some singing almost every evening. The Italians sang a variety of songs—barca-

150

rolles, provincial airs, &c.; in several of which I recognized parts of our favorite operas and sentimental songs. They often joined in a song, taking the different parts, which produced a fine effect, as many of them had good voices, and all sang with spirit. One young man, in particular, had a falsetto as clear as a clarinet.

The greater part of the crews of the vessels came ashore every evening, and we passed the time in going about from one house to another, and listening to all manner of languages. The Spanish was the common ground upon which we all met; for everyone knew more or less of that. We had now, out of forty or fifty, representatives from almost every nation under the sun—two Englishmen, three Yankees, two Scotchmen, two Welshmen, one Irishman, three Frenchmen (two of whom were Normans, and the third from Gascony), one Dutchman, one Austrian, two or three Spaniards (from old Spain), half a dozen Spanish Americans and half-breeds, two native Indians from Chile and the island of Chiloe, one Negro, one mulatto, about twenty Italians, from all parts of Italy, as many more Sandwich Islanders, one Tahitian, and one Kanaka from the Marquesas Islands.

The night before the vessels were ready to sail, all the Europeans united and had an entertainment at the *Rosa*'s hide house, and we had songs of every nation and tongue. A German gave us "Ach! Mein Lieber Augustin!"; the three Frenchmen roared through the Marseilles Hymn; the English and Scotchmen gave us "Rule Britannia," and "Wha'll Be King but Charlie?" the Italians and Spaniards screamed through some national affairs, for which I was none the wiser; and we three Yankees made an attempt at "The Star-Spangled Banner." After these national tributes had been paid, the Austrian gave us a pretty little love song, and the Frenchmen sang a spirited thing—"Sentinelle! O Prenez Garde à Vous!" —and then followed the *mélange* which might have been expected. When I left them, the *aguardiente* and annisou were pretty well in their heads, they were all singing and talking at once, and their peculiar national oaths were getting as plenty as pronouns.

The next day, the two vessels got under way for the windward, and left us in quiet possession of the beach. Our numbers were somewhat enlarged by the opening of the new houses, and the "society" of the beach was a little changed.

In charge of the *Catalina's* house was an old Scotchman, Robert, who, like most of his countrymen, had some education, and, like many of them, was rather pragmatical, and had a ludicrously solemn conceit of himself. He employed his time in taking care of his pigs, chickens, turkeys, dogs, &c., and in smoking his long pipe. Everything was as neat as a pin in the house, and he was as regular in his hours as a chronometer, but, as he kept very much by himself, was not a great addition to our society. He hardly spent a cent all the time he was on the beach, and the others said he was no shipmate. He had been a petty officer on board the British frigate *Dublin*, Captain Lord James Townshend, and had great ideas of his own importance. The man in charge of the *Rosa's* house, Schmidt, was an Austrian, but spoke, read, and wrote four languages with ease and correctness. German was his native tongue, but being born near the borders of Italy, and having sailed out of Genoa, the Italian was almost as familiar to him as his own language. He was six years on board of an English man-of-war, where he learned to speak our language easily, and also to read and write it. He had been several years in Spanish vessels, and had acquired that language so well that he could read books in it. He was between forty and fifty years of age, and was a singular mixture of the man-of-war's-man and Puritan. He talked a great deal about propriety and steadiness, and gave good advice to the youngsters and Kanakas, but seldom went up to the town without coming down "three sheets in the wind." One holiday, he and old Robert (the Scotchman from the *Catalina*) went up to the town, and got so "cosy," talking over old stories and giving each other good advice, that they came down, double-backed, on a horse, and both rolled off into the sand as soon as the horse stopped. This put an end to their pretensions, and they never heard the last of it from the rest of the men. On the night of the entertainment at the *Rosa's* house, I saw old Schmidt (that was the Austrian's name) standing up by a hogshead, holding on by both hands, and calling out to himself, "Hold on, Schmidt! Hold on, my good fellow, or you'll be on your back!" Still, he was an intelligent, good-natured old fellow, and had a chest full of books, which he willingly lent me to read. In the same house with him were a Frenchman and an Englishman, the latter a regular-built "man-o'-war jack," a thorough seaman, a hearty, generous fellow, and, at the same time, a drunken, dissolute dog. He made it a point to get drunk every time he went to the presidio, when he always managed to sleep on the road, and have his money stolen from him. These, with a Chilean and half a dozen Kanakas, formed the addition to our company.

In about six weeks from the time when the *Pilgrim* sailed, we had all the hides which she left us cured and stowed away; and having cleared up the ground and emptied the vats, and set everything in order, had nothing more to do, until she should come down again, but to supply ourselves with wood. Instead of going twice a week for this purpose, we determined to give one whole week to getting wood, and then we should have enough to last us half through the summer. Accordingly we started off every morning, after an early breakfast, with our hatchets in hand, and cut wood until the sun was over the point—which was our mark for noon, as there was not a watch on the beach—and then came back to dinner, and after dinner started off again with our handcart and ropes, and carted and "backed" it down until sunset. This we kept up for a week, until we had collected several cords—enough to last us for six or eight weeks—when we "knocked off" altogether, much to my joy; for, though I liked straying in the woods, and cutting, very well, yet the "backing" the wood for so great a distance, over an uneven country, was, without exception, the hardest work I had ever done. I usually had to kneel down, and contrive to heave the load, which was well strapped together, upon my back, and then rise up and start off with it, up the hills and down the vales, sometimes through thickets, the rough points sticking into the skin and tearing the clothes, so that, at the end of the week I had hardly a whole shirt to my back.

We were now through all our work, and had nothing more to do until the *Pilgrim* should come down again. We had nearly got through our provisions too, as well as our work; for our officer had been very wasteful of them, and the tea, flour, sugar, and molasses were all gone. We suspected him of sending them up to the town; and he always treated the squaws with molasses when they came down to the beach. Finding wheat coffee and dry bread rather poor living, we clubbed together, and I went to the town on horseback, with a great salt bag behind the saddle, and a few reals in my pocket, and brought back the bag full of onions, beans, pears, watermelons, and other fruits; for the young woman who tended the garden, finding that I belonged to the American ship, and that we were short of provisions, put in a larger portion. With these we lived like fighting cocks for a week or two, and had, besides, what the sailors call a "blowout on sleep," not turning out in the morning until breakfast was ready. I employed several days in overhauling my chest, and mending up all my old clothes, until I had put everything in order, "patch upon patch, like a sand barge's mainsail." Then I took hold of Bowditch's *Navigator*, which I had always with me. I had been through the greater part of it, and now went carefully over it from beginning to end, working out most of the examples. That done, and there being no signs of the *Pilgrim*, I made a descent upon old Schmidt, and borrowed and read all the books there were upon the beach. Such a dearth was there of these latter articles, that anything, even a little child's storybook, or the half of a shipping calendar, seemed a treasure. I actually read a jest book through, from beginning to end, in one day, as I should a novel, and enjoyed it much. At last, when I thought that there were no more to be had, I found at the bottom of old Schmidt's chest, "Mandeville, a Romance, by Godwin, in five volumes." This I had never read, but Godwin's name was enough, and, after the wretched trash I had devoured, anything bearing the name of an intellectual man was a prize indeed. I bore it off, and for two days I was up early and late, reading with all my might, and actually drinking in delight. It is no extravagance to say that it was like a spring in a desert land.

From the sublime to the ridiculous—so, with me, from Mandeville to hide curing—was but a step; for—

*Wednesday, July 18th,* brought us the brig *Pilgrim* from the windward. As she came in, we found that she was a good deal altered in her appearance. Her short topgallant masts were up, her bowlines all unrove (except to the courses), the quarter boom irons off her lower yards, her jack crosstrees sent down, several blocks got rid of, running rigging rove in new places, and numberless other changes of the same character. Then, too, there was a new voice giving orders, and a new face on the quarterdeck—a short, dark-complexioned man, in a green jacket and a high leather cap. These changes, of course, set the whole beach on the *qui vive*, and we were all waiting for the boat to come ashore, that we might have things explained. At length, after the sails were furled and the anchor carried out, her boat pulled ashore, and the news soon flew that the expected ship had arrived at Santa Barbara, and that Captain Thompson had taken command of her, and her captain, Faucon, had taken the *Pilgrim*, and was the green-jacketed man on the quarterdeck. The boat put directly off again, without giving us time to ask any more questions, and we were obliged to wait till night, when we took a little skiff, that lay on the beach, and paddled off. When I stepped aboard, the second mate called me aft, and gave me a large bundle, directed to me, and marked "Ship *Alert*." This was what I had longed for, yet I refrained from opening it until I went ashore. Diving down into the forecastle, I found the same old crew, and was really glad to see them again. Numerous inquiries passed as to the new ship, the latest news from Boston, &c., &c. Stimson had received letters from home, and nothing remarkable had happened. The *Alert* was agreed on all hands to be a fine ship, and a large one: "Larger than the *Rosa*," "Big enough to carry off all the hides in California," "Rail as high as a man's head," "A crack ship," "A regular dandy," &c., &c. Captain Thompson took command of her, and she went directly up to Monterey; thence she was to go to San Francisco, and probably would not be in San Diego under two or three months. Some of the *Pilgrim's* crew found old shipmates aboard of her, and spent an hour or two in her forecastle the evening before she sailed. They said her decks were as white as snow, holystoned every morning, like a man-of-war's; everything on board "shipshape and Bristol fashion"; a fine crew, three mates, a sailmaker and carpenter, and all complete. "They've got a *man* for mate of that ship, and not a bloody *sheep* about decks!" "A mate that knows his duty, and makes everybody do theirs, and won't be imposed upon by either captain or crew." After collecting all the information we could get on this point, we asked something about their new captain. He had hardly been on board long enough for them to know much about him, but he had taken hold strong, as soon as he took command, shifting the topgallant masts, and unreeving all the studding-sail gear and half the running rigging, the very first day.

Having got all the news we could, we pulled ashore; and as soon as we reached the house, I, as might be supposed, fell directly to opening my bundle, and found a reasonable supply of duck, flannel shirts, shoes, &c., and, what was still more valuable, a packet of eleven letters. These I sat up nearly all night reading, and put them carefully away, to be reread again and again at my leisure. Then came half a dozen newspapers, the last of which gave notice of Thanksgiving, and of the clearance of "ship *Alert*, Edward H. Faucon, master, for Callao and California, by Bryant, Sturgis & Co." Only those who have been on distant voyages, and after a long absence received a newspaper from home, can understand the delight that they give one. I read every part of them—the houses to let, things lost or stolen, auction sales, and all. Nothing carries you so entirely to a place, and makes you feel so perfectly at home, as a newspaper. The very name of Boston *Daily Advertiser* "sounded hospitably upon the ear."

The *Pilgrim* discharged her hides, which set us at work again, and in a few days we were in the old routine of dry hides, wet hides, cleaning, beating, &c. Captain Faucon came quietly up to me, as I was sitting upon a stretched hide, cutting the meat from it with my knife, and asked me how I liked California, and repeated: *"Tityre, tu patulae recubans sub tegmine fagi."* Very apropos, thought I, and, at the same time, shows that you have studied Latin. However, it was kind of him, and an attention from a captain is a thing not to be slighted. Thompson's majesty could not have bent to it, in the sight of so many mates and men; but Faucon was a man of education, literary habits, and good social position, and held things at their right value.

*Saturday, July 11th.* The *Pilgrim* set sail for the windward, and left us to go on in our old way. Having laid in such a supply of wood, and the days being now long, and invariably pleasant, we had a good deal of time to ourselves. The duck I received from home I soon made up into trousers and frocks, and, having formed the remnants of the duck into a cap, I displayed myself, every Sunday, in a complete suit of my own make, from head to foot. Reading, mending, sleeping, with occasional excursions into the bush, with the dogs, in search of coyotes, hares, and rabbits, or to encounter a rattlesnake, and now and then a visit to the presidio, filled up our spare time after hide curing was over for the day. Another amusement which we sometimes indulged in was "burning the water" for crawfish. For this purpose we procured a pair of "grains," with a long staff like a harpoon, and, making torches with tarred rope twisted round a long pine stick, took the only boat on the beach, a small skiff, and with a torchbearer in the bow, a steersman in the stern, and one man on each side with the grains, went off, on dark nights, to burn the water. This is fine sport. Keeping within a few rods of the shore, where the water is not more than three or four feet deep, with a clear, sandy bottom, the torches light everything up so that one could almost have seen a pin among the grains of sand. The crawfish are an easy prey, and we used soon to get a load of them. The other fish were more difficult to catch, yet we frequently speared a number of them, of various kinds and sizes. The *Pilgrim* brought us a supply of fish hooks, which we had never had before on the beach, and for several days we went down to the Point, and caught a quantity of cod and mackerel. On one of these expeditions, we saw a battle between two Sandwich Islanders and a shark. "Johnny" had been playing about our boat for some time, driving away the fish, and showing his teeth at our bait, when we missed him, and in a few minutes heard a great shouting between two Kanakas who were fishing on the rock opposite to us: *"E hana hana make i ka ia nui!" "E pii mai aikane!"* &c., &c.; and saw them pulling away on a stout line, and "Johnny Shark" floundering at the other end. The line soon broke; but the Kanakas would not let him off so easily, and sprang directly into the water after him. Now came the tug of war. Before he could get into deep water, one of them seized him by the tail, and ran up with him upon the beach; but Johnny twisted round, and turning his head under his body, and showing his teeth in the vicinity of the Kanaka's hand, made him let go and spring out of the way. The shark now turned tail and made the best of his way, by flapping and floundering, toward deep water; but here again, before he was fairly off, the other Kanaka seized him by the tail, and made a spring toward the beach, his companion at the same time paying away upon him with stones and a large stick. As soon, however, as the shark could turn, the man was obliged to let go his hold; but the instant he made toward deep water, they were both behind him, watching their chance to seize him. In this way the battle went on for some time, the shark, in a rage, splashing and twisting about, and the

Kanakas, in high excitement, yelling at the top of their voices. But the shark at last got off, carrying away a hook and line, and not a few severe bruises.

## CHAPTER XXI

We kept up a constant connection with the presidio, and by the close of the summer I had added much to my vocabulary, beside having made the acquaintance of nearly everybody in the place, and acquired some knowledge of the character and habits of the people, as well as of the institutions under which they live.

California was discovered in 1534 by Ximenes, or in 1536 by Cortes—I cannot settle which—and was subsequently visited by many other adventurers, as well as commissioned voyagers of the Spanish crown. It was found to be inhabited by numerous tribes of Indians, and to be in many parts extremely fertile; to which, of course, were added rumors of gold mines, pearl fishery, &c. No sooner was the importance of the country known than the Jesuits obtained leave to establish themselves in it, to Christianize and enlighten the Indians. They established missions in various parts of the country toward the close of the seventeenth century, and collected the natives about them, baptizing them into the Church, and teaching them the arts of civilized life. To protect the Jesuits in their missions, and at the same time to support the power of the crown over the civilized Indians, two forts were erected and garrisoned—one at San Diego, and the other at Monterey. These were called presidios, and divided the command of the whole country between them. Presidios have since been established at Santa Barbara, San Francisco, and other places, dividing the country into large districts, each with its presidio, and governed by a *comandante*. The soldiers, for the most part, married civilized Indians; and thus, in the vicinity of each presidio, sprung up, gradually, small towns. In the course of time, vessels began to come into the ports to trade with the missions and receive hides in return; and thus began the great trade of California. Nearly all the cattle in the country belonged to the missions, and they employed their Indians—who became, in fact, their serfs—in tending their vast herds. In the year 1793, when Vancouver visited San Diego, the missions had obtained great wealth and power, and are accused of having depreciated the country with the sovereign, that they might be allowed to retain their possessions. On the expulsion of the Jesuits from the Spanish dominions, the missions passed into the hands of the Franciscans, though without any essential change in their management. Ever since the independence of Mexico, the missions had been going down; until, at last, a law was passed, stripping them of all their possessions, and confining the priests to their spiritual duties, at the same time declaring all the Indians free and independent rancheros. The change in the condition of the Indians was, as may be supposed, only nominal; they are virtually serfs, as much as they ever were. But in the missions the change was complete. The priests have now no power, except in their religious character, and the great possessions of the missions are given over to be preyed upon by the harpies of the civil power, who are sent there in the capacity of *administradores*, to settle up the concerns; and who usually end, in a few years, by making themselves fortunes, and leaving their stewardships worse than they found them. The dynasty of the priests was much more acceptable to the people of the country, and, indeed, to everyone concerned with the country, by trade or otherwise, than that of the *administradores*. The priests were connected permanently to one mission, and felt the necessity of keeping up its credit. Accordingly the debts of the missions were regularly paid, and the people were, in the main, well treated, and attached to those who had spent their whole lives among them. But the *administradores* are strangers sent from Mexico, having no interest in the country, not identified in any way with their charge, and, for the most part, men of desperate fortunes—broken-down politicians and soldiers—whose only *missions in decay*

object is to retrieve their condition in as short a time as possible. The change had been made but a few years before our arrival upon the coast, yet, in that short time, the trade was much diminished, credit impaired, and the venerable missions were going rapidly to decay.

The external political arrangements remain the same. There are four or more presidios, having under their protection the various missions, and the pueblos, which are towns formed by the civil power and containing no mission or presidio. The most northerly presidio is San Francisco, the next Monterey, the next Santa Barbara, including the mission of the same, San Luis Obispo, and Santa Buenaventura, which is said to be the best mission in the whole country, having fertile soil and rich vineyards. The last, and most southerly, is San Diego, including the mission of the same, San Juan Capistrano, the Pueblo de los Angeles, the largest town in California, with the neighboring mission of San Gabriel. The priests, in spiritual matters, are subject to the Archbishop of Mexico, and in temporal matters to the governor general, who is the great civil and military head of the country.

The government of the country is an arbitrary democracy, having no common law, and nothing that we should call a judiciary. Their only laws are made and unmade at the caprice of the legislature, and are as variable as the legislature itself. They pass through the form of sending representatives to the congress at Mexico, but as it takes several months to go and return, and there is very little communication between the capital and this distant province, a member usually stays there as permanent member, knowing very well that there will be revolutions at home before he can write and receive an answer; and if another member should be sent, he has only to challenge him, and decide the contested election in that way.

Revolutions are matters of frequent occurrence in California. They are got up by men who are at the foot of the ladder and in desperate circumstances, just as a new political organization may be started by such men in our own country. The only object, of course, is the loaves and fishes; and instead of "caucusing," paragraphing, libeling, feasting, promising, and lying, they take muskets and bayonets, and, seizing upon the presidio and customhouse, divide the spoils, and declare a new dynasty. As for justice, they know little law but will and fear. A Yankee, who had been naturalized and become a Catholic, and had married in the country, was sitting in his house at the Pueblo de los Angeles, with his wife and children, when a Mexican with whom he had had a difficulty entered the house and stabbed him to the heart before them all. The murderer was seized by some Yankees who had settled there, and kept in confinement until a statement of the whole affair could be sent to the governor general. The governor general refused to do anything about it, and the countrymen of the murdered man, seeing no prospect of justice being administered, gave notice that, if nothing was done, they should try the man themselves. It chanced that, at this time, there was a company of some thirty or forty trappers and hunters from the Western States, with their rifles, who had made their headquarters at the Pueblo; and these, together with the Americans and Englishmen in the place, who were between twenty and thirty in number, took possession of the town, and, waiting a reasonable time, proceeded to try the man according to the forms in their own country. A judge and jury were appointed, and he was tried, convicted, sentenced to be shot, and carried out before the town blindfolded. The names of all the men were then put into a hat, and each one pledging himself to perform his duty, twelve names were drawn out, and the men took their stations with their rifles, and, firing at the word, laid him dead. He was decently buried, and the piace was restored quietly to the proper authorities. A general, with titles enough for an hidalgo, was at San Gabriel, and issued a proclamation as long as the foretop bowline, threatening destruction to the rebels, but never stirred from his fort; for forty Kentucky hunters, with their rifles, and a dozen of Yankees and Englishmen, were a match for a whole regiment of hungry, drawling, lazy half-breeds. This affair happened while we were at San Pedro (the port of the Pueblo), and we had the particulars from those who were on the spot. A few months afterward, another man was murdered on the highroad between the Pueblo and San Luis Rey by his own wife and a man with whom she ran off. The foreigners pursued and shot them both, according to one story. According to another version, nothing was done about it, as the parties were natives, and a man whom I frequently saw in San Diego was pointed out as the murderer. Perhaps they were two cases that had got mixed.

*inequal Justice*

When a crime has been committed by Indians, justice, or rather vengeance, is not so tardy. One Sunday afternoon, while I was at San Diego, an Indian was sitting on his horse, when another, with whom he had had some difficulty, came up to him, drew a long knife, and plunged it directly into the horse's heart. The Indian sprang from his falling horse, drew out the knife, and plunged it into the other Indian's breast, over his shoulder, and laid him dead. The fellow was seized at once, clapped into the *calabozo*, and kept there until an answer could be received from Monterey. A few weeks afterward I saw the poor wretch, sitting on the bare ground, in front of the *calabozo*, with his feet chained to a stake, and handcuffs about his wrists. I knew there was very little hope for him. Although the deed was done in hot blood, the horse on which he was sitting being his own, and a favorite with him, yet he was an Indian, and that was enough. In about a week after I saw him, I heard that he had been shot. These few instances will serve to give one a notion of the distribution of justice in California.

In their domestic relations, these people are not better than in their public. The men are thriftless, proud, extravagant, and very much given to gaming; and the women have but little education, and a good deal of beauty, and their morality, of course, is none of the best; yet the instances of infidelity are much less frequent than one would at first suppose. In fact, one vice is set over against another; and thus something like a balance is obtained. If the women have but little virtue, the jealousy of their husbands is extreme, and their revenge deadly and almost certain. A few inches of cold steel has been the punishment of many an unwary man, who has been guilty, perhaps, of nothing more than indiscretion. The difficulties of the attempt are numerous, and the consequences of discovery fatal, in the better classes. With the unmarried women, too, great watchfulness is used. The main object of the parents is to marry their daughters well, and to this a fair name is necessary. The sharp eyes of a *dueña*, and the ready weapons of a father or brother, are a protection which the characters of most of them—men and women—render by no means useless; for the very men who would lay down their lives to avenge the dishonor of their own family would risk the same lives to complete the dishonor of another.

Of the poor Indians very little care is taken. The priests, indeed, at the missions are said to keep them very strictly, and some rules are usually made by the alcaldes to punish their misconduct; yet it all amounts to but little. Indeed, to show the entire want of any sense of morality or domestic duty among them, I have frequently known an Indian to bring his wife, to whom he was lawfully married in the church, down to the beach, and carry her back again, dividing with her the money which she had got from the sailors. If any of the girls were discovered by the alcalde to be open evil livers, they were whipped, and kept at work sweeping the square of the presidio, and carrying mud and bricks for the buildings; yet a few reals would generally buy them off. Intemperance, too, is a common vice among the Indians. The Mexicans, on the contrary, are abstemious, and I do not remember ever having seen a Mexican intoxicated.

Such are the people who inhabit a country embracing four or five hundred miles of seacoast, with several good harbors; with fine forests in the north; the waters filled with fish, and the plains covered with thousands of herds of cattle; blessed with a climate than which there can be no better in the world; free from all manner of diseases, whether epidemic or endemic; and with a soil in which corn yields from seventy to eighty fold. In the hands of an enterprising people, what a country this might be, we are ready to say. Yet how long would a people remain so, in such a country? The Americans (as those from the United States are called) and Englishmen, who are fast filling up the principal towns, and getting the trade into their hands, are indeed more industrious and effective than the Mexicans; yet their children are brought up Mexicans in most respects, and if the "California fever" (laziness) spares the first generation, it is likely to attack the second.

# CHAPTER XXII

*Saturday, July 18th.* This day sailed the Mexican hermaphrodite brig *Fazio,* for San Blas and Mazatlán. This was the brig which was driven ashore at San Pedro in a southeaster, and had been lying at San Diego to repair and take in her cargo. The owner of her had had a good deal of difficulty with the government about the duties, &c., and her sailing had been delayed for several weeks; but everything having been arranged, she got under way with a light breeze, and was floating out of the harbor, when two horsemen came dashing down to the beach at full speed, and tried to find a boat to put off after her; but there being none then at hand, they offered a handful of silver to any Kanaka who would swim off and take a letter on board. One of the Kanakas, an active, well-made young fellow, instantly threw off everything but his duck trousers, and, putting the letter into his hat, swam off after the vessel. Fortunately the wind was very light, and the vessel was going slowly, so that, although she was nearly a mile off when he started, he gained on her rapidly. He went through the water leaving a wake like a small steamboat. I certainly never saw such swimming before. They saw him coming from the deck, but did not heave to, suspecting the nature of his errand; yet, the wind continuing light, he swam alongside, and got on board, and delivered his letter. The captain read the letter, told the Kanaka there was no answer, and, giving him a glass of brandy, left him to jump overboard and find the best of his way to the shore. The Kanaka swam in for the nearest point of land, and in about an hour made his appearance at the hide house. He did not seem at all fatigued, had made three or four dollars, got a glass of brandy, and was in high spirits. The brig kept on her course, and the government officers, who had come down to forbid her sailing, went back, each with something very like a flea in his ear, having depended upon extorting a little more money from the owner.

It was now nearly three months since the *Alert* arrived at Santa Barbara, and we began to expect her daily. About half a mile behind the hide house was a high hill, and every afternoon, as soon as we had done our work, someone of us walked up to see if there was a sail in sight, coming down before the regular trades. Day after day we went up the hill, and came back disappointed. I was anxious for her arrival, for I had been told by letter that the owners in Boston, at the request of my friends, had written to Captain Thompson to take me on board the *Alert*, in case she returned to the United States before the *Pilgrim*; and I, of course, wished to know whether the order had been received, and what was the destination of the ship. One year, more or less, might be of small consequence to others, but it was everything to me. It was now just a year since we sailed from Boston, and, at the shortest, no vessel could expect to get away under eight or nine months, which would make our absence two years in all. This would be pretty long, but would not be fatal. It would not necessarily be decisive of my future life. But one year more might settle the matter. I might be a sailor for life; and although I had pretty well made up my mind to it before I had my letters from home, yet, as soon as an opportunity was held out to me of returning, and the prospect of another kind of life was opened to me, my anxiety to return, and, at least, to have the chance of deciding upon my course for myself, was beyond measure. Besides that, I wished to be "equal to either fortune," and to qualify myself for an officer's berth, and a hide house was no place to learn seamanship in. I had become experienced in hide curing, and everything went on smoothly, and I had many opportunities of becoming acquainted with the people, and much leisure for reading and studying navigation; yet practical seamanship could only be got on board ship, therefore I determined to ask to be taken on board the ship when she arrived. By the first of August we finished curing all our hides, stored them away, cleaned out our vats (in which latter work we spent two days, up to our knees in mud and the sediments of six months' hide curing, in a stench which would drive a donkey from his breakfast), and got all in readiness for the arrival of the ship, and had another leisure interval of three or four weeks. I spent these, as usual, in reading, writing, studying, making and mending my clothes, and getting my wardrobe in complete readiness in case I should go on board the ship; and in fishing, ranging the woods with the dogs, and in occasional visits to the presidio and mission. A good deal of my time was passed in taking care of a little puppy, which I had selected from thirty-six that were born within three days of one another at our house. He was a fine, promising pup, with four white paws, and all the rest of his body of a dark brown. I built a little kennel for him, and kept him fastened there, away from the other dogs, feeding and disciplining him myself. In a few weeks I brought him into complete subjection, and he grew nicely, was much attached to me, and bade fair to be one of the leading dogs on the beach. I called him Bravo, and all I regretted at the thought of leaving the beach was parting from him and the Kanakas.

Day after day we went up the hill, but no ship was to be seen, and we began to form all sorts of conjectures as to her whereabouts; and the theme of every evening's conversation at the different houses, and in our afternoon's *paseo* upon the beach, was the ship—where she could be, had she been to San Francisco, how many hides she would bring, &c., &c.

*Tuesday, August 25th.* This morning the officer in charge of our house went off beyond the point a-fishing, in a small canoe, with two Kanakas; and we were sitting quietly in our room at the hide house, when, just before noon, we heard a complete yell of "Sail ho!" breaking out from all parts of the beach at once, from the Kanakas' oven to the *Rosa*'s hide house. In an instant everyone was out of his house, and there was a tall, gallant ship, with royals and skysails set, bending over before the strong afternoon breeze, and coming rapidly round the point. Her yards were braced sharp up; every sail was set, and drew well; the stars and stripes were flying from her mizzen peak, and, having the tide in her favor, she came up like a race horse. It was nearly six months since a new vessel had entered San Diego, and, of course, everyone was wide awake. She certainly made a fine appearance. Her light sails were taken in, as she passed the low, sandy tongue of land, and clewing up her head sails, she rounded handsomely to under her mizzen topsail, and let go her anchor at about a cable's length from the shore. In a few minutes the topsail yards were manned, and all three of the topsails furled at once. From the fore-topgallant yard, the men slid down the stay to furl the jib, and from the mizzen-topgallant yard, by the stay, into the maintop, and thence to the yard; and the men on the topsail yards came down the lifts to the yardarms of the courses. The sails were furled with great care, the bunts triced up by jiggers, and the jibs stowed in cloth. The royal yards were then struck, tackles got upon the yardarms and the stay, the longboat hoisted out, a large anchor carried astern, and the ship moored. This was the *Alert*.

The gig was lowered away from the quarter, and a boat's crew of fine lads, between the ages of fourteen and eighteen, pulled the captain ashore. The gig was a light whaleboat, handsomely painted, and fitted up with cushions and tiller-ropes in the stern sheets. We immediately attacked the boat's crew, and got very thick with them in a few minutes. We had much to ask about Boston, their passage out, &c., and they were very curious to know about the kind of life we were leading upon the beach. One of them offered to exchange with me, which was just what I wanted, and we had only to get the permission of the captain.

After dinner the crew began discharging their hides, and, as we had nothing to do at the hide houses, we were ordered aboard to help them. I had now my first opportunity of seeing the ship which I hoped was to be my home for the next year. She looked as well on board as she did from without. Her decks were wide and roomy (there being no poop or house on deck, which disfigures the after part of most of our vessels), flush fore and aft, and as white as flax, which the crew told us was from constant use of holystones. There was no foolish gilding and gingerbread work, to take the eye of landsmen and passengers, but everything was "ship-shape." There was no rust, no dirt, no rigging hanging slack, no fag ends of ropes and "Irish pendants" aloft, and the yards were squared "to a *t*" by lifts and braces. The mate was a hearty fellow, with a roaring voice, and always wide awake. He was "a man, every inch of him," as the sailors said; and though "a bit of a horse," and "a hard customer," yet he was generally liked by the crew. There was also a second and third mate, a carpenter, sailmaker, steward, and cook, and twelve hands before the mast. She had on board seven thousand hides, which she had collected at the windward, and also horns and tallow. All these we began discharging from both gangways at once into the two boats, the second mate having charge of the launch, and the third mate of the pinnace. For several days we were employed in this way, until all the hides were taken out, when the crew began taking in ballast, and we returned to our old work, hide curing.

*Saturday, August 29th.* Arrived, brig *Catalina*, from the windward.

*Sunday, August 30th.* This was the first Sunday that the *Alert*'s crew had been in San Diego, and of course they were all for going up to see the town. The Indians came down early, with horses to let for the day, and those of the crew who could obtain liberty went off to the presidio and mission, and did not return until night. I had seen enough of San Diego, and went on board and spent the day with some of the crew, whom I found quietly at work in the forecastle, either mending and washing their clothes, or reading and writing. They told me that the ship stopped at Callao on the passage out, and lay there three weeks. She had a passage of a little over eighty days from Boston to Callao, which is one of the shortest on record. There they left the *Brandywine* frigate, and some smaller American ships of war, and the English frigate *Blonde*, and a French seventy-four. From Callao they came directly to California, and had visited every port on the coast, including San Francisco. The forecastle in which they lived was large, tolerably well lighted by bull's-eyes, and, being kept perfectly clean, had quite a comfortable appearance; at least, it was far better than the little, black, dirty hole in which I had lived so many months on board the *Pilgrim*. By the regulations of the ship, the forecastle was cleaned out every morning; and the crew, being very neat, kept it clean by some regulations of their own, such as having a large spitbox always under the steps and between the bits, and obliging every man to hang up his wet clothes, &c. In addition to this, it was holystoned every Saturday morning. In the after part of the ship was a handsome cabin, a dining room, and a trade room, fitted out with shelves, and furnished with all sorts of goods. Between these and the forecastle was the "between decks," as high as the gun deck of a frigate, being six feet and a half, under the beams. These between decks were holystoned regularly, and kept in the most perfect order; the carpenter's bench and tools being in one part, the sailmaker's in another, and the boatswain's locker, with the spare rigging, in a third. A part of the crew slept here, in hammocks swung fore and aft from the beams, and triced up every morning. The sides of the between decks were clapboarded, the knees and stanchions of iron, and the latter made to unship. The crew said she was as tight as a drum, and a fine sea boat, her only fault being—that of most fast ships—that she was wet forward. When she was going, as she sometimes would, eight or nine knots on a wind, there would not be a dry spot forward of the gangway. The men told great stories of her sailing, and had entire confidence in her as a "lucky ship." She was seven years old, had always been in the Canton trade, had never met with an accident of any consequence, nor made a passage that was not shorter than the average. The third mate, a young man about eighteen years of age, nephew of one of the owners, had been in the ship from a small boy, and "believed in the ship"; and the chief mate thought as much of her as he would of a wife and family.

The ship lay about a week longer in port, when, having discharged her cargo and taken in ballast, she prepared to get under way. I now made my application to the captain to go on board. He told me that I could go home in the ship when she sailed (which I knew before); and, finding that I wished to be on board while she was on the coast, said he had no objection, if I could find one of my own age to exchange with me for the time. This I easily accomplished, for they were glad to change the scene by a few months on shore, and, moreover, escape the winter and the southeasters; and I went on board the next day, with my chest and hammock, and found myself once more afloat.

# CHAPTER XXIII

*Tuesday, September 8th.* This was my first day's duty on board the ship; and though a sailor's life is a sailor's life wherever it may be, yet I found everything very different here

from the customs of the brig *Pilgrim*. After all hands were
called at daybreak, three minutes and a half were allowed
for the men to dress and come on deck, and if any were
longer than that, they were sure to be overhauled by the
mate, who was always on deck, and making himself heard
all over the ship. The head pump was then rigged, and the
decks washed down by the second and third mates; the chief
mate walking the quarterdeck, and keeping a general super-
vision, but not deigning to touch a bucket or a brush. Inside
and out, fore and aft, upper deck and between decks, steerage
and forecastle, rail, bulwarks, and waterways, were washed,
scrubbed, and scraped with brooms and canvas, and the
decks were wet and sanded all over, and then holystoned.
The holystone is a large, soft stone, smooth on the bottom,
with long ropes attached to each end, by which the crew
keep it sliding fore and aft over the wet, sanded decks. Smaller
hand stones, which the sailors call "prayerbooks," are used
to scrub in among the crevices and narrow places, where
the large holystone will not go. An hour or two we were
kept at this work, when the head pump was manned, and
all the sand washed off the decks and sides. Then came
swabs and squilgees; and, after the decks were dry, each one
went to his particular morning job. There were five boats belonging to the ship—launch, pinnace, jolly boat, larboard quarter
boat, and gig—each of which had a coxswain, who had charge
of it, and was answerable for the order and cleanness of it.
The rest of the cleaning was divided among the crew; one
having the brass and composition work about the capstan;
another, the bell, which was of brass, and kept as bright as
a gilt button; a third, the harness cask; another, the man-rope
stanchions; others, the steps of the forecastle and hatchways,
which were hauled up and holystoned. Each of these jobs
must be finished before breakfast; and in the meantime the
rest of the crew filled the scuttle butt, and the cook scraped
his kids (wooden tubs out of which sailors eat), and polished
the hoops, and placed them before the galley to await inspection. When the decks were dry, the lord paramount made
his appearance on the quarterdeck, and took a few turns,
eight bells were struck, and all hands went to breakfast.
Half an hour was allowed for breakfast, when all hands were
called again; the kids, pots, bread bags, &c., stowed away;
and, this morning, preparations were made for getting under

way. We paid out on the chain by which we swung, hove in
on the other, catted the anchor, and hove short on the first.
This work was done in shorter time than was usual on board
the brig; for though everything was more than twice as large
and heavy, the cat block being as much as a man could lift,
and the chain as large as three of the *Pilgrim*'s, yet there
was a plenty of room to move about in, more discipline and
system, more men, and more goodwill. Each seemed ambitious to do his best. Officers and men knew their duty, and
all went well. As soon as she was hove short, the mate, on
the forecastle, gave the order to loose the sails; and, in an
instant all sprung into the rigging, up the shrouds, and out
on the yards, scrambling by one another—the first up, the
best fellow—cast off the yardarm gaskets and bunt gaskets,
and one man remained on each yard, holding the bunt
jigger with a turn round the tye, all ready to let go, while
the rest laid down to man the sheets and halyards. The mate
then hailed the yards—"All ready forward?" "All ready the
crossjack yards?" &c., &c., and "Aye, aye, sir!" being returned
from each—the word was given to let go; and, in the
twinkling of an eye, the ship, which had shown nothing but
her bare yards, was covered with her loose canvas, from the
royal mastheads to the decks. All then came down, except
one man in each top, to overhaul the rigging, and the topsails
were hoisted and sheeted home, the three yards going to
the masthead at once, the larboard watch hoisting the fore,
the starboard watch the main, and five light hands (of whom
I was one), picked from the two watches, the mizzen. The
yards were then trimmed, the anchor weighed, the cat block
hooked on, the fall stretched out, manned by "all hands and
the cook," and the anchor brought to the head with "Cheerly,
men!" in full chorus. The ship being now under way, the
light sails were set, one after another, and she was under
full sail before she had passed the sandy point. The fore
royal, which fell to my lot (as I was in the mate's watch),
was more than twice as large as that of the *Pilgrim*, and,
though I could handle the brig's easily, I found my hands
full with this, especially as there were no jacks to the ship,
everything being for neatness, and nothing left for Jack to
hold on by but his "eyelids."

As soon as we were beyond the point, and all sail out, the
order was given, "Go below, the watch!" and the crew said

*better atmosphere than on the Pilgrim*

that, ever since they had been on the coast, they had had
"watch and watch" while going from port to port; and, in
fact, all things showed that, though strict discipline was kept,
and the utmost was required of every man in the way of his
duty, yet, on the whole, there was good usage on board.
Each one knew that he must be a man, and show himself
such when at his duty, yet all were satisfied with the treatment; and a contented crew, agreeing with one another, and
finding no fault, was a contrast indeed with the small, hard-
used, dissatisfied, grumbling, desponding crew of the *Pilgrim*.

It being the turn of our watch to go below, the men set
themselves to work, mending their clothes, and doing other
little things for themselves; and I, having got my wardrobe
in complete order at San Diego, had nothing to do but to
read. I accordingly overhauled the chests of the crew, but
found nothing that suited me exactly, until one of the men
said he had a book which "told all about a great highway-
man," at the bottom of his chest, and, producing it, I found,
to my surprise and joy, that it was nothing else than Bulwer's
*Paul Clifford*. I seized it immediately, and, going to my
hammock, lay there, swinging and reading, until the watch
below was out. The between decks clear, the hatchways open,
a cool breeze blowing through them, the ship under easy
way—everything was comfortable. I had just got well into
the story when eight bells were struck, and we were all
ordered to dinner. After dinner came our watch on deck for
four hours, and at four o'clock I went below again, turned
into my hammock, and read until the dog watch. As lights
were not allowed after eight o'clock, there was no reading
in the night watch. Having light winds and calms, we were
three days on the passage, and each watch below, during the
daytime, I spent in the same manner, until I had finished my
book. I shall never forget the enjoyment I derived from it.
To come across anything with the slightest claims to literary
merit was so unusual that this was a feast to me. The brilliancy of the book, the succession of capital hits, and the
lively and characteristic sketches kept me in a constant state
of pleasing sensations. It was far too good for a sailor. I could
not expect such fine times to last long.

While on deck, the regular work of the ship went on. The
sailmaker and carpenter worked between decks, and the
crew had their work to do upon the rigging, drawing yarns,

making spun yarn, &c., as usual in merchantmen. The night watches were much more pleasant than on board the *Pilgrim*. There, there were so few in a watch that, one being at the wheel and another on the lookout, there was no one left to talk with; but here we had seven in a watch, so that we had long yarns in abundance. After two or three night watches, I became well acquainted with the larboard watch. The sail-maker was the head man of the watch, and was generally considered the most experienced seaman on board. He was a thoroughbred old man-of-war's-man, had been at sea twenty-two years, in all kinds of vessels—men-of-war, privateers, slavers, and merchantmen—everything except whalers, which a thorough man-of-war or merchant seaman looks down upon, and will always steer clear of if he can. He had, of course, been in most parts of the world, and was remarkable for drawing a long bow. His yarns frequently stretched through a watch, and kept all hands awake. They were amusing from their improbability, and, indeed, he never expected to be believed, but spun them merely for amusement; and as he had some humor and a good supply of man-of-war slang and sailor's salt phrases, he always made fun. Next to him in age and experience, and, of course, in standing in the watch, was an Englishman named Harris, of whom I shall have more to say hereafter. Then came two or three Americans, who had been the common run of European and South American voyages, and one who had been in a "spouter," and, of course, had all the whaling stories to himself. Last of all was a broad-backed, thickheaded, Cape Cod * boy, who had been in mackerel schooners, and was making his first voyage in a square-rigged vessel. He was born in Hingham, and of course was called "Bucketmaker." The other watch was composed of about the same number. A tall, fine-looking Frenchman, with coal-black whiskers and curly hair, a first-rate seaman, named John (one name is enough for a sailor), was the head man of the watch. Then came two Americans (one of whom had been a dissipated young man of some property and respectable connections, and was reduced to duck trousers and monthly wages), a German, an English lad, named Ben, who belonged on the mizzen-topsail yard with me, and was a good sailor for his

* Sailors call men from any part of the coast of Massachusetts south of Boston Cape Cod men.

years, and two Boston boys just from the public schools. The
carpenter sometimes mustered in the starboard watch, and
was an old sea dog, a Swede by birth, and accounted the best
helmsman in the ship. This was our ship's company, besides
cook and steward, who were blacks, three mates, and the
captain.

The second day out, the wind drew ahead, and we had
to beat up the coast; so that, in tacking ship, I could see the
regulations of the vessel. Instead of going wherever was
most convenient, and running from place to place, wherever
work was to be done, each man had his station. A regular
tacking-and-wearing bill was made out. The chief mate commanded on the forecastle, and had charge of the head sails
and the forward part of the ship. Two of the best men in
the ship, the sailmaker from our watch, and John, the Frenchman, from the other, worked the forecastle. The third mate
commanded in the waist, and, with the carpenter and one
man, worked the main tack and bowline; the cook, *ex officio*,
the foresheet, and the steward the main. The second mate
had charge of the afteryards, and let go the lee fore and
main braces. I was stationed at the weather crossjack braces;
three other light hands at the lee; one boy at the spanker
sheet and guy; a man and a boy at the main topsail, topgallant, and royal braces; and all the rest of the crew—men
and boys—tallied on to the main brace. Everyone here knew
his station, must be there when all hands were called to put
the ship about, and was answerable for the ropes committed
to him. Each man's rope must be let go and hauled in at
the order, properly made fast, and neatly coiled away when
the ship was about. As soon as all hands are at their stations,
the captain, who stands on the weather side of the quarterdeck, makes a sign to the man at the wheel to put it down, and
calls out, "Helm's a lee'!" "Helm's a lee'!" answers the mate
on the forecastle, and the head sheets are let go. "Raise
tacks and sheets!" says the captain; "tacks and sheets!" is
passed forward, and the foretack and mainsheet are let go.
The next thing is to haul taut for a swing. The weather crossjack braces and the lee main braces are belayed together
upon two pins, and ready to be let go, and the opposite
braces hauled taut. "Main topsail haul!" shouts the captain;
the braces are let go; and if he has chosen his time well,
the yards swing round like a top; but if he is too late, or too

soon, it is like drawing teeth. The afteryards are then braced up and belayed, the mainsheet hauled aft, the spanker eased over to leeward, and the men from the braces stand by the head yards. "Let go and haul!" says the captain; the second mate lets go the weather forebraces, and the men haul in to leeward. The mate, on the forecastle, looks out for the head yards. "*Well* the fore-topsail yard!" "Topgallant yard's *well!*" "Royal yard too much! Haul in to windward! So! Well *that!*" "Well *all!*" Then the starboard watch board the main tack, and the larboard watch lay forward and board the foretack and haul down the jib sheet, clapping a tackle upon it if it blows very fresh. The afteryards are then trimmed, the captain generally looking out for them himself. "Well the crossjack * yard!" "Small pull the main-topgallant yard!" "Well *that!*" "Well the mizzen-topsail yard!" "Crossjack yards all *well!*" "Well all aft!" "Haul taut to windward!" Everything being now trimmed and in order, each man coils up the rigging at his own station, and the order is given, "Go below, the watch!"

During the last twenty-four hours of the passage, we beat off and on the land, making a tack about once in four hours, so that I had sufficient opportunity to observe the working of the ship; and certainly it took no more men to brace about this ship's lower yards, which were more than fifty feet square, than it did those of the *Pilgrim*, which were not much more than half the size; so much depends upon the manner in which the braces run, and the state of the blocks; and Captain Wilson, of the *Ayacucho*, who was afterward a passenger with us, upon a trip to windward, said he had no doubt that our ship worked two men lighter than his brig. This light working of the ship was owing to the attention and seamanship of Captain Faucon. He had reeved anew nearly all the running rigging of the ship, getting rid of useless blocks, putting single blocks for double wherever he could, using pendent blocks, and adjusting the purchases scientifically.

*Friday, September 11th.* This morning, at four o'clock, went below, San Pedro point being about two leagues ahead, and the ship going on under studding sails. In about an hour we were waked up by the hauling of the chain about decks, and in a few minutes, "All hands ahoy!" was called;

* Pronounced *croj-ac*.

and we were all at work, hauling in and making up the studding sails, overhauling the chain forward, and getting the anchors ready. "The *Pilgrim* is there at anchor," said someone, as we were running about decks; and, taking a moment's look over the rail, I saw my old friend, deeply laden, lying at anchor inside of the kelp. In coming to anchor, as well as in tacking ship, each one had his station and duty. The light sails were clewed up and furled, the courses hauled up, and the jibs down; then came the topsails in the buntlines, and the anchor let go. As soon as she was well at anchor, all hands lay aloft to furl the topsails; and this, I soon found, was a great matter on board this ship; for every sailor knows that a vessel is judged of, a good deal, by the furl of her sails. The third mate, sailmaker, and the larboard watch went upon the fore-topsail yard; the second mate, carpenter, and the starboard watch, upon the main; and I, and the English lad, and the two Boston boys, and the young Cape Cod man, furled the mizzen topsail. This sail belonged to us altogether to reef and to furl, and not a man was allowed to come upon our yard. The mate took us under his special care, frequently making us furl the sail over three or four times, until we got the bunt up to a perfect cone, and the whole sail without a wrinkle. As soon as each sail was hauled up and the bunt made, the jigger was bent on to the slack of the buntlines, and the bunt triced up, on deck. The mate then took his place between the knightheads to "twig" the fore, on the windlass to twig the main, and at the foot of the mainmast for the mizzen; and if anything was wrong— too much bunt on one side, clews too taut or too slack, or any sail abaft the yard—the whole must be dropped again. When all was right, the bunts were triced well up, the yard-arm gaskets passed, so as not to leave a wrinkle forward of the yard—short gaskets, with turns close together.

From the moment of letting go the anchor, when the captain ceases his care of things, the chief mate is the great man. With a voice like a young lion, he was hallooing in all directions, making everything fly, and, at the same time, doing everything well. He was quite a contrast to the worthy, quiet, unobtrusive mate of the *Pilgrim*, not a more estimable man, perhaps, but a far better mate of a vessel; and the entire change in Captain Thompson's conduct, since he took command of the ship, was owing, no doubt, in a great measure, to this fact. If the chief officer wants force, discipline slackens, everything gets out of joint, and the captain interferes continually; that makes a difficulty between them, which encourages the crew, and the whole ends in a three-sided quarrel. But Mr. Brown (a Marblehead man) wanted no help from anybody, took everything into his own hands, and was more likely to encroach upon the authority of the master than to need any spurring. Captain Thompson gave his directions to the mate in private, and, except in coming to anchor, getting under way, tacking, reefing topsails, and other "all-hands work," seldom appeared in person. This is the proper state of things; and while this lasts, and there is a good understanding aft, everything will go on well.

Having furled all the sails, the royal yards were next to be sent down. The English lad and myself sent down the main, which was larger than the *Pilgrim*'s main-topgallant yard; two more light hands the fore, and one boy the mizzen. This order we kept while on the coast, sending them up and down every time we came in and went out of port. They were all tripped and lowered together, the main on the starboard side, and the fore and mizzen to port. No sooner was she all snug, than tackles were got up on the yards and stays, and the longboat and pinnace hove out. The swinging booms were then guyed out, and the boats made fast by guess-warps, and everything in harbor style. After breakfast, the hatches were taken off, and everything got ready to receive hides from the *Pilgrim*. All day, boats were passing and repassing, until we had taken her hides from her, and left her in ballast trim. These hides made but little show in our hold, though they had loaded the *Pilgrim* down to the water's edge. This changing of the hides settled the question of the destination of the two vessels, which had been one of some speculation with us. We were to remain in the ward ports, while the *Pilgrim* was to sail, the next morning, for San Francisco. After we had knocked off work, and cleared up decks for the night, my friend Stimson came on board, and spent an hour with me in our berth between decks. The *Pilgrim*'s crew envied me my place on board the ship, and seemed to think that I had got a little to windward of them, especially in the matter of going home first. Stimson was determined to go home in the *Alert*, by begging or buying. If Captain Thompson would not let him come on other terms, he would purchase an exchange with someone of the crew. The prospect of another year after the *Alert* should sail was rather "too much of the monkey." About seven o'clock the mate came down into the steerage in fine trim for fun, roused the boys out of the berth, turned up the carpenter with his fiddle, sent the steward with lights to put in the between decks, and set all hands to dancing. The between decks were high enough to allow of jumping, and being clear, and white from holystoning, made a good dancing hall. Some of the *Pilgrim*'s crew were in the forecastle, and they all turned to and had a regular sailor's shuffle till eight bells. The Cape Cod boy could dance the true fisherman's jig, barefooted, knocking with his heels, and slapping the decks with his bare feet, in time with the music. This was a favorite amusement of the mate's, who used to stand at the steerage door, looking on, and if the boys would not dance, hazed them round with a rope's end, much to the entertainment of the men.

The next morning, according to the orders of the agent, the *Pilgrim* set sail for the windward, to be gone three or four months. She got under way with no fuss, and came so near us as to throw a letter on board, Captain Faucon standing at the tiller himself, and steering her as he would a mackerel smack. When Captain Thompson was in command of the *Pilgrim*, there was as much preparation and ceremony as there would be in getting a seventy-four under way. Captain Faucon was a sailor, every inch of him. He knew what a ship was, and was as much at home in one as a cobbler in his stall. I wanted no better proof of this than the opinion of the ship's crew, for they had been six months under his command, and knew him thoroughly, and if sailors allow their captain to be a good seaman, you may be sure he is one, for that is a thing they are not usually ready to admit. To find fault with the seamanship of the captain is a crew's reserved store for grumbling.

After the *Pilgrim* left us, we lay three weeks at San Pedro, from the eleventh of September until the second of October, engaged in the usual port duties of landing cargo, taking off hides, &c., &c. These duties were much easier, and went on much more agreeably, than on board the *Pilgrim*. "The more the merrier" is the sailor's maxim, and, by a division of labor, a boat's crew of a dozen could take off all the hides brought down in a day without much trouble; and on shore, as well as on board, a goodwill, and no discontent or grumbling, make everything go well. The officer, too, who usually went with us, the third mate, was a pleasant young fellow, and made no unnecessary trouble; so that we generally had a sociable time, and were glad to be relieved from the restraint of the ship. While here, I often thought of the miserable, gloomy weeks we had spent in this dull place, in the brig—discontent and hard usage on board, and four hands to do all the work on shore. Give me a big ship. There is more room, better outfit, better regulation, more life, and more company. Another thing was better arranged here: we had a regular gig's crew. A light whaleboat, handsomely painted, and fitted out with stern seats, yoke and tiller ropes, hung on the starboard quarter, and was used as the gig. The youngest lad in the ship, a Boston boy about fourteen years old, was coxswain of this boat, and had the entire charge of her, to keep her clean and have her in readiness to go and come at any hour. Four light hands, of about the same size and age, of whom I was one, formed her crew. Each had his oar and seat numbered, and we were obliged to be in our places, have our oars scraped white, our tholepins in, and the fenders over the side. The bowman had charge of the boat hook and painter, and the coxswain of the rudder, yoke, and stern sheets. Our duty was to carry the captain and agent about, and passengers off and on, which last was no trifling duty, as the people on shore have no boats, and every purchaser, from the boy who buys his pair of shoes, to the trader who buys his casks and bales, was to be brought off and taken ashore in our boat. Some days, when people were coming and going fast, we were in the boat, pulling off and on, all day long, with hardly time for our meals, making, as we lay nearly three miles offshore, from thirty to forty miles' rowing in a day. Still, we thought it the best berth in the ship; for when the gig was employed, we had nothing to do with the cargo, except with small bundles which the passengers took with them, and no hides to carry. Besides, we had the opportunity of seeing everybody, making acquaintances, and hearing the news. Unless the captain or agent was in the boat, we had no officer with us, and often had fine times with the passengers, who were always willing to talk and joke with us. Frequently, too, we were obliged to wait several hours on shore, when we would haul the boat up on the beach, and, leaving one to watch her, go to the nearest house, or spend the time in strolling about the beach, picking up shells, or playing hop-scotch, and other games, on the hard sand. The others of the crew never left the ship, except for bringing heavy goods and taking off hides; and though we were always in the water, the surf hardly leaving us a dry thread from morning till night, yet we were young, and the climate was good, and we thought it much better than the quiet, humdrum drag and pull on board ship. We made the acquaintance of nearly half California; for, besides carrying everybody in our boat—men, women, and children—all the messages, letters, and light packages went by us, and, being known by our dress, we found a ready reception everywhere.

At San Pedro, we had none of this amusement, for, there being but one house in the place, there was nothing to see and no company. All the variety that I had was riding, once a week, to the nearest rancho,* to order a bullock down to the ship.

The brig *Catalina* came in from San Diego, and, being bound to windward, we both got under way at the same time, for a trial of speed up to Santa Barbara, a distance of about eighty miles. We hove up and got under sail about eleven o'clock at night, with a light land breeze, which died away toward morning, leaving us becalmed only a few miles from our anchoring place. The *Catalina*, being a small vessel, of less than half our size, put out sweeps and got a boat ahead, and pulled out to sea during the night, so that she had the sea breeze earlier and stronger than we did, and we had the mortification of seeing her standing up the coast with a fine breeze, the sea all ruffled about her, while we were becalmed inshore. When the sea breeze died away, she was nearly out of sight; and, toward the latter part of the afternoon, the regular northwest wind setting in fresh, we braced sharp upon it, took a pull at every sheet, tack, and halyard, and stood after her in fine style, our ship being very good upon a taut bowline. We had nearly five hours of splendid sailing, beating up to windward by long stretches in- and offshore, and evidently gaining upon the *Catalina* at every tack. When this breeze left us, we were so near as to count the painted ports

---

* This was Sepulveda's rancho, where there was a fight, during our war with Mexico in 1846, between some United States troops and the Mexicans, under Don Andrés Pico.

on her side. Fortunately, the wind died away when we were
on our inward tack, and she on her outward, so we were
inshore and caught the land breeze first, which came off upon
our quarter, about the middle of the first watch. All hands
were turned up, and we set all sail, to the skysails and the
royal studding sails; and with these, we glided quietly through
the water, leaving the *Catalina,* which could not spread so
much canvas as we, gradually astern, and, by daylight, were
off Santa Buenaventura, and our competitor nearly out of
sight. The sea breeze, however, favored her again, while we
were becalmed under the headland, and laboring slowly along,
and she was abreast of us by noon. Thus we continued, ahead,
astern, and abreast of each other, alternately; now far out at
sea, and again close in under the shore. On the third morning
we came into the great bay of Santa Barbara two hours behind the brig, and thus lost the bet; though if the race had
been to the point, we should have beaten her by five or six
hours. This, however, settled the relative sailing of the vessels,
for it was admitted that although she, being small and light,
could gain upon us in very light winds, yet whenever there was
breeze enough to set us a-going, we walked away from her
like hauling in a line; and, in beating to windward, which is
the best trial of a vessel, had much the advantage.

*Sunday, October 4th.* This was the day of our arrival; and,
somehow or other, our captain seemed to manage, not only to
sail, but to come into port, on a Sunday. The main reason for
sailing on Sunday is not, as many people suppose, because it
is thought a lucky day but because it is a leisure day. During
the six days the crew are employed upon the cargo and other
ship's works, and, Sunday being their only day of rest, whatever additional work can be thrown into it is so much gain to
the owners. This is the reason of our coasters and packets generally sailing on Sunday. Thus it was with us nearly all the
time we were on the coast, and many of our Sundays were
lost entirely to us. The Catholics on shore do not, as a general
thing, do regular trading or make journeys on Sunday, but the
American has no national religion, and likes to show his independence of priestcraft by doing as he chooses on the Lord's
Day.

Santa Barbara looked very much as it did when I left it
five months before: the long sand beach, with the heavy rollers,
breaking upon it in a continual roar, and the little town, em-

bedded on the plain, girt by its amphitheater of mountains. Day after day the sun shone clear and bright upon the wide bay and the red roofs of the houses, everything being as still as death, the people hardly seeming to earn their sunlight. Daylight was thrown away upon them. We had a few visitors, and collected about a hundred hides, and every night, at sundown, the gig was sent ashore to wait for the captain, who spent his evenings in the town. We always took our monkey jackets with us, and flint and steel, and made a fire on the beach with the driftwood and the bushes which we pulled from the neighboring thickets, and lay down by it, on the sand. Sometimes we would stray up to the town, if the captain was likely to stay late, and pass the time at some of the houses, in which we were almost always well received by the inhabitants. Sometimes earlier and sometimes later, the captain came down; when, after a good drenching in the surf, we went aboard, changed our clothes, and turned in for the night—yet not for all the night, for there was the anchor watch to stand.

This leads me to speak of my watchmate for nine months—and, taking him all in all, the most remarkable man I had ever seen—Tom Harris. An hour, every night, while lying in port, Harris and I had the deck to ourselves, and walking fore and aft, night after night, for months, I learned his character and history, and more about foreign nations, the habits of different people, and especially the secrets of sailors' lives and hardships, and also of practical seamanship, in which he was abundantly capable of instructing me, than I could ever have learned elsewhere. His memory was perfect, seeming to form a regular chain, reaching from his earliest childhood up to the time I knew him, without a link wanting. His power of calculation, too, was extraordinary. I called myself pretty quick at figures, and had been through a course of mathematical studies; but, working by my head, I was unable to keep within sight of this man, who had never been beyond his arithmetic. He carried in his head, not only a logbook of the voyage, which was complete and accurate, and from which no one thought of appealing, but also an accurate registry of the cargo, knowing where each thing was stowed, and how many hides we took in at each port.

One night he made a rough calculation of the number of hides that could be stowed in the lower hold, between the fore-

and mainmasts, taking the depth of hold and breadth of beam (for he knew the dimensions of every part of a ship before he had been long on board), and the average area and thickness of a hide; and he came surprisingly near the number, as it afterward turned out. The mate frequently came to him to know the capacity of different parts of the vessel, and he could tell the sailmaker very nearly the amount of canvas he would want for each sail in the ship; for he knew the hoist of every mast, and spread of each sail, on the head and foot, in feet and inches. When we were at sea, he kept a running account, in his head, of the ship's way—the number of knots and the courses—and, if the courses did not vary much during the twenty-four hours, by taking the whole progress and allowing so many eighths southing or northing, to so many easting or westing, he would make up his reckoning just before the captain took the sun at noon, and often came very near the mark. He had, in his chest, several volumes giving accounts of inventions in mechanics, which he read with great pleasure, and made himself master of. I doubt if he forgot anything that he read. The only thing in the way of poetry that he ever read was Falconer's "Shipwreck," which he was charmed with, and pages of which he could repeat. He said he could recall the name of every sailor that had ever been his shipmate, and also of every vessel, captain, and officer, and the principal dates of each voyage; and a sailor whom we afterward fell in with, who had been in a ship with Harris nearly twelve years before, was much surprised at having Harris tell him things about himself which he had entirely forgotten. His facts, whether dates or events, no one thought of disputing; and his opinions few of the sailors dared to oppose, for, right or wrong, he always had the best of the argument with them. His reasoning powers were striking. I have had harder work maintaining an argument with him in a watch, even when I knew myself to be right, and he was only doubting, than I ever had before, not from his obstinacy, but from his acuteness. Give him only a little knowledge of his subject, and, among all the young men of my acquaintance at college, there is not one whom I had not rather meet in an argument than this man. I never answered a question from him, or advanced an opinion to him, without thinking more than once. With an iron memory, he seemed to have your whole past conversation at command, and if you said a thing now which ill agreed with

something you had said months before, he was sure to have
you on the hip. In fact, I felt, when with him, that I was with
no common man. I had a positive respect for his powers of
mind, and thought, often, that if half the pains had been
spent upon his education which are thrown away yearly in
our colleges, he would have made his mark. Like many self-
taught men of real merit, he overrated the value of a regular
education; and this I often told him, though I had profited by
his error; for he always treated me with respect, and often
unnecessarily gave way to me, from an overestimate of my
knowledge. For the intellectual capacities of all the rest of
the crew—captain and all—he had a sovereign contempt.
He was a far better sailor, and probably a better navigator,
than the captain, and had more brains than all the after part
of the ship put together. The sailors said, "Tom's got a head
as long as the bowsprit," and if anyone fell into an argument
with him, they would call out, "Ah, Jack! You had better
drop that as you would a hot potato, for Tom will turn you
inside out before you know it!"

I recollect his posing me once on the subject of the Corn
Laws. I was called to stand my watch, and, coming on deck,
found him there before me; and we began, as usual, to walk
fore and aft, in the waist. He talked about the Corn Laws;
asked me my opinion about them, which I gave him, and my
reasons, my small stock of which I set forth to the best advantage, supposing his knowledge on the subject must be less
than mine, if, indeed, he had any at all. When I had got
through, he took the liberty of differing from me, and brought
arguments and facts which were new to me, and to which I
was unable to reply. I confessed that I knew almost nothing
of the subject, and expressed my surprise at the extent of his
information. He said that, a number of years before, while
at a boardinghouse in Liverpool, he had fallen in with a
pamphlet on the subject, and, as it contained calculations, had
read it very carefully, and had ever since wished to find someone who could add to his stock of knowledge on the question.
Although it was many years since he had seen the book, and
it was a subject with which he had had no previous acquaintance, yet he had the chain of reasoning, founded upon principles of political economy, fully in his memory; and his facts,
so far as I could judge, were correct; at least, he stated them
with precision. The principles of the steam engine, too, he

was familiar with, having been several months on board a steamboat, and made himself master of its secrets. He knew every lunar star in both hemispheres, and was a master of the quadrant and sextant. The men said he could take a meridian altitude of the sun from a tar bucket. Such was the man, who, at forty, was still a dog before the mast, at twelve dollars a month. The reason of this was to be found in his past life, as I had it, at different times, from himself.

He was an Englishman, a native of Ilfracombe, in Devonshire. His father was skipper of a small coaster from Bristol, and, dying, left him, when quite young, to the care of his mother, by whose exertions he received a common-school education, passing his winters at school and his summers in the coasting trade until his seventeenth year, when he left home to go upon foreign voyages. Of this mother he spoke with the greatest respect, and said that she was a woman of a strong mind, and had an excellent system of education, which had made respectable men of his three brothers, and failed in him only from his own indomitable obstinacy. One thing he mentioned, in which he said his mother differed from all other mothers that he had ever seen disciplining their children; that was, that when he was out of humor and refused to eat, instead of putting his plate away, saying that his hunger would bring him to it in time, she would stand over him and oblige him to eat it—every mouthful of it. It was no fault of hers that he was what I saw him; and so great was his sense of gratitude for her efforts, though unsuccessful, that he determined, when the voyage should end, to embark for home with all the wages he should get, to spend with and for his mother, if perchance he should find her alive.

After leaving home, he had spent nearly twenty years sailing upon all sorts of voyages, generally out of the ports of New York and Boston. Twenty years of vice! Every sin that a sailor knows, he had gone to the bottom of. Several times he had been hauled up in the hospitals, and as often the great strength of his constitution had brought him out again in health. Several times, too, from his acknowledged capacity, he had been promoted to the office of chief mate, and as often his conduct when in port, especially his drunkenness, which neither fear nor ambition could induce him to abandon, put him back into the forecastle. One night, when giving me an account of his life, and lamenting the years of manhood he had thrown away, "There," said he, "in the forecastle, at the foot of those steps, a chest of old clothes, is the result of twenty-two years of hard labor and exposure—worked like a horse, and treated like a dog." As he had grown older, he began to feel the necessity of some provision for his later years, and came gradually to the conviction that rum had been his worst enemy. One night, in Havana, a young shipmate of his was brought aboard drunk, with a dangerous gash in his head, and his money and new clothes stripped from him. Harris had been in hundreds of such scenes as these, but in his then state of mind it fixed his determination, and he resolved never to taste a drop of strong drink of any kind. He signed no pledge, and made no vow, but relied on his own strength of purpose. The first thing with him was a reason, and then a resolution, and the thing was done. The date of his resolution he knew, of course, to the very hour. It was three years before I became acquainted with him, and during all that time nothing stronger than cider or coffee had passed his lips. The sailors never thought of enticing Tom to take a glass, any more than they would of talking to the ship's compass. He was now a temperate man for life, and capable of filling any berth in a ship, and many a high station there is on shore which is held by a meaner man.

He understood the management of a ship upon scientific principles, and could give the reason for hauling every rope; and a long experience, added to careful observation at the time, gave him a knowledge of the expedients and resorts for times of hazard, for which I became much indebted to him, as he took the greatest pleasure in opening his stores of information to me, in return for what I was enabled to do for him. Stories of tyranny and hardship which had driven men to piracy; of the incredible ignorance of masters and mates, and of horrid brutality to the sick, dead, and dying; as well as of the secret knavery and impositions practiced upon seamen by connivance of the owners, landlords, and officers—all these he had, and I could not but believe them; for he made the impression of an exact man, to whom exaggeration was falsehood; and his statements were always credited. I remember, among other things, his speaking of a captain whom I had known by report, who never handed a thing to a sailor, but put it on deck and kicked it to him; and of another, who was highly connected in Boston, who absolutely murdered a

lad from Boston who went out with him before the mast to
Sumatra, by keeping him hard at work while ill of the coast
fever, and obliging him to sleep in the close steerage. (The
same captain has since died of the same fever on the same
coast.)

In fact, taking together all that I learned from him of seamanship, of the history of sailors' lives, of practical wisdom,
and of human nature under new circumstances and strange
forms of life—a great history from which many are shut out—
I would not part with the hours I spent in the watch with that
man for the gift of many hours to be passed in study and
intercourse with even the best of society.

# CHAPTER XXIV

*Sunday, October 11th.* Set sail this morning for the leeward;
passed within sight of San Pedro, and, to our great joy, did
not come to anchor, but kept directly on to San Diego, where
we arrived and moored ship on—

*Thursday, October 15th.* Found here the Italian ship *La
Rosa*, from the windward, which reported the brig *Pilgrim*
at San Francisco, all well. Everything was as quiet here as
usual. We discharged our hides, horns, and tallow, and were
ready to sail again on the following Sunday. I went ashore to
my old quarters, and found the gang at the hide house going
on in the even tenor of their way, and spent an hour or two,
after dark, at the oven, taking a whiff with my old Kanaka
friends, who really seemed glad to see me again, and saluted
me as the *aikane* of the Kanakas. I was grieved to find that
my poor dog Bravo was dead. He had sickened and died
suddenly the very day after I sailed in the *Alert*.

Sunday was again, as usual, our sailing day, and we got under way with a stiff breeze, which reminded us that it was the latter part of the autumn, and time to expect southeasters once more. We beat up against a strong head wind, under reefed topsails, as far as San Juan, where we came to anchor nearly three miles from the shore, with slip ropes on our cables, in the old southeaster style of last winter. On the passage up, we had an old sea captain on board, who had married and settled in California, and had not been on salt water for more than fifteen years. He was surprised at the changes and improvements that had been made in ships, and still more at the manner in which we carried sail; for he was really a little frightened, and said that while we had topgallant sails on, he should have been under reefed topsails. The working of the ship, and her progress to windward, seemed to delight him, for he said she went to windward as though she were kedging.

*Tuesday, October 20th.* Having got everything ready, we set the agent ashore, who went up to the mission to hurry down the hides for the next morning. This night we had the strictest orders to look out for southeasters; and the long, low clouds seemed rather threatening. But the night passed over without any trouble, and early the next morning we hove out the long-boat and pinnace, lowered away the quarter boats, and went ashore to bring off our hides. Here we were again, in this romantic spot—a perpendicular hill, twice the height of the ship's masthead, with a single circuitous path to the top, and long sand beach at its base, with the swell of the whole Pacific breaking high upon it, and our hides ranged in piles on the overhanging summit. The captain sent me, who was the only one of the crew that had ever been there before, to the top to count the hides and pitch them down. There I stood again, as six months before, throwing off the hides, and watching them, pitching and scaling, to the bottom, while the men, dwarfed by the distance, were walking to and fro on the beach, carrying the hides, as they picked them up, to the distant boats, upon the tops of their heads. Two or three boatloads were sent off, until at last all were thrown down, and the boats nearly loaded again, when we were delayed by a dozen or twenty hides which had lodged in the recesses of the bank, and which we could not reach by any missiles, as the general line of the side was exactly perpendicular, and these places were caved in, and could not be seen or reached from the top. As hides are worth in Boston twelve and a half cents a pound, and the captain's commission was 1 per cent, he determined not to give them up, and sent on board for a pair of topgallant-studding-sail halyards, and requested some-one of the crew to go to the top and come down by the hal-yards. The older sailors said the boys, who were light and active, ought to go; while the boys thought that strength and experience were necessary. Seeing the dilemma, and feeling myself to be near the medium of these requisites, I offered my services, and went up, with one man to tend the rope, and prepared for the descent.

We found a stake fastened strongly into the ground, and apparently capable of holding my weight, to which we made one end of the halyard well fast, and, taking the coil, threw it over the brink. The end, we saw, just reached to a landing place, from which the descent to the beach was easy. Having nothing on but shirt, trousers, and hat, the common sea rig of warm weather, I had no stripping to do, and began my descent by taking hold of the rope with both hands, and slipping down, sometimes with hands and feet round the rope, and sometimes breasting off with one hand and foot against the precipice, and holding on to the rope with the other. In this way I descended until I came to a place which shelved in, and in which the hides were lodged. Keeping hold of the rope with one hand, I scrambled in, and by aid of my feet and the other hand succeeded in dislodging all the hides, and continued on my way. Just below this place, the precipice pro-jected again, and, going over the projection, I could see noth-ing below me but the sea and the rocks upon which it broke, and a few gulls flying in midair. I got down in safety, pretty well covered with dirt; and for my pains was told, "What a d——d fool you were to risk your life for half a dozen hides!"

While we were carrying the hides to the boat, I perceived, what I had been too busy to observe before, that heavy black clouds were rolling up from seaward, a strong swell heaving in, and every sign of a southeaster. The captain hurried every-thing. The hides were pitched into the boats, and, with some difficulty, and by wading nearly up to our armpits, we got the boats through the surf, and began pulling aboard. Our gig's crew towed the pinnace astern of the gig, and the launch was towed by six men in the jolly boat. The ship was lying three miles off, pitching at her anchor, and the farther we pulled, the heavier grew the swell. Our boat stood nearly up and down several times; the pinnace parted her towline, and we expected every moment to see the launch swamped. At length we got alongside, our boats half full of water; and now came the greatest trouble of all—unloading the boats in a heavy sea, which pitched them about so that it was almost impossible to stand in them, raising them sometimes even with the rail, and again dropping them below the bends. With great difficulty we got all the hides aboard and stowed under hatches, the yard and stay tackles hooked on, and the launch and pinnace hoisted, chocked, and griped. The quarter boats were then hoisted up, and we began heaving in on the chain. Getting the anchor was no easy work in such a sea, but as we were not coming back to this port, the captain determined not to slip. The ship's head pitched into the sea, and the water rushed through the hawseholes, and the chain surged so as almost to unship the barrel of the windlass. "Hove short, sir!" said the mate. "Aye, aye! Weather-bit your chain and loose the topsails! Make sail on her, men—with a will!" A few moments served to loose the topsails, which were furled with reefs, to sheet them home, and hoist them up. "Bear a hand!" was the order of the day; and everyone saw the necessity of it, for the gale was already upon us. The ship broke out her own anchor, which we catted and fished, after a fashion, and were soon close-hauled, under reefed sails, standing off from the lee shore and rocks against a heavy head sea. The fore course was given to her, which helped her a little; but as she hardly held her own against the sea, which was setting her to leeward, "Board the main tack!" shouted the captain, when the tack was carried forward and taken to the windlass, and all hands called to the handspikes. The great sail bellied out horizontally, as though it would lift up the mainstay; the blocks rattled and flew about; but the force of machinery was too much for her. "Heave ho! Heave and pawl! Yo, heave, hearty, ho!" and, in time with the song, by the force of twenty strong arms, the windlass came slowly round, pawl after pawl, and the weather clew of the sail was brought down to the waterways. The starboard watch hauled aft the sheet, and the ship tore through the water like a mad horse, quivering and shaking at every joint, and dashing from her head the foam, which flew off at each blow, yards and *loss of hides = late return*

yards to leeward. A half hour of such sailing served our turn, when the clews of the sail were hauled up, the sail furled, and the ship, eased of her press, went more quietly on her way. Soon after, the foresail was reefed, and we mizzentopmen were sent up to take another reef in the mizzen topsail. This was the first time I had taken a weather earing, and I felt not a little proud to sit astride of the weather yardarm, pass the earing, and sing out, "Haul out to leeward!" From this time until we got to Boston the mate never suffered anyone but our own gang to go upon the mizzen-topsail yard, either for reefing or furling, and the young English lad and I generally took the earings between us.

Having cleared the point and got well out to sea, we squared away the yards, made more sail, and stood on, nearly before the wind, for San Pedro. It blew strong, with some rain, nearly all night, but fell calm toward morning, and the gale having blown itself out, we came to—

*Thursday, October 22nd,* at San Pedro, in the old southeaster berth, a league from shore, with a slip rope on the cable, reefs in the topsails, and rope yarns for gaskets. Here we lay ten days, with the usual boating, hide carrying, rolling of cargo up the steep hill, walking barefooted over stones, and getting drenched in salt water.

The third day after our arrival, the *Rosa* came in from San Juan, where she went the day after the southeaster. Her crew said it was as smooth as a mill pond after the gale, and she took off nearly a thousand hides, which had been brought down for us, and which we lost in consequence of the southeaster. This mortified us: not only that an Italian ship should have got to windward of us in the trade, but because every thousand hides went toward completing the forty thousand which we were to collect before we could say good-bye to California.

While lying here, we shipped one new hand, an Englishman, of about six and twenty years, who was an acquisition, as he proved to be a good sailor, could sing tolerably, and, what was of more importance to me, had a good education and a somewhat remarkable history. He called himself George P. Marsh, professed to have been at sea from a small boy, and to have served his time in the smuggling trade between Germany and the coasts of France and England. Thus he accounted for his knowledge of the French language, which he spoke and read as well as he did English; but his cutter education would not account for his English, which was far too good to have been learned in a smuggler; for he wrote an uncommonly handsome hand, spoke with great correctness, and frequently, when in private talk with me, quoted from books, and a showed knowledge of the customs of society, and particularly of the formalities of the various English courts of law and of Parliament, which surprised me. Still he would give no other account of himself than that he was educated in a smuggler. A man whom we afterward fell in with, who had been a shipmate of George's a few years before, said that he heard, at the boardinghouse from which they shipped, that George had been at a college (probably a naval one, as he knew no Latin or Greek), where he learned French and mathematics. He was not the man by nature that Harris was. Harris had made everything of his mind and character in spite of obstacles; while this man had evidently been born in a different rank, and educated early in life accordingly, but had been a vagabond, and done nothing for himself since. Neither had George the character, strength of mind, or memory of Harris; yet there was about him the remains of a pretty good education, which enabled him to talk quite up to his brains, and a high spirit and amenability to the point of honor which years of a dog's life had not broken. After he had been a little while on board, we learned from him his adventures of the last two years, which we afterward heard confirmed in such a manner as put the truth of them beyond a doubt.

He sailed from New York in the year 1833, if I mistake not, before the mast, in the brig *Lascar*, for Canton. She was sold in the East Indies, and he shipped at Manila, in a small schooner, bound on a trading voyage among the Ladrone and Pelew Islands. On one of the latter islands their schooner was wrecked on a reef, and they were attacked by the natives, and, after a desperate resistance, in which all their number, except the captain, George, and a boy, were killed or drowned, they surrendered, and were carried bound, in a canoe, to a neighboring island. In about a month after this, an opportunity occurred by which one of their number might get away. I have forgotten the circumstances, but only one could go, and they gave way to the captain, upon his promising to send them aid if he escaped. He was successful in his attempt; got on board an American vessel, went back to Manila, and thence to America, without making any effort for their rescue, or, indeed, as George afterward discovered, without even mentioning their case to anyone in Manila. The boy that was with George died, and he being alone, and there being no chance for his escape, the natives soon treated him with kindness, and even with attention. They painted him, tattooed his body (for he would never consent to be marked in the face or hands), gave him two or three wives, and, in fact, made a pet of him. In this way he lived for thirteen months, in a delicious climate, with plenty to eat, half naked, and nothing to do. He soon, however, became tired, and went round the island, on different pretences, to look out for a sail. One day he was out fishing in a small canoe with another man, when he saw a large sail to windward, about a league and a half off, passing abreast of the island and standing westward. With some difficulty, he persuaded the islander to go off with him to the ship, promising to return with a good supply of rum and tobacco. These articles, which the islanders had got a taste of from American traders, were too strong a temptation for the fellow, and he consented. They paddled off in the track in which the ship was bound, and lay to until she came down to them. George stepped on board the ship, nearly naked, painted from head to foot, and in no way distinguishable from his companion until he began to speak. Upon this the people on board were not a little astonished, and, having learned his story, the captain had him washed and clothed, and, sending away the poor astonished native with a knife or two and some tobacco and calico, took George with him on the voyage. This was the ship *Cabot,* of New York, Captain Low. She was bound to Manila, from across the Pacific; and George did seaman's duty in her until her arrival in Manila, when he left her, and shipped in a brig bound to the Sandwich Islands. From Oahu, he came, in the British brig *Clementine,* to Monterey, as second officer, where, having some difficulty with the captain, he left her, and, coming down the coast, joined us at San Pedro. Nearly six months after this, among some papers we received by an arrival from Boston, we found a letter from Captain Low, of the *Cabot,* published immediately upon his arrival at New York, giving all the particulars just as we had them from George. The letter was published for the information of the friends of George, and Captain Low added that he left him at Manila to go to Oahu, and he had heard nothing of him since.

George had an interesting journal of his adventures in the Pelew Islands, which he had written out at length, in a handsome hand, and in correct English.*

# CHAPTER XXV

*Sunday, November 1st.* Sailed this day (Sunday again) for Santa Barbara, where we arrived on the fifth. Coming round Santa Buenaventura, and nearing the anchorage, we saw two vessels in port, a large full-rigged, and a small, hermaphrodite brig. The former, the crew said, must be the *Pilgrim;* but I had been too long in the *Pilgrim* to be mistaken in her, and I was right in differing from them; for, upon nearer

---

* In the spring of 1841, a seafaring man called at my rooms, in Boston, and said he wished to see me, as he knew something about a man I had spoken of in my book. He then told me that he was second mate of the bark *Mary Frazer,* which sailed from Batavia in company with the *Cabot,* bound to Manila, that when off the Pelew Islands they fell in with a canoe with two natives on board, who told them that there was an American ship ahead, out of sight, and that they had put a white man on board of her. The bark gave the canoe a tow for a sort distance. When the *Mary Frazer* arrived at Manila, they found the *Cabot* there; and my informant said that George came on board several times, and told the same story that I had given of him in this book. He said the name of George's schooner was the *Dash,* and that she was wrecked, and attacked by the natives, as George had told me.

This man, whose name was Beauchamp, was second mate of the *Mary Frazer* when she took the missionaries to Oahu. He became religious during the passage, and joined the mission church at Oahu upon his arrival. When I saw him, he was master of a bark.

approach, her long, low, sheer, sharp bows and raking masts told quite another story. "Man-of-war brig," said some of them; "Baltimore clipper," said others; the *Ayacucho*, thought I; and soon the broad folds of the beautiful banner of St. George—white field with blood-red border and cross—were displayed from her peak. A few minutes put it beyond a doubt, and we were lying by the side of the *Ayacucho*, which had sailed from San Diego about nine months before, while we were lying there in the *Pilgrim*. She had since been to Valparaiso, Callao, and the Sandwich Islands, and had just come upon the coast. Her boat came on board, bringing Captain Wilson; and in half an hour the news was all over the ship that there was a war between the United States and France. Exaggerated accounts reached the forecastle. Battles had been fought, a large French fleet was in the Pacific, &c., &c.; and one of the boat's crew of the *Ayacucho* said that, when they left Callao, a large French frigate and the American frigate *Brandywine*, which were lying there, were going outside to have a battle, and that the English frigate *Blonde* was to be umpire, and see fair play. Here was important news for us. Alone, on an unprotected coast, without an American man-of-war within some thousands of miles, and the prospect of a voyage home through the whole length of the Pacific and Atlantic Oceans! A French prison seemed a much more probable place of destination than the good port of Boston. However, we were too salt to believe every yarn that comes into the forecastle, and waited to hear the truth of the matter from higher authority. By means of the supercargo's clerk I got the amount of the matter, which was that the governments had had a difficulty about the payment of a debt; that war had been threatened and prepared for, but not actually declared, although it was pretty generally anticipated. This was not quite so bad, yet was no small cause of anxiety. But we cared very little about the matter ourselves. "Happy go lucky" with Jack! We did not believe that a French prison would be much worse than "hide droghing" on the coast of California; and no one who has not been a long, dull voyage, shut up in one ship, can conceive of the effect of monotony upon one's thoughts and wishes. The prospect of a change is a green spot in the desert, and the probability of great events and exciting scenes creates a feeling of delight, and sets life in motion, so as to give a pleasure which anyone not in the some state would be unable to explain. In fact, a more jovial night we had not passed in the forecastle for months. All seemed in unaccountably high spirits. An undefined anticipation of radical changes, of new scenes and great doings, seemed to have possessed everyone, and the common drudgery of the vessel appeared contemptible. Here was a new vein opened, a grand theme of conversation and a topic for all sorts of discussions. National feeling was wrought up. Jokes were cracked upon the only Frenchman in the ship, and comparisons made between "old horse" and "soup meager," &c., &c.

We remained in uncertainty as to this war for more than two months, when an arrival from the Sandwich Islands brought us the news of an amicable arrangement of the difficulties.

The other vessel which we found in port was the hermaphrodite brig *Avon*, from the Sandwich Islands. She was fitted up in handsome style; fired a gun, and ran her ensign up and down, at sunrise and sunset; had a band of four or five pieces of music on board, and appeared rather like a pleasure yacht than a trader; yet, in connection with the *Loriotte, Clementine, Bolivar, Convoy*, and other small vessels, belonging to sundry Americans at Oahu, she carried on a considerable trade, legal and illegal, in otter skins, silks, teas, &c., as well as hides and tallow.

The second day after our arrival, a full-rigged brig came round the point from the northward, sailed leisurely through the bay, and stood off again for the southeast in the direction of the large island of Catalina. The next day the *Avon* got under way, and stood in the same direction, bound for San Pedro. This might do for marines and Californians, but we knew the ropes too well. The brig was never again seen on the coast, and the *Avon* went into San Pedro in about a week with a replenished cargo of Canton and American goods.

This was one of the means of escaping the heavy duties the Mexicans lay upon all imports. A vessel comes on the coast, enters a moderate cargo at Monterey, which is the only customhouse, and commences trading. In a month or more, having sold a large part of her cargo, she stretches over to Catalina, or other of the large, uninhabited islands which lie off the coast, in a trip from port to port, and supplies herself with choice goods from a vessel from Oahu, which has been lying off and on the islands, waiting for her. Two days after the sailing of the *Avon*, the *Loriotte* came in from the leeward, and without doubt had also a snatch at the brig's cargo.

*Tuesday, November 10th.* Going ashore, as usual, in the gig, just before sundown, to bring off the captain, we found, upon taking in the captain and pulling off again, that our ship, which lay the farthest out, had run up her ensign. This meant "Sail ho!" of course, but as we were within the point we could see nothing. "Give way, boys! Give way! Lay out on your oars, and long stroke!" said the captain; and stretching to the whole length of our arms, bending back again so that our backs touched the thwarts, we sent her through the water like a rocket. A few minutes of such pulling opened the islands, one after another, in range of the point, and gave us a view of the canal, where was a ship, under topgallant sails, standing in, with a light breeze, for the anchorage. Putting the boat's head in the direction of the ship, the captain told us to lay out again; and we needed no spurring, for the prospect of boarding a new ship, perhaps from home, hearing the news, and having something to tell of when we got back, was excitement enough for us, and we gave way with a will. Captain Nye, of the *Loriotte*, who had been an old whaleman, was in the stern sheets, and fell mightily into the spirit of it. "Bend your backs, and break your oars!" said he. "Lay me on, Captain Bunker!" "There she flukes!" and other exclamations current among whalemen. In the meantime it fell flat calm, and, being within a couple of miles of the ship, we expected to board her in a few minutes, when a breeze sprung up, dead ahead for the ship, and she braced up and stood off toward the islands, sharp on the larboard tack, making good way through the water. This, of course, brought us up, and we had only to "ease larboard oars, pull round starboard!" and go aboard the *Alert*, with something very like a flea in the ear. There was a light land breeze all night, and the ship did not come to anchor until the next morning.

As soon as her anchor was down we went aboard, and found her to be the whaleship *Wilmington and Liverpool Packet*, of New Bedford, last from the "offshore ground," with nineteen hundred barrels of oil. A "spouter" we knew her to be, as soon as we saw her, by her cranes and boats, and by her stump topgallant masts, and a certain slovenly look to the sails, rigging, spars, and hull; and when we got on board, we found everything to correspond, spouter fashion. She had a false deck, which was rough and oily, and cut up in every direction by the chimes of oil casks; her rigging was slack, and turning white, paint worn off the spars and blocks, clumsy seizings, straps without covers, and "home-ward-bound splices" in every direction. Her crew, too, were not in much better order. Her captain was a slab-sided Quaker, in a suit of brown, with a broad-brimmed hat, bending his long legs as he moved about decks, with his head down, like a sheep, and the men looked more like fishermen and farmers than they did like sailors.

Though it was by no means cold weather (we having on only our red shirts and duck trousers), they all had on woolen trousers—not blue and shipshape, but of all colors, brown, drab, gray, aye, and *green*—with suspenders over their shoulders, and pockets to put their hands in. This, added to Guernsey frocks, striped comforters about the neck, thick cowhide boots, woolen caps, and a strong, oily smell, and a decidedly green look, will complete the description. Eight or ten were on the fore-topsail yard, and as many more in the main, furling the topsails, while eight or ten were hanging about the forecastle, doing nothing. This was a strange sight for a vessel coming to anchor; so we went up to them, to see what was the matter. One of them, a stout, hearty-looking fellow, held out his leg and said he had the scurvy; another had cut his hand; and others had got nearly well, but said that there were plenty aloft to furl the sails, so they were "sogering" on the forecastle. There was only one "splicer" on board, a fine-looking old tar, who was in the bunt of the fore-topsail. He was probably the only thorough marlinespike seaman in the ship, before the mast. The mates, of course, and the boat steerers, and also two or three of the crew, had been to sea before, but only on whaling voyages; and the greater part of the crew were raw hands, just from the bush, and had not yet got the hayseed out of their hair. The mizzen topsail hung in the buntlines until every-thing was furled forward. Thus a crew of thirty men were half an hour in doing what would have been done in the

*Alert,* with eighteen hands to go aloft, in fifteen or twenty minutes.*

We found they had been at sea six or eight months, and had no news to tell us, so we left them, and promised to get liberty to come on board in the evening for some curiosities. Accordingly, as soon as we were knocked off in the evening and were through supper, we obtained leave, took a boat, and went aboard and spent an hour or two. They gave us pieces of whalebone, and the teeth and other parts of curious sea animals, and we exchanged books with them—a practice very common among ships in foreign ports, by which you get rid of the books you have read and reread, and a supply of new ones in their stead, and Jack is not very nice as to their comparative value.†

*Thursday, November 12th.* This day was quite cool in the early part, and there were black clouds about; but as it was often so in the morning, nothing was apprehended, and all the captains went ashore together to spend the day. Toward noon the clouds hung heavily over the mountains, coming halfway down the hills that encircle the town of Santa Barbara, and a heavy swell rolled in from the southeast. The mate immediately ordered the gig's crew away, and, at the same time, we saw boats pulling ashore from the other vessels. Here was a grand chance for a rowing match, and everyone did his best. We passed the boats of the *Ayacucho* and *Loriotte,* but could not hold our own with the long six-oared boat of the whaleship. They reached the breakers before us; but here we had the advantage of them, for, not being used to the surf, they were obliged to wait to see us beach our boat, just as, in the same place, nearly a year

* I have been told that this description of a whaleman has given offense to the whale-trading people of Nantucket, New Bedford, and the Vineyard. It is not exaggerated; and the appearance of such a ship and crew might well impress a young man trained in the ways of a ship of the style of the *Alert.* Long observation has satisfied me that there are no better seamen, so far as handling a ship is concerned, and none so venturous and skillful navigators, as the masters and officers of our whalemen. But never, either on this voyage, or in a subsequent visit to the Pacific and its islands, was it my fortune to fall in with a whaleship whose appearance, and the appearance of whose crew, gave signs of strictness of discipline and seaman-like neatness. Probably these things are impossibilities, from the nature of the business, and I may have made too much of them.

† This visiting between the crews of ships at sea is called, among whalemen, "gamming."

before, we, in the *Pilgrim*, were glad to be taught by a boat's crew of Kanakas.

We had hardly got the boats beached, and their heads pointed out to sea, before our old friend Bill Jackson, the handsome English sailor, who steered the *Loriotte*'s boat, called out that his brig was adrift; and, sure enough, she was dragging her anchors, and drifting down into the bight of the bay. Without waiting for the captain (for there was no one on board the brig but the mate and steward), he sprung into the boat, called the Kanakas together, and tried to put off. But the Kanakas, though capital water dogs, were frightened by their vessel's being adrift, and by the emergency of the case, and seemed to lose their faculties. Twice their boat filled, and came broadside upon the beach. Jackson swore at them for a parcel of savages, and promised to flog every one of them. This made the matter no better; when we came forward, he told the Kanakas to take their seats in the boat, and, going two on each side, walked out with her till it was up to our shoulders, and gave them a shove, when, giving way with their oars, they got her safely into the long, regular swell. In the meantime, boats had put off to the *Loriotte* from our ship and the whaler, and, coming all on board the brig together, they let go the other anchor, paid out chain, braced the yards to the wind, and brought the vessel up.

In a few minutes, the captains came hurrying down, on the run; and there was no time to be lost, for the gale promised to be a severe one, and the surf was breaking upon the beach, three deep, higher and higher every instant. The *Ayacucho*'s boat, pulled by four Kanakas, put off first, and as they had no rudder or steering oar, would probably never have got off, had we not waded out with them as far as the surf would permit. The next that made the attempt was the whaleboat, for we, being the most experienced "beach-combers," needed no help, and stayed till the last. Whalemen make the best boats' crews in the world for a long pull, but this landing was new to them, and, notwithstanding the examples they had had, they slewed round and were hove up —boat, oars, and men—all together, high and dry upon the sand. The second time they filled, and had to turn their boat over, and set her off again. We could be of no help to them, for they were so many as to be in one another's way, without the addition of our numbers. The third time they got off, though not without shipping a sea which drenched them all, and half filled their boat, keeping them baling until they reached their ship. We now got ready to go off, putting the boat's head out; English Ben and I, who were the largest, standing on each side of the bows to keep her head out to the sea, two more shipping and manning the two after oars, and the captain taking the steering oar. Two or three Mexicans, who stood upon the beach looking at us, wrapped their cloaks about them, shook their heads, and muttered, "*Caramba!*" They had no taste for such doings; in fact, the hydrophobia is a national malady, and shows itself in their persons as well as their actions.

Watching for a "smooth chance," we determined to show the other boats the way it should be done, and, as soon as ours floated, ran out with her, keeping her head out, with all our strength, and the help of the captain's oar, and the two after oarsmen giving way regularly and strongly, until our feet were off the ground, we tumbled into the bows, keeping perfectly still, from fear of hindering the others. For some time it was doubtful how it would go. The boat stood nearly up and down in the water, and the sea, rolling from under her, let her fall upon the water with a force which seemed almost to stave her bottom in. By quietly sliding two oars forward, along the thwarts, without impeding the rowers, we shipped two bow oars, and thus, by the help of four oars and the captain's strong arm, we got safely off, though we shipped several seas, which left us half full of water. We pulled alongside of the *Loriotte*, put her skipper on board, and found her making preparations for slipping, and then pulled aboard our own ship. Here Mr. Brown, always "on hand," had got everything ready, so that we had only to hook on the gig and hoist it up, when the order was given to loose the sails. While we were on the yards, we saw the *Loriotte* under way, and, before our yards were mast-headed, the *Ayacucho* had spread her wings, and, with yards braced sharp up, was standing athwart our hawse. There is no prettier sight in the world than a full-rigged, clipper-built brig, sailing sharp on the wind. In a minute more our slip rope was gone, the head yards filled away, and we were off. Next came the whaler; and in half an hour from the time when four vessels were lying quietly at anchor, without a

rag out, or a sign of motion, the bay was deserted, and four
white clouds were moving over the water to seaward. Being
sure of clearing the point, we stood off with our yards a little
braced in, while the *Ayacucho* went off with a taut bowline,
which brought her to windward of us. During all this day,
and the greater part of the night, we had the usual southeaster entertainment, a gale of wind, with occasional rain,
and finally topped off with a drenching rain of three or four
hours. At daybreak the clouds thinned off and rolled away,
and the sun came up clear. The wind, instead of coming out
from the northward, as is usual, blew steadily and freshly
from the anchoring ground. This was bad for us, for, being
"flying light," with little more than ballast trim, we were in
no condition for showing off on a taut bowline, and had
depended upon a fair wind, with which, by the help of our
light sails and studding sails, we meant to have been the
first at the anchoring ground; but the *Ayacucho* was a good
league to windward of us, and was standing in in fine style.
The whaler, however, was as far to leeward of us, and the
*Loriotte* was nearly out of sight, among the islands, up the
canal. By hauling every brace and bowline, and clapping
watch tackles upon all the sheets and halyards, we managed
to hold our own, and drop the leeward vessels a little in
every tack. When we reached the anchoring ground, the
*Ayacucho* had got her anchor, furled her sails, squared her
yards, and was lying as quietly as if nothing had happened.

We had our usual good luck in getting our anchor without letting go another, and were all snug, with our boats
at the boom ends, in half an hour. In about two hours more
the whaler came in, and made a clumsy piece of work in
getting her anchor, being obliged to let go her best bower,
and, finally, to get out a kedge and a hawser. They were
heave-ho-ing, stopping and unstopping, pawling, catting, and
fishing for three hours; and the sails hung from the yards
all the afternoon, and were not furled until sundown. The
*Loriotte* came in just after dark, and let go her anchor, making no attempt to pick up the other until the next day.

This affair led to a dispute as to the sailing of our ship
and the *Ayacucho*. Bets were made between the captains,
and the crews took it up in their own way; but as she was
bound to leeward and we to windward, and merchant captains cannot deviate, a trial never took place; and perhaps

it was well for us that it did not, for the *Ayacucho* had been eight years in the Pacific, in every part of it—Valparaiso, Sandwich Islands, Canton, California, and all—and was called the fastest merchantman that traded in the Pacific, unless it was the brig *John Gilpin,* and perhaps the ship *Ann McKim,* of Baltimore.

*Saturday, November 14th.* This day we got under way, with the agent and several Mexicans of note, as passengers, bound up to Monterey. We went ashore in the gig to bring them off with their baggage, and found them waiting on the beach, and a little afraid about going off, as the surf was running very high. This was nuts to us, for we liked to have a Mexican wet with salt water; and then the agent was very much disliked by the crew, one and all; and we hoped, as there was no officer in the boat, to have a chance to duck them, for we knew that they were such "marines" that they would not know whether it was our fault or not. Accordingly, we kept the boat so far from shore as to oblige them to wet their feet in getting into her; and then waited for a good high comber, and, letting the head slue a little round, sent the whole force of the sea into the stern sheets, drenching them from head to feet. The Mexicans sprang out of the boat, swore, and shook themselves, and protested against trying it again; and it was with the greatest difficulty that the agent could prevail upon them to make another attempt. The next time we took care, and went off easily enough, and pulled aboard. The crew came to the side to hoist in their baggage, and heartily enjoyed the half-drowned looks of the company.

Everything being now ready, and the passengers aboard, we ran up the ensign and broad pennant (for there was no man-of-war, and we were the largest vessel on the coast), and the other vessels ran up their ensigns. Having hove short, cast off the gaskets, and made the bunt of each sail fast by the jigger, with a man on each yard, at the word the whole canvas of the ship was loosed, and with the greatest rapidity possible everything was sheeted home and hoisted up, the anchor tripped and catheaded, and the ship under headway. We were determined to show the "spouter" how things could be done in a smart ship, with a good crew, though not more than half his numbers. The royal yards were all crossed at once, and royals and skysails set, and, as we had the wind

*Competition among ships*

free, the booms were run out, and all were aloft, active as cats, laying out on the yards and booms, reeving the studding-sail gear; and sail after sail the captain piled upon her, until she was covered with canvas, her sails looking like a great white cloud resting upon a black speck. Before we doubled the point, we were going at a dashing rate, and leaving the shipping far astern. We had a fine breeze to take us through the canal, as they call this bay of forty miles long by ten wide. The breeze died away at night, and we were becalmed all day on Sunday, about halfway between Santa Barbara and Point Conception. Sunday night we had a light, fair wind, which set us up again; and having a fine sea breeze on the first part of Monday we had the prospect of passing, without any trouble, Point Conception, the Cape Horn of California, where, the sailors say, it begins to blow the first of January, and blows until the last of December. Toward the latter part of the afternoon, however, the regular northwest wind, as usual, set in, which brought in our studding sails, and gave us the chance of beating round the Point, which we were now just abreast of, and which stretched off into the Pacific, high, rocky, and barren, forming the central point of the coast for hundreds of miles north and south. A capful of wind will be a bagful here, and before night our royals were furled, and the ship was laboring hard under her topgallant sails. At eight bells our watch went below, leaving her with as much sail as she could stagger under, the water flying over the forecastle at every plunge. It was evidently blowing harder, but then there was not a cloud in the sky, and the sun had gone down bright.

We had been below but a short time, before we had the usual premonitions of a coming gale—seas washing over the whole forward part of the vessel, and her bows beating against them with a force and sound like the driving of piles. The watch, too, seemed very busy trampling about decks, and singing out at the ropes. A sailor can tell, by the sound, what sail is coming in; and, in a short time, we heard the top-gallant sails come in, one after another, and then the flying jib. This seemed to ease her a good deal, and we were fast going off to the land of Nod, when, *bang, bang, bang* on the scuttle, and "All hands, reef topsails, ahoy!" started us out of our berths; and, it not being very cold weather, we had nothing extra to put on, and were soon on deck. I shall never forget the fineness of the sight. It was a clear, and rather a chilly night; the stars were twinkling with an intense brightness, and as far as the eye could reach there was not a cloud to be seen. The horizon met the sea in a defined line. A painter could not have painted so clear a sky. There was not a speck upon it. Yet it was blowing great guns from the northwest. When you can see a cloud to windward, you feel that there is a place for the wind to come from; but here it seemed to come from nowhere. No person could have told from the heavens, by their eyesight alone, that it was not a still summer's night. One reef after another, we took in the topsails, and before we could get them hoisted up we heard a sound like a short, quick rattling of thunder, and the jib was blown to atoms out of the boltrope. We got the topsails set, and the fragments of the jib stowed away, and the fore-topmast staysail set in its place, when the great mainsail gaped open, and the sail ripped from head to foot. "Lay up on that main yard and furl the sail, before it blows to tatters!" shouted the captain; and in a moment we were up, gathering the remains of it upon the yard. We got it wrapped round the yard, and passed gaskets over it as snugly as possible, and were just on deck again, when, with another loud rent, which was heard throughout the ship, the fore-topsail, which had been double-reefed, split in two athwart-ships, just below the reef band, from earing to earing. Here again it was: down yard, haul out reef tackles, and lay out upon the yard for reefing. By hauling the reef tackles chock-ablock we took the strain from the other earings, and passing the close-reef earing, and knotting the points carefully, we succeeded in setting the sail, close-reefed.

We had but just got the rigging coiled up, and were waiting to hear, "Go below, the watch!" when the main royal worked loose from the gaskets, and blew directly out to lee-ward, flapping, and shaking the mast like a wand. Here was a job for somebody. The royal must come in or be cut adrift, or the mast would be snapped short off. All the light hands in the starboard watch were sent up one after another, but they could do nothing with it. At length, John, the tall French-man, the head of the starboard watch (and a better sailor never stepped upon a deck), sprang aloft, and, by the help of his long arms and legs, succeeded, after a hard struggle —the sail blowing over the yardarm to leeward, and the

skysail adrift directly over his head—in smothering it and
frapping it with long pieces of sennit. He came very near
being blown or shaken from the yard several times, but he
was a true sailor, every finger a fish hook. Having made the
sail snug, he prepared to send the yard down, which was a
long and difficult job; for, frequently, he was obliged to stop,
and hold on with all his might for several minutes, the ship
pitching so as to make it impossible to do anything else at
that height. The yard at length came down safe, and, after
it, the fore and mizzen royal yards were sent down. All hands
were then sent aloft, and for an hour or two we were hard
at work, making the booms well fast, unreeving the studding-
sail and royal and skysail gear, getting rolling ropes on the
yard, setting up the weather breast backstays, and making
other preparations for a storm. It was a fine night for a
gale; just cool and bracing enough for quick work, without
being cold, and as bright as day. It was sport to have a gale
in such weather as this. Yet it blew like a hurricane. The
wind seemed to come with a spite, an edge to it, which
threatened to scrape us off the yards. The force of the wind
was greater than I had ever felt it before; but darkness, cold,
and wet are the worst parts of a storm, to a sailor.

Having got on deck again, we looked round to see what
time of night it was, and whose watch. In a few minutes
the man at the wheel struck four bells, and we found that
the other watch was out, and our own half out. Accordingly,
the starboard watch went below, and left the ship to us for
a couple of hours, yet with orders to stand by for a call.

Hardly had they got below, before away went the fore-
topmast staysail, blown to ribands. This was a small sail,
which we could manage in the watch, so that we were not
obliged to call up the other watch. We laid out upon the bowsprit, where we were under water half the time, and took
in the fragments of the sail, and, as she must have some
headsail on her, prepared to bend another staysail. We got
the new one out into the nettings; seized on the tack, sheets,
and halyards, and the hanks; manned the halyards, cut adrift
the frapping lines, and hoisted away; but before it was halfway up the stay it was blown all to pieces. When we belayed
the halyards, there was nothing left but the boltrope. Now
large eyes began to show themselves in the foresail, and,
knowing that it must soon go, the mate ordered us upon the

yard to furl it. Being unwilling to call up the watch who
had been on deck all night, he roused out the carpenter, sailmaker, cook, and steward, and with their help we manned
the foreyard, and, after nearly half an hour's struggle mas-
tered the sail, and got it well furled round the yard. The
force of the wind had never been greater than at this moment.
In going up the rigging, it seemed absolutely to pin us down
to the shrouds; and, on the yard, there was no such thing
as turning a face to windward. Yet here was no driving sleet,
and darkness, and wet, and cold, as off Cape Horn; and
instead of stiff oilcloth suits, southwester caps, and thick
boots, we had on hats, round jackets, duck trousers, light
shoes, and everything light and easy. These things make a
great difference to a sailor. When we got on deck, the man
at the wheel struck eight bells (four o'clock in the morning),
and "All Starbowlines, ahoy!" brought the other watch up,
but there was no going below for us. The gale was now at
its height, "blowing like scissors and thumbscrews"; the
captain was on deck; the ship, which was light, rolling and
pitching as though she would shake the long sticks out of
her, and the sails were gaping open and splitting in every
direction. The mizzen topsail, which was a comparatively
new sail, and close-reefed, split from head to foot, in the
bunt; the fore-topsail went, in one rent, from clew to earing,
and was blowing to tatters; one of the chain bobstays parted;
the spritsail yard sprung in the slings; the martingale had
slued away off to leeward; and, owing to the long dry weather,
the lee rigging hung in large bights at every lurch. One of
the main-topgallant shrouds had parted; and, to crown all,
the galley had got adrift, and gone over to leeward, and the
anchor on the lee bow had worked loose, and was thumping
the side. Here was work enough for all hands for half a
day. Our gang laid out on the mizzen-topsail yard, and after
more than half an hour's hard work, furled the sail, though
it bellied out over our heads, and again, by a slat of the wind,
blew in under the yard with a fearful jerk, and almost threw
us off from the footropes.

Double gaskets were passed round the yards, rolling tackles
and other gear boused taut, and everything made as secure
as it could be. Coming down, we found the rest of the crew
just coming down the forerigging, having furled the tattered
topsail, or, rather, swathed it round the yard, which looked

like a broken limb, bandaged. There was no sail now on the
ship but the spanker and the close-reefed main topsail, which
still held good. But this was too much after sail, and order
was given to furl the spanker. The brails were hauled up,
and all the light hands in the starboard watch sent out on
the gaff to pass the gaskets; but they could do nothing with
it. The second mate swore at them for a parcel of "sogers,"
and sent up a couple of the best men; but they could do no
better, and the gaff was lowered down. All hands were now
employed in setting up the lee rigging, fishing the spritsail
yard, lashing the galley, and getting tackles upon the martingale, to bouse it to windward. Being in the larboard watch,
my duty was forward, to assist in setting up the martingale.
Three of us were out on the martingale guys and backropes
for more than half an hour, carrying out, hooking and un-
hooking the tackles, several times buried in the seas, until
the mate ordered us in, from fear of our being washed off.
The anchors were then to be taken up on the rail, which
kept all hands on the forecastle for an hour, though every
now and then the seas broke over it, washing the rigging off
to leeward, filling the lee scuppers breast-high, and washing
chock aft to the taffrail.

Having got everything secure again, we were promising
ourselves some breakfast, for it was now nearly nine o'clock
in the forenoon, when the main topsail showed evident signs
of giving way. Some sail must be kept on the ship, and the
captain ordered the fore and main spencer gaffs to be lowered
down, and the two spencers (which were storm sails, brand-
new, small, and made of the strongest canvas) to be got
up and bent; leaving the main topsail to blow away, with
a blessing on it, if it would only last until we could set the
spencers. These we bent on very carefully, with strong
robands and seizings, and, making tackles fast to the clews,
boused them down to the waterways. By this time the main
topsail was among the things that have been, and we went
aloft to stow away the remnant of the last sail of all those
which were on the ship twenty-four hours before. The
spencers were now the only whole sails on the ship, and,
being strong and small, and near the deck, presenting but
little surface to the wind above the rail, promised to hold
out well. Hove to under these, and eased by having no sail

above the tops, the ship rose and fell, and drifted off to lee-ward like a line-of-battle ship.

It was now eleven o'clock, and the watch was sent below to get breakfast, and at eight bells (noon), as everything was snug, although the gale had not in the least abated, the watch was set, and the other watch and idlers sent below. For three days and three nights the gale continued with un-abated fury, and with singular regularity. There were no lulls, and very little variation in its fierceness. Our ship, being light, rolled so as almost to send the fore yardarm under water, and drifted off bodily to leeward. All this time there was not a cloud to be seen in the sky, day or night; no, not so large as a man's hand. Every morning the sun rose cloudless from the sea, and set again at night in the sea, in a flood of light. The stars, too, came out of the blue one after another, night after night, unobscured, and twinkled as clear as on a still, frosty night at home, until the day came upon them. All this time the sea was rolling in im-mense surges, white with foam, as far as the eye could reach, on every side, for we were now leagues and leagues from shore.

The between decks being empty, several of us slept there in hammocks, which are the best things in the world to sleep in during a storm; it not being true of them, as it is of another kind of bed, "when the wind blows the cradle will rock"; for it is the ship that rocks, while they hang vertically from the beams. During these seventy-two hours we had nothing to do but to turn in and out, four hours on deck, and four below, eat, sleep, and keep watch. The watches were only varied by taking the helm in turn, and now and then by one of the sails, which were furled, blowing out of the gaskets, and getting adrift, which sent us up on the yards, and by getting tackles on different parts of the rigging, which were slack. Once the wheel rope parted, which might have been fatal to us, had not the chief mate sprung instantly with a relieving tackle to windward, and kept the tiller up, till a new rope could be rove. On the morning of the twen-tieth, at daybreak, the gale had evidently done its worst, and had somewhat abated; so much so that all hands were called to bend new sails, although it was still blowing as hard as two common gales. One at a time, and with great difficulty and labor, the old sails were unbent and sent down by the buntlines, and three new topsails, made for the homeward passage round Cape Horn, which had never been bent, were got up from the sail room, and, under the care of the sail-maker, were fitted for bending, and sent up by the halyards into the tops, and, with stops and frapping lines, were bent to the yards, close-reefed, sheeted home, and hoisted. These were bent one at a time, and with the greatest care and difficulty. Two spare courses were then got up and bent in the same manner and furled, and a storm jib, with the bonnet off, bent and furled to the boom. It was twelve o'clock before we got through, and five hours of more exhausting labor I never experienced; and no one of that ship's crew, I will venture to say, will ever desire again to unbend and bend five large sails in the teeth of a tremendous northwester. Toward night a few clouds appeared in the horizon, and, as the gale moderated, the usual appearance of driving clouds relieved the face of the sky. The fifth day after the commencement of the storm, we shook a reef out of each topsail, and set the reefed foresail, jib, and spanker, but it was not until after eight days of reefed topsails that we had a whole sail on the ship, and then it was quite soon enough, for the captain was anxious to make up for leeway, the gale having blown us half the distance to the Sandwich Islands.

Inch by inch, as fast as the gale would permit, we made sail on the ship, for the wind still continued ahead, and we had many days' sailing to get back to the longitude we were in when the storm took us. For eight days more we beat to windward under a stiff topgallant breeze, when the wind shifted and became variable. A light southeaster, to which we could carry a reefed topmast studding sail, did wonders for our dead reckoning.

*Friday, December 4th.* After a passage of twenty days, we arrived at the mouth of the bay of San Francisco.

# CHAPTER XXVI

Our place of destination had been Monterey, but as we were to the northward of it when the wind hauled ahead, we made a fair wind for San Francisco. This large bay, which lies in latitude 37° 58', was discovered by Sir Francis Drake, and by him represented to be (as indeed it is) a magnificent bay, containing several good harbors, great depth of water, and surrounded by a fertile and finely wooded country. About thirty miles from the mouth of the bay, and on the southeast side, is a high point, upon which the presidio is built. Behind this point is the little harbor, or bight, called Yerba Buena, in which trading vessels anchor, and, near it, the Mission of Dolores. There was no other habitation on this side of the bay, except a shanty of rough boards put up by a man named Richardson, who was doing a little trading between the vessels and the Indians.* Here, at anchor, and the only vessel, was a brig under Russian colors, from Sitka, in Russian America, which had come down to winter, and to take in a supply of tallow and grain, great quantities of which latter article are raised in the missions at the head of the bay. The second day after our arrival we went on board the brig, it being Sunday, as a matter of curiosity; and there was enough there to gratify it. Though no larger than the *Pilgrim*, she had five or six officers, and a crew of between twenty and thirty; and such a stupid and greasy-looking set I never saw before. Although it was quite comfortable weather and we had nothing on but straw hats, shirts, and duck trousers, and were barefooted, they had, every man of them, double-soled boots, coming up to the knees, and well greased; thick woolen trousers, frocks, waistcoats, pea jackets, woolen caps, and everything in true Novaya Zemlya rig; and in the warmest days they made no change. The clothing of one of these men would weigh nearly as much as that of half our crew. They had brutish faces, looked like the antipodes of sailors, and apparently dealt in nothing but grease. They lived upon grease; ate it, drank

* The next year Richardson built a one-story adobe house on the same spot, which was long afterward known as the oldest house in the great city of San Francisco.

it, slept in the midst of it, and their clothes were covered with it. To a Russian, grease is the greatest luxury. They looked with greedy eyes upon the tallow bags as they were taken into the vessel, and, no doubt, would have eaten one up whole, had not the officer kept watch over it. The grease appeared to fill their pores, and to come out in their hair and on their faces. It seems as if it were this saturation which makes them stand cold and rain so well. If they were to go into a warm climate, they would melt and die of the scurvy.

The vessel was no better than the crew. Everything was in the oldest and most inconvenient fashion possible: running trusses and lifts on the yards, and large hawser cables, coiled all over the decks, and served and parceled in all directions. The topmasts, topgallant masts, and studding-sail booms were nearly black for want of scraping, and the decks would have turned the stomach of a man-of-war's-man. The galley was down in the forecastle; and there the crew lived, in the midst of the steam and grease of the cooking, in a place as hot as an oven, and apparently never cleaned out. Five minutes in the forecastle was enough for us, and we were glad to get into the open air. We made some trade with them, buying Indian curiosities, of which they had a great number; such as beadwork, feathers of birds, fur moccasins, &c. I purchased a large robe, made of the skins of some animal, dried and sewed nicely together, and covered all over on the outside with thick downy feathers, taken from the breasts of various birds, and arranged with their different colors so as to make a brilliant show.

A few days after our arrival the rainy season set in, and for three weeks it rained almost every hour, without cessation. This was bad for our trade, for the collecting of hides is managed differently in this port from what it is in any other on the coast. The Mission of Dolores, near the anchorage, has no trade at all; but those of San José, Santa Clara, and others situated on the large creeks or rivers which run into the bay, and distant between fifteen and forty miles from the anchorage, do a greater business in hides than any in California. Large boats, or launches, manned by Indians, and capable of carrying from five to six hundred hides apiece, are attached to the missions, and sent down to the vessels with hides, to bring away goods in return. Some of the crews of the vessels are obliged to go and come in the boats, to look out for the hides and goods. These are favorite expeditions with the sailors in fine weather; but now, to be gone three or four days, in open boats, in constant rain, without any shelter, and with cold food, was hard service. Two of our men went up to Santa Clara in one of these boats, and were gone three days, during all which time they had a constant rain, and did not sleep a wink, but passed three long nights walking fore and aft the boat, in the open air. When they got on board they were completely exhausted, and took a watch below of twelve hours. All the hides, too, that came down in the boats were soaked with water, and unfit to put below, so that we were obliged to trice them up to dry, in the intervals of sunshine or wind, upon all parts of the vessel. We got up tricing lines from the jib-boom end to each arm of the foreyard, and thence to the main and crossjack yardarms. Between the tops, too, and the mast-heads, from the fore to the main swifters, and thence to the mizzen rigging, and in all directions athwartships, tricing lines were run, and strung with hides. The head stays and guys and the spritsail yard were lined, and, having still more, we got out the swinging booms, and strung them and the forward and after guys with hides. The rail, fore and aft, the windlass, capstan, the sides of the ship, and every vacant place on deck were covered with wet hides, on the least sign of an interval for drying. Our ship was nothing but a mass of hides, from the catharpings to the water's edge, and from the jib-boom end to the taffrail.

One cold, rainy evening, about eight o'clock, I received orders to get ready to start for San José at four the next morning, in one of these Indian boats, with four days' provisions. I got my oilcloth clothes, southwester, and thick boots ready, and turned into my hammock early, determined to get some sleep in advance, as the boat was to be alongside before daybreak. I slept on till all hands were called in the morning; for, fortunately for me, the Indians, intentionally or from mistaking their orders, had gone off alone in the night, and were far out of sight. Thus I escaped three or four days of very uncomfortable service.

Four of our men, a few days afterward, went up in one of the quarter boats to Santa Clara, to carry the agent, and remained out all night in a drenching rain, in the small boat, in which there was not room for them to turn round;

*Angel Island = wood*

the agent having gone up to the mission and left the men to their fate, making no provision for their accommodation, and not even sending them anything to eat. After this they had to pull thirty miles, and when they got on board were so stiff that they could not come up the gangway ladder. This filled up the measure of the agent's unpopularity, and never after this could he get anything done for him by the crew; and many a delay and vexation, and many a good ducking in the surf, did he get to pay up old scores, or "square the yards with the bloody quill driver."

Having collected nearly all the hides that were to be procured, we began our preparations for taking in a supply of wood and water, for both of which San Francisco is the best place on the coast. A small island, about two leagues from the anchorage, called by us Wood Island, and by the Mexicans Isla de los Angeles, was covered with trees to the water's edge; and to this two of our crew, who were Kennebec men, and could handle an ax like a plaything, were sent every morning to cut wood, with two boys to pile it up for them. In about a week they had cut enough to last us a year, and the third mate, with myself and three others, were sent over in a large, schooner-rigged open launch, which we had hired of the mission, to take in the wood, and bring it to the ship. We left the ship about noon, but owing to a strong head wind, and a tide which here runs four or five knots, did not get into the harbor, formed by two points of the island, where the boats lie, until sundown. No sooner had we come to, than a strong southeaster, which had been threatening us all day, set in, with heavy rain and a chilly air. We were in rather a bad situation: an open boat, a heavy rain, and a long night; for in winter, in this latitude, it was dark nearly fifteen hours. Taking a small skiff which we had brought with us, we went ashore, but discovered no shelter, for everything was open to the rain; and, collecting a little wood, which we found by lifting up the leaves and brush, and a few mussels, we put aboard again, and made the best preparations in our power for passing the night. We unbent the mainsail, and formed an awning with it over the after part of the boat, made a bed of wet logs of wood, and, with our jackets on, lay down, about six o'clock, to sleep. Finding the rain running down upon us, and our jackets getting wet through, and the rough, knotty logs rather indifferent couches, we turned out; and, taking an iron pan which we brought with us, we wiped it out dry, put some stones around it, cut the wet bark from some sticks, and, striking a light, made a small fire in the pan. Keeping some sticks near to dry, and covering the whole over with a roof of boards, we kept up a small fire, by which we cooked our mussels, and ate them, rather for an occupation than from hunger. Still it was not ten o'clock, and the night was long before us, when one of the party produced an old pack of Spanish cards from his monkey-jacket pocket, which we hailed as a great windfall; and, keeping a dim, flickering light by our fagots, we played game after game, till one or two o'clock, when, becoming really tired, we went to our logs again, one sitting up at a time, in turn, to keep watch over the fire. Toward morning the rain ceased, and the air became sensibly colder, so that we found sleep impossible, and sat up, watching for daybreak. No sooner was it light than we went ashore, and began our preparations for loading our vessel. We were not mistaken in the coldness of the weather, for a white frost was on the ground, and—a thing we had never seen before in California—one or two little puddles of fresh water were skimmed over with a thin coat of ice. In this state of the weather, and before sunrise, in the gray of the morning, we had to wade off, nearly up to our hips in water, to load the skiff with the wood by armfuls. The third mate remained on board the launch, two more men stayed in the skiff to load and manage it, and all the water work, as usual, fell upon the two youngest of us; and there we were with frost on the ground, wading forward and back, from the beach to the boat, with armfuls of wood, barefooted, and our trousers rolled up. When the skiff went off with her load, we could only keep our feet from freezing by racing up and down the beach on the hard sand, as fast as we could go. We were all day at this work, and toward sundown, having loaded the vessel as deep as she would bear, we hove up our anchor and made sail, beating out of the bay. No sooner had we got into the large bay than we found a strong tide setting us out to seaward, a thick fog which prevented our seeing the ship, and a breeze too light to set us against the tide, for we were as deep as a sand barge. By the utmost exertions, we saved ourselves from being carried out to sea, and were glad to reach the leewardmost point of the island, where we came to, and prepared to pass another night, more uncomfortable than the first, for we were loaded up to the gunwale, and had only a choice among logs and sticks for a resting place. The next morning we made sail at slack water, with a fair wind, and got on board by eleven o'clock, when all hands were turned to to unload and stow away the wood, which took till night.

Having now taken in all our wood, the next morning a water party was ordered off with all the casks. From this we escaped, having had a pretty good siege with the wooding. The water party were gone three days, during which time they narrowly escaped being carried out to sea, and passed one day on an island, where one of them shot a deer, great numbers of which overrun the islands and hills of San Francisco Bay.

While not off on these wood and water parties, or up the rivers to the missions, we had easy times on board the ship. We were moored, stem and stern, within a cable's length of the shore, safe from southeasters, and with little boating to do; and, as it rained nearly all the time, awnings were put over the hatchways, and all hands sent down between decks, where we were at work, day after day, picking oakum, until we got enough to calk the ship all over, and to last the whole voyage. Then we made a whole suit of gaskets for the voyage home, a pair of wheel ropes from strips of green hide, great quantities of spun yarn, and everything else that could be made between decks. It being now midwinter and in high latitude, the nights were very long, so that we were not turned to until seven in the morning, and were obliged to knock off at five in the evening, when we got supper; which gave us nearly three hours before eight bells, at which time the watch was set.

As we had now been about a year on the coast, it was time to think of the voyage home; and, knowing that the last two or three months of our stay would be very busy ones, and that we should never have so good an opportunity to work for ourselves as the present, we all employed our evenings in making clothes for the passage home, and more especially for Cape Horn. As soon as supper was over and the kids cleared away, and each man had taken his smoke, we seated ourselves on our chests round the lamp, which swung from a beam, and went to work each in his own way, some making hats, others trousers, others jackets, &c., &c., and no one was idle. The boys who could not sew well enough to make their own clothes laid up grass into sennit for the men, who sewed for them in return. Several of us clubbed together and bought a large piece of twilled cotton, which we made into trousers and jackets, and, giving them several coats of linseed oil, laid them by for Cape Horn. I also sewed and covered a tarpaulin hat, thick and strong enough to sit upon, and made myself a complete suit of flannel underclothing for bad weather. Those who had no southwester caps made them; and several of the crew got up for themselves tarpaulin jackets and trousers, lined on the inside with flannel. Industry was the order of the day, and everyone did something for himself; for we knew that as the season advanced, and we went further south, we should have no evenings to work in.

*Friday, December 25th.* This day was Christmas; and, as it rained all day long, and there were no hides to take in, and nothing especial to do, the captain gave us a holiday (the first we had had, except Sundays, since leaving Boston), and plum duff for dinner. The Russian brig, following the Old Style, had celebrated their Christmas eleven days before, when they had a grand blowout, and (as our men said) drank, in the forecastle, a barrel of gin, ate up a bag of tallow, and made a soup of the skin.

*Sunday, December 27th.* We had now finished all our business at this port, and, it being Sunday, we unmoored ship and got under way, firing a salute to the Russian brig, and another to the presidio, which were both answered. The *comandante* of the presidio, Don Guadalupe Vallejo, a young man, and the most popular, among the Americans and English, of any man in California, was on board when we got under way. He spoke English very well, and was suspected of being favorably inclined to foreigners.

We sailed down this magnificent bay with a light wind, the tide, which was running out, carrying us at the rate of four or five knots. It was a fine day; the first of entire sunshine we had had for more than a month. We passed directly under the high cliff on which the presidio is built, and stood into the middle of the bay, from whence we could see small bays making up into the interior, large and beautifully wooded islands, and the mouths of several small rivers. If California ever be-

*Future of SF.*

comes a prosperous country, this bay will be the center of its prosperity. The abundance of wood and water; the extreme fertility of its shores; the excellence of its climate, which is as near to being perfect as any in the world; and its facilities for navigation, affording the best anchoring grounds in the whole western coast of America—all fit it for a place of great importance.

The tide leaving us, we came to anchor near the mouth of the bay, under a high and beautifully sloping hill, upon which herds of hundreds and hundreds of red deer, and the stag, with his high branching antlers, were bounding about, looking at us for a moment, and then starting off, affrighted at the noises which we made for the purpose of seeing the variety of their beautiful attitudes and motions.

At midnight, the tide having turned, we hove up our anchor and stood out of the bay, with a fine starry heaven above us, the first we had seen for many weeks. Before the light northerly winds, which blow here with the regularity of trades, we worked slowly along, and made Point Año Nuevo, the northerly point of the Bay of Monterey, on Monday afternoon. We spoke, going in, the brig *Diana,* of the Sandwich Islands, from the northwest coast, last from Sitka. She was off the point at the same time with us, but did not get in to the anchoring ground until an hour or two after us. It was ten o'clock on Tuesday morning when we came to anchor. Monterey looked just as it did when I saw it last, which was eleven months before, in the brig *Pilgrim.* The pretty lawn on which it stands, as green as sun and rain could make it; the pine wood on the south; the small river on the north side; the adobe houses, with their white walls and red-tiled roofs, dotted about on the green; the low, white presidio, with its soiled tricolored flag flying, and the discordant din of drums and trumpets of the noon parade—all brought up the scene we had witnessed here with so much pleasure nearly a year before, when coming from a long voyage, and from our unprepossessing reception at Santa Barbara. It seemed almost like coming to a home.

# CHAPTER XXVII

The only other vessel in the port was a Russian government bark from Sitka, mounting eight guns (four of which we found to be Quakers), and having on board the ex-governor, who was going in her to Mazatlán, and thence overland to Vera Cruz. He offered to take letters, and deliver them to the American consul at Vera Cruz, whence they could be easily forwarded to the United States. We accordingly made up a packet of letters, almost everyone writing, and dating them "January 1st, 1836." The governor was true to his promise, and they all reached Boston before the middle of March; the shortest communication ever yet made across the country.

The brig *Pilgrim* had been lying in Monterey through the latter part of November, according to orders, waiting for us. Day after day Captain Faucon went up to the hill to look out for us, and at last gave us up, thinking we must have gone down in the gale which we experienced off Point Conception, and which had blown with great fury over the whole coast, driving ashore several vessels in the snuggest ports. An English brig, which had put into San Francisco, lost both her anchors, the *Rosa* was driven upon a mudbank in San Diego, and the *Pilgrim*, with great difficulty, rode out the gale in Monterey, with three anchors ahead. She sailed early in December for San Diego and *intermedios*.

As we were to be here over Sunday, and Monterey was the best place to go ashore on the whole coast, and we had had no liberty day for nearly three months, everyone was for going ashore. On Sunday morning, as soon as the decks were washed, and we were through breakfast, those who had obtained liberty began to clean themselves, as it is called, to go ashore. Buckets of fresh water, cakes of soap, large coarse towels—and we went to work scrubbing one another, on the forecastle. Having gone through this, the next thing was to step into the head, one on each side, with a bucket apiece, and duck one another, by drawing up water and heaving over each other, while we were stripped to a pair of trousers. Then came the rigging-up. The usual outfit of pumps, white stockings, loose white duck trousers, blue jackets, clean

*dressing up*

checked shirts, black kerchiefs, hats well varnished, with a fathom of black ribbon over the left eye, a silk handkerchief flying from the outside jacket pocket, and four or five dollars tied up in the back of the neckerchief, and we were "all right." One of the quarter boats pulled us ashore, and we streamed up to the town. I tried to find the church, in order to see the worship, but was told that there was no service, except a mass early in the morning; so we went about the town, visiting the Americans and English, and the Mexicans whom we had known when we were here before. Toward noon we procured horses, and rode out to the Carmel Mission, which is about a league from the town, where we got something in the way of a dinner—beef, eggs, frijoles, tortillas, and some middling wine—from the *mayordomo,* who, of course, refused to make any charge, as it was the Lord's gift, yet received our present, as a gratuity, with a low bow, a touch of the hat, and *"Diós se lo pague!"*

After this repast we had a fine run, scouring the country on our fleet horses, and came into town soon after sundown. Here we found our companions, who had refused to go to ride with us, thinking that a sailor has no more business with a horse than a fish has with a balloon. They were moored, stem and stern, in a grogshop, making a great noise, with a crowd of Indians and hungry half-breeds about them, and with a fair prospect of being stripped and dirked, or left to pass the night in the *calabozo.* With a great deal of trouble we managed to get them down to the boats, though not without many angry looks and interferences from the Mexicans, who had marked them out for their prey. The *Diana*'s crew—a set of worthless outcasts, who had been picked up at the islands from the refuse of whaleships—were all as drunk as beasts, and had a set-to on the beach with their captain, who was in no better state than themselves. They swore they would not go aboard, and went back to the town, were robbed and beaten, and lodged in the *calabozo,* until the next day, when the captain brought them out. Our forecastle, as usual after a liberty day, was a scene of tumult all night long, from the drunken ones. They had just got to sleep toward morning, when they were turned up with the rest, and kept at work, all day in the water, carrying hides, their heads aching so that they could hardly stand. This is sailor's pleasure.

Nothing worthy of remark happened while we were here,

except a little boxing match on board our own ship, which
gave us something to talk about. Our broad-backed, big-
headed Cape Cod boy, about sixteen years old, had been
playing the bully, for the whole voyage, over a slender, deli-
cate-looking boy from one of the Boston schools, and over
whom he had much the advantage in strength, age, and experience in the ship's duty, for this was the first time the Boston
boy had been on salt water. The latter, however, had "picked
up his crumbs," was learning his duty, and getting strength
and confidence daily, and began to assert his rights against
his oppressor. Still, the other was his master, and, by his
superior strength, always tackled with him and threw him
down. One afternoon, before we were turned to, these boys
got into a violent squabble in the between decks, when George
(the Boston boy) said he would fight Nat if he could have
fair play. The chief mate heard the noise, dove down the
hatchway, hauled them both up on deck, and told them to
shake hands and have no more trouble for the voyage, or
else they should fight till one gave in for beaten. Finding
neither willing to make an offer of reconciliation, he called
all hands up (for the captain was ashore, and he could do
as he chose aboard), ranged the crew in the waist, marked a
line on the deck, brought the two boys up to it, making them
"toe the mark"; then made the bight of a rope fast to a belaying pin, and stretched it across the deck, bringing it just above
their waists. "No striking below the rope!" And there they
stood, one on each side of it, face to face, and went at it like
two gamecocks. The Cape Cod boy, Nat, put in his double-
fisters, starting the blood, and bringing the black-and-blue
spots all over the face and arms of the other, whom we expected to see give in every moment; but, the more he was
hurt, the better he fought. Again and again he was knocked
nearly down, but up he came again and faced the mark, as
bold as a lion, again to take the heavy blows, which sounded
so as to make one's heart turn with pity for him. At length
he came up to the mark for the last time, his shirt torn from
his body, his face covered with blood and bruises, and his
eyes flashing fire, and swore he would stand there until one
or the other was killed, and set to like a young fury. "Hurrah in the bow!" said the men, cheering him on. "Never say
die, while there's a shot in the locker!" Nat tried to close with
him, knowing his advantage, but the mate stopped that, say-

ing there should be fair play, and no fingering. Nat then came up to the mark, but looked white about the mouth, and his blows were not given with half the spirit of his first. Something was the matter. I was not sure whether he was cowed, or, being good-natured, he did not care to beat the boy any more. At all events he faltered. He had always been master, and had nothing to gain and everything to lose; while the other fought for honor and freedom, and under a sense of wrong. It was soon over. Nat gave in—apparently not much hurt—and never afterward tried to act the bully over the boy. We took George forward, washed him in the deck tub, complimented his pluck, and from this time he became somebody on board, having fought himself into notice. Mr. Brown's plan had a good effect, for there was no more quarreling among the boys for the rest of the voyage.

*Wednesday, January 6th, 1836.* Set sail from Monterey, with a number of Mexicans as passengers, and shaped our course for Santa Barbara. The *Diana* went out of the bay in company with us, but parted from us off Point Pinos, being bound to the Sandwich Islands. We had a smacking breeze for several hours, and went along at a great rate until night, when it died away, as usual, and the land breeze set in, which brought us upon a taut bowline. Among our passengers was a young man who was a good representation of a decayed gentleman. He reminded me much of some of the characters in *Gil Blas*. He was of the aristocracy of the country, his family being of pure Spanish blood, and once of considerable importance in Mexico. His father had been governor of the province, and, having amassed a large property, settled at San Diego, where he built a large house with a courtyard in front, kept a retinue of Indians, and set up for the grandee of that part of the country. His son was sent to Mexico, where he received an education, and went into the first society of the capital. Misfortune, extravagance, and the want of any manner of getting interest on money soon ate the estate up, and Don Juan Bandini returned from Mexico, accomplished, poor, and proud, and without any office or occupation, to lead the life of most young men of the better families— dissipated and extravagant when the means are at hand; ambitious at heart, and impotent in act; often pinched for bread; keeping up an appearance of style, when their poverty is known to each half-naked Indian boy in the street, and standing in dread of every small trader and shopkeeper in the place. He had a slight and elegant figure, moved gracefully, danced and waltzed beautifully, spoke good Castilian, with a pleasant and refined voice and accent, and had, throughout, the bearing of a man of birth and figure. Yet here he was, with his passage given him (as I afterward learned), for he had not the means of paying for it, and living upon the charity of our agent. He was polite to everyone, spoke to the sailors, and gave four reals—I dare say the last he had in his pocket—to the steward, who waited upon him. I could not but feel pity for him, especially when I saw him by the side of his fellow-passenger and townsman, a fat, coarse, vulgar, pretentious fellow of a Yankee trader, who had made money in San Diego, and was eating out the vitals of the Bandinis, fattening upon their extravagance, grinding them in their poverty, having mortgages on their lands, forestalling their cattle, and already making an inroad upon their jewels, which were their last hope.

Don Juan had with him a retainer, who was as much like many of the characters in *Gil Blas* as his master. He called himself a private secretary, though there was no writing for him to do, and he lived in the steerage with the carpenter and sailmaker. He was certainly a character; could read and write well; spoke good Spanish; had been over the greater part of Spanish America, and lived in every possible situation, and served in every conceivable capacity, though generally in that of confidential servant to some man of figure. I cultivated this man's acquaintance, and during the five weeks that he was with us—for he remained on board until we arrived at San Diego—I gained a greater knowledge of the state of political parties in Mexico, and the habits and affairs of the different classes of society, than I could have learned from almost anyone else. He took great pains in correcting my Spanish, and supplying me with colloquial phrases, and common terms and exclamations, in speaking. He lent me a file of late newspapers from the city of Mexico, which were full of the triumphal reception of Santa Anna, who had just returned from Tampico after a victory, and with the preparations for his expedition against the Texans. "Viva Santa Anna!" was the byword everywhere, and it had even reached California, though there were still many here, among whom was Don Juan Bandini, who were opposed to his government, and intriguing to bring in Bustamente. Santa Anna, they said, was for breaking down the missions; or, as they termed it, *"Santa Anna no quiere religión."* Yet I had no doubt that the office of *administrador* of San Diego would reconcile Don Juan to any dynasty, and any state of the church. In these papers, too, I found scraps of American and English news; but which were so unconnected, and I was so ignorant of everything preceding them for eighteen months past, that they only awakened a curiosity which they could not satisfy. One article spoke of Taney as *Justicia Mayor de los Estados Unidos* (what had become of Marshall—was he dead, or banished?), and another made known, by news received from Veracruz, that *El Vizconde Melbourne* had returned to the office of *primer ministro* in place of Sir Roberto Peel. (Sir Robert Peel had been minister, then? And where were Earl Grey and the Duke of Wellington?) Here were the outlines of grand political overturns, the filling up of which I was left to imagine at my leisure.

The second morning after leaving Monterey, we were off Point Conception. It was a bright, sunny day, and the wind, though strong, was fair; and everything was in striking contrast with our experience in the same place two months before, when we were drifting off from a northwester under a fore and main spencer. "Sail ho!" cried a man who was rigging out a topgallant-studding-sail boom. "Where away?" "Weather beam, sir!" and in a few minutes a full-rigged brig was seen standing out from under Point Conception. The studding-sail halyards were let go, and the yards boom-ended, the afteryards braced aback, and we waited her coming down. She rounded to, backed her main topsail, and showed her decks full of men, four guns on a side, hammock nettings, and everything man-of-war fashion, except that there was no boatswain's whistle, and no uniforms on the quarterdeck. A short, square-built man, in a rough gray jacket, with a speaking trumpet in hand, stood in the weather hammock nettings. "Ship ahoy!" "Hallo!" "What ship is that, pray?" *"Alert."* "Where are you from, pray?" &c., &c. She proved to be the brig *Convoy*, from the Sandwich Islands, engaged in otter hunting among the islands which lie along the coast. Her armament was because of her being a *contrabandista.* The otter are very numerous among these islands, and, being of great value, the government require a heavy sum for a license

to hunt them, and lay a high duty upon every one shot or
carried out of the country. This vessel had no license, and
paid no duty, besides being engaged in smuggling goods on
board other vessels trading on the coast, and belonging to the
same owners in Oahu. Our captain told him to look out for
the Mexicans, but he said they had not an armed vessel of
his size in the whole Pacific. This was without doubt the same
vessel that showed herself off Santa Barbara a few months
before. These vessels frequently remain on the coast for years,
without making port, except at the islands for wood and
water, and an occasional visit to Oahu for a new outfit.

*Sunday, January 10th.* Arrived at Santa Barbara, and on
the following Wednesday slipped our cable and went to sea,
on account of a southeaster. Returned to our anchorage the
next day. We were the only vessel in the port. The *Pilgrim*
had passed through the canal and hove to off the town, nearly
six weeks before, on her passage down from Monterey, and
was now at the leeward. She heard here of our safe arrival
at San Francisco.

Great preparations were making on shore for the marriage
of our agent, who was to marry Doña Anita de la Guerra de
Noriego y Corillo, youngest daughter of Don Antonio Noriego,
the grandee of the place, and the head of the first family in
California. Our steward was ashore three days, making pastry
and cake, and some of the best of our stores were sent off
with him. On the day appointed for the wedding, we took
the captain ashore in the gig, and had orders to come for him
at night, with leave to go up to the house and see the fandango. Returning on board, we found preparations making
for a salute. Our guns were loaded and run out, men appointed
to each, cartridges served out, matches lighted, and all the
flags ready to be run up. I took my place at the starboard after
gun, and we all waited for the signal from on shore. At ten
o'clock the bride went up with her sister to the confessional,
dressed in deep black. Nearly an hour intervened, when the
great doors of the mission church opened, the bells rang out
a loud, discordant peal, the private signal for us was run up
by the captain ashore, the bride, dressed in complete white,
came out of the church with the bridegroom, followed by a
long procession. Just as she stepped from the church door,
a small white cloud issued from the bows of our ship, which
was full in sight, the loud report echoed among the sur-

rounding hills and over the bay, and instantly the ship was dressed in flags and pennants from stem to stern. Twenty-three guns followed in regular succession, with an interval of fifteen seconds between each, when the cloud blew off, and our ship lay dressed in her colors all day. At sundown another salute of the same number of guns was fired, and all the flags run down. This we thought was pretty well—a gun every fifteen seconds—for a merchantman with only four guns and a dozen or twenty men.

After supper, the gig's crew were called, and we rowed ashore, dressed in our uniform, beached the boat, and went up to the fandango. The bride's father's house was the principal one in the place, with a large court in front, upon which a tent was built, capable of containing several hundred people. As we drew near, we heard the accustomed sound of violins and guitars, and saw a great motion of the people within. Going in, we found nearly all the people of the town—men, women, and children—collected and crowded together, leaving barely room for the dancers; for on these occasions no invitations are given, but everyone is expected to come, though there is always a private entertainment within the house for particular friends. The old women sat down in rows, clapping their hands to the music, and applauding the young ones. The music was lively, and among the tunes we recognized several of our popular airs, which we, without doubt, have taken from the Spanish. In the dancing I was much disappointed. The women stood upright, with their hands down by their sides, their eyes fixed upon the ground before them, and slided about without any perceptible means of motion; for their feet were invisible, the hem of their dresses forming a circle about them, reaching to the ground. They looked as grave as though they were going through some religious ceremony, their faces as little excited as their limbs; and on the whole, instead of the spirited, fascinating Spanish dances which I had expected, I found the Californian fandango, on the part of the women at least, a lifeless affair. The men did better. They danced with grace and spirit, moving in circles round their nearly stationary partners, and showing their figures to advantage.

A great deal was said about our friend Don Juan Bandini, and when he did appear, which was toward the close of the evening, he certainly gave us the most graceful dancing that

I had ever seen. He was dressed in white pantaloons, neatly
made, a short jacket of dark silk gaily figured, white stockings and thin morocco slippers upon his very small feet.
His slight and graceful figure was well adapted to dancing,
and he moved about with the grace and daintiness of a
young fawn. An occasional touch of the toe to the ground
seemed all that was necessary to give him a long interval of
motion in the air. At the same time he was not fantastic
or flourishing, but appeared to be rather repressing a strong
tendency to motion. He was loudly applauded, and danced
frequently toward the close of the evening. After the supper,
the waltzing began, which was confined to a very few of the
gente de razón, and was considered a high accomplishment,
and a mark of aristocracy. Here, too, Don Juan figured
greatly, waltzing with the sister of the bride (Doña Angustia,
a handsome woman and a general favorite) in a variety of
beautiful figures, which lasted as much as half an hour, no
one else taking the floor. They were repeatedly and loudly
applauded, the old men and women jumping out of their
seats in admiration, and the young people waving their hats
and handkerchiefs. The great amusement of the evening—
owing to its being the Carnival—was the breaking of eggs
filled with cologne, or other essences, upon the heads of
the company. The women bring a great number of these
secretly about them, and the amusement is to break one
upon the head of a gentleman when his back is turned. He
is bound in gallantry to find out the lady and return the
compliment, though it must not be done if the person sees
you. A tall, stately don, with immense gray whiskers, and
a look of great importance, was standing before me, when
I felt a light hand on my shoulder, and, turning round, saw
Doña Angustia (whom we all knew, as she had been up to
Monterey, and down again, in the Alert), with her finger
upon her lip, motioning me gently aside. I stepped back a
little, when she went up behind the don, and with one hand
knocked off his huge sombrero, and at the same instant,
with the other, broke the egg upon his head, and springing
behind me, was out of sight in a moment. The don turned
slowly round, the cologne running down his face and over
his clothes, and a loud laugh breaking out from every
quarter. He looked round in vain for some time, until the
direction of so many laughing eyes showed him the fair

offender. She was his niece, and a great favorite with him, so old Don Domingo had to join in the laugh. A great many such tricks were played, and many a war of sharp maneuvering was carried on between couples of the younger people, and at every successful exploit a general laugh was raised.

Another of their games I was for some time at a loss about. A pretty young girl was dancing, named—after what would appear to us an almost sacrilegious custom of the country— Espíritu Santo, when a young man went behind her and placed his hat directly upon her head, letting it fall down over her eyes, and sprang back among the crowd. She danced for some time with the hat on, when she threw it off, which called forth a general shout, and the young man was obliged to go out upon the floor and pick it up. Some of the ladies, upon whose heads hats had been placed, threw them off at once, and a few kept them on throughout the dance, and took them off at the end, and held them out in their hands, when the owner stepped out, bowed, and took it from them. I soon began to suspect the meaning of the thing, and was afterward told that it was a compliment, and an offer to become the lady's gallant for the rest of the evening, and to wait upon her home. If the hat was thrown off, the offer was refused, and the gentleman was obliged to pick up his hat amid a general laugh. Much amusement was caused sometimes by gentlemen putting hats on the ladies' heads, without permitting them to see whom it was done by. This obliged them to throw them off, or keep them on at a venture, and when they came to discover the owner the laugh was turned upon one or the other.

The captain sent for us about ten o'clock, and we went aboard in high spirits, having enjoyed the new scene much, and were of great importance among the crew, from having so much to tell, and from the prospect of going every night until it was over; for these fandangos generally last three days. The next day, two of us were sent up to the town, and took care to come back by way of Señor Noriego's, and take a look into the booth. The musicians were again there, upon their platform, scraping and twanging away, and a few people, apparently of the lower classes, were dancing. The dancing is kept up, at intervals, throughout the day, but the crowd, the spirit, and the élite come in at night. The next night, which was the last, we went ashore in the same

manner, until we got almost tired of the monotonous twang
of the instruments, the drawling sounds which the women
kept up, as an accompaniment, and the slapping of the
hands in time with the music, in place of castanets. We
found ourselves as great objects of attention as any persons
or anything at the place. Our sailor dresses—and we took
great pains to have them neat and shipshape—were much
admired, and we were invited, from every quarter, to give
them an American dance; but after the ridiculous figure
some of our countrymen cut in dancing after the Mexicans,
we thought it best to leave it to their imaginations. Our
agent, with a tight black swallow-tailed coat just imported
from Boston, a high stiff cravat, looking as if he had been
pinned and skewered, with only his feet and hands left
free, took the floor just after Bandini, and we thought they
had had enough of Yankee grace.

The last night they kept it up in great style, and were
getting into a high go, when the captain called us off to go
aboard, for, it being southeaster season, he was afraid to
remain on shore long; and it was well he did not, for that
night we slipped our cables, as a crowner to our fun ashore,
and stood off before a southeaster, which lasted twelve hours,
and returned to our anchorage the next day.

## CHAPTER XXVIII

*Monday, February 1st.* After having been in port twenty-one
days, we sailed for San Pedro, where we arrived on the
following day, having gone "all fluking," with the weather
clew of the mainsail hauled up, the yards braced in a little,
and the lower studding sail just drawing; the wind hardly

shifting a point during the passage. Here we found the *Ayacucho* and the *Pilgrim*, which last we had not seen since the eleventh of September, nearly five months; and I really felt something like an affection for the old brig which had been my first home, and in which I had spent nearly a year, and got the first rough and tumble of a sea life. She, too, was associated in my mind with Boston, the wharf from which we sailed, anchorage in the stream, leave-taking, and all such matters, which were now to me like small links connecting me with another world, which I had once been in, and which, please God, I might yet see again. I went on board the first night, after supper; found the old cook in the galley, playing upon the fife which I had given him as a parting present; had a hearty shake of the hand from him; and dove down into the forecastle, where were my old shipmates, the same as ever, glad to see me; for they had nearly given us up as lost, especially when they did not find us in Santa Barbara. They had been at San Diego last, had been lying at San Pedro nearly a month, and had received three thousand hides from the Pueblo. But—"*Sic vos non vobis*"—these we took from her the next day, which filled us up, and we both got under way on the fourth, she bound to San Francisco again, and we to San Diego, where we arrived on the sixth.

We were always glad to see San Diego; it being the depot, and a snug little place, and seeming quite like home, especially to me, who had spent a summer there. There was no vessel in port, the *Rosa* having sailed for Valparaiso and Cádiz, and the *Catalina* for Callao, nearly a month before. We discharged our hides, and in four days were ready to sail again for the windward; and, to our great joy, *for the last time!* Over thirty thousand hides had been already collected, cured, and stowed away in the house, which, together with what we should collect, and the *Pilgrim* would bring down from San Francisco, would make out our cargo. The thought that we were actually going up for the last time, and that the next time we went round San Diego point it would be "homeward bound," brought things so near a close that we felt as though we were just there, though it must still be the greater part of a year before we could see Boston.

I spent one evening, as had been my custom, at the oven with the Sandwich Islanders; but it was far from being the

usual noisy, laughing time. It has been said that the greatest
curse to each of the South Sea Islands was the first man
who discovered it; and everyone who knows anything of
the history of our commerce in those parts knows how much
truth there is in this; and that the white men, with their
vices, have brought in diseases before unknown to the
islanders, which are now sweeping off the native population
of the Sandwich Islands at the rate of one-fortieth of the
entire population annually. They seem to be a doomed people.
The curse of a people calling themselves Christians seems
to follow them everywhere; and even here, in this obscure
place, lay two young islanders, whom I had left strong,
active young men, in the vigor of health, wasting away under
a disease which they would never have known but for their
intercourse with people from Christian America and Europe.
One of them was not so ill, and was moving about, smoking
his pipe, and talking, and trying to keep up his spirits; but
the other, who was my friend and *aikane*, Hope, was the
most dreadful object I had ever seen in my life—his eyes
sunken and dead, his cheeks fallen in against his teeth, his
hands looking like claws; a dreadful cough, which seemed
to rack his whole shattered system, a hollow, whispering
voice, and an entire inability to move himself. There he lay,
upon a mat, on the ground, which was the only floor of the
oven, with no medicine, no comforts, and no one to care
for or help him but a few Kanakas, who were willing
enough, but could do nothing. The sight of him made me
sick and faint. Poor fellow! During the four months that I
lived upon the beach, we were continually together, in work
and in our excursions in the woods and upon the water. I
felt a strong affection for him, and preferred him to any of
my own countrymen there; and I believe there was nothing
which he would not have done for me. When I came into the
oven he looked at me, held out his hand, and said, in a low
voice, but with a delightful smile, *"Aloha, aikane! Aloha
nui!"* I comforted him as well as I could, and promised to
ask the captain to help him from the medicine chest, and
told him I had no doubt the captain would do what he
could for him, as he had worked in our employ for several
years, both on shore and aboard our vessels on the coast.
I went aboard and turned into my hammock, but I could
not sleep.

Thinking, from my education, that I must have some knowledge of medicine, the Kanakas had insisted upon my examining him carefully; and it was not a sight to be forgotten. One of our crew, an old man-of-war's-man of twenty years' standing, who had seen sin and suffering in every shape, and whom I afterward took to see Hope, said it was dreadfully worse than anything he had ever seen, or even dreamed of. He was horror-struck, as his countenance showed; yet he had been among the worst cases in our naval hospitals. I could not get the thought of the poor fellow out of my head all night—his dreadful suffering, and his apparently inevitable horrible end.

The next day I told Captain Thompson of Hope's state, and asked him if he would be so kind as to go and see him.

"What—a d——d Kanaka?"

"Yes, sir," said I, "but he has worked four years for our vessels, and has been in the employ of our owners, both on shore and aboard."

"Oh, he be d——d!" said the captain, and walked off.

This man died afterward of a fever on the deadly coast of Sumatra; and God grant he had better care taken of him in his sufferings than he ever gave to anyone else.

Finding nothing was to be got from the captain, I consulted an old shipmate, who had much experience in these matters, and got a recipe from him, which he kept by him. With this I went to the mate, and told him the case. Mr. Brown had been entrusted with the general care of the medicine chest, and although a driving fellow, and a taut hand in a watch, he had good feelings, and was inclined to be kind to the sick. He said that Hope was not strictly one of the crew, but, as he was in our employ when taken sick, he should have the medicines; and he got them and gave them to me, with leave to go ashore at night. Nothing could exceed the delight of the Kanakas, when I came, bringing the medicines. All their terms of affection and gratitude were spent upon me, and in a sense wasted (for I could not understand half of them), yet they made all known by their manner. Poor Hope was so much revived at the bare thought of anything being done for him that he seemed already stronger and better. I knew he must die as he was, and he could but die under the medicines, and any chance was worth running. An oven exposed to every wind and change of weather is no place to take calomel; but nothing else would do, and strong remedies must be used, or he was gone. The applications, internal and external, were powerful, and I gave him strict directions to keep warm and sheltered, telling him it was his only chance for life. Twice after this I visited him, having only time to run up, while waiting in the boat. He promised to take his medicines regularly while we were up the coast, until we returned, and insisted upon it that he was doing better.

We got under way on the tenth, bound up to San Pedro, and had three days of calm and head winds, making but little progress. On the fourth, we took a stiff southeaster, which obliged us to reef our topsails. While on the yard, we saw a sail on the weather bow, and in about half an hour passed the *Ayacucho*, under double-reefed topsails, beating down to San Diego. Arrived at San Pedro on the fourth day, and came to in the old place, a league from shore, with no other vessel in port, and the prospect of three weeks or more of dull life, rolling goods up a slippery hill, carrying hides on our heads over sharp stones, and, perhaps, slipping for a southeaster.

There was but one man in the only house here, and him I shall always remember as a good specimen of a California ranger. He had been a tailor in Philadelphia, and, getting intemperate and in debt, joined a trapping party, and went to the Columbia River, and thence down to Monterey, where he spent everything, left his party, and came to the Pueblo de los Angeles to work at his trade. Here he went dead to leeward among the *pulperías*, gambling rooms, &c., and came down to San Pedro to be moral by being out of temptation. He had been in the house several weeks, working hard at his trade, upon orders which he had brought with him, and talked much of his resolution, and opened his heart to us about his past life. After we had been here some time, he started off one morning, in fine spirits, well dressed, to carry the clothes which he had been making to the Pueblo, and saying that he would bring back his money and some fresh orders the next day. The next day came, and a week passed, and nearly a fortnight, when one day, going ashore, we saw a tall man, who looked like our friend the tailor, getting out of the back of an Indian's cart, which had just come down from the Pueblo. He stood for the house, but we bore up after him;

when, finding that we were overhauling him, he hove to and spoke us. Such a sight! Barefooted, with an old pair of trousers tied round his waist by a piece of green hide, a soiled cotton shirt, and a torn Indian hat; "cleaned out" to the last real, and completely "used up." He confessed the whole matter; acknowledged that he was on his back; and now he had a prospect of a fit of the horrors for a week, and of being worse than useless for months. This is a specimen of the life of half of the Americans and English who are adrift along the coasts of the Pacific and its islands—commonly called "beachcombers." One of the same stamp was Russell, who was master of the hide house at San Diego while I was there, but had been afterward dismissed for his misconduct. He spent his own money, and nearly all the stores among the half-bloods upon the beach, and went up to the presidio, where he lived the life of a desperate "loafer," until some rascally deed sent him off "between two days," with men on horseback, dogs, and Indians in full cry after him, among the hills. One night he burst into our room at the hide house, breathless, pale as a ghost, covered with mud, and torn by thorns and briers, nearly naked, and begged for a crust of bread, saying he had neither eaten nor slept for three days. Here was the great *Mr.* Russell, who a month before was "Don Tomás," *capitán de la playa, maestro de la casa,* &c., &c., begging food and shelter of Kanakas and sailors. He stayed with us till he had given himself up, and was dragged off to the *calabozo.*

Another, and a more amusing, specimen was one whom we saw at San Francisco. He had been a lad on board the ship *California,* in one of her first voyages, and ran away and commenced ranchero, gambling, stealing horses, &c. He worked along up to San Francisco, and was living on a rancho near there while we were in port. One morning, when we went ashore in the boat, we found him at the landing place, dressed in California style—a wide hat, faded velveteen trousers, and a blanket thrown over his shoulders—and wishing to go off in the boat, saying he was going to *pasear* with our captain a little. We had many doubts of the reception he would meet with; but he seemed to think himself company for anyone. We took him aboard, landed him at the gangway, and went about our work, keeping an eye upon the quarter-deck, where the captain was walking. The lad went up to him with complete assurance, and, raising his hat, wished him a good afternoon. Captain Thompson turned round, looked at him from head to foot, and, saying coolly, "Hallo! Who the hell are you?" kept on his walk. This was a rebuff not to be mistaken, and the joke passed about among the crew by winks and signs at different parts of the ship. Finding himself disappointed at headquarters, he edged along forward to the mate, who was overseeing some work upon the forecastle, and tried to begin a yarn; but it would not do. The mate had seen the reception he had met with aft, and would have no cast-off company. The second mate was aloft, and the third mate and myself were painting the quarter boat, which hung by the davits, so he betook himself to us; but we looked at each other, and the officer was too busy to say a word. From us, he went to one and another of the crew, but the joke had got before him, and he found everybody busy and silent. Looking over the rail a few moments afterward, we saw him at the galley door talking with the cook. This was indeed a comedown, from the highest seat in the synagogue to a seat in the galley with the black cook. At night, too, when supper was called, he stood in the waist for some time, hoping to be asked down with the officers, but they went below, one after another, and left him. His next chance was with the carpenter and sailmaker, and he lounged round the after hatchway until the last had gone down. We had now had fun enough out of him, and, taking pity on him, offered him a pot of tea, and a cut at the kid, with the rest, in the forecastle. He was hungry, and it was growing dark, and he began to see that there was no use in playing the *caballero* any longer, and came down into the forecastle, put into the "grub" in sailor's style, threw off all his airs, and enjoyed the joke as much as anyone; for a man must take a joke among sailors. He gave us an account of his adventures in the country, roguery and all, and was very entertaining. He was a smart, unprincipled fellow, was in many of the rascally doings of the country, and gave us a great deal of interesting information as to the ways of the world we were in.

*Saturday, February 13th.* Were called up at midnight to slip for a violent northeaster; for this miserable hole of San Pedro is thought unsafe in almost every wind. We went off with a flowing sheet, and hove to under the lee of Catalina

Island, where we lay three days, and then returned to our anchorage.

*Tuesday, February 23rd.* This afternoon a signal was made from the shore, and we went off in the gig, and found the agent's clerk, who had been up to the Pueblo, waiting at the landing place, with a package under his arm, covered with brown paper and tied carefully with twine. No sooner had we shoved off than he told us there was good news from Santa Barbara. "What's that?" said one of the crew. "Has the bloody agent slipped off the hooks? Has the old bundle of bones got him at last?" "No; better than that. The *California* has arrived." Letters, papers, news, and, perhaps, friends on board! Our hearts were all up in our mouths, and we pulled away like good fellows, for the precious packet could not be opened except by the captain. As we pulled under the stern, the clerk held up the package, and called out to the mate, who was leaning over the taffrail, that the *California* had arrived.

"Hurrah!" said the mate, so as to be heard fore and aft. "*California* come, and news from Boston!"

Instantly there was a confusion on board which no one would understand who had not been in the same situation. All discipline seemed for a moment relaxed.

"What's that, Mr. Brown?" said the cook, putting his head out of the galley. "*California* come?"

"Aye, aye, you angel of darkness, and there's a letter for you from Bullknop 'treet, number two-two-five—green door and brass knocker!"

The packet was sent down into the cabin, and everyone waited to hear of the result. As nothing came up, the officers began to feel that they were acting rather a child's part, and turned the crew to again; and the same strict discipline was restored, which prohibits speech between man and man while at work on deck; so that, when the steward came forward with letters for the crew, each man took his letters, carried them below to his chest, and came up again immediately, and not a letter was read until we had cleared up decks for the night.

An overstrained sense of manliness is the characteristic of seafaring men. This often gives an appearance of want of feeling, and even of cruelty. From this, if a man comes within an ace of breaking his neck and escapes, it is made a joke of; and no notice must be taken of a bruise or a cut; and any expression of pity, or any show of attention, would look sisterly, and unbecoming a man who has to face the rough and tumble of such a life. From this cause, too, the sick are neglected at sea, and, whatever sailors may be ashore, a sick man finds little sympathy or attention, forward or aft. A man, too, can have nothing peculiar or sacred on board ship; for all the nicer feelings they take pride in disregarding, both in themselves and others. A "thin-skinned" man could hardly live on shipboard. One would be torn raw unless he had the hide of an ox. A moment of natural feeling for home and friends, and then the frigid routine of sea life returned. Jokes were made upon those who showed any interest in the expected news, and everything near and dear was made common stock for rude jokes and unfeeling coarseness, to which no exception could be taken by anyone.

Supper, too, must be eaten before the letters were read; and when, at last, they were brought out, they all got round anyone who had a letter, and expected to hear it read aloud, and have it all in common. If anyone went by himself to read, it was, "Fair play, there, and no skulking!" I took mine and went into the sailmaker's berth, where I could read it without interruption. It was dated August, just a year from the time I had sailed from home, and everyone was well, and no great change had taken place. Thus, for one year, my mind was set at ease, yet it was already six months from the date of the letter, and what another year would bring to pass, who could tell? Everyone away from home thinks that some great thing must have happened, while to those at home there seems to be a continued monotony and lack of incident.

As much as my feelings were taken up by my own news from home, I could not but be amused by a scene in the steerage. The carpenter had been married just before leaving Boston, and during the voyage had talked much about his wife, and had to bear and forbear, as every man known to be married must, aboard ship; yet the certainty of hearing from his wife by the first ship seemed to keep up his spirits. The *California* came, the packet was brought on board, no one was in higher spirits than he; but when the letters came forward, there was none for him. The captain looked again, but there was no mistake. Poor "Chips" could eat no supper. He was completely down in the mouth. "Sails" (the sailmaker) tried to comfort him, and told him he was a bloody fool to give up his grub for any woman's daughter, and reminded him that he had told him a dozen times that he'd never see or hear from his wife again.

"Ah!" said Chips, "you don't know what it is to have a wife, and——"

"Don't I?" said Sails; and then came, for the hundredth time, the story of his coming ashore at New York, from the *Constellation* frigate, after a cruise of four years round the Horn—being paid off with over five hundred dollars—marrying, and taking a couple of rooms in a four-story house—furnishing the rooms (with a particular account of the furniture, including a dozen flag-bottomed chairs, which he always dilated upon whenever the subject of furniture was alluded to)—going off to sea again, leaving his wife half-pay like a fool—coming home and finding her "off, like Bob's horse, with nobody to pay the reckoning"; furniture gone, flag-bottomed chairs and all, and with it his "long togs," the half-pay, his beaver hat, and white linen shirts. His wife he never saw or heard of from that day to this, and never wished to. Then followed a sweeping assertion, not much to the credit of the sex, in which he has Pope to back him. "Come, Chips, cheer up like a man, and take some hot grub! Don't be made a fool of by anything in petticoats! As for your wife, you'll never see her again; she was 'up keeleg and off' before you were outside of Cape Cod. You've hove your money away like a fool; but every man must learn once, just as I did; so you'd better square the yards with her, and make the best of it."

This was the best consolation Sails had to offer, but it did not seem to be just the thing the carpenter wanted; for, during several days, he was very much dejected, and bore with difficulty the jokes of the sailors, and with still more difficulty their attempts at advice and consolation, of most of which the sailmaker's was a good specimen.

*Thursday, February 25th.* Set sail for Santa Barbara, where we arrived on Sunday, the twenty-eighth. We just missed seeing the *California,* for she had sailed three days before, bound to Monterey, to enter her cargo and procure her license, and thence to San Francisco, &c. Captain Arthur left files of Boston papers for Captain Thompson, which, after they had been read and talked over in the cabin, I procured from my friend the third mate. One file was of all the Boston *Transcripts* for the month of August, 1835, and the rest were about a dozen *Daily Advertisers* and *Couriers* of different dates. After all, there is nothing in a strange land like a newspaper from home. Even a letter, in many respects, is nothing in comparison with it. It carries you back to the spot better than anything else. It is almost equal to clairvoyance. The names of the streets, with the things advertised, are almost as good as seeing the signs; and while reading "Boy lost!" one can almost hear the bell and well-known voice of "Old Wilson," crying the boy as "strayed, stolen, *or mislaid!*" Then there was the "Commencement at Cambridge," and the full account of the exercises at the graduating of my own class. A list of all those familiar names (beginning as usual with Abbot, and ending with W), which, as I read them over, one by one, brought up their faces and characters as I had known them in the various scenes of college life. Then I imagined them upon the stage, speaking their orations, dissertations, colloquies, &c., with the familiar gestures and tones of each, and tried to fancy the manner in which each would handle his subject. ———, handsome, showy, and superficial; ———, with his strong head, clear brain, cool self-possession; ———, modest, sensitive, and underrated; ———, the mouthpiece of the debating clubs, noisy, vaporous, and democratic; and so, following. Then I could see them receiving their A.B.'s from the dignified, feudal-looking President, with his *"auctoritate mihi commissa,"* and walking off the stage with their diplomas in their hands; while upon the same day their classmate was walking up and down California beach with a hide upon his head.

Every watch below, for a week, I pored over these papers, until I was sure there could be nothing in them that had escaped my attention, and was ashamed to keep them any longer.

*Saturday, March 5th.* This was an important day in our almanac, for it was on this day that we were first assured that our voyage was really drawing to a close. The captain gave orders to have the ship ready for getting under way; and observed that there was a good breeze to take us down to San Pedro. Then we were not going up to windward. Thus much was certain, and was soon known fore and aft; and when we went in the gig to take him off, he shook hands with the people on the beach, and said that he did not expect to see Santa Barbara again. This settled the matter, and sent a thrill of pleasure through the heart of everyone in the boat. We pulled off with a will, saying to ourselves (I can speak for myself at least), "Good-bye, Santa Barbara! This is the last pull here! No more duckings in your breakers, and slipping from your cursed southeasters!" The news was soon known aboard, and put life into everything when we were getting under way. Each one was taking his last look at the mission, the town, the breakers on the beach, and swearing that no money would make him ship to see them again; and when all hands tallied on to the catfall, the chorus of "Time for us to go!" was raised for the first time, and joined in, with full swing, by everybody. One would have thought we were on our voyage home, so near did it seem to us, though there were yet three months for us on the coast.

We left here the young Englishman, George Marsh, of whom I have before spoken, who was wrecked upon the Pelew Islands. He left us to take the berth of second mate on board the *Ayacucho*, which was lying in port. He was well qualified for this post, and his education would enable him to rise to any situation on board ship. I felt really sorry to part from him. There was something about him which excited my curiosity; for I could not, for a moment, doubt that he was well born, and, in early life, well bred. There was the latent gentleman about him, and the sense of honor, and no little of the pride, of a young man of good family. The situation was offered him only a few hours before we sailed; and though he must give up returning to America, yet I have no doubt that the change from a dog's berth to an officer's was too agreeable to his feelings to be declined. We pulled him on board the *Ayacucho*, and when he left the boat he gave each of its crew a piece of money except myself, and shook hands with me, nodding his head, as much as to say "We understand each other," and sprang on board. Had I known, an hour sooner, that he was to leave us, I would have made an effort to get from him the true history of his birth and early life. He knew that I had no faith in th story which he told the crew about them, and perhaps, in the moment of parting from me, probably forever, he would have given me the true account. Whether I shall ever meet him again, or whether his manuscript narrative of his adventures in the Pelew Islands, which would be creditable to him and interesting to the world, will ever see the light, I cannot tell. His is one of those cases which are more numerous than those suppose who have never lived anywhere but in their own homes, and never walked but in one line from their cradles to their graves. We must come down from our heights, and leave our straight paths for the byways and low places of life, if we would learn truths by strong contrasts; and in hovels, in forecastles, and among our own outcasts in foreign lands, see what has been wrought among our fellow-creatures by accident, hardship, or vice.

Two days brought us to San Pedro, and two days more (to our no small joy) gave us our last view of that place, which was universally called the Hell of California, and seemed designed in every way for the wear and tear of sailors. Not even the last view could bring out one feeling of regret. No thanks, thought I, as we left the hated shores in the distance, for the hours I have walked over your stones barefooted, with hides on my head—for the burdens I have carried up your steep, muddy hill—for the duckings in your surf—and for the long days and longer nights passed on your desolate hill, watching piles of hides, hearing the sharp bark of your eternal coyotes, and the dismal hooting of your owls.

As I bade good-bye to each successive place, I felt as though one link after another were struck from the chain of my servitude. Having kept close in shore for the land breeze, we passed the Mission of San Juan Capistrano the same night, and saw distinctly, by the bright moonlight, the cliff which I had gone down by a pair of halyards in search of a few paltry hides. *"Forsan et haec olim,"* thought I, and took my last look of that place, too. And on the next morning we were under the high point of San Diego. The flood tide took us swiftly in, and we came to opposite our hide house, and prepared to get everything in trim for a long stay. This was our last port. Here we were to discharge everything from the ship, clean her out, smoke her, take in our hides, wood, and water, and set sail for Boston. While all this was doing, we were to lie still in one place, the port a safe one, and no fear of southeasters. Accordingly, having picked out a good berth in the stream, with a smooth beach opposite for a

landing place, and within two cables' length of our hide
house, we moored ship, unbent the sails, sent down the topgallant yards and the studding-sail booms, and housed the
topgallant masts. The boats were then hove out and all the
sails, the spare spars, the stores, the rigging not rove, and,
in fact, everything which was not in daily use, sent ashore,
and stowed away in the house. Then went our hides and
horns, and we left hardly anything in the ship but her
ballast, and this we made preparations to heave out the next
day. At night, after we had knocked off, and were sitting
round in the forecastle, smoking and talking, and taking
sailor's pleasure, we congratulated ourselves upon being in
that situation in which we had wished ourselves every time
we had come into San Diego. "If we were only here for
the last time," we had often said, "with our topgallant
masts housed and our sails unbent!"—and now we had our
wish. Six weeks, or two months, of the hardest work we had
yet seen, but not the most disagreeable or trying, was before
us, and then—"Good-bye to California!"

# CHAPTER XXIX

We turned in early, knowing that we might expect an early
call; and sure enough, before the stars had quite faded, "All
hands ahoy!" and we were turned to, heaving out ballast. A
regulation of the port forbids any ballast to be thrown overboard; accordingly, our longboat was lined inside with rough
boards and brought alongside the gangway, but where one
tubful went into the boat, twenty went overboard. This is done
by every vessel, as it saves more than a week of labor, which

would be spent in loading the boats, rowing them to the point, and unloading them. When any people from the presidio were on board, the boat was hauled up and the ballast thrown in; but when the coast was clear, she was dropped astern again, and the ballast fell overboard. This is one of those petty frauds which many vessels practice in ports of inferior foreign nations, and which are lost sight of among the deeds of greater weight which are hardly less common. Fortunately, a sailor, not being a free agent in work aboard ship, is not accountable; yet the fact of being constantly employed, without thought, in such things begets an indifference to the rights of others.

Friday, and a part of Saturday, we were engaged in this work, until we had thrown out all but what we wanted under our cargo on the passage home; when, as the next day was Sunday, and a good day for smoking ship, we cleared everything out of the cabin and forecastle, made a slow fire of charcoal, birch bark, brimstone, and other matters, on the ballast in the bottom of the hold, calked up the hatches and every open seam, and pasted over the cracks of the windows, and the slides of the scuttles and companionway. Wherever smoke was seen coming out, we calked and pasted and, so far as we could, made the ship smoke-tight. The captain and officers slept under the awning which was spread over the quarterdeck; and we stowed ourselves away under an old studding sail, which we drew over one side of the forecastle. The next day, from fear that something might happen in the way of fire, orders were given for no one to leave the ship, and, as the decks were lumbered up, we could not wash them down, so we had nothing to do all day long. Unfortunately, our books were where we could not get at them, and we were turning about for something to do, when one man recollected a book he had left in the galley. He went after it, and it proved to be Woodstock. This was a great windfall, and as all could not read it at once, I, being the scholar of the company, was appointed reader. I got a knot of six or eight about me, and no one could have had a more attentive audience. Some laughed at the "scholars," and went over the other side of the forecastle to work and spin their yarns; but I carried the day, and had the cream of the crew for my hearers. Many of the reflections, and the political parts, I omitted, but all the narrative they were delighted with; especially the descriptions of the Puritans, and the sermons and harangues of the Roundhead soldiers. The gallantry of Charles, Dr. Radcliffe's plots, the knavery of "trusty Tompkins"—in fact, every part seemed to chain their attention. Many things which, while I was reading, I had a misgiving about, thinking them above their tastes, I was surprised to find them enter into completely.

I read nearly all day, until sundown; when, as soon as supper was over, as I had nearly finished, they got a light from the galley; and, by skipping what was less interesting, I carried them through to the marriage of Everard, and the restoration of Charles the Second, before eight o'clock.

The next morning, we took the battens from the hatches, and opened the ship. A few stifled rats were found, and what bugs, cockroaches, fleas, and other vermin there might have been on board must have unrove their lifelines before the hatches were opened. The ship being now ready, we covered the bottom of the hold over, fore and aft, with dried brush for dunnage, and, having leveled everything away, we were ready to take in our cargo. All the hides that had been collected since the *California* left the coast (a little more than two years), amounting to about forty thousand, had been cured, dried, and stowed away in the house, waiting for our good ship to take them to Boston.

Now began the operation of taking in our cargo, which kept us hard at work, from the gray of the morning till starlight, for six weeks, with the exception of Sundays, and of just time to swallow our meals. To carry the work on quicker, a division of labor was made. Two men threw the hides down from the piles in the house, two more picked them up and put them on a long horizontal pole, raised a few feet from the ground, where they were beaten by two more with flails, somewhat like those used in threshing wheat. When beaten, they were taken from this pole by two more, and placed upon a platform of boards; and ten or a dozen men, with their trousers rolled up, and hides upon their heads, were constantly going back and forth from the platform to the boat, which was kept off where she would just float. The throwing the hides upon the pole was the most difficult work, and required a sleight of hand which was only to be got by long practice. As I was known for a hide curer, this post was assigned to me, and I continued at it for six or eight days, tossing, in that time, from eight to ten thousand hides, until my wrists became so lame that I gave in, and was transferred to the gang that was employed in filling the boats, where I remained for the rest of the time. As we were obliged to carry the hides on our heads from fear of their getting wet, we each had a piece of sheepskin sewed into the inside of our hats, with the wool next our heads, and thus were able to bear the weight, day after day, which might otherwise have worn off our hair, and borne hard upon our skulls. Upon the whole, ours was the best berth, for though the water was nipping cold early in the morning and late at night, and being so continually wet was rather an exposure, yet we got rid of the constant dust and dirt from the beating of the hides, and, being all of us young and hearty, did not mind the exposure. The older men of the crew, whom it would have been imprudent to keep in the water, remained on board with the mate, to stow the hides away, as fast as they were brought off by the boats.

We continued at work in this manner until the lower hold was filled to within four feet of the beams, when all hands were called aboard to begin "steeving." As this is a peculiar operation, it will require a minute description.

Before stowing the hides, as I have said, the ballast is leveled off, just above the keelson, and then loose dunnage is placed upon it, on which the hides rest. The greatest care is used in stowing, to make the ship hold as many hides as possible. It is no mean art, and a man skilled in it is an important character in California. Many a dispute have I heard raging high between professed "beachcombers," as to whether the hides should be stowed "shingling," or "back-to-back and flipper-to-flipper"; upon which point there was an entire and bitter division of sentiment among the *savants*. We adopted each method at different periods of the stowing, and parties ran high in the forecastle, some siding with "old Bill" in favor of the former, and others scouting him and relying upon "English Bob" of the *Ayacucho*, who had been eight years in California, and was willing to risk his life and limb for the latter method. At length a compromise was effected, and a middle course of shifting the ends and backs at every lay was adopted, which worked well, and which each party granted was better than that of the other, though inferior to its own.

Having filled the ship up, in this way, to within four feet of her beams, the process of steeving began, by which a hundred hides are got into a place where scarce one could be forced by hand, and which presses the hides to the utmost, sometimes starting the beams of the ship, resembling in its effects the jackscrews which are used in stowing cotton. Each morning we went ashore, and beat and brought off as many hides as we could steeve in a day, and, after breakfast, went down into the hold, where we remained at work until night, except a short spell for dinner. The length of the hold, from stem to stern, was floored off level; and we began with raising a pile in the after part, hard against the bulkhead of the run, and filling it up to the beams, crowding in as many as we could by hand and pushing in with oars, when a large "book" was made of from twenty-five to fifty hides, doubled at the backs, and placed one within another, so as to leave but one outside hide for the book. An opening was then made between two hides in the pile, and the back of the outside hide of the book inserted. Above and below this book were placed smooth strips of wood, well greased, called "ways," to facilitate the sliding in of the book. Two long, heavy spars, called steeves, made of the strongest wood, and sharpened off like a wedge at one end, were placed with their wedge ends into the inside of the hide which was the center of the book, and to the other end of each straps were fitted, into which large tackles * were hooked, composed each of two huge purchase blocks, one hooked to the strap on the end of the steeve, and the other into a dog, fastened into one of the beams, as far aft as it could be got. When this was arranged, and the ways greased upon which the book was to slide, the falls of the tackles were stretched forward, and all hands tallied on, and boused away upon them until the book was well entered, when these tackles were nippered, straps and toggles clapped upon the falls, and two more luff tackles hooked on, with dogs, in the same manner; and thus, by luff upon luff, the power was multiplied, until into a pile in which one hide more could not be crowded by hand, a hundred or a hundred and fifty were often driven by this complication of purchases. When the last luff was hooked on, all hands were called to the rope—cook, steward, and all—and ranging

* This word, when used to signify a pulley or purchase formed by blocks and a rope, is always by seamen pronounced tā-kl.

ourselves at the falls, one behind the other, sitting down on
the hides, with our heads just even with the beams, we set
taut upon the tackles, and striking up a song, and all lying
back at the chorus, we boused the tackles home, and drove
the large books chock in out of sight.

The sailors' songs for capstans and falls are of a peculiar
kind, having a chorus at the end of each line. The burden
is usually sung by one alone, and, at the chorus, all hands
join in—and the louder the noise, the better. With us, the
chorus seemed almost to raise the decks of the ship, and might
be heard at a great distance ashore. A song is as necessary
to sailors as the drum and fife to a soldier. They must pull
together as soldiers must step in time, and they can't pull
in time, or pull with a will, without it. Many a time, when
a thing goes heavy, with one fellow yo-ho-ing, a lively song,
like "Heave, to the Girls!" "Nancy O!" "Jack Crosstree,"
"Cheerly, men," &c., has put life and strength into every arm.
We found a great difference in the effect of the various
songs in driving in the hides. Two or three songs would
be tried, one after the other, with no effect—not an inch
could be got upon the tackles; when a new song, struck up,
seemed to hit the humor of the moment, and drove the
tackles "two blocks" at once. "Heave Round Hearty!" "Captain Gone Ashore!" "Dandy Ship and a Dandy Crew," and
the like might do for common pulls, but on an emergency,
when we wanted a heavy, "raise-the-dead pull," which should
start the beams of the ship, there was was nothing like "Time
for Us to Go!" "Round the Corner," "Tally High Ho! You
Know," or "Hurrah! Hurrah! My Hearty Bullies!"

This was the most lively part of our work. A little boating
and beach work in the morning; then twenty or thirty men
down in a close hold, where we were obliged to sit down and
slide about, passing hides, and rousing about the great steeves,
tackles, and dogs, singing out at the falls, and seeing the
ship filling up every day. The work was as hard as it could
well be. There was not a moment's cessation from Monday
morning till Saturday night, when we were generally beaten
out, and glad to have a full night's rest, a wash and shift of
clothes, and a quiet Sunday. During all this time—which
would have startled Dr. Graham—we lived upon almost
nothing but fresh beef—fried beefsteaks, three times a day,
morning, noon, and night. At morning and night we had a

quart of tea to each man, and an allowance of about a pound of hard bread a day; but our chief article of food was beef. A mess, consisting of six men, had a large wooden kid piled up with beefsteaks, cut thick, and fried in fat, with the grease poured over them. Round this we sat, attacking it with our jackknives and teeth, and with the appetite of young lions, and sent back an empty kid to the galley. This was done three times a day. How many pounds each man ate in a day I will not attempt to compute. A whole bullock (we ate liver and all) lasted us but four days. Such devouring of flesh, I will venture to say, is not often seen. What one man ate in a day, over a hearty man's allowance, would make an English peasant's heart leap into his mouth. Indeed, during all the time we were upon the coast, our principal food was fresh beef, and every man had perfect health; but this was a time of especial devouring, and what we should have done without meat I cannot tell. Once or twice, when our bullocks failed, and we were obliged to make a meal upon dry bread and water, it seemed like feeding upon shavings. Light and dry, feeling unsatisfied, and, at the same time, full, we were glad to see four quarters of a bullock, just killed, swinging from the foretop. Whatever theories may be started by sedentary men, certainly no men could have gone through more hard work and exposure for sixteen months in more perfect health, and without ailings and failings, than our ship's crew, let them have lived upon Hygeia's own baking and dressing.

*Friday, April 15th.* Arrived, brig *Pilgrim*, from the windward. It was a sad sight for her crew to see us getting ready to go off the coast, while they, who had been longer on the coast than the *Alert*, were condemned to another year's hard service. I spent an evening on board, and found them making the best of the matter, and determined to rough it out as they might. But Stimson, after considerable negotiating and working, had succeeded in persuading my English friend, Tom Harris—my companion in the anchor watch—for thirty dollars, some clothes, and an intimation from Captain Faucon that he should want a second mate before the voyage was over, to take his place in the brig as soon as she was ready to go up to windward.

The first opportunity I could get to speak to Captain Faucon, I asked him to step up to the oven and look at Hope, whom he knew well, having had him on board his vessel. He went to see him at once, and said that he was doing pretty well, but there was so little medicine on board the brig, and she would be so long on the coast, that he could spare none for him, but that Captain Arthur would take care of him when he came down in the *California*, which would be in a week or more. I had been to see Hope the first night after we got into San Diego this last time, and had frequently since spent the early part of a night in the oven. I hardly expected, when I left him to go to windward, to find him alive upon my return. He was certainly as low as he could well be when I left him, and what would be the effect of the medicines that I gave him I hardly then dared to conjecture. Yet I knew that he must die without them. I was not a little rejoiced, therefore, and relieved, upon our return, to see him decidedly better. The medicines were strong, and took hold and gave a check to the disorder which was destroying him; and, more than that, they had begun the work of exterminating it. I shall never forget the gratitude that he expressed. All the Kanakas attributed his escape solely to my knowledge, and would not be persuaded that I had not all the secrets of the physical system open to me and under my control. My medicines, however, were gone, and no more could be got from the ship, so that his life was left to hang upon the arrival of the *California*.

*Sunday, April 24th.* We had now been nearly seven weeks in San Diego, and had taken in the greater part of our cargo, and were looking out every day for the arrival of the *California*, which had our agent on board; when, this afternoon, some Kanakas, who had been over the hill for rabbits and to fight rattlesnakes, came running down the path, singing out, "Sail ho!" with all their might. Mr. Hatch, our third mate, was ashore, and, asking them particularly about the size of the sail, &c., and learning that it was *"Moku—Nui Moku,"* hailed our ship, and said that the *California* was on the other side of the point. Instantly all hands were turned up, the bow guns run out and loaded, the ensign and broad pennant set, the yards squared by lifts and braces, and everything got ready to make a fair appearance. The instant she showed her nose round the point we began our salute. She came in under topgallant sails, clewed up and furled her sails in good order, and came to within swinging distance of us. It being Sunday, and nothing to do, all hands were on the forecastle, criticizing the newcomer. She was a good, substantial ship, not quite so long as the *Alert*, wall-sided and kettle-bottomed, after the latest fashion of south-shore cotton-and-sugar wagons; strong, too, and tight, and a good average sailer, but with no pretensions to beauty, and nothing in the style of a "crack ship." Upon the whole, we were perfectly satisfied that the *Alert* might hold up her head with a ship twice as smart as she.

At night some of us got a boat and went on board, and found a large, roomy forecastle (for she was squarer forward than the *Alert*), and a crew of a dozen or fifteen men and boys sitting around on their chests, smoking and talking, and ready to give a welcome to any of our ship's company. It was just seven months since they left Boston, which seemed but yesterday to us. Accordingly, we had much to ask; for though we had seen the newspapers which she had brought, yet these were the very men who had been in Boston, and seen everything with their own eyes. One of the green hands was a Boston boy, from one of the public schools, and, of course, knew many things which we wished to ask about, and, on inquiring the names of our two Boston boys, found that they had been schoolmates of his. Our men had hundreds of questions to ask about Ann Street, the boardinghouses, the ships in port, the rate of wages, and other matters.

Among her crew were two English man-of-war's-men, so that, of course, we soon had music. They sang in the true sailor's style, and the rest of the crew, which was a remarkably musical one, joined in the choruses. They had many of the latest sailor songs, which had not yet got about among our merchantmen, and which they were very choice of. They began soon after we came on board, and kept it up until after two bells, when the second mate came forward and called, "The *Alert*s away!" Battle songs, drinking songs, boat songs, love songs, and everything else, they seemed to have a complete assortment of, and I was glad to find that "All in the Downs," "Poor Tom Bowline," "The Bay of Biscay," "List, Ye Landsmen!" and other classical songs of the sea still held their places. In addition to these, they had picked up at the theaters and other places a few songs of a little more genteel cast, which they were very proud of; and I shall never forget hearing an old salt, who had broken his voice by hard drinking on shore, and bellowing from the masthead in a hundred northwesters, singing—with all manner of ungovernable trills and quavers, in the high notes breaking into a rough falsetto, and in the low ones growling along like the dying away of the boatswain's "All hands ahoy!" down the hatchway—"Oh, No, We Never Mention Him."

> "Perhaps, like me, he struggles with
> Each feeling of regret;
> But if he's loved as I have loved,
> He never can forget!"

The last line he roared out at the top of his voice, breaking each word into half a dozen syllables. This was very popular, and Jack was called upon every night to give them his "sentimental song." No one called for it more loudly than I, for the complete absurdity of the execution, and the sailors' perfect satisfaction in it, were ludicrous beyond measure.

The next day the *California* began unloading her cargo; and her boats' crews, in coming and going, sang their boat songs, keeping time with their oars. This they did all day long for several days, until their hides were all discharged, when a gang of them were sent on board the *Alert* to help us steeve our hides. This was a windfall for us, for they had a set of new songs for the capstan and fall, and ours had got nearly worn out by six weeks' constant use. I have no doubt that this timely reinforcement of songs hastened our work several days.

Our cargo was now nearly all taken in, and my old friend, the *Pilgrim*, having completed her discharge, unmoored, to set sail the next morning on another long trip to windward. I was just thinking of her hard lot, and congratulating myself upon my escape from her, when I received a summons into the cabin. I went aft, and there found, seated round the cabin table, my own captain, Captain Faucon of the *Pilgrim*, and Mr. Robinson, the agent. Captain Thompson turned to me and asked abruptly:

"Dana, do you want to go home in the ship?"

"Certainly, sir," said I. "I expect to go home in the ship."

"Then," said he, "you must get someone to go in your place on board the *Pilgrim*."

I was so completely "taken aback" by this sudden intimation that for a moment I could make no reply. I thought it

would be hopeless to attempt to prevail upon any of the
ship's crew to take twelve months more upon California in
the brig. I knew, too, that Captain Thompson had received
orders to bring me home in the *Alert,* and he had told me,
when I was at the hide house, that I was to go home in her;
and even if this had not been so, it was cruel to give me no
notice of the step they were going to take, until a few hours
before the brig would sail. As soon as I had got my wits about
me, I put on a bold front, and told him plainly that I had a
letter in my chest informing me that he had been written to
by the owners in Boston to bring me home in the ship; and,
moreover, that he had told me that he had such instructions,
and that I was to return in the ship.

To have this told him, and to be opposed in such a manner,
was more than my lord paramount had been used to. He
turned fiercely upon me, and tried to look me down, and face
me out of my statement; but finding that that wouldn't do,
and that I was entering upon my defense in such a way as
would show to the other two that he was in the wrong, he
changed his ground, and pointed to the shipping papers of the
*Pilgrim,* from which my name had never been erased, and
said that there was my name—that I belonged to her—that he
had an absolute discretionary power—and, in short, that I
must be on board the *Pilgrim* by the next morning with my
chest and hammock, or have someone ready to go in my
place, and that he would not hear another word from me.
No court of star chamber could proceed more summarily with
a poor devil than this trio was about to do with me; con-
demning me to a punishment worse than a Botany Bay exile,
and to a fate which might alter the whole current of my
future life; for two years more in California might have made
me a sailor for the rest of my days. I felt all this, and saw the
necessity of being determined. I repeated what I had said,
and insisted upon my right to return in the ship. I—

> ". . . raised my arm, and tauld my crack,
>     Before them a'."

But it would have all availed me nothing had I been "some
poor body" before this absolute, domineering tribunal. But
they saw that I would not go, unless *"vi et armis,"* and they
knew that I had friends and interest enough at home to make

them suffer for any injustice they might do me. It was probably this that turned the scale; for the captain changed his tone entirely, and asked me if, in case anyone went in my place, I would give him the same sum that Stimson gave Harris to exchange with him. I told them that if anyone was sent on board the brig I should pity him, and be willing to help him to that, or almost any amount, but would not speak of it as an exchange.

"Very well," said he. "Go forward about your business, and send English Ben here to me!"

I went forward with a light heart, but feeling as much anger and contempt as I could well contain between my teeth. English Ben was sent aft, and in a few moments came forward, looking as though he had received his sentence to be hanged. The captain had told him to get his things ready to go on board the brig the next morning; and that I would give him thirty dollars and a suit of clothes. The hands had "knocked off" for dinner, and were standing about the forecastle, when Ben came forward and told his story. I could see plainly that it made a great excitement, and that, unless I explained the matter to them, the feeling would be turned against me. Ben was a poor English boy, a stranger in Boston, and without friends or money; and, being an active, willing lad, and a good sailor for his years, was a general favorite. "Oh, yes!" said the crew. "The captain has let you off because you are a gentleman's son, and taken Ben because he is poor, and has got nobody to say a word for him." I knew that this was too true to be answered, but I excused myself from any blame, and told them that I had a right to go home, at all events. This pacified them a little, but Jack had got a notion that a poor lad was to be imposed upon, and did not distinguish very clearly; and though I knew that I was in no fault, and, in fact, had barely escaped the grossest injustice, yet I felt that my berth was getting to be a disagreeable one. The notion that I was not "one of them," which, by a participation in all their labor and hardships, and having no favor shown me, and never asserting myself among them, had been laid asleep, was beginning to revive. But far stronger than any feeling for myself was the pity I felt for the poor lad. He had depended upon going home in the ship; and from Boston was going immediately to Liverpool, to see his friends. Besides this, having begun the voyage with very few clothes, he had taken up the greater part of his wages in the slop chest, and it was every day a losing concern to him; and, like all the rest of the crew, he had a hearty hatred of California, and the prospect of eighteen months or two years more of hide droghing seemed completely to break down his spirit. I had determined not to go myself, happen what would, and I knew that the captain would not dare to attempt to force me. I knew, too, that the two captains had agreed together to get someone, and that unless I could prevail upon somebody to go voluntarily, there would be no help for Ben. From this consideration, though I had said that I would have nothing to do with an exchange, I did my best to get someone to go voluntarily. I offered to give an order upon the owners in Boston for six months' wages, and also all the clothes, books, and other matters which I should not want upon the voyage home. When this offer was published in the ship, and the case of poor Ben set forth in strong colors, several, who would not dream of going themselves, were busy in talking it up to others, who, they thought, might be tempted to accept it; and, at length, a Boston boy, a harum-scarum lad, a great favorite, Harry May, whom we called Harry Bluff, and who did not care what country or ship he was in, if he had clothes enough and money enough—partly from pity for Ben, and partly from the thought he should have "cruising money" for the rest of his stay—came forward, and offered to go and "sling his hammock in the bloody hooker." Lest his purpose should cool, I signed an order for the sum upon the owners in Boston, gave him all the clothes I could spare, and sent him aft to the captain, to let him know what had been done. The skipper accepted the exchange, and was, doubtless, glad to have it pass off so easily. At the same time he cashed the order, which was endorsed to him,* and the next morning the lad went aboard the brig, apparently in good spirits, having shaken hands with each of us and wished us a pleasant passage home, jingling the money in his pockets, and calling out, "Never say die, while there's a shot in the locker." The same boat carried off Harris, my old watchmate, who had previously made an exchange with my friend Stimson.

I was sorry to part with Harris. Nearly two hundred hours

* When our crew were paid off in Boston, the owners answered the orders of Stimson and me, but refused to deduct the amount from the payroll saying that the exchanges were made under compulsion.

(as we had calculated it) had we walked the ship's deck together, at anchor watch, when all hands were below, and talked over and over every subject which came within the ken of either of us. He gave me a strong grip with his hand; and I told him, if he came to Boston, not to fail to find me out, and let me see my old watchmate. The same boat brought on board Stimson, who had begun the voyage with me from Boston, and, like me, was going back to his family and to the society in which he had been born and brought up. We congratulated each other upon finding what we had long talked over and wished for thus brought about; and none on board the ship were more glad than ourselves to see the old brig standing round the point, under full sail. As she passed abreast of us, we all collected in the waist, and gave her three loud, hearty cheers, waving our hats in the air. Her crew sprang into the rigging and chains, and answered us with three as loud, to which we, after the nautical custom, gave one in return. I took my last look of their familiar faces as they passed over the rail, and saw the old black cook put his head out of the galley, and wave his cap over his head. Her crew flew aloft to loose the topgallant sails and royals; the two captains waved their hands to each other; and, in ten minutes, we saw the last inch of her white canvas, as she rounded the point.

Relieved as I was to see her well off (and I felt like one who had just sprung from an iron trap which was closing upon him), I had yet a feeling of regret at taking the last look at the old craft in which I had spent a year, and the first year, of my sailor's life, which had been my first home in the new world into which I had entered, and with which I had associated so many events—my first leaving home, my first crossing the equator, Cape Horn, Juan Fernández, death at sea, and other things, serious and common. Yet, with all this, and the sentiment I had for my old shipmates condemned to another term of California life, the thought that we were done with it, and that one week more would see us on our way to Boston, was a cure for everything.

*Friday, May 6th,* completed the getting in of our cargo, and was a memorable day in our calendar. The time when we were to take in our last hide we had looked forward to, for sixteen months, as the first bright spot. When the last hide was stowed away, the hatches calked down, the tarpaulins battened onto them, the longboat hoisted in and secured, and the

decks swept down for the night—the chief mate sprang upon
the top of the longboat, called all hands into the waist, and,
giving us a signal by swinging his cap over his head, we gave
three long, loud cheers, which came from the bottom of our
hearts, and made the hills and valleys ring again. In a moment we heard three in answer from the *California*'s crew,
who had seen us taking in our longboat: "the cry they heard
—its meaning knew."

The last week we had been occupied in taking in a supply
of wood and water for the passage home, and in bringing on
board the spare spars, sails, &c. I was sent off with a party
of Indians to fill the water casks, at a spring about three miles
from the shipping and near the town, and was absent three
days, living at the town, and spending the daytime in filling
the casks and transporting them on oxcarts to the landing
place, whence they were taken on board by the crew with
boats. This being all done with, we gave one day to bending
our sails, and at night every sail, from the courses to the skysails, was bent, and every studding sail ready for setting.

Before our sailing, an unsuccessful attempt was made by
one of the crew of the *California* to effect an exchange with
one of our number. It was a lad, between fifteen and sixteen
years of age, who went by the name of "The Reefer," having
been a midshipman in an East India Company's ship. His singular character and story had excited our interest ever since
the ship came into the port. He was a delicate, slender little
fellow, with a beautiful pearly complexion, regular features;
forehead as white as marble, black hair curling beautifully
round it; tapering, delicate fingers; small feet, soft voice, gen-
tle manners, and, in fact, every sign of having been well born
and bred. At the same time there was something in his expression which showed a slight deficiency of intellect. How
great the deficiency was, or what it resulted from; whether he
was born so; whether it was the result of disease or accident;
or whether, as some said, it was brought on by his distress of
mind during the voyage—I cannot say. From his account of
himself, and from many circumstances which were known in
connection with his story, he must have been the son of a man
of wealth. His mother was an Italian. He was probably a natural son, for in scarcely any other way could the incidents of
his early life be accounted for. He said that his parents did
not live together, and he seemed to have been ill treated by

his father. Though he had been delicately brought up, and indulged in every way (and he had then with him trinkets which had been given him at home), yet his education had been sadly neglected; and when only twelve years old, he was sent as midshipman in the Company's service. His own story was, that he afterward ran away from home, upon a difficulty which he had with his father, and went to Liverpool, whence he sailed in the ship *Rialto*, Captain Holmes, for Boston. Captain Holmes endeavored to get him a passage back, but, there being no vessel to sail for some time, the boy left him, and went to board at a common sailor's boardinghouse in Ann Street, where he supported himself for a few weeks by selling some of his valuables. At length, according to his own account, being desirous of returning home, he went to a shipping office, where the shipping articles of the *California* were open. Upon asking where the ship was going, he was told by the shipping master that she was bound to California. Not knowing where that was, he told him that he wanted to go to Europe, and asked if California was in Europe. The shipping master answered him in a way which the boy did not understand, and advised him to ship. The boy signed the articles, received his advance, laid out a little of it in clothes, and spent the rest, and was ready to go on board, when, upon the morning of sailing, he heard that the ship was bound upon the Northwest Coast, on a two or three years' voyage, and was not going to Europe. Frightened at this prospect, he slipped away when the crew was going aboard, wandered up into another part of the town, and spent all the forenoon in straying about the Common, and the neighboring streets. Having no money, and all his clothes and other things being in his chest on board, and being a stranger, he became tired and hungry, and ventured down toward the shipping, to see if the vessel had sailed. He was just turning the corner of a street, when the shipping master, who had been in search of him, popped upon him, seized him, and carried him on board. He cried and struggled, and said he did not wish to go in the ship; but the topsails were at the masthead, the fasts just ready to be cast off, and everything in the hurry and confusion of departure, so that he was hardly noticed; and the few who did inquire about the matter were told that it was merely a boy who had spent his advance and tried to run away. Had the owners of the vessel known anything of the matter, they would doubtless have interfered; but they either knew nothing of it, or heard, like the rest, that it was only an unruly boy who was sick of his bargain. As soon as the boy found himself actually at sea, and upon a voyage of two or three years in length, his spirits failed him; he refused to work, and became so miserable that Captain Arthur took him into the cabin, where he assisted the steward, and occasionally pulled and hauled about decks. He was in this capacity when we saw him; and though it was much better for him than the life in a forecastle, and the hard work, watching, and exposure, which his delicate frame could not have borne, yet, to be joined with a black fellow in waiting upon a man whom he probably looked upon as but little, in point of education and manners, above one of his father's servants, was almost too much for his spirit to bear. Had he entered upon this situation of his own free will, he could have endured it; but to have been deceived, and, in addition to that, forced into it, was intolerable. He made every effort to go home in our ship, but his captain refused to part with him except in the way of exchange, and that he could not effect. If this account of the whole matter, which we had from the boy, and which was confirmed by the crew, be correct, I cannot understand why Captain Arthur should have refused to let him go, especially as he had the name, not only with that crew, but with all he had ever commanded, of an unusually kindhearted man. The truth is, the unlimited power which merchant captains have upon long voyages on strange coasts takes away the sense of responsibility, and too often, even in men otherwise well disposed, gives growth to a disregard for the rights and feelings of others. The lad was sent on shore to join the gang at the hide house, from whence, I was afterward rejoiced to hear, he effected his escape, and went down to Callao in a small Spanish schooner; and from Callao he probably returned to England.

Soon after the arrival of the *California*, I spoke to Captain Arthur about Hope, the Kanaka; and as he had known him on the voyage before, and liked him, he immediately went to see him, gave him proper medicines, and, under such care, he began rapidly to recover. The Saturday night before our sailing I spent an hour in the oven, and took leave of my Kanaka friends; and, really, this was the only thing connected with leaving California which was in any way unpleasant. I felt an interest and affection for many of these simple, truehearted men, such as I never felt before but for a near relation. Hope shook me by the hand; said he should soon be well again, and ready to work for me when I came upon the coast, next voyage, as officer of the ship; and told me not to forget, when I became captain, how to be kind to the sick. Old "Mr. Bingham" and "King Mannini" went down to the boat with me, shook me heartily by the hand, wished us a good voyage, and went back to the oven, chanting one of their deep, monotonous, improvised songs, the burden of which I gathered to be about us and our voyage.

*Sunday, May 8th.* This promised to be our last day in California. Our forty thousand hides and thirty thousand horns, besides several barrels of otter and beaver skins, were all stowed below, and the hatches calked down.* All our spare spars were taken on board and lashed, our water casks secured, and our livestock, consisting of four bullocks, a dozen sheep, a dozen or more pigs, and three or four dozens of poultry, were all stowed away in their different quarters; the bullocks in the longboat, the sheep in a pen on the fore hatch, the pigs in a sty under the bows of the longboat, and the poultry in their proper coop, and the jolly boat was full of hay for the sheep and bullocks. Our unusually large cargo, together with the stores for a five months' voyage, brought the ship channels down into the water. In addition to this, she had been steeved so thoroughly, and was so bound by the compression of her cargo, forced into her by machinery so powerful, that she was like a man in a straitjacket, and would be but a dull sailer until she had worked herself loose.

The *California* had finished discharging her cargo, and was to get under way at the same time with us. Having washed down decks and got breakfast, the two vessels lay side by side, in complete readiness for sea, our ensigns hanging from the peaks, and our tall spars reflected from the glassy surface of the river, which, since sunrise, had been unbroken by a ripple. At length a few whiffs came across the water, and, by eleven o'clock, the regular northwest wind set steadily in. There was no need of calling all hands, for we had all been

* We had also a small quantity of gold dust, which Mexicans or Indians had brought down to us from the interior. It was not uncommon for our ships to bring a little, as I have since learned from the owners. I heard rumors of gold discoveries, but they attracted little or no attention, and were not followed up.

hanging about the forecastle the whole forenoon, and were ready for a start upon the first sign of a breeze. Often we turned our eyes aft upon the captain, who was walking the deck, with every now and then a look to windward. He made a sign to the mate, who came forward, took his station deliberately between the knightheads, cast a glance aloft, and called out, "All hands, lay aloft and loose the sails!" We were half in the rigging before the order came, and never since we left Boston were the gaskets off the yards, and the rigging overhauled, in a shorter time. "All ready forward, sir!" "All ready the main!" "Crossjack yards all ready, sir!" "Lay down, all hands but one on each yard!" The yardarm and bunt gaskets were cast off; and each sail hung by the jigger, with one man standing by the tie to let it go. At the same moment that we sprang aloft, a dozen hands sprang into the rigging of the *California*, and in an instant were all over her yards; and her sails, too, were ready to be dropped at the word. In the meantime our bow gun had been loaded and run out, and its discharge was to be the signal for dropping the sails. A cloud of smoke came out of our bows; the echoes of the gun rattled our farewell among the hills of California, and the two ships were covered, from head to foot, with their white canvas. For a few minutes all was uproar and apparent confusion; men jumping about like monkeys in the rigging; ropes and blocks flying, orders given and answered amid the confused noises of men singing out at the ropes. The topsails came to the mastheads with "Cheerly, men!" and, in a few minutes, every sail was set, for the wind was light. The head sails were backed, the windlass came round "slip—slap" to the cry of the sailors. "Hove short, sir," said the mate. "Up with him!" "Aye, aye, sir." A few hearty and long heaves, and the anchor showed its head. "Hook cat!" The fall was stretched along the decks; all hands laid hold. "Hurrah, for the last time," said the mate; and the anchor came to the cathead to the tune of "Time for Us to Go," with a rollicking chorus. Everything was done quick, as though it *was* for the last time. The head yards were filled away, and our ship began to move through the water on her homeward-bound course.

The *California* had got under way at the same moment, and we sailed down the narrow bay abreast, and were just off the mouth, and, gradually drawing ahead of her, were on the point of giving her three parting cheers, when suddenly we found ourselves stopped short, and the *California* ranging fast ahead of us. A bar stretches across the mouth of the harbor, with water enough to float common vessels, but, being low in the water, and having kept well to leeward, as we were bound to the southward, we had stuck fast, while the *California*, being light, had floated over.

We kept all sail on, in the hope of forcing over, but, failing in this, we hove aback, and lay waiting for the tide, which was on the flood, to take us back into the channel. This was something of a damper to us, and the captain looked not a little mortified and vexed. "This is the same place where the *Rosa* got ashore, sir," observed our redheaded second mate, most malapropos. A malediction on the *Rosa*, and him, too, was all the answer he got, and he slunk off to leeward. In a few minutes the force of the wind and the rising of the tide backed us into the stream, and we were on our way to our old anchoring place, the tide setting swiftly up, and the ship barely manageable in the light breeze. We came to in our old berth opposite the hide house, whose inmates were not a little surprised to see us return. We felt as though we were tied to California; and some of the crew swore that they never should get clear of the "bloody" * coast.

In about half an hour, which was near high water, the order was given to man the windlass, and again the anchor was catted; but there was no song, and not a word was said about the last time. The *California* had come back on finding that we had returned, and was hove to, waiting for us, off the point. This time we passed the bar safely, and were soon up with the *California*, who filled away, and kept us company. She seemed desirous of a trial of speed, and our captain accepted the challenge, although we were loaded down to the bolts of our chain plates, as deep as a sand barge, and bound so taut with our cargo that we were no more fit for a race than a man in fetters; while our antagonist was in her best trim. Being clear of the point, the breeze became stiff, and the royal masts bent under our sails, but we would not take them in until we saw three boys spring aloft into the rigging of the *California;* when they were all furled at once, but with orders to our boys to stay aloft at the topgallant mastheads and loose them again at the word. It was my duty to furl the fore royal; and, while standing by to loose it again, I had a fine view of

* This is a common expletive among sailors, and suits any purpose.

the scene. From where I stood, the two vessels seemed nothing but spars and sails, while their narrow decks, far below, slanting over by the force of the wind aloft, appeared hardly capable of supporting the great fabrics raised upon them. The *California* was to windward of us, and had every advantage; yet, while the breeze was stiff, we held our own. As soon as it began to slacken, she ranged a little ahead, and the order was given to loose the royals. In an instant the gaskets were off and the bunt dropped. "Sheet home the fore royal! Weather sheet's home!" "Lee sheet's home!" "Hoist away, sir!" is bawled from aloft. "Overhaul your clew lines!" shouts the mate. "Aye, aye, sir! All clear!" "Taut leech—belay! Well the lee brace; haul taut to windward"—and the royals are set. These brought us up again; but, the wind continuing light, the *California* set hers, and it was soon evident that she was walking away from us. Our captain then hailed, and said that he should keep off to his course; adding, "She isn't the *Alert* now. If I had her in your trim she would have been out of sight by this time." This was good-naturedly answered from the *California*, and she braced sharp up, and stood close upon the wind up the coast; while we squared away our yards, and stood before the wind to the south-southwest. The *California*'s crew manned her weather rigging, waved their hats in the air, and gave us three hearty cheers, which we answered as heartily, and the customary single cheer came back to us from over the water. She stood on her way, doomed to eighteen months' or two years' hard service upon that hated coast, while we were making our way to our home, to which every hour and every mile was bringing us nearer.

As soon as we parted company with the *California*, all hands were sent aloft to set the studding sails. Booms were rigged out, tacks and halyards rove, sail after sail packed upon her, until every available inch of canvas was spread, that we might not lose a breath of the fair wind. We could now see how much she was cramped and deadened by her cargo; for with a good breeze on her quarter, and every stitch of canvas spread, we could not get more than six knots out of her. She had no more life in her than if she were waterlogged. The log was hove several times; but she was doing her best. We had hardly patience with her, but the older sailors said, "Stand by! You'll see her work herself loose in a week or two, and then she'll walk up to Cape Horn like a race horse."

When all sail had been set, and the decks cleared up, the *California* was a speck in the horizon, and the coast lay like a low cloud along the northeast. At sunset they were both out of sight, and we were once more upon the ocean, where sky and water meet.

# CHAPTER XXX

At eight o'clock all hands were called aft, and the watches set for the voyage. Some changes were made; but I was glad to find myself still in the larboard watch. Our crew was somewhat diminished; for a man and a boy had gone in the *Pilgrim;* another was second mate of the *Ayacucho;* and a fourth, Harry Bennett, the oldest man of the crew, had broken down under the hard work and constant exposure on the coast, and, having had a stroke of the palsy, was left behind at the hide house, under the charge of Captain Arthur. The poor fellow wished very much to come home in the ship; and he ought to have been brought home in her. But a live dog is better than a dead lion, and a sick sailor belongs to nobody's mess; so he was sent ashore with the rest of the lumber, which was only in the way. He had come on board, with his chest, in the morning, and tried to make himself useful about decks; but his shuffling feet and weak arms led him into trouble, and some words were said to him by the mate. He had the spirit of a man, and had become a little tender, perhaps weakened in mind, and said, "Mr. Brown, I always did my duty aboard until I was sick. If you don't want me, say so, and I'll go ashore." "Bring up his chest," said Mr. Brown, and poor Bennett went down into a boat and was taken ashore, with tears in his eyes. He loved the ship and the crew, and wished to get home, but could not bear to be treated as a "soger" or loafer on board. This was the only hardhearted thing I ever knew Mr. Brown to do.

By these diminutions, we were shorthanded for a voyage round Cape Horn in the dead of winter. Beside Stimson and myself, there were only five in the forecastle; who, together with four boys in the steerage, the sailmaker, carpenter, cook, and steward, composed the crew. In addition to this, we were only four days out, when the sailmaker, who was the oldest and best seaman on board, was taken with the palsy, and was useless for the rest of the voyage. The constant wading in the water, in all weathers, to take off hides, together with the other labors, is too much for men even in middle life, and for any who have not good constitutions. (Beside these two men of ours, the second officer of the *California* and the carpenter of the *Pilgrim*, as we afterward learned, broke down under the work, and the latter died at Santa Barbara. The young man, too, Henry Mellus, who came out with us from Boston in the *Pilgrim*, had to be taken from his berth before the mast and made clerk, on account of a fit of rheumatism which attacked him soon after he came upon the coast.) By the loss of the sailmaker, our watch was reduced to five, of whom two were boys, who never steered but in fine weather, so that the other two and myself had to stand at the wheel four hours apiece out of every twenty-four; and the other watch had only four helmsmen. "Never mind—we're homeward bound!" was the answer to everything; and we should not have minded this, were it not for the thought that we should be off Cape Horn in the very dead of winter. It was now the first part of May; and two months would bring us off the Cape in July, which is the worst month in the year there; when the sun rises at nine and sets at three, giving eighteen hours' night, and there is snow and rain, gales and high seas, in abundance.

The prospect of meeting this in a ship half-manned, and loaded so deep that every heavy sea must wash her fore and aft, was by no means pleasant. The *Alert*, in her passage out, doubled the Cape in the month of February, which is mid-summer; and we came round in the *Pilgrim* in the latter part of October, which we thought was bad enough. There was only one of our crew who had been off there in the winter, and that was in a whaleship, much lighter and higher than our ship; yet he said they had man-killing weather for twenty days without intermission, and their decks were swept twice, and they were all glad enough to see the last of it. The *Brandywine* frigate, also, in her recent passage round, had sixty days off the Cape, and lost several boats by the heavy seas. All this was for our comfort; yet pass it we must; and all hands agreed to make the best of it.

During our watches below we overhauled our clothes, and made and mended everything for bad weather. Each of us had made for himself a suit of oilcloth or tarpaulin, and these we got out, and gave thorough coatings of oil or tar, and hung upon the stays to dry. Our stout boots, too, we covered over with a thick mixture of melted grease and tar. Thus we took advantage of the warm sun and fine weather of the Pacific to prepare for its other face. In the forenoon watches below, our forecastle looked like the workshop of what a sailor is—a Jack-at-all-trades. Thick stockings and drawers were darned and patched; mittens dragged from the bottom of the chest and mended; comforters made for the neck and ears; old flannel shirts cut up to line monkey jackets; southwesters were lined with flannel, and a pot of paint smuggled forward to give them a coat on the outside; and everything turned to hand; so that, although two years had left us but a scanty wardrobe, yet the economy and invention which necessity teaches a sailor soon put each of us in pretty good trim for bad weather, before we had seen the last of the fine. Even the cobbler's art was not out of place. Several old shoes were very decently repaired, and with waxed ends, an awl, and the top of an old boot, I made me quite a respectable sheath for my knife.

There was one difficulty, however, which nothing that we could do would remedy; and that was the leaking of the forecastle, which made it very uncomfortable in bad weather, and rendered half of the berths tenantless. The tightest ships, in a long voyage, from the constant strain which is upon the bowsprit, will leak more or less round the heel of the bowsprit and the bitts, which come down into the forecastle; but, in addition to this, we had an unaccountable leak on the starboard bow, near the cathead, which drove us from the forward berths on that side, and, indeed, when she was on the starboard tack, from all the forward berths. One of the after berths, too, leaked in very bad weather; so that in a

ship which was in other respects unusually tight, and brought
her cargo to Boston perfectly dry, we had, after every effort
made to prevent it, in the way of calking and leading, a forecastle with only three dry berths for seven of us. However, as
there is never but one watch below at a time, by "turning in
and out," we did pretty well. And there being in our watch
but three of us who lived forward, we generally had a dry
berth apiece in bad weather.*

All this, however, was but anticipation. We were still in
fine weather in the North Pacific, running down the northeast
trades, which we took on the second day after leaving San
Diego.

*Sunday, May 15th*, one week out, we were in latitude
14° 56' N., lon. 116° 14' W., having gone, by reckoning, over
thirteen hundred miles in seven days. In fact, ever since leaving San Diego, we had had a fair wind, and as much as we
wanted of it. For seven days our lower and topmast studding
sails were set all the time, and our royals and topgallant studding sails whenever she could stagger under them. Indeed, the
captain had shown, from the moment we got to sea, that he
was to have no boy's play, but that the ship was to carry all
she could, and that he was going to make up by "cracking on"
to her what she wanted in lightness. In this way we frequently
made three degrees of latitude, besides something in longitude,
in the course of twenty-four hours. Our days we spent in the
usual ship's work. The rigging which had become slack from
being long in port was to be set up; breast backstays got up;
studding-sail booms rigged upon the main yard; and royal
studding sails got ready for the light trades; ringtail set; and
new rigging fitted, and sails made ready for Cape Horn. For,
with a ship's gear, as well as a sailor's wardrobe, fine weather
must be improved to get ready for the bad to come. Our
forenoon watch below, as I have said, was given to our own
work, and our night watches were spent in the usual manner—
a trick at the wheel, a lookout on the forecastle, a nap on a
coil of rigging under the lee of the rail; a yarn round the
windlass end; or, as was generally my way, a solitary walk

* On removing the cathead, after the ship arrived at Boston, it was
found that there were two holes under it which had been bored for the
purpose of driving treenails, and which, accidentally, had not been
plugged up when the cathead was placed over them. This provoking
little piece of negligence caused us great discomfort.

fore and aft, in the weather waist, between the windlass end and the main tack. Every wave that she threw aside brought us nearer home, and every day's observation at noon showed a progress which, if it continued, would, in less than five months, take us into Boston Bay. This is the pleasure of life at sea—fine weather, day after day, without interruption; fair wind, and aplenty of it; and homeward bound. Everyone was in good humor; things went right; and all was done with a will. At the dog watch, all hands came on deck, and stood round the weather side of the forecastle, or sat upon the windlass, and sung sea songs and those ballads of pirates and highwaymen which sailors delight in. Home, too, and what we should do when we got there, and when and how we should arrive, was no infrequent topic. Every night, after the kids and pots were put away, and we had lighted our pipes and cigars at the galley, and gathered about the windlass, the first question was:

"Well, Dana, what was the latitude today?"

"Why, fourteen, north; and she has been going seven knots ever since."

"Well, this will bring us to the line in five days."

"Yes, but these trades won't last twenty-four hours longer," says an old salt, pointing with the sharp of his hand to leeward. "I know that by the look of the clouds."

Then came all manner of calculations and conjectures as to the continuance of the wind, the weather under the line, the southeast trades, &c., and rough guesses as to the time the ship would be up with the Horn; and some, more venturous, gave her so many days to Boston Light, and offered to bet that she would not exceed it.

"You'd better wait till you get round Cape Horn," says an old croaker.

"Yes," says another, "you may see Boston, but you've got to 'smell hell' before that good day."

Rumors also of what had been said in the cabin, as usual, found their way forward. The steward had heard the captain say something about the Straits of Magellan, and the man at the wheel fancied he had heard him tell the "passenger" that, if he found the wind ahead and the weather very bad off the Cape, he should stick her off for New Holland, and come home round the Cape of Good Hope.

This passenger—the first and only one we had had, except

to go from port to port, on the coast—was no one else than a
gentleman whom I had known in my smoother days, and the
last person I should have expected to see on the coast of
California—Professor Nuttall, of Cambridge. I had left him
quietly seated in the chair of Botany and Ornithology in Harvard University, and the next I saw of him, he was strolling
about San Diego beach, in a sailor's pea jacket, with a wide
straw hat, and barefooted, with his trousers rolled up to his
knees, picking up stones and shells. He had traveled overland
to the Northwest Coast, and come down in a small vessel to
Monterey. There he learned that there was a ship at the leeward about to sail for Boston, and, taking passage in the
*Pilgrim,* which was then at Monterey, he came slowly along,
visiting the intermediate ports, and examining the trees, plants,
earths, birds, &c., and joined us at San Diego shortly before
we sailed. The second mate of the *Pilgrim* told me that they
had an old gentleman on board who knew me, and came
from the college that I had been in. He could not recollect
his name, but said he was a "sort of an oldish man," with
white hair, and spent all his time in the bush, and along the
beach, picking up flowers and shells and such truck, and
had a dozen boxes and barrels full of them. I thought over
everybody who would be likely to be there, but could fix
upon no one; when, the next day, just as we were about to
shove off from the beach, he came down to the boat in the
rig I have described, with his shoes in his hand, and his pockets full of specimens. I knew him at once, though I should
hardly have been more surprised to have seen the Old South
steeple shoot up from the hide house. He probably had no
more difficulty in recognizing me. As we left home about the
same time, we had nothing to tell each other; and, owing to
our different situations on board, I saw but little of him on the
passage home. Sometimes, when I was at the wheel of a calm
night, and the steering required little attention, and the officer
of the watch was forward, he would come aft and hold a short
yarn with me; but this was against the rules of the ship, as is,
in fact, all intercourse between passengers and the crew. I
was often amused to see the sailors puzzled to know what to
make of him, and to hear their conjectures about him and his
business. They were as much at a loss as our old sailmaker
was with the captain's instruments in the cabin. He said there
were three—the *chro*-nometer, the *chre*-nometer, and the *the*-

nometer. The *Pilgrim*'s crew called Mr. Nuttall "Old Curious," from his zeal for curiosities; and some of them said that he was crazy, and that his friends let him go about and amuse himself in this way. Why else a rich man (sailors call every man rich who does not work with his hands, and who wears a long coat and cravat) should leave a Christian country and come to such a place as California to pick up shells and stones, they could not understand. One of them, however, who had seen something more of the world ashore, set all to rights, as he thought: "Oh, 'vast there! You don't know anything about them craft. I've seen them colleges and know the ropes. They keep all such things for cur'osities, and study 'em, and have men a purpose to go and get 'em. This old chap knows what he's about. He a'n't the child you take him for. He'll carry all these things to the college, and if they are better than any that they have had before, he'll be head of the college. Then, by and by, somebody else will go after some more, and if they beat him he'll have to go again, or else give up his berth. That's the way they do it. This old covey knows the ropes. He has worked a traverse over 'em, and come 'way out here where nobody's ever been afore, and where they'll never think of coming." This explanation satisfied Jack; and as it raised Mr. Nuttall's credit, and was near enough to the truth for common purposes, I did not disturb it.

With the exception of Mr. Nuttall, we had no one on board but the regular ship's company and the livestock. Upon the stock we had made a considerable inroad. We killed one of the bullocks every four days, so that they did not last us up to the line. We, or rather, the cabin, then began upon the sheep and the poultry, for these never come into Jack's mess.*

---

* The customs as to the allowance of "grub" are very nearly the same in all American merchantmen. Whenever a pig is killed, the sailors have one mess from it. The rest goes to the cabin. The smaller livestock, poultry, &c., the sailors never taste. And indeed they do not complain of this, for it would take a great deal to supply them with a good meal; and without the accompaniments (which could hardly be furnished to them), it would not be much better than salt beef. But even as to the salt beef, they are scarcely dealt fairly with; for whenever a barrel is opened, before any of the beef is put into the harness cask, the steward comes up and picks it all over, and takes out the best pieces (those that have any fat in them) for the cabin. This was done in both the vessels I was in, and the men said that it was usual in other vessels. Indeed, it is made no secret, and some of the crew are usually called to help in assorting and putting away the pieces. By this arrangement the hard, dry pieces, which the sailors call "old horse," come to their share.

The pigs were left for the latter part of the voyage, for they are sailors, and can stand all weathers. We had an old sow on board, the mother of a numerous progeny, who had been twice round the Cape of Good Hope and once round Cape Horn. The last time going round was very nearly her death. We heard her squealing and moaning one dark night after it had been snowing and hailing for several hours, and, climbing over into the sty, we found her nearly frozen to death. We got some straw, an old sail, and other things, and wrapped her up in a corner of the sty, where she stayed until we came into fine weather again.

*Wednesday, May 18th.* Lat. 9° 54′ N., lon. 113° 17′ W. The northeast trades had now left us, and we had the usual variable winds, the "doldrums," which prevail near the line, together with some rain. So long as we were in these latitudes, we had but little rest in our watch on deck at night; for, as the winds were light and variable, and we could not lose a breath, we were all the watch bracing the yards, and taking in and making sail, and "humbugging" with our flying kites. A little puff of wind on the larboard quarter, and then: "Larboard forebraces!" and studding-sail booms were rigged out, studding sails set alow and aloft, the yards trimmed, and jibs and spanker in; when it would come as calm as a duck pond, the man at the wheel standing with the palm of his hand up,

---

There is a singular piece of rhyme, traditional among sailors, which they say over such pieces of beef. I do not know that it ever appeared in print before. When seated round the kid, if a particularly bad piece is found, one of them takes it up, and addresses it thus:

> " 'Old horse! Old horse! What brought you here?'
> 'From Sacarap' to Portland Pier
> I've carted stone this many a year;
> Till, killed by blows and sore abuse,
> They salted me down for sailors' use.
> The sailors they do me despise;
> They turn me over and damn my eyes;
> Cut off my meat, and scrape my bones,
> And pitch me over to Davy Jones.' "

There is a story current among seamen, that a beef dealer was convicted, at Boston, of having sold old horse for ship's stores, instead of beef, and had been sentenced to be confined in jail until he should eat the whole of it; and that he is now lying in Boston jail. I have heard this story often, on board other vessels besides those of our own nation. It is very generally believed, and is always highly commended, as a fair instance of retaliatory justice.

feeling for the wind. "Keep her off a little!" "All aback forward, sir!" cries a man from the forecastle. Down go the braces again; in come the studding sails, all in a mess, which half an hour won't set right; yards braced sharp up, and she's on the starboard tack, close-hauled. The studding sails must now be cleared away, and set up in the tops and on the booms, and the gear cut off and made fast. By the time this is done, and you are looking out for a soft plank for a nap—"Lay aft here, and square in the head yards!" and the studding sails are all set again on the starboard side. So it goes until it is eight bells—call the watch, heave the log; relieve the wheel; and go below, the larboard watch.

*Sunday, May 22nd.* Lat. 5° 14' N., lon. 166° 45' W. We were now a fortnight out, and within five degrees of the line, to which two days of good breeze would take us; but we had, for the most part, what the sailors call "an Irishman's hurricane—right up and down." This day it rained nearly all day, and, being Sunday and nothing to do, we stopped up the scuppers and filled the decks with rain water, and, bringing all our clothes on deck, had a grand wash, fore and aft. When this was through, we stripped to our drawers, and taking pieces of soap, with strips of canvas for towels, we turned to and soaped, washed, and scrubbed one another down, to get off, as we said, the California grime; for the common wash in salt water, which is all that Jack can get, being on an allowance of fresh, had little efficacy, and was more for taste than utility. The captain was below all the afternoon, and we had something nearer to Saturnalia than anything we had yet seen; for the mate came into the scuppers, with a couple of boys to scrub him, and got into a contest with them in heaving water. By unplugging the holes, we let the soapsuds off the decks, and in a short time had a new supply of clear rain water, in which we had a grand rinsing. It was surprising to see how much soap and fresh water did for the complexions of many of us; how much of what we supposed to be tan and sea-blacking we got rid of. The next day, the sun rising clear, the ship was covered, fore and aft, with clothes of all sorts, hanging out to dry.

As we approached the line, the wind became more easterly, and the weather clearer, and in twenty days from San Diego—

*Saturday, May 28th,* at about 3 P.M., with a fine breeze from the east-southeast, we crossed the equator. In twenty-

four hours after crossing the line, we took, which was very
unusual, the regular southeast trades. These winds come a
little from the eastward of southeast, and with us they blew
directly from the east-southeast, which was fortunate for us,
as our course was south-by-west, and we could thus go one
point free. The yards were braced so that every sail drew,
from the spanker to the flying jib; and, the upper yards being
squared in a little, the fore and main topgallant studding sails
were set, and drew handsomely. For twelve days this breeze
blew steadily, not varying a point, and just so fresh that we
could carry our royals; and during the whole time we hardly
started a brace. Such progress did we make that at the end
of seven days from the time we took the breeze, on—

*Sunday, June 5th,* we were in lat. 19° 29′ S., and lon. 118°
01′ W., having made twelve hundred miles in seven days, very
nearly upon a taut bowline. Our good ship was getting to be
herself again, and had increased her rate of sailing more than
one-third since leaving San Diego. The crew ceased complain-
ing of her, and the officers hove the log every two hours with
evident satisfaction. This was glorious sailing. A steady breeze;
the light trade-wind clouds over our heads; the incomparable
temperature of the Pacific—neither hot nor cold; a clear sun
every day, and clear moon and stars every night, and new
constellations rising in the south, and the familiar ones sinking
in the north, as we went on our course, "stemming nightly
toward the pole." Already we had sunk the North Star and
the Great Bear, while the Southern Cross appeared well above
the southern horizon, and all hands looked out sharp to the
southward for the Magellan Clouds, which, each succeeding
night, we expected to make. "The next time we see the North
Star," said one, "we shall be standing to the northward, the
other side of the Horn." This was true enough, and no doubt
it would be a welcome sight, for sailors say that in coming
home from round Cape Horn, or the Cape of Good Hope,
the North Star is the first land you make.

These trades were the same that in the passage out in the
*Pilgrim* lasted nearly all the way from Juan Fernández to the
line; blowing steadily on our starboard quarter for three
weeks, without our starting a brace, or even brailing down the
skysails. Though we had now the same wind, and were in the
same latitude with the *Pilgrim* on her passage out, yet we were
nearly twelve hundred miles to the westward of her course;

for the captain, depending upon the strong southwest winds
which prevail in high southern latitudes during the winter
months, took the full advantage of the trades, and stood well
to the westward, so far that we passed within about two hundred miles of Ducie Island.

It was this weather and sailing that brought to my mind a
little incident that occurred on board the *Pilgrim*, while we
were in the same latitude. We were going along at a great
rate, dead before the wind, with studding sails out on both
sides, alow and aloft, on a dark night, just after midnight, and
everything as still as the grave, except the washing of the
water by the vessel's side; for, being before the wind, with a
smooth sea, the little brig, covered with canvas, was doing
great business with very little noise. The other watch was
below, and all our watch, except myself and the man at the
wheel, were asleep under the lee of the boat. The second mate,
who came out before the mast, and was always very "thick"
with me, had been holding a yarn with me, and just gone aft
to his place on the quarterdeck, and I had resumed my usual
walk to and from the windlass end, when, suddenly, we heard
a loud scream coming from ahead, apparently directly from
under the bows. The darkness, and complete stillness of the
night, and the solitude of the ocean, gave to the sound a
dreadful and almost supernatural effect. I stood perfectly still,
and my heart beat quick. The sound woke up the rest of the
watch, who stood looking at one another. "What, in the name
of God, is that?" said the second mate, coming slowly forward. The first thought I had was that it might be a boat, with
the crew of some wrecked vessel, or perhaps the boat of some
whaleship, out overnight, and we had run it down in the darkness. Another scream—but less loud than the first. This started
us, and we ran forward, and looked over the bows, and over
the sides, to leeward, but nothing was to be seen or heard.
What was to be done? Heave the ship aback, and call the captain? Just at this moment, in crossing the forecastle, one of the
men saw a light below, and, looking down the scuttle, saw
the watch all out of their berths, and afoul of one poor fellow,
dragging him out of his berth, and shaking him, to wake him
out of a nightmare. They had been waked out of their sleep,
and as much alarmed at the scream as we were, and were
hesitating whether to come on deck, when the second sound,
proceeding directly from one of the berths, revealed the cause

of the alarm. The fellow got a good shaking for the trouble he had given. We made a joke of the matter; and we could well laugh, for our minds were not a little relieved by its ridiculous termination.

We were now close upon the southern tropical line, and, with so fine a breeze, were daily leaving the sun behind us, and drawing nearer to Cape Horn, for which it behooved us to make every preparation. Our rigging was all overhauled and mended, or changed for new, where it was necessary; new and strong bobstays fitted in the place of the chain ones, which were worn out; the spritsail yard and martingale guys and backropes set well taut; brand-new fore and main braces rove; topgallant sheets, and wheelropes, made of green hide, laid up in the form of rope, were stretched and fitted; and new topsail clew lines, &c., rove; new fore-topmast backstays fitted; and other preparations made in good season, that the ropes might have time to stretch and become limber before we got into cold weather.

*Sunday, June 12th.* Lat. 26° 04′ S., lon. 116° 31′ W. We had now lost the regular trades, and had the winds variable, principally from the westward, and kept on in a southerly course, sailing very nearly upon a meridian, and at the end of the week—

*Sunday, June 19th,* were in lat. 34° 15′ S., and lon. 116° 38′ W.

# CHAPTER XXXI

There began now to be a decided change in the appearance of things. The days became shorter and shorter; the sun running lower in its course each day, and giving less and less heat, and the nights so cold as to prevent our sleeping on deck;

the Magellan Clouds in sight, of a clear, moonless night; the skies looking cold and angry; and, at times, a long, heavy, ugly sea, setting in from the southward, told us what we were coming to. Still, however, we had a fine, strong breeze, and kept on our way under as much sail as our ship would bear. Toward the middle of the week, the wind hauled to the southward, which brought us upon a taut bowline, made the ship meet, nearly head on, the heavy swell which rolled from that quarter; and there was something not at all encouraging in the manner in which she met it. Being still so deep and heavy, she wanted the buoyancy which should have carried her over the seas, and she dropped heavily into them, the water washing over the decks; and every now and then, when an unusually large sea met her fairly upon the bows, she struck it with a sound as dead and heavy as that with which a sledgehammer falls upon the pile, and took the whole of it in upon the forecastle, and, rising, carried it aft in the scuppers, washing the rigging off the pins, and carrying along with it everything which was loose on deck. She had been acting in this way all of our forenoon watch below; as we could tell by the washing of the water over our heads, and the heavy breaking of the seas against her bows, only the thickness of a plank from our heads, as we lay in our berths, which are directly against the bows. At eight bells, the watch was called, and we came on deck, one hand going aft to take the wheel, and another going to the galley to get the grub for dinner. I stood on the forecastle, looking at the seas, which were rolling high, as far as the eye could reach, their tops white with foam, and the body of them of a deep indigo blue, reflecting the bright rays of the sun. Our ship rose slowly over a few of the largest of them, until one immense fellow came rolling on, threatening to cover her, and which I was sailor enough to know, by the "feeling of her" under my feet, she would not rise over. I sprang upon the knightheads, and, seizing hold of the forestay, drew myself up upon it. My feet were just off the stanchion when the bow struck fairly into the middle of the sea, and it washed the ship fore and aft, burying her in the water. As soon as she rose out of it, I looked aft, and everything forward of the mainmast, except the longboat, which was griped and double-lashed down to the ringbolts, was swept off clear. The galley, the pigsty, the hencoop, and a large sheep pen which had been built upon the fore hatch, were all gone in the twinkling of an eye, leaving the deck as clean as a chin new reaped, and not a stick left to show where anything had stood. In the scuppers lay the galley, bottom up, and a few boards floating about—the wreck of the sheep pen—and half a dozen miserable sheep floating among them, wet through, and not a little frightened at the sudden change that had come upon them. As soon as the sea had washed by, all hands sprang up out of the forecastle to see what had become of the ship; and in a few moments the cook and Old Bill crawled out from under the galley, where they had been lying in the water, nearly smothered, with the galley over them. Fortunately, it rested against the bulwarks, or it would have broken some of their bones. When the water ran off, we picked the sheep up, and put them in the longboat, got the galley back in its place, and set things a little to rights; but, had not our ship had uncommonly high bulwarks and rail, everything must have been washed overboard, not excepting Old Bill and the cook. Bill had been standing at the galley door, with the kid of beef in his hand for the forecastle mess, when away he went, kid, beef, and all. He held onto the kid to the last, like a good fellow, but the beef was gone, and when the water had run off we saw it lying high and dry, like a rock at low tide—nothing could hurt *that*. We took the loss of our beef very easily, consoling ourselves with the recollection that the cabin had more to lose than we; and chuckled not a little at seeing the remains of the chicken pie and pancakes floating in the scuppers. "This will never do!" was what some said, and everyone felt. Here we were, not yet within a thousand miles of the latitude of Cape Horn, and our decks swept by a sea not one half so high as we must expect to find there. Some blamed the captain for loading his ship so deep when he knew what he must expect; while others said that the wind was always southwest, off the Cape, in the winter and that, running before it, we should not mind the seas so much. When we got down into the forecastle, Old Bill, who was somewhat of a croaker— having met with a great many accidents at sea—said that, if that was the way she was going to act, we might as well make our wills, and balance the books at once, and put on a clean shirt. " 'Vast there, you bloody old owl! You're always hanging out blue lights! You're frightened by the ducking you got in the scuppers, and can't take a joke! What's the use in being always on the lookout for Davy Jones?" "Stand by!" says another, "and we'll get an afternoon watch below, by this scrape"; but in this they were disappointed, for at two bells all hands were called and set to work, getting lashings upon everything on deck; and the captain talked of sending down the long topgallant masts; but as the sea went down toward night, and the wind hauled abeam, we left them standing, and set the studding sails.

The next day all hands were turned to upon unbending the old sails, and getting up the new ones; for a ship, unlike people on shore, puts on her best suit in bad weather. The old sails were sent down, and three new topsails, and new fore and main courses, jib, and fore-topmast staysail, which were made on the coast and never had been used, were bent, with a complete set of new earings, robands, and reef points; and reef tackles were rove to the courses, and spilling lines to the topsails. These, with new braces and clew lines fore and aft, gave us a good suit of running rigging.

The wind continued westerly, and the weather and sea less rough since the day on which we shipped the heavy sea, and we were making great progress under studding sails, with our light sails all set, keeping a little to the eastward of south; for the captain, depending upon westerly winds off the Cape, had kept so far to the westward that, though we were within about five hundred miles of the latitude of Cape Horn, we were nearly seventeen hundred miles to the westward of it. Through the rest of the week we continued on with a fair wind, gradually, as we got more to the southward, keeping a more easterly course, and bringing the wind on our larboard quarter, until—

*Sunday, June 26th,* when, having a fine, clear day, the captain got a lunar observation, as well as his meridian altitude, which made us in lat. 47° 50′ S., lon. 113° 49′ W.; Cape Horn bearing, according to my calculations, ESE. ½ E., and distant eighteen hundred miles.

*Monday, June 27th.* During the first part of this day the wind continued fair, and, as we were going before it, it did not feel very cold, so that we kept at work on deck in our common clothes and round jackets. Our watch had an afternoon watch below for the first time since leaving San Diego; and, having inquired of the third mate what the latitude was at noon, and made our usual guesses as to the time she would need to be up with the Horn, we turned in for a nap. We were sleeping away "at the rate of knots," when three knocks on the scuttle and "All hands, ahoy!" started us from our berths. What could be the matter? It did not appear to be blowing hard, and, looking up through the scuttle, we could see that it was a clear day overhead; yet the watch were taking in sail. We thought there must be a sail in sight, and that we were about to heave to and speak her; and were just congratulating ourselves upon it—for we had seen neither sail nor land since we left port—when we heard the mate's voice on deck (he turned in "all-standing," and was always on deck the moment he was called), singing out to the men who were taking in the studding sails, and asking where his watch were. We did not wait for a second call, but tumbled up the ladder; and there, on the starboard bow, was a bank of mist, covering sea and sky, and driving directly for us. I had seen the same before in my passage round in the *Pilgrim*, and knew what it meant, and that there was no time to be lost. We had nothing on but thin clothes, yet there was not a moment to spare, and at it we went.

The boys of the other watch were in the tops, taking in the topgallant studding sails, and the lower and topmast studding sails were coming down by the run. It was nothing but "haul down and clew up," until we got all the studding sails in, and the royals, flying jib, and mizzen-topgallant sail furled, and the ship kept off a little, to take the squall. The fore and main topgallant sails were still on her, for the "old man" did not mean to be frightened in broad daylight, and was determined to carry sail till the last minute. We all stood waiting for its coming, when the first blast showed us that it was not to be trifled with. Rain, sleet, snow, and wind enough to take our breath from us, and make the toughest turn his back to windward! The ship lay nearly over upon her beam ends; the spars and rigging snapped and cracked; and her topgallant masts bent like whipsticks. "Clew up the fore and main topgallant sails!" shouted the captain, and all hands sprang to the clew lines. The decks were standing nearly at an angle of forty-five degrees, and the ship going like a mad steed through the water, the whole forward part of her in a smother of foam. The halyards were let go, and the yard clewed down, and the sheets started, and in a few minutes the sails smothered and kept in by clew lines and buntlines. "Furl 'em, sir?" asked the mate. "Let go the topsail halyards, fore and aft!" shouted the captain in answer, at the top of his voice. Down came the topsail yards, the reef tackles were manned and hauled out, and we climbed up to windward, and sprang into the weather rigging. The violence of the wind, and the hail and sleet, driving nearly horizontally across the ocean, seemed actually to pin us down to the rigging. It was hard work making head against them. One after another we got out upon the yards. And here we had work to do; for our new sails had hardly been bent long enough to get the stiffness out of them, and the new earings and reef points, stiffened with the sleet, knotted like pieces of iron wire. Having only our round jackets and straw hats on, we were soon wet through, and it was every moment growing colder. Our hands were soon numbed, which, added to the stiffness of everything else, kept us a good while on the yard. After we had got the sail hauled upon the yard, we had to wait a long time for the weather earing to be passed; but there was no fault to be found, for French John was at the earing, and a better sailor never laid out on a yard; so we leaned over the yard and beat our hands upon the sail to keep them from freezing. At length the word came: "Haul out to leeward," and we seized the reef points and hauled the band taut for the lee earing. "Taut band—knot away," and we got the first reef fast, and were just going to lay down, when: "Two reefs—two reefs!" shouted the mate, and we had a second reef to take, in the same way. When this was fast we went down on deck, manned the halyards to leeward, nearly up to our knees in water, set the topsail, and then laid aloft on the main-topsail yard, and reefed that sail in the same manner; for, as I have before stated, we were a good deal reduced in numbers, and, to make it worse, the carpenter, only two days before, had cut his leg with an ax, so that he could not go aloft. This weakened us so that we could not well manage more than one topsail at a time, in such weather as this, and, of course, each man's labor was doubled. From the main-topsail yard, we went upon the main yard, and took a reef in the mainsail. No sooner had we got on deck than: "Lay aloft there, and close-reef mizzen topsail!" This called me; and, being nearest to the rigging, I got first aloft, and out to the weather earing. English Ben was up just after me, and took the lee earing, and the rest of our gang were soon on the yard, and began to fist the sail, when the

mate considerately sent up the cook and steward to help us.
I could now account for the long time it took to pass the
other earings, for, to do my best, with a strong hand to help
me at the dog's ear, I could not get it passed until I heard
them beginning to complain in the bunt. One reef after
another we took in, until the sail was close-reefed, when we
went down and hoisted away at the halyards. In the meantime,
the jib had been furled and the staysail set, and the ship under
her reduced sail had got more upright, and was under
management; but the two topgallant sails were still hanging
in the buntlines, and slatting and jerking as though they
would take the masts out of her. We gave a look aloft, and
knew that our work was not done yet; and, sure enough,
no sooner did the mate see that we were on deck than: "Lay
aloft there, four of you, and furl the topgallant sails!" This
called me again, and two of us went aloft up the forerigging,
and two more up the main, upon the topgallant yards. The
shrouds were now iced over, the sleet having formed a crust
round all the standing rigging, and on the weather side of the
masts and yards. When we got upon the yard, my hands
were so numb that I could not have cast off the knot of the
gasket if it were to save my life. We both lay over the yard
for a few seconds, beating our hands upon the sail, until we
started the blood into our fingers' ends, and at the next
moment our hands were in a burning heat. My companion
on the yard was a lad (the boy George Somerby), who came
out in the ship a weak, puny boy, from one of the Boston
schools, "no larger than a spritsail-sheet knot," nor "heavier
than a paper of lamp black," and "not strong enough to haul
a shad off a gridiron," but who was now "as long as a spare
topmast, strong enough to knock down an ox, and hearty
enough to eat him." We fisted the sail together, and, after
six or eight minutes of hard hauling and pulling and beating
down the sail, which was about as stiff as sheet iron, we
managed to get it furled; and snugly furled it must be, for we
knew the mate well enough to be certain that if it got adrift
again we should be called up from our watch below, at any
hour of the night, to furl it.

I had been on the lookout for a chance to jump below
and clap on a thick jacket and southwester; but when we
got on deck we found that eight bells had been struck, and
the other watch gone below, so that there were two hours

of dog watch for us, and aplenty of work to do. It had now
set in for a steady gale from the southwest; but we were
not yet far enough to the southward to make a fair wind
of it, for we must give Tierra del Fuego a wide berth. The
decks were covered with snow, and there was a constant
driving of sleet. In fact, Cape Horn had set in with good
earnest. In the midst of all this, and before it became dark,
we had all the studding sails to make up and stow away,
and then to lay aloft and rig in all the booms, fore and aft,
and coil away the tacks, sheets, and halyards. This was pretty
tough work for four or five hands, in the face of a gale
which almost took us off the yards, and with ropes so stiff
with ice that it was almost impossible to bend them. I was
nearly half an hour out on the end of the foreyard, trying
to coil away and stop down the topmast-studding sail tack
and lower halyards. It was after dark when we got through,
and we were not a little pleased to hear four bells struck,
which sent us below for two hours, and gave us each a pot
of hot tea with our cold beef and bread, and, what was
better yet, a suit of thick, dry clothing, fitted for the weather,
in place of our thin clothes, which were wet through and
now frozen stiff.

This sudden turn, for which we were so little prepared,
was as unacceptable to me as to any of the rest; for I had
been troubled for several days with a slight toothache, and
this cold weather and wetting and freezing were not the best
things in the world for it. I soon found that it was getting
strong hold, and running over all parts of my face; and
before the watch was out I went aft to the mate, who had
charge of the medicine chest, to get something for it. But
the chest showed like the end of a long voyage, for there was
nothing that would answer but a few drops of laudanum,
which must be saved for an emergency; so I had only to bear
the pain as well as I could.

When we went on deck at eight bells, it had stopped snowing, and there were a few stars out, but the clouds were
still black, and it was blowing a steady gale. Just before
midnight, I went aloft and sent down the mizzen royal yard,
and had the good luck to do it to the satisfaction of the mate,
who said it was done "out of hand and shipshape." The
next four hours below were but little relief to me, for I lay
awake in my berth the whole time, from the pain in my

face, and heard every bell strike, and, at four o'clock, turned out with the watch, feeling little spirit for the hard duties of the day. Bad weather and hard work at sea can be borne up against very well if one only has spirit and health; but there is nothing brings a man down, at such a time, like bodily pain and want of sleep. There was, however, too much to do to allow time to think; for the gale of yesterday, and the heavy seas we met with a few days before, while we had yet ten degrees more southing to make, had convinced the captain that we had something before us which was not to be trifled with, and orders were given to send down the long topgallant masts. The topgallant and royal yards were accordingly struck, the flying jib boom rigged in, and the topgallant masts sent down on deck, and all lashed together by the side of the longboat. The rigging was then sent down and coiled away below, and everything made snug aloft. There was not a sailor in the ship who was not rejoiced to see these sticks come down; for, so long as the yards were aloft, on the least sign of a lull, the topgallant sails were loosed, and then we had to furl them again in a snow squall, and "shin" up and down single ropes caked with ice, and send royal yards down in the teeth of a gale coming right from the south pole. It was an interesting sight, too, to see our noble ship, dismantled of all her top hamper of long tapering masts and yards, and boom pointed with spear head, which ornamented her in port; and all that canvas, which a few days before had covered her like a cloud, from the truck to the water's edge, spreading far out beyond her hull on either side, now gone; and she stripped, like a wrestler for the fight. It corresponded, too, with the desolate character of her situation—alone, as she was, battling with storms, wind, and ice, at this extremity of the globe, and in almost constant night.

*Friday, July 1st.* We were now nearly up to the latitude of Cape Horn, and having over forty degrees of easting to make, we squared away the yards before a strong westerly gale, shook a reef out of the fore-topsail, and stood on our way, east-by-south, with the prospect of being up with the Cape in a week or ten days. As for myself, I had had no sleep for forty-eight hours; and the want of rest, together with constant wet and cold, had increased the swelling, so that my face was nearly as large as two, and I found it impossible to get my mouth open wide enough to eat. In this state, the steward applied to the captain for some rice to boil for me, but he only got a "No, d—— you! Tell him to eat salt junk and hard bread, like the rest of them." This was, in truth, what I expected. However, I did not starve, for Mr. Brown, who was a man as well as a sailor, and had always been a good friend to me, smuggled a pan of rice into the galley, and told the cook to boil it for me, and not let the "old man" see it. Had it been fine weather, or in port, I should have gone below and lain by until my face got well; but in such weather as this, and shorthanded as we were, it was not for me to desert my post; so I kept on deck, and stood my watch and did my duty as well as I could.

*Saturday, July 2nd.* This day the sun rose fair, but it ran too low in the heavens to give any heat, or thaw out our sails and rigging; yet the sight of it was pleasant; and we had a steady "reef-topsail breeze" from the westward. The atmosphere, which had previously been clear and cold, for the last few hours grew damp, and had a disagreeable, wet chilliness in it; and the man who came from the wheel said he heard the captain tell the "passenger" that the thermometer had fallen several degrees since morning, which he could not account for in any other way than by supposing that there must be ice near us; though such a thing was rarely heard of in this latitude at this season of the year. At twelve o'clock we went below, and had just got through dinner, when the cook put his head down the scuttle and told us to come on deck and see the finest sight that we had ever seen. "Where away, Doctor?" * asked the first man who was up. "On the larboard bow." And there lay, floating in the ocean, several miles off, an immense, irregular mass, its top and points covered with snow, and its center of a deep indigo color. This was an iceberg, and of the largest size, as one of our men said who had been in the Northern Ocean. As far as the eye could reach, the sea in every direction was of a deep-blue color, the waves running high and fresh, and sparkling in the light, and in the midst lay this immense mountain island, its cavities and valleys thrown into deep shade, and its points and pinnacles glittering in the sun. All hands were soon on deck, looking at it, and admiring in various ways its beauty and grandeur. But no description

* The cook's title in all vessels.

can give any idea of the strangeness, splendor, and, really, the sublimity, of the sight. Its great size—for it must have been from two to three miles in circumference, and several hundred feet in height; its slow motion, as its base rose and sank in the water, and its high points nodded against the clouds; the dashing of the waves upon it, which, breaking high with foam, lined its base with a white crust; and the thundering sound of the cracking of the mass, and the breaking and tumbling down of huge pieces; together with its nearness and approach, which added a slight element of fear—all combined to give to it the character of true sublimity. The main body of the mass was, as I have said, of an indigo color, its base crusted with frozen foam; and as it grew thin and transparent toward the edges and top, its color shaded off from a deep blue to the whiteness of snow. It seemed to be drifting slowly toward the north, so that we kept away and avoided it. It was in sight all the afternoon; and when we got to leeward of it the wind died away, so that we lay to quite near it for a greater part of the night. Unfortunately, there was no moon, but it was a clear night, and we could plainly mark the long, regular heaving of the stupendous mass, as its edges moved slowly against the stars, now revealing them, and now shutting them in. Several times in our watch loud cracks were heard, which sounded as though they must have run through the whole length of the iceberg, and several pieces fell down with a thundering crash, plunging heavily into the sea. Toward morning a strong breeze sprang up, and we filled away, and left it astern, and at daylight it was out of sight. The next day, which was—

*Sunday, July 3rd,* the breeze continued strong, the air exceedingly chilly, and the thermometer low. In the course of the day we saw several icebergs of different sizes, but none so near as the one which we saw the day before. Some of them, as well as we could judge, at the distance at which we were, must have been as large as that, if not larger. At noon we were in lat. 55° 12′ S., and supposed lon. 89° 5′ W. Toward night the wind hauled to the southward, and headed us off our course a little, and blew a tremendous gale; but this we did not mind, as there was no rain nor snow, and we were already under close sail.

*Monday, July 4th.* This was Independence Day in Boston. What firing of guns, and ringing of bells, and rejoicings of

all sorts, in every part of our country! The ladies (who have
not gone down to Nahant, for a breath of cool air and sight
of the ocean) walking the streets with parasols over their
heads, and the dandies in their white pantaloons and silk
stockings! What quantities of ice cream have been eaten, and
how many loads of ice brought into the city from a distance,
and sold out by the lump and the pound! The smallest of
the islands which we saw today would have made the fortune
of poor Jack, if he had had it in Boston; and I dare say he
would have had no objection to being there with it. This, to
be sure, was no place to keep the Fourth of July. To keep
ourselves warm, and the ship out of the ice, was as much as
we could do. Yet no one forgot the day; and many were the
wishes and conjectures and comparisons, both serious and
ludicrous, which were made among all hands. The sun shone
bright as long as it was up, only that a scud of black clouds
was ever and anon driving across it. At noon we were in lat.
54° 27′ S., and lon. 85° 5′ W., having made a good deal of
easting, but having lost in our latitude by the heading off of
the wind. Between daylight and dark—that is, between nine
o'clock and three—we saw thirty-four ice islands of various
sizes; some no bigger than the hull of our vessel, and others
apparently nearly as large as the one that we first saw; though,
as we went on, the islands became smaller and more numerous; and, at sundown of this day, a man at the masthead
saw large tracts of floating ice, called "field ice," at the
southeast. This kind of ice is much more dangerous than the
large islands, for those can be seen at a distance, and kept
away from; but the field ice, floating in great quantities,
and covering the ocean for miles and miles, in pieces of every
size—large, flat, and broken cakes, with here and there an
island rising twenty and thirty feet, and as large as the ship's
hull—this it is very difficult to sheer clear of. A constant
lookout was necessary; for many of these pieces, coming with
the heave of the sea, were large enough to have knocked a
hole in the ship, and that would have been the end of us;
for no boat (even if we could have got one out) could have
lived in such a sea; and no man could have lived in a boat
in such weather. To make our condition still worse, the wind
came out due east, just after sundown, and it blew a gale
dead ahead, with hail and sleet and a thick fog, so that we
could not see half the length of the ship. Our chief reliance,

the prevailing westerly gales, was thus cut off; and here we were, nearly seven hundred miles to the westward of the Cape, with a gale dead from the eastward, and the weather so thick that we could not see the ice, with which we were surrounded, until it was directly under our bows. At 4 P.M. (it was then quite dark) all hands were called, and sent aloft, in a violent squall of hail and rain, to take in sail. We had now all got on our "Cape Horn rig"—thick boots, south-westers coming down over our neck and ears, thick trousers and jackets, and some with oilcloth suits over all. Mittens, too, we wore on deck, but it would not do to go aloft with them, as, being wet and stiff, they might let a man slip overboard, for all the hold he could get upon a rope; so we were obliged to work with bare hands, which, as well as our faces, were often cut with the hailstones, which fell thick and large. Our ship was now all cased with ice—hull, spars, and standing rigging—and the running rigging so stiff that we could hardly bend it so as to belay it, or, still less, take a knot with it; and the sails frozen. One at a time (for it was a long piece of work and required many hands) we furled the courses, mizzen topsail, and fore-topmast staysail, and close-reefed the fore and main topsails, and hove the ship to under the fore, with the main hauled up by the clew lines and buntlines, and ready to be sheeted home, if we found it necessary to make sail to get to windward of an ice island. A regular look-out was then set, and kept by each watch in turn, until the morning. It was a tedious and anxious night. It blew hard the whole time, and there was an almost constant driving of either rain, hail, or snow. In addition to this, it was "as thick as muck," and the ice was all about us. The captain was on deck nearly the whole night, and kept the cook in the galley, with a roaring fire, to make coffee for him, which he took every few hours, and once or twice gave a little to his officers; but not a drop of anything was there for the crew. The captain, who sleeps all the daytime, and comes and goes at night as he chooses, can have his brandy-and-water in the cabin, and his hot coffee at the galley; while Jack, who has to stand through everything, and work in wet and cold, can have nothing to wet his lips or warm his stomach. This was a "temperance ship" by her articles, and, like too many such ships, the temperance was all in the forecastle. The sailor, who only takes his one glass as it is dealt out to him, is in danger of being drunk; while the captain, upon whose self-possession and cool judgment the lives of all depend, may be trusted with any amount, to drink at his will. Sailors will never be convinced that rum is a dangerous thing by taking it away from them and giving it to the officers; nor can they see a friend in that temperance which takes from them what they have always had, and gives them nothing in the place of it. By seeing it allowed to their officers, they will not be convinced that it is taken from them for their good; and by receiving nothing in its place, they will not believe that it is done in kindness. On the contrary, many of them look upon the change as a new instrument of tyranny. Not that they prefer rum. I never knew a sailor who had been a month away from the grogshops who would not prefer a pot of hot coffee or chocolate, in a cold night, to all the rum afloat. They all say that rum only warms them for a time; yet, if they can get nothing better, they will miss what they have lost. The momentary warmth and glow from drinking it; the break and change which it makes in a long, dreary watch by the mere calling all hands aft and serving of it out; and the simply having some event to look forward to and to talk about—all give it an importance and a use which no one can appreciate who has not stood his watch before the mast. On my passage out, the *Pilgrim* was not under temperance articles, and grog was served out every middle and morning watch, and after every reefing of topsails; and, though I had never drunk rum before, nor desire to again, I took my allowance then at the capstan, as the rest did, merely for the momentary warmth it gave the system, and the change in our feelings and aspect of our duties on the watch. At the same time, as I have said, there was not a man on board who would not have pitched the rum to the dogs (I have heard them say so a dozen times) for a pot of coffee or chocolate; or even for our common beverage, "water bewitched and tea begrudged," as it was.* The temperance

---

* The proportions of the ingredients of the tea that was made for us (and ours, as I have before stated, was a favorable specimen of American merchantmen) were a pint of tea and a pint and a half of molasses to about three gallons of water. These are all boiled down together in the "coppers," and, before serving it out, the mess is stirred up with a stick, so as to give each man his fair share of sweetening and tea leaves. The tea for the cabin is, of course, made in the usual way, in a teapot, and drunk with sugar.

reform is the best thing that ever was undertaken for the sailor; but when the grog is taken from him, he ought to have something in its place. As it is now, in most vessels, it is a mere saving to the owners; and this accounts for the sudden increase of temperance ships, which surprised even the best friends of the cause. If every merchant, when he struck grog from the list of the expenses of his ship, had been obliged to substitute as much coffee, or chocolate, as would give each man a potful when he came off the topsail yard, on a stormy night, I fear Jack might have gone to ruin on the old road.*

But this is not doubling Cape Horn. Eight hours of the night our watch was on deck, and during the whole of that time we kept a bright lookout—one man on each bow, another in the bunt of the foreyard, the third mate on the scuttle, one man on each quarter, and another always standing by the wheel. The chief mate was everywhere, and commanded the ship when the captain was below. When a large piece of ice was seen in our way, or drifting near us, the word was passed along, and the ship's head turned one way and another; and sometimes the yards squared or braced up. There was little else to do than to look out; and we had the sharpest eyes in the ship on the forecastle. The only variety was the monotonous voice of the lookout forward: "Another island!" "Ice ahead!" "Ice on the lee bow!" "Hard up the helm!" "Keep her off a little!" "Stead-y!"

In the meantime the wet and cold had brought my face into such a state that I could neither eat nor sleep; and though I stood it out all night, yet, when it became light, I was in such a state that all hands told me I must go below, and lie by for a day or two, or I should be laid up for a long

---

* I do not wish these remarks, so far as they relate to the saving of expense in the outfit, to be applied to the owners of our ship, for she was supplied with an abundance of stores of the best kind that are given to seamen; though the dispensing of them is necessarily left to the captain. And I learned, on our return, that the captain withheld many of the stores from us, from mere ugliness. He brought several barrels of flour home, but would not give us the usual twice-a-week duff, and so as to other stores. Indeed, so high was the reputation of "the employ" among men and officers for the character and outfit of their vessels, and for their liberality in conducting their voyages, that when it was known that they had the *Alert* fitting out for a long voyage, and that hands were to be shipped at a certain time—a half hour before the time, as one of the crew told me, sailors were steering down the wharf, hopping over the barrels, like a drove of sheep.

time. When the watch was changed I went into the steerage, and took off my hat and comforter, and showed my face to the mate, who told me to go below at once, and stay in my berth until the swelling went down, and gave the cook orders to make a poultice for me, and said he would speak to the captain.

I went below and turned in, covering myself over with blankets and jackets, and lay in my berth nearly twenty-four hours, half asleep and half awake, stupid from the dull pain. I heard the watch called, and the men going up and down, and sometimes a noise on deck, and a cry of "Ice," but I gave little attention to anything. At the end of twenty-four hours the pain went down, and I had a long sleep, which brought me back to my proper state; yet my face was so swollen and tender that I was obliged to keep my berth for two or three days longer. During the two days I had been below, the weather was much the same that it had been—head winds, and snow and rain; or, if the wind came fair, too foggy, and the ice too thick, to run. At the end of the third day the ice was very thick; a complete fog bank covered the ship. It blew a tremendous gale from the eastward, with sleet and snow, and there was every promise of a dangerous and fatiguing night. At dark, the captain called all hands aft, and told them that not a man was to leave the deck that night; that the ship was in the greatest danger, any cake of ice might knock a hole in her, or she might run on an island and go to pieces. No one could tell whether she would be a ship the next morning. The lookouts were then set, and every man was put in his station. When I heard what was the state of things, I began to put on my clothes to stand it out with the rest of them, when the mate came below and, looking at my face, ordered me back to my berth, saying that if we went down, we should all go down together, but if I went on deck I might lay myself up for life. This was the first word I had heard from aft; for the captain had done nothing, nor inquired how I was, since I went below.

In obedience to the mate's orders, I went back to my berth; but a more miserable night I never wish to spend. I never felt the curse of sickness so keenly in my life. If I could only have been on deck with the rest where something was to be done and seen and heard, where there were fellow-beings for companions in duty and danger; but to be cooped

up alone in a black hole, in equal danger, but without the
power to do, was the hardest trial. Several times, in the
course of the night, I got up, determined to go on deck; but
the silence which showed that there was nothing doing, and
the knowledge that I might make myself seriously ill, for
no purpose, kept me back. It was not easy to sleep, lying, as
I did, with my head directly against the bows, which might
be dashed in by an island of ice, brought down by the very
next sea that struck her. This was the only time I had been ill
since I left Boston, and it was the worst time it could have
happened. I felt almost willing to bear the plagues of Egypt
for the rest of the voyage, if I could but be well and strong
for that one night. Yet it was a dreadful night for those on
deck. A watch of eighteen hours, with wet and cold and
constant anxiety, nearly wore them out; and when they came
below at nine o'clock for breakfast, they almost dropped
asleep on their chests, and some of them were so stiff that
they could with difficulty sit down. Not a drop of anything
had been given them during the whole time (though the
captain, as on the night that I was on deck, had his coffee
every four hours), except that the mate stole a potful of
coffee for two men to drink behind the galley, while he kept
a lookout for the captain. Every man had his station, and
was not allowed to leave it; and nothing happened to break
the monotony of the night, except once setting the main
topsail, to run clear of a large island to leeward, which they
were drifting fast upon. Some of the boys got so sleepy and
stupefied that they actually fell asleep at their posts; and the
young third mate, Mr. Hatch, whose post was the exposed
one of standing on the fore scuttle, was so stiff, when he was
relieved, that he could not bend his knees to get down. By a
constant lookout, and a quick shifting of the helm, as the
islands and pieces came in sight, the ship went clear of
everything but a few small pieces, though daylight showed
the ocean covered for miles. At daybreak it fell a dead calm,
and with the sun the fog cleared a little, and a breeze sprung
up from the westward, which soon grew into a gale. We had
now a fair wind, daylight, and comparatively clear weather;
yet, to the surprise of everyone, the ship continued hove to.
"Why does not he run?" "What is the captain about?" was
asked by everyone; and from questions it soon grew into
complaints and murmurings. When the daylight was so short,

it was too bad to lose it, and a fair wind, too, which everyone
had been praying for. As hour followed hour, and the captain
showed no sign of making sail, the crew became impatient,
and there was a good deal of talking and consultation together
on the forecastle. They had been beaten out with the exposure
and hardship, and impatient to get out of it, and this unaccountable delay was more than they could bear in quietness,
in their excited and restless state. Some said the captain was
frightened, completely cowed by the dangers and difficulties
that surrounded us, and was afraid to make sail; while
others said that in his anxiety and suspense he had made a
free use of brandy and opium, and was unfit for his duty.
The carpenter, who was an intelligent man, and a thorough
seaman, and had great influence with the crew, came down
into the forecastle, and tried to induce them to go aft and
ask the captain why he did not run, or request him, in the
name of all hands, to make sail. This appeared to be a very
reasonable request, and the crew agreed that if he did not
make sail before noon they would go aft. Noon came, and
no sail was made. A consultation was held again, and it was
proposed to take the ship from the captain and give the
command of her to the mate, who had been heard to say
that if he could have his way the ship would have been
half the distance to the Cape before night, ice or no ice.
And so irritated and impatient had the crew become, that
even this proposition, which was open mutiny, was entertained, and the carpenter went to his berth, leaving it tacitly
understood that something serious would be done if things
remained as they were many hours longer. When the carpenter
left, we talked it all over, and I gave my advice strongly
against it. Another of the men, too, who had known something of the kind attempted in another ship by a crew who
were dissatisfied with their captain, and which was followed
with serious consequences, was opposed to it. Stimson, who
soon came down, joined us, and we determined to have
nothing to do with it. By these means the crew were soon
induced to give it up for the present, though they said they
would not lie where they were much longer without knowing
the reason.

The affair remained in this state until four o'clock, when
an order came forward for all hands to come aft upon
the quarterdeck. In about ten minutes they came forward

again, and the whole affair had been blown. The carpenter, prematurely, and without any authority from the crew, had sounded the mate as to whether he would take command of the ship, and intimated an intention to displace the captain; and the mate, as in duty bound, had told the whole to the captain, who immediately sent for all hands aft. Instead of violent measures, or, at least, an outbreak of quarterdeck bravado, threats, and abuse, which they had every reason to expect, a sense of common danger and common suffering seemed to have tamed his spirit, and begotten in him something like a humane fellow-feeling; for he received the crew in a manner quiet, and even almost kind. He told them what he had heard, and said that he did not believe that they would try to do any such thing as was intimated; that they had always been good men, obedient, and knew their duty, and he had no fault to find with them, and asked them what they had to complain of; said that no one could say that he was slow to carry sail (which was true enough), and that, as soon as he thought it was safe and proper, he should make sail. He added a few words about their duty in their present situation, and sent them forward, saying that he should take no further notice of the matter; but, at the same time, told the carpenter to recollect whose power he was in, and that if he heard another word from him he would have cause to remember him to the day of his death.

This language of the captain had a very good effect upon the crew, and they returned quietly to their duty.

For two days more the wind blew from the southward and eastward, and in the short intervals when it was fair, the ice was too thick to run; yet the weather was not so dreadfully bad, and the crew had watch and watch. I still remained in my berth, fast recovering, yet not well enough to go safely on deck. And I should have been perfectly useless; for, from having eaten nothing for nearly a week, except a little rice which I forced into my mouth the last day or two, I was as weak as an infant. To be sick in a forecastle is miserable indeed. It is the worst part of a dog's life, especially in bad weather. The forecastle shut up tight to keep out the water and cold air; the watch either on deck or asleep in their berths; no one to speak to; the pale light of the single lamp, swinging to and fro from the beam, so dim that one can scarcely see, much less read, by it; the water dropping from the beams and carlings and running down the sides, and the forecastle so wet and dark and cheerless, and so lumbered up with chests and wet clothes, that sitting up is worse than lying in the berth. These are some of the evils. Fortunately, I needed no help from anyone, and no medicine; and if I had needed help I don't know where I should have found it. Sailors are willing enough, but it is true, as is often said— no one ships for nurse on board a vessel. Our merchant ships are always undermanned, and if one man is lost by sickness, they cannot spare another to take care of him. A sailor is always presumed to be well, and if he's sick he's a poor dog. One has to stand his wheel, and another his lookout, and the sooner he gets on deck again the better.

Accordingly, as soon as I could possibly go back to my duty, I put on my thick clothes and boots and southwester, and made my appearance on deck. I had been but a few days below, yet everything looked strangely enough. The ship was cased in ice—decks, sides, masts, yards, and rigging. Two close-reefed topsails were all the sail she had on, and every sail and rope was frozen so stiff in its place that it seemed as though it would be impossible to start anything. Reduced, too, to her topmasts, she had altogether a most forlorn and crippled appearance. The sun had come up brightly; the snow was swept off the decks and ashes thrown upon them so that we could walk, for they had been as slippery as glass. It was, of course, too cold to carry on any ship's work, and we had only to walk the deck and keep ourselves warm. The wind was still ahead, and the whole ocean, to the eastward, covered with islands and field ice. At four bells the order was given to square away the yards, and the man who came from the helm said that the captain had kept her off to NNE. What could this mean? The wildest rumors got adrift. Some said that he was going to put into Valparaiso and winter, and others that he was going to run out of the ice and cross the Pacific, and go home round the Cape of Good Hope. Soon, however, it leaked out, and we found that we were running for the Straits of Magellan. The news soon spread through the ship, and all tongues were at work talking about it. No one on board had been through the Straits; but I had in my chest an account of the passage of the ship *A. J. Donelson*, of New York, through those Straits a few years before. The account was given by the captain, and the representation was as favorable as possible. It was soon read by everyone on board, and various opinions pronounced. The determination of our captain had at least this good effect; it gave us something to think and talk about, made a break in our life, and diverted our minds from the monotonous dreariness of the prospect before us. Having made a fair wind of it, we were going off at a good rate, and leaving the thickest of the ice behind us. This, at least, was something.

Having been long enough below to get my hands well warmed and softened, the first handling of the ropes was rather tough; but a few days hardened them, and as soon as I got my mouth open wide enough to take in a piece of salt beef and hard bread, I was all right again.

*Sunday, July 10th.* Lat. 54° 10′, lon. 79° 07′. This was our position at noon. The sun was out bright; the ice was all left behind, and things had quite a cheering appearance. We brought our wet pea jackets and trousers on deck, and hung them up in the rigging, that the breeze and the few hours of sun might dry them a little; and, by leave of the cook, the galley was nearly filled with stockings and mittens, hung round to be dried. Boots, too, were brought up; and, having got a little tar and slush from below, we gave them thick coats. After dinner all hands were turned to, to get the anchors over the bows, bend on the chains, &c. The fish tackle was got up, fish davit rigged out, and, after two or three hours of hard and cold work, both the anchors were ready for instant use, a couple of kedges got up, a hawser coiled away upon the fore hatch, and the deep-sea lead line overhauled and made ready. Our spirits returned with having something to do; and when the tackle was manned to bouse the anchor home, notwithstanding the desolation of the scene, we struck up "Cheerly, men!" in full chorus. This pleased the mate, who rubbed his hands and cried out, "That's right, my boys; never say die! That sounds like the old crew!" and the captain came up, on hearing the song, and said to the passenger, within hearing of the man at the wheel, "That sounds like a lively crew. They'll have their song so long as there're enough left for a chorus!"

This preparation of the cable and anchors was for the passage of the Straits; for, as they are very crooked, and with a variety of currents, it is necessary to come frequently to anchor. This was not, by any means, a pleasant prospect;

for, of all the work that a sailor is called upon to do in cold weather, there is none so bad as working the ground tackle. The heavy chain cables to be hauled and pulled about decks with bare hands; wet hawsers, slip ropes, and buoy ropes to be hauled aboard, dripping in water, which is running up your sleeves, and freezing; clearing hawse under the bows; getting under way and coming to at all hours of the night and day, and a constant lookout for rocks and sands and turns of tides—these are some of the disagreeables of such a navigation to a common sailor. Fair or foul, he wants to have nothing to do with the ground tackle between port and port. One of our hands, too, had unluckily fallen upon a half of an old newspaper which contained an account of the passage, through the Straits, of a Boston brig, called, I think, the *Peruvian*, in which she lost every cable and anchor she had, got aground twice, and arrived at Valparaiso in distress. This was set off against the account of the *A. J. Donelson*, and led us to look forward with less confidence to the passage, especially as no one on board had ever been through, and we heard that the captain had no very satisfactory charts. However, we were spared any further experience on the point; for the next day, when we must have been near the Cape of Pillars, which is the southwest point of the mouth of the Straits, a gale set in from the eastward, with a heavy fog, so that we could not see half the ship's length ahead. This, of course, put an end to the project for the present; for a thick fog and a gale blowing dead ahead are not the most favorable circumstances for the passage of difficult and dangerous straits. This weather, too, seemed likely to last for some time, and we could not think of beating about the mouth of the Straits for a week or two, waiting for a favorable opportunity; so we braced up on the larboard tack, put the ship's head due south, and stuck her off for Cape Horn again.

# CHAPTER XXXII

In our first attempt to double the Cape, when we came up to the latitude of it, we were nearly seventeen hundred miles to the westward, but, in running for the Straits of Magellan, we stood so far to the eastward that we made our second attempt at a distance of not more than four or five hundred miles; and we had great hopes, by this means, to run clear of the ice; thinking that the easterly gales, which had prevailed for a long time, would have driven it to the westward. With the wind about two points free, the yards braced in a little, and two close-reefed topsails and a reefed foresail on the ship, we made great way toward the southward; and almost every watch, when we came on deck, the air seemed to grow colder, and the sea to run higher. Still we saw no ice, and had great hopes of going clear of it altogether, when, one afternoon, about three o'clock, while we were taking a *siesta* during our watch below, "All hands!" was called in a loud and fearful voice. "Tumble up here, men— tumble up—don't stop for your clothes—before we're upon it!" We sprang out of our berths and hurried upon deck. The loud, sharp voice of the captain was heard giving orders, as though for life or death, and we ran aft to the braces, not waiting to look ahead, for not a moment was to be lost. The helm was hard up, the afteryards shaking, and the ship in the act of wearing. Slowly, with the stiff ropes and iced rigging, we swung the yards round, everything coming hard and with a creaking and rending sound, like pulling up a plank which has been frozen into the ice. The ship wore round fairly, the yards were steadied, and we stood off on the other tack, leaving behind us, directly under our larboard quarter, a large ice island, peering out of the mist, and reaching high above our tops; while astern, and on either side of the island, large tracts of field ice were dimly seen, heaving and rolling in the sea. We were now safe, and standing to the northward; but, in a few minutes more, had it not been for the sharp lookout of the watch, we should have been fairly upon the ice, and left our ship's old bones adrift in the Southern Ocean. After standing to the northward a few hours, we wore ship, and, the wind having hauled, we stood to the southward and eastward. All night long a bright lookout was kept from every part of the deck; and whenever ice was seen on the one bow or the other, the helm was shifted and the yards braced, and, by quick working of the ship, she was kept clear. The accustomed cry of "Ice ahead!" "Ice on the lee bow!" "Another island!" in the same tones, and with the same orders following them, seemed to bring us directly back to our old position of the week before. During our watch on deck, which was from twelve to four, the wind came out ahead, with a pelting storm of hail and sleet, and we lay hove to, under a close-reefed fore-topsail, the whole watch. During the next watch it fell calm with a drenching rain until daybreak, when the wind came out to the westward, and the weather cleared up, and showed us the whole ocean, in the course which we should have steered, had it not been for the head wind and calm, completely blocked up with ice. Here, then, our progress was stopped, and we wore ship, and once more stood to the northward and eastward; not for the Straits of Magellan, but to make another attempt to double the Cape, still farther to the eastward; for the captain was determined to get round if perseverance could do it, and the third time, he said, never failed.

With a fair wind, we soon ran clear of the field ice, and by noon had only the stray islands floating far and near upon the ocean. The sun was out bright, the sea of a deep blue, fringed with the white foam of the waves, which ran high before a strong southwester; our solitary ship tore on through the open water as though glad to be out of her confinement; and the ice islands lay scattered here and there, of various sizes and shapes, reflecting the bright rays of the sun, and drifting slowly northward before the gale. It was a contrast to much that we had lately seen, and a spectacle not only of beauty, but of life; for it required but little fancy to imagine these islands to be animate masses which had broken loose from the "thrilling regions of thick-ribbed ice," and were working their way, by wind and current, some alone, and some in fleets, to milder climes. No pencil has ever yet given anything like the true effect of an iceberg. In a picture, they are huge, uncouth masses, stuck in the sea, while their chief beauty and grandeur—their slow, stately motion, the whirling of the snow about their summits, and the fearful groaning and cracking of their parts—the picture cannot give. This is the large iceberg, while the small and distant islands, floating on the smooth sea, in the light of a clear day, look like little floating fairy isles of sapphire.

From a northeast course we gradually hauled to the eastward, and after sailing about two hundred miles, which brought us as near to the western coast of Terra del Fuego as was safe, and having lost sight of the ice altogether, for the third time we put the ship's head to the southward, to try the passage of the Cape. The weather continued clear and cold, with a strong gale from the westward, and we were fast getting up with the latitude of the Cape, with a prospect of soon being round. One fine afternoon, a man who had gone into the foretop to shift the rolling tackles sung out at the top of his voice, and with evident glee, "Sail ho!" Neither land nor sail had we seen since leaving San Diego; and only those who have traversed the length of a whole ocean alone can imagine what an excitement such an announcement produced on board. "Sail ho!" shouted the cook, jumping out of his galley; "Sail ho!" shouted a man, throwing back the slide of the scuttle, to the watch below, who were soon out of their berths and on deck; and "Sail ho!" shouted the captain down the companionway to the passenger in the cabin. Besides the pleasure of seeing a ship and human beings in so desolate a place, it was important for us to speak a vessel, to learn whether there was ice to the eastward, and to ascertain the longitude; for we had no chronometer, and had been drifting about so long that we had nearly lost our reckoning; and opportunities for lunar observations are not frequent or sure in such a place as Cape Horn. For these various reasons the excitement in our little community was running high, and conjectures were made, and everything thought of for which the captain would hail, when the man aloft sung out, "Another sail, large on the weather bow!" This was a little odd, but so much the better, and did not shake our faith in their being sails. At length the man in the top hailed, and said he believed it was land, after all. "Land in your eye!" said the mate, who was looking through the telescope. "They are ice islands, if I can see a hole through a ladder"; and a few moments showed the mate to be right; and all our expectations fled; and instead of what we most wished to see we had what we most dreaded, and what we hoped we had seen the last of. We soon, however, left these astern, having passed within about two miles of them, and at sundown the horizon was clear in all directions.

Having a fine wind, we were soon up with and passed the latitude of the Cape, and, having stood far enough to the southward to give it a wide berth, we began to stand to the eastward, with a good prospect of being round and steering to the northward, on the other side, in a very few days. But ill luck seemed to have lighted upon us. Not four hours had we been standing on in this course before it fell dead calm, and in half an hour it clouded up, a few straggling blasts, with spits of snow and sleet, came from the eastward, and in an hour more we lay hove to under a close-reefed main-topsail, drifting bodily off to leeward before the fiercest storm that we had yet felt, blowing dead ahead, from the eastward. It seemed as though the genius of the place had been roused at finding that we had nearly slipped through his fingers, and had come down upon us with tenfold fury. The sailors said that every blast, as it shook the shrouds, and whistled through the rigging, said to the old ship, "No, you don't! No, you don't!"

For eight days we lay drifting about in this manner. Sometimes—generally toward noon—it fell calm; once or twice a round copper ball showed itself for a few moments in the place where the sun ought to have been, and a puff or two came from the westward, giving some hope that a fair wind had come at last. During the first two days we made sail for these puffs, shaking the reefs out of the topsails and boarding the tacks of the courses; but finding that it only made work for us when the gale set in again, it was soon given up, and we lay to under our close reefs. We had less snow and hail than when we were farther to the westward, but we had an abundance of what is worse to a sailor in cold weather—drenching rain. Snow is blinding, and very bad when coming upon a coast, but, for genuine discomfort, give me rain with freezing weather. A snowstorm is exciting, and it does not wet through the clothes (a fact important to a sailor); but a constant rain there is no escaping from. It wets to the skin, and makes all protection vain. We had long ago run through all our dry clothes, and as sailors have no other way of drying them than by the sun, we had nothing to do but to put on those which were the least wet. At the end of each

watch, when we came below, we took off our clothes and
wrung them out; two taking hold of a pair of trousers, one
at each end—and jackets in the same way. Stockings, mittens,
and all were wrung out also, and then hung up to drain and
chafe dry against the bulkheads. Then, feeling of all our
clothes, we picked out those which were the least wet, and
put them on, so as to be ready for a call, and turned in,
covered ourselves up with blankets, and slept until three
knocks on the scuttle and the dismal sound of "All Starbowlines ahoy! Eight bells, there below! Do you hear the news?"
drawled out from on deck, and the sulky answer of "Aye,
aye!" from below, sent us up again.

On deck all was dark, and either a dead calm, with the
rain pouring steadily down, or, more generally, a violent
gale dead ahead, with rain pelting horizontally, and occasional
variations of hail and sleet; decks afloat with water swashing
from side to side, and constantly wet feet, for boots could
not be rung out like drawers, and no composition could stand
the constant soaking. In fact, wet and cold feet are inevitable
in such weather, and are not the least of those items which
go to make up the grand total of the discomforts of a winter
passage round Cape Horn. Few words were spoken between
the watches as they shifted; the wheel was relieved, the
mate took his place on the quarterdeck, the lookouts in the
bows; and each man had his narrow space to walk fore and
aft in, or rather to swing himself forward and back in, from
one belaying pin to another, for the decks were too slippery
with ice and water to allow of much walking. To make a
walk, which is absolutely necessary to pass away the time,
one of us hit upon the expedient of sanding the decks; and
afterward, whenever the rain was not so violent as to wash
it off, the weather side of the quarterdeck and a part of the
waist and forecastle were sprinkled with the sand which we
had on board for holystoning, and thus we made a good
promenade, where we walked fore and aft, two and two, hour
after hour, in our long, dull, and comfortless watches. The
bells seemed to be an hour or two apart, instead of half an
hour, and an age elapsed before the welcome sound of eight
bells. The sole object was to make the time pass on. Any
change was sought for which would break the monotony of
the time; and even the two hours' trick at the wheel, which
came round to us in turn, once in every other watch, was

looked upon as a relief. The never-failing resource of long yarns, which eke out many a watch, seemed to have failed us now; for we had been so long together that we had heard each other's stories told over and over again till we had them by heart; each one knew the whole history of each of the others, and we were fairly and literally talked out. Singing and joking we were in no humor for; and, in fact, any sound of mirth or laughter would have struck strangely upon our ears, and would not have been tolerated any more than whistling or a wind instrument. The last resort, that of speculating upon the future, seemed now to fail us; for our discouraging situation, and the danger we were really in (as we expected every day to find ourselves drifted back among the ice), "clapped a stopper" upon all that. From saying "*when* we get home," we began insensibly to alter it to "*if* we get home," and at last the subject was dropped by a tacit consent.

In this state of things, a new light was struck out, and a new field opened, by a change in the watch. One of our watch was laid up for two or three days by a bad hand (for in cold weather the least cut or bruise ripens into a sore), and his place was supplied by the carpenter. This was a windfall, and there was a contest who should have the carpenter to walk with him. As "Chips" was a man of some little education, and he and I had had a good deal of intercourse with each other, he fell in with me in my walk. He was a Finn, but spoke English well, and gave me long accounts of his country—the customs, the trade, the towns, what little he knew of the government (I found he was no friend of Russia), his voyages, his first arrival in America, his marriage and courtship; he had married a countrywoman of his, a dressmaker, whom he met with in Boston. I had very little to tell him of my quiet, sedentary life at home; and in spite of our best efforts, which had protracted these yarns through five or six watches, we fairly talked each other out, and I turned him over to another man in the watch, and put myself upon my own resources.

I commenced a deliberate system of time-killing, which united some profit with a cheering up of the heavy hours. As soon as I came on deck, and took my place and regular walk, I began with repeating over to myself in regular order a string of matters which I had in my memory—the multiplication table and the tables of weights and measures; the

Kanaka numerals; then the states of the Union, with their capitals; the counties of England, with their shire towns; and the kings of England, in their order, and other things. This carried me through my facts, and, being repeated deliberately, with long intervals, often eked out the first two bells. Then came the Ten Commandments, the thirty-ninth chapter of Job, and a few other passages from Scripture. The next in the order, which I seldom varied from, came Cowper's "Castaway," which was a great favorite with me, its solemn measure and gloomy character, as well as the incident it was founded upon, making it well suited to a lonely watch at sea. Then his lines to Mary, his address to the Jackdaw, and a short extract from "Table Talk" (I abounded in Cowper, for I happened to have a volume of his poems in my chest); *"Ille et nefasto"* from Horace, and Goethe's *"Erlkönig."* After I had got through these, I allowed myself a more general range among everything that I could remember, both in prose and verse. In this way, with an occasional break by relieving the wheel, heaving the log, and going to the scuttle butt for a drink of water, the longest watch was passed away; and I was so regular in my silent recitations that, if there was no interruption by ship's duty, I could tell very nearly the number of bells by my progress.

Our watches below were no more varied than the watch on deck. All washing, sewing, and reading was given up, and we did nothing but eat, sleep, and stand our watch, leading what might be called a Cape Horn life. The forecastle was too uncomfortable to sit up in; and whenever we were below, we were in our berths. To prevent the rain and the sea water which broke over the bows from washing down, we were obliged to keep the scuttle closed, so that the forecastle was nearly airtight. In this little, wet, leaky hole, we were all quartered, in an atmosphere so bad that our lamp, which swung in the middle from the beams, sometimes actually burned blue, with a large circle of foul air about it. Still, I was never in better health than after three weeks of this life. I gained a great deal of flesh, and we all ate like horses. At every watch when we came below, before turning in, the bread barge and beef kid were overhauled. Each man drank his quart of hot tea night and morning, and glad enough we were to get it; for no nectar and ambrosia were sweeter to the lazy immortals than was a pot of hot tea, a hard biscuit, and a slice of cold salt beef to us after a watch on deck. To be sure, we were mere animals, and, had this life lasted a year instead of a month, we should have been little better than the ropes in the ship. Not a razor, nor a brush, nor a drop of water, except the rain and the spray, had come near us all the time; for we were on an allowance of fresh water; and who would strip and wash himself in salt water on deck, in the snow and ice, with the thermometer at zero?

After about eight days of constant easterly gales, the wind hauled occasionally a little to the southward, and blew hard, which, as we were well to the southward, allowed us to brace in a little, and stand on under all the sail we could carry. These turns lasted but a short while, and sooner or later it set in again from the old quarter; yet at each time we made something, and were gradually edging along to the eastward. One night, after one of these shifts of the wind, and when all hands had been up a great part of the time, our watch was left on deck, with the mainsail hanging in the buntlines, ready to be set if necessary. It came on to blow worse and worse, with hail and snow beating like so many furies upon the ship, it being as dark and thick as night could make it. The mainsail was blowing and slatting with a noise like thunder, when the captain came on deck and ordered it to be furled. The mate was about to call all hands, when the captain stopped him, and said that the men would be beaten out if they were called up so often; that, as our watch must stay on deck, it might as well be doing that as anything else. Accordingly, we went upon the yard; and never shall I forget that piece of work. Our watch had been so reduced by sickness, and by some having been left in California, that, with one man at the wheel, we had only the third mate and three beside myself to go aloft; so that at most we could only attempt to furl one yardarm at a time. We manned the weather yardarm, and set to work to make a furl of it. Our lower masts being short, and our yards very square, the sail had a head of nearly fifty feet, and a short leech, made still shorter by the deep reef which was in it, which brought the clew away out on the quarters of the yard, and made a bunt nearly as square as the mizzen-royal yard. Beside this difficulty, the yard over which we lay was cased with ice, the gaskets and rope of the foot and leech of the sail as stiff and hard as a piece of leather hose, and the sail itself about as pliable as though it had been made of sheets of sheathing copper. It blew a perfect hurricane, with alternate blasts of snow, hail, and rain. We had to "fist" the sail with bare hands. No one could trust himself to mittens, for if he slipped he was a gone man. All the boats were hoisted in on deck, and there was nothing to be lowered for him. We had need of every finger God had given us. Several times we got the sail upon the yard, but it blew away again before we could secure it. It required men to lie over the yard to pass each turn of the gaskets, and when they were passed it was almost impossible to knot them so that they would hold. Frequently we were obliged to leave off altogether and take to beating our hands upon the sail to keep them from freezing. After some time—which seemed forever—we got the weather side stowed after a fashion, and went over to leeward for another trial. This was still worse, for the body of the sail had been blown over to leeward, and, as the yard was acockbill by the lying over of the vessel, we had to light it all up to windward. When the yardarms were furled, the bunt was all adrift again, which made more work for us. We got all secure at last, but we had been nearly an hour and a half upon the yard, and it seemed an age. It had just struck five bells when we went up, and eight were struck soon after we came down. This may seem slow work; but considering the state of everything, and that we had only five men to a sail with just half as many square yards of canvas in it as the mainsail of the *Independence*, a sixty-gun ship, which musters seven hundred men at her quarters, it is not wonderful that we were no quicker about it. We were glad enough to get on deck, and still more to go below. The oldest sailor in the watch said, as he went down, "I shall never forget that main yard; it beats all my going a-fishing. Fun is fun, but furling one yardarm of a course at a time, off Cape Horn, is no better than mankilling."

During the greater part of the next two days, the wind was pretty steady from the southward. We had evidently made great progress, and had good hope of being soon up with the Cape, if we were not there already. We could put but little confidence in our reckoning, as there had been no opportunities for an observation, and we had drifted too much to allow of our dead reckoning being anywhere near the mark. If it would clear off enough to give a chance for an observation, or if we could make land, we should know where we were;

and upon these, and the chances of falling in with a sail from the eastward, we depended almost entirely.

*Friday, July 22d.* This day we had a steady gale from the southward, and stood on under close sail, with the yards eased a little by the weather braces, the clouds lifting a little, and showing signs of breaking away. In the afternoon, I was below with Mr. Hatch, the third mate, and two others, filling the bread locker in the steerage from the casks, when a bright gleam of sunshine broke out and shone down the companion-way, and through the skylight, lighting up everything below, and sending a warm glow through the hearts of all. It was a sight we had not seen for weeks—an omen, a godsend. Even the roughest and hardest face acknowledged its influence. Just at that moment we heard a loud shout from all parts of the deck, and the mate called out down the companionway to the captain, who was sitting in the cabin. What he said we could not distinguish, but the captain kicked over his chair, and was on deck at one jump. We could not tell what it was; and, anxious as we were to know, the discipline of the ship would not allow of our leaving our places. Yet, as we were not called, we knew there was no danger. We hurried to get through with our job, when, seeing the steward's black face peering out of the pantry, Mr. Hatch hailed him to know what was the matter. "Lan'o, to be sure, sir! No you hear 'em sing out, 'Lan'o'? De cap'em say 'im Cape Horn!"

This gave us a new start, and we were soon through our work and on deck; and there lay the land, fair upon the larboard beam, and slowly edging away upon the quarter. All hands were busy looking at it—the captain and mates from the quarterdeck, the cook from his galley, and the sailors from the forecastle; and even Mr. Nuttall, the passenger, who had kept in his shell for nearly a month, and hardly been seen by anybody, and whom we had almost forgotten was on board, came out like a butterfly, and was hopping round as bright as a bird.

The land was the island of Staten Land, just to the eastward of Cape Horn; and a more desolate-looking spot I never wish to set eyes upon—bare, broken, and girt with rocks and ice, with here and there, between the rocks and broken hillocks, a little stunted vegetation of shrubs. It was a place well suited to stand at the junction of the two oceans, beyond the reach of human cultivation, and encounter the blasts and snows of a perpetual winter. Yet, dismal as it was, it was a pleasant sight to us; not only as being the first land we had seen, but because it told us that we had passed the Cape—were in the Atlantic—and that, with twenty-four hours of this breeze, we might bid defiance to the Southern Ocean. It told us, too, our latitude and longitude better than any observation; and the captain now knew where we were, as well as if we were off the end of Long Wharf.

In the general joy, Mr. Nuttall said he should like to go ashore upon the island and examine a spot which probably no human being had ever set foot upon; but the captain intimated that he would see the island, specimens and all, in—another place, before he would get out a boat or delay the ship one moment for him.

We left the land gradually astern; and at sundown had the Atlantic Ocean clear before us.

# CHAPTER XXXIII

It is usual, in voyages round the Cape from the Pacific, to keep to the eastward of the Falkland Islands; but as there had now set in a strong, steady, and clear southwester, with every prospect of its lasting, and we had had enough of high latitudes, the captain determined to stand immediately to the northward, running inside the Falkland Islands. Accordingly, when the wheel was relieved at eight o'clock, the order was given to keep her due north, and all hands were turned up to square away the yards and make sail. In a moment the news ran through the ship that the captain was keeping her off, with her nose straight for Boston, and Cape Horn over her taffrail. It was a moment of enthusiasm. Everyone was on the alert, and even the two sick men turned out to lend a hand at the halyards. The wind was now due southwest, and blowing a gale to which a vessel close-hauled could have shown no more than a single close-reefed sail; but as we were going before it, we could carry on. Accordingly, hands were sent aloft, and a reef shaken out of the topsails, and the reefed foresail set. When we came to masthead the topsail yards, with all hands at the halyards, we struck up "Cheerly, men," with a chorus which might have been heard halfway to Staten Land. Under her increased sail, the ship drove on through the water. Yet she could bear it well; and the captain sang out from the quarterdeck, "Another reef out of that fore-topsail, and give it to her!" Two hands sprang aloft; the frozen reef points and earings were cast adrift, the halyards manned, and the sail gave out her increased canvas to the gale. All hands were kept on deck to watch the effect of the change. It was as much as she could well carry, and with a heavy sea astern it took two men at the wheel to steer her. She flung the foam from her bows, the spray breaking aft as far as the gangway. She was going at a prodigious rate. Still everything held. Preventer braces were reeved and hauled taut, tackles got upon the backstays, and everything done to keep all snug and strong. The captain walked the deck at a rapid stride, looked aloft at the sails, and then to windward; the mate stood in the gangway, rubbing his hands, and talking aloud to the ship: "Hurrah, old bucket! The Boston girls have got hold of the towrope!" and the like; and we were on the forecastle, looking to see how the spars stood it, and guessing the rate at which she was going, when the captain called out, "Mr. Brown, get up the topmast studding sail! What she can't carry she may drag!" The mate looked a moment; but he would let no one be before him in daring. He sprang forward. "Hurrah, men! Rig out the topmast-studding-sail boom! Lay aloft, and I'll send the rigging up to you!" We sprang aloft into the top; lowered a girtline down, by which we hauled up the rigging; rove the tacks and halyards; ran out the boom and lashed it fast, and sent down the lower halyards as a preventer. It was a clear starlight night, cold and blowing; but everybody worked with a will. Some, indeed, looked as though they thought the "old man" was mad, but no one said a word. We had had a new topmast studding sail made with a reef in it—a thing hardly ever heard of, and which the sailors had ridiculed a good deal, saying that when it was time to reef a studding sail it was time to take it in. But we found a use for it now; for, there being a reef in the topsail, the studding sail could not be set without one in it also. To be sure, a studding sail with reefed topsails was rather a novelty; yet there was some reason in it, for if we carried that away we should lose only a sail and a boom; but a whole topsail might have carried away the mast and all.

While we were aloft the sail had been got out, bent to the yard, reefed, and ready for hoisting. Waiting for a good opportunity, the halyards were manned and the yard hoisted fairly up to the block; but when the mate came to shake the cat's-paw out of the downhaul, and we began to boom-end the sail, it shook the ship to her center. The boom buckled up and bent like a whipstick, and we looked every moment to see something go; but, being of the short, tough upland spruce, it bent like whalebone, and nothing could break it. The carpenter said it was the best stick he had ever seen. The strength of all hands soon brought the tack to the boom end, and the sheet was trimmed down, and the preventer and the weather brace hauled taut to take off the strain. Every rope yarn seemed stretched to the utmost, and every thread of canvas; and with this sail added to her, the ship sprang through the water like a thing possessed. The sail being nearly all forward, it lifted her out of the water, and she seemed actually to jump from sea to sea. From the time her keel was laid, she had never been so driven; and had it been life or death with every one of us, she could not have borne another stitch of canvas.

Finding that she would bear the sail, the hands were sent below, and our watch remained on deck. Two men at the wheel had as much as they could do to keep her within three points of her course, for she steered as wild as a young colt. The mate walked the deck, looking at the sails, and then over the side to see the foam fly by her, slapping his hands upon his thighs and talking to the ship: "Hurrah, you jade, you've got the scent! You know where you're going!" And when she leaped over the seas, and almost out of the water, and trembled to her very keel, the spars and masts snapping and creaking: "There she goes! There she goes—handsomely! As long as she cracks she holds!" while we stood with the rigging laid down fair for letting go, and ready to take in sail and clear away, if anything went. At four bells we hove the log, and she was going eleven knots fairly; and had it not been for the sea from aft, which sent the chip home, and threw her continually off her course, the log would have shown her to have been going somewhat faster. I went to the wheel with a young fellow from the Kennebec, Jack Stewart, who was a good helmsman, and for two hours we had our hands full. A few minutes showed us that our monkey jackets must come off; and, cold as it was, we stood in our shirt sleeves in a perspiration, and were glad enough to have it eight bells, and the wheel relieved. We turned in and slept as well as we could, though the sea made a constant roar under her bows, and washed over the forecastle like a small cataract.

At four o'clock we were called again. The same sail was still on the vessel, and the gale, if there was any change, had increased a little. No attempt was made to take the studding sail in; and, indeed, it was too late now. If we had started anything toward taking it in, either tack or halyards, it would have blown to pieces, and carried something away with it. The only way now was to let everything stand, and if the gale went down, well and good; if not, something must go— the weakest stick or rope first—and then we could get it in. For more than an hour she was driven on at such a rate that she seemed to crowd the sea into a heap before her; and the water poured over the spritsail yard as it would over a dam. Toward daybreak the gale abated a little, and she was just beginning to go more easily along, relieved of the pressure, when Mr. Brown, determined to give her no respite, and depending upon the wind's subsiding as the sun rose, told us to get along the lower studding sail. This was an immense sail, and held wind enough to last a Dutchman a week, hove to. It was soon ready, the boom topped up, preventer guys rove, and the idlers called up to man the halyards; yet such was still the force of the gale that we were nearly an hour setting the sail, carried away the outhaul in doing it, and came very near snapping off the swinging boom. No sooner was it set than the ship tore on again like one mad, and began to steer wilder than ever. The men at the wheel were puffing and blowing at their work, and the helm was going hard up and hard down, constantly. Add to this, the gale did not lessen as the day came on, but the sun rose in clouds. A sudden lurch threw the man from the weather wheel across the deck and against the side. The mate sprang to the wheel, and the man, regaining his feet, seized the spokes, and they hove the wheel up just in time to save the ship from broaching to, though as she came up the studding-sail boom stood at an angle of forty-five degrees. She had evidently more on her than she could bear; yet it was in vain to try to take it in—the clew line was not strong enough, and they were thinking of cutting away, when another wide yaw and a come-to snapped the guys, and the swinging boom came in with a crash against the lower rigging. The outhaul block gave way, and the topmast-studding-sail boom bent in a manner which I never before supposed a stick could bend. I had my eye on it when the guys parted, and it made one spring and buckled up so as to form nearly a half-circle, and sprang out again to its shape. The clew line gave way at the first pull; the cleat to which the halyards were belayed was wrenched off, and the sail blew round the spritsail yard and head guys, which gave us a bad job to get it in. A half hour served to clear all away, and she was suffered to drive on with her topmast studding sail set, it being as much as she could stagger under.

During all this day and the next night we went on under the same sail, the gale blowing with undiminished violence; two men at the wheel all the time; watch and watch, and nothing to do but to steer and look out for the ship, and be blown along; until the noon of the next day—

*Sunday, July 24th,* when we were in lat. 50° 27' S., lon. 62° 13' W., having made four degrees of latitude in the last twenty-four hours. Being now to the northward of the Falkland Islands, the ship was kept off, northeast, for the equator; and with her head for the equator, and Cape Horn over her taff-rail, she went gloriously on; every heave of the sea leaving the Cape astern, and every hour bringing us nearer to home and to warm weather. Many a time, when blocked up in the ice, with everything dismal and discouraging about us, had we said, if we were only fairly round, and standing north on the other side, we should ask for no more; and now we had it all, with a clear sea and as much wind as a sailor could pray for. If the best part of a voyage is the last part, surely we had all now that we could wish. Everyone was in the highest spirits, and the ship seemed as glad as any of us at getting out of her confinement. At each change of the watch, those coming on deck asked those going below, "How does she go along?" and got, for answer, the rate, and the customary addition: "Aye, and the Boston girls have had hold of the towrope all the watch." Every day the sun rose higher in the horizon, and the nights grew shorter; and at coming on deck each morning there was a sensible change in the temperature. The ice, too, began to melt from off the rigging and spars, and, except a little which remained in the tops and round the hounds of the lower masts, was soon gone. As we left the gale behind us, the reefs were shaken out of the topsails, and sail made as fast as she could bear it; and every time all hands were sent to the halyards, a song was called for, and we hoisted away with a will.

Sail after sail was added, as we drew into fine weather; and in one week after leaving Cape Horn, the long topgallant masts were got up, topgallant and royal yards crossed, and the ship restored to her fair proportions.

The Southern Cross and the Magellan Clouds settled lower and lower in the horizon; and so great was our change of latitude that each succeeding night we sank some constellation in the south, and raised another in the northern horizon.

*Sunday, July 31st.* At noon we were in lat. 36° 41' S., lon. 38° 08' W.; having traversed the distance of two thousand miles, allowing for changes of course, in nine days. A thousand miles in four days and a half! This is equal to steam.

Soon after eight o'clock the appearance of the ship gave evidence that this was the first Sunday we had yet had in fine weather. As the sun came up clear, with the promise of a fair, warm day, and, as usual on Sunday, there was no work going on, all hands turned to upon clearing out the forecastle. The wet and soiled clothes which had accumulated there during the past month were brought up on deck; the chests moved; brooms, buckets of water, swabs, scrubbing brushes, and scrapers carried down and applied, until the forecastle floor was as white as chalk, and everything neat and in order. The bedding from the berths was then spread on deck, and dried and aired; the deck tub filled with water; and a grand washing begun of all the clothes which were brought up. Shirts, frocks, drawers, trousers, jackets, stockings, of every shape and color, wet and dirty, many of them moldy from having been lying a long time wet in a foul corner—these were all washed and scrubbed out, and finally towed overboard for half an hour; and then made fast in the rigging to dry. Wet boots and shoes were spread out to dry in sunny places on deck; and the whole ship looked like a back yard on a washing day. After we had done with our clothes, we began upon our persons. A little fresh water, which we had saved from our allowance, was put in buckets, and, with soap and towels, we had what sailors call a fresh-water wash. The same bucket, to be sure, had to go through several hands, and was spoken for by one after another, but as we rinsed off in salt water, pure from the ocean, and the fresh was used only to start the accumulated grime and blackness of five weeks, it was held of little consequence. We soaped down and scrubbed one another with towels and pieces of canvas, stripping to it; and then, getting into the head, threw buckets of water upon each other. After this came shaving, and combing, and brushing; and when, having spent the first part of the day in this way, we sat down on the forecastle, in the afternoon, with clean duck trousers and shirts on, washed, shaved, and combed, and looking a dozen shades lighter for it, reading, sewing, and talking at our ease, with a clear sky and warm sun over our heads, a steady breeze over the larboard quarter, studding sails out alow and aloft, and all the flying kites abroad—we felt that we had got back into the pleasantest part of a sailor's life. At sunset the clothes were all taken down from the rigging, clean and dry, and stowed neatly away in our chests; and our southwesters, thick boots, Guernsey frocks, and other accompaniments of bad weather put out of the way, we hoped, for the rest of the voyage, as we expected to come upon the coast early in the autumn.

Notwithstanding all that has been said about the beauty of a ship under full sail, there are very few who have ever seen a ship, literally, under all her sail. A ship coming in or going out of port, with her ordinary sails, and perhaps two or three studding sails, is commonly said to be under full sail; but a ship never has all her sail upon her, except when she has a light, steady breeze, very nearly, but not quite, dead aft, and so regular that it can be trusted, and is likely to last for some time. Then, with all her sails, light and heavy, and studding sails, on each side, alow and aloft, she is the most glorious moving object in the world. Such a sight very few, even some who have been at sea a good deal, have ever beheld; for from the deck of your own vessel you cannot see her, as you would a separate object.

One night, while we were in these tropics, I went out to the end of the flying-jib boom upon some duty, and, having finished it, turned round, and lay over the boom for a long time, admiring the beauty of the sight before me. Being so far out from the deck, I could look at the ship as at a separate vessel; and there rose up from the water, supported only by the small black hull, a pyramid of canvas, spreading out far beyond the hull, and towering up almost, as it seemed in the indistinct night air, to the clouds. The sea was as still as an inland lake; the light trade wind was gently and steadily breathing from astern; the dark-blue sky was studded with the tropical stars; there was no sound but the rippling of the water under the stem; and the sails were spread out, wide and high, the two lower studding sails stretching on each side far beyond the deck; the topmast studding sails like wings to the topsails; the topgallant studding sails spreading fearlessly out above them; still higher, the two royal studding sails, looking like two kites flying from the same string; and, highest of all, the little skysail, the apex of the pyramid, seeming actually to touch the stars, and to be out of reach of human hand. So quiet, too, was the sea, and so steady the breeze, that if these sails had been sculptured marble they could not have been more motionless. Not a ripple upon the surface of the canvas; not even a quivering of the extreme edges of the sail, so perfectly were they distended by the breeze. I was so lost in the sight that I forgot the presence of the man who came out with me, until he said (for he, too, rough old man-of-war's-man as he was, had been gazing at the show), half to himself, still looking at the marble sails, "How quietly they do their work!"

The fine weather brought work with it, as the ship was to be put in order for coming into port. To give a landsman some notion of what is done on board ship, it may be truly said that all the first part of a passage is spent in getting a ship ready for sea, and the last part in getting her ready for port. She is, as sailors say, like a lady's watch, always out of repair. The new, strong sails, which we had up off Cape Horn, were to be sent down, and the old set, which were still serviceable in fine weather, to be bent in their place; all the rigging to be set up, fore and aft; the masts stayed; the standing rigging to be tarred down; lower and topmast rigging to be rattled down, fore and aft; the ship scraped inside and out, and painted; decks varnished; new and neat knots, seizings and coverings, to be fitted; and every part put in order, to

look well to the owner's eye, and to all critics, on coming into
Boston. This, of course, was a long matter; and all hands
were kept on deck at work for the whole of each day, during
the rest of the voyage. Sailors call this hard usage; but the
ship must be in crack order; and "We're homeward bound"
was the answer to everything.

We went on for several days, employed in this way, nothing
remarkable occurring; and, at the latter part of the week, fell
in with the southeast trades, blowing about east-southeast,
which brought them nearly two points abaft our beam. They
blew strong and steady, so that we hardly started a rope, until
we were beyond their latitude. The first day of "all hands,"
one of those little incidents occurred, which are nothing in
themselves, but are great matters in the eyes of a ship's company, as they serve to break the monotony of a voyage, and
afford conversation to the crew for days afterward. These
things, too, are often interesting, as they show the customs
and states of feeling on shipboard.

In merchant vessels, the captain gives his orders, as to
the ship's work, to the mate, in a general way, and leaves
the execution of them, with the particular ordering, to him.
This has become so fixed a custom that it is like a law, and
is never infringed upon by a wise master, unless his mate is
no seaman; in which case the captain must often oversee
things for himself. This, however, could not be said of our
chief mate, and he was very jealous of any encroachment
upon the borders of his authority.

On Monday morning the captain told him to stay the fore-
topmast plumb. He accordingly came forward, turned all
hands to, with tackles on the stays and backstays, coming up
with the seizings, hauling here, belaying there, and full of
business, standing between the knightheads to sight the mast—
when the captain came forward, and also began to give orders.
This made confusion, and the mate left his place and went
aft, saying to the captain:

"If you come forward, sir, I'll go aft. One is enough on the
forecastle."

This produced a reply, and another fierce answer; and the
words flew, fists were doubled up, and things looked threat-
eningly.

"I'm master of this ship."

"Yes, sir, and I'm mate of her, and know my place! My place is forward, and yours is aft."

"My place is where I choose! I command the *whole* ship, and you are mate only so long as I choose!"

"Say the word, Captain Thompson, and I'm done! I can do a man's work aboard! I didn't come through the cabin windows! If I'm not mate, I can be man," &c., &c.

This was all fun for us, who stood by, winking at each other, and enjoying the contest between the higher powers. The captain took the mate aft; and they had a long talk, which ended in the mate's returning to his duty. The captain had broken through a custom, which is a part of the common law of a ship, and without reason, for he knew that his mate was a sailor, and needed no help from him; and the mate was excusable for being angry. Yet, in strict law, he was wrong, and the captain right. Whatever the captain does is right, *ipso facto*, and any opposition to it is wrong on board ship; and every officer and man knows this when he signs the ship's articles. It is a part of the contract. Yet there has grown up in merchant vessels a series of customs, which have become a well-understood system, and have somewhat the force of prescriptive law. To be sure, all power is in the captain, and the officers hold their authority only during his will, and the men are liable to be called upon for any service; yet, by breaking in upon these usages, many difficulties have occurred on board ship, and even come into courts of justice, which are perfectly unintelligible to anyone not acquainted with the universal nature and force of these customs. Many a provocation has been offered, and a system of petty oppression pursued toward men, the force and meaning of which would appear as nothing to strangers, and doubtless do appear so to many "longshore" juries and judges.

The next little diversion was a battle on the forecastle, one afternoon, between the mate and the steward. They had been on bad terms the whole voyage, and had threatened a rupture several times. Once, on the coast, the mate had seized the steward, when the steward suddenly lowered his head, and pitched it straight into Mr. Brown's stomach, butting him against the galley, grunting at every shove, and calling out, "You, Brown!" Mr. Brown looked white in the face, and the heaviest blows he could give seemed to have no effect on the

Negro's head. He was pulled off by the second mate, and Mr. Brown was going at him again, when the captain separated them; and Mr. Brown told his tale to the captain, adding "and, *moreover, he called me Brown!*" From this time, "moreover, he called me Brown," became a byword on board. Mr. Brown went aft, saying, "I've promised it to you, and now you've got it." But he did not seem to be sure which had "got it"; nor did we. We knew Mr. Brown would not leave the thing in that equivocal position all the voyage, if he could help it. This afternoon the mate asked the steward for a tumbler of water, and he refused to get it for him, saying that he waited upon nobody but the captain; and here he had the custom on his side. But, in answering, he committed the unpardonable offense of leaving off the handle to the mate's name. This enraged the mate, who called him a "black soger," and at it they went, clenching, striking, and rolling over and over; while we stood by, looking on and enjoying the fun. The darky tried to butt him, as before, but the mate got him down, and held him, the steward singing out, "Let me go, Mr. Brown, or there'll be blood spilt!" In the midst of this, the captain came on deck, separated them, took the steward aft, and gave him half a dozen with a rope's end. The steward tried to justify himself, but he had been heard to talk of spilling blood and that was enough to earn him his flogging; and the captain did not choose to inquire any further. Mr. Brown was satisfied to let him alone after that, as he had, on the whole, vindicated his superiority in the eyes of the crew.

# CHAPTER  XXXIV

The same day, I met with one of those narrow escapes which are so often happening in a sailor's life. I had been aloft nearly all the afternoon, at work, standing for as much as an hour on the fore-topgallant yard, which was hoisted up, and hung only by the tie; when, having got through my work, I balled up my yarns, took my serving board in my hand, laid hold deliberately of the topgallant rigging, took one foot from the yard, and was just lifting the other, when the tie parted, and down the yard fell. I was safe, by my hold upon the rigging, but it made my heart beat quick. Had the tie parted one instant sooner, or had I stood an instant longer on the yard, I should inevitably have been thrown violently from the height of ninety or a hundred feet, overboard; or, what is worse, upon the deck. However, "a miss is as good as a mile"; a saying which sailors very often have occasion to use. An escape is always a joke on board ship. A man would be ridiculed who should make a serious matter of it. A sailor knows too well that his life hangs upon a thread to wish to be often reminded of it; so, if a man has an escape, he keeps it to himself, or makes a joke of it. I have often known a man's life to be saved by an instant of time, or by the merest chance —the swinging of a rope—and no notice taken of it. One of our boys, off Cape Horn, reefing topsails of a dark night when there were no boats to be lowered away, and where, if a man fell overboard, he must be left behind, lost his hold of the reef point, slipped from the foot rope, and would have been in the water in a moment, when the man who was next to him on the yard, French John, caught him by the collar of his jacket, and hauled him up upon the yard, with, "Hold on, another time, you young monkey, and be d——d to you!" and that was all that was heard about it.

*Sunday, August 7th.* Lat. 25° 59′ S., lon. 27° 0′ W. Spoke the English bark *Mary Catherine,* from Bahia, bound to Calcutta. This was the first sail we had fallen in with, and the first time we had seen a human form or heard the human voice, except of our own number, for nearly a hundred days. The very yo-ho-ing of the sailors at the ropes sounded sociably upon the ear. She was an old, damaged-looking craft, with a high poop and topgallant forecastle, and sawed off square, stem and stern, like a true English "tea wagon," and with a run like a sugar box. She had studding sails out alow and aloft, with a light but steady breeze, and her captain said he could not get more than four knots out of her, and thought he should have a long passage. We were going six on an easy bowline.

The next day, about 3 P.M., passed a large corvette-built ship, close upon the wind, with royals and skysails set fore and aft, under English colors. She was standing south-by-east, probably bound round Cape Horn. She had men in her tops, and black mastheads; heavily sparred, with sails cut to a *t*, and other marks of a man-of-war. She sailed well, and presented a fine appearance, the proud, feudal-looking banner of St. George—the cross in a blood-red field—waving from the mizzen. We probably were nearly as fine a sight, with our studding sails spread far out beyond the ship on either side, and rising in a pyramid to royal studding sails and skysails, burying the hull in canvas and looking like what the whalemen on the Banks, under their stump topgallant masts, call "a Cape Horner under a cloud of sail."

*Friday, August 12th.* At daylight made the island of Trinidad, situated in lat. 20° 28′ S., lon. 29° 08′ W. at 12 M., it bore NW. ½ N., distant twenty-seven miles. It was a beautiful day, the sea hardly ruffled by the light trades, and the island looking like a small blue mound rising from a field of glass. Such a fair and peaceful-looking spot is said to have been, for a long time, the resort of a band of pirates, who ravaged the tropical seas.

*Thursday, August 18th.* At 3 P.M., made the island of Fernando Noronha, lying in lat. 3° 55′ S., lon. 32° 35′ W.; and between twelve o'clock Friday night and one o'clock Saturday morning crossed the equator, for the fourth time since leaving Boston, in lon. 35° W.; having been twenty-seven days from Staten Land—a distance, by the courses we had made, of more than four thousand miles.

We were now to the northward of the line, and every day added to our latitude. The Magellan Clouds, the last sign of south latitude, had long been sunk, and the North Star, the Great Bear, and the familiar signs of northern latitudes were rising in the heavens. Next to seeing land, there is no sight which makes one realize more that he is drawing near home, than to see the same heavens under which he was born, shining at night over his head. The weather was extremely hot, with the usual tropical alternations of a scorching sun and squalls of rain; yet not a word was said in complaint of the heat, for we all remembered that only three or four weeks

before we would have given our all to be where we now
were. We had aplenty of water, too, which we caught by
spreading an awning, with shot thrown in to make hollows.
These rain squalls came up in the manner usual between the
tropics. A clear sky; burning, vertical sun; work going lazily
on, and men about decks with nothing but duck trousers,
checked shirts, and straw hats; the ship moving as lazily
through the water; the man at the helm resting against the
wheel, with his hat drawn over his eyes; the captain below,
taking an afternoon nap; the passenger leaning over the taffrail, watching a dolphin following slowly in our wake; the
sailmaker mending an old topsail on the lee side of the quarterdeck; the carpenter working at his bench, in the waist;
the boys making sennit; the spun-yarn winch whizzing round
and round, and the men walking slowly fore and aft with the
yarns. A cloud rises to windward, looking a little black; the
skysails are brailed down; the captain puts his head out of
the companionway, looks at the cloud, comes up, and begins
to walk the deck. The cloud spreads and comes on; the tub
of yarns, the sail, and other matters are thrown below, and the
skylight and booby hatch put on, and the slide drawn over the
forecastle. "Stand by the royal halyards"; and the man at the
wheel keeps a good weather helm, so as not to be taken
aback. The squall strikes her. If it is light, the royal yards
are clewed down, and the ship keeps on her way; but if the
squall takes strong hold, the royals are clewed up, fore and
aft; light hands lay aloft and furl them; topgallant yards are
clewed down, flying jib hauled down, and the ship kept off
before it, the man at the helm laying out his strength to
heave the wheel up to windward. At the same time a drenching rain, which soaks one through in an instant. Yet no one
puts on a jacket or cap; for if it is only warm, a sailor does
not mind a ducking; and the sun will soon be out again. As
soon as the force of the squall has passed, though to a common eye the ship would seem to be in the midst of it: "Keep
her up to her course again!" "Keep her up, sir" (answer).*
"Hoist away the topgallant yards!" "Run up the flying jib!"
"Lay aloft, you boys, and loose the royals!" and all sail is on
her again before she is fairly out of the squall; and she is
going on in her course. The sun comes out once more, hotter

* A man at the wheel is required to repeat every order given him. A
simple "Aye, aye, sir" is not enough there.

than ever, dries up the decks and the sailors' clothes; the hatches are taken off; the sail got up and spread on the quarterdeck; spun-yarn winch set a-whirling again; rigging coiled up; captain goes below; and every sign of an interruption disappears.

These scenes, with occasional dead calms, lasting for hours, and sometimes for days, are fair specimens of the Atlantic tropics. The nights were fine; and as we had all hands all day, the watch were allowed to sleep on deck at night, except the man at the wheel, and one lookout on the forecastle. This was not so much expressly allowed as winked at. We could do it if we did not ask leave. If the lookout was caught napping, the whole watch was kept awake. We made the most of this permission, and stowed ourselves away upon the rigging, under the weather rail, on the spars, under the windlass, and in all the snug corners; and frequently slept out the watch, unless we had a wheel or a lookout. And we were glad enough to get this rest; for under the "all-hands" system, out of every other thirty-six hours we had only four below; and even an hour's sleep was a gain not to be neglected. One would have thought so to have seen our watch some nights, sleeping through a heavy rain. And often have we come on deck, and, finding a dead calm and a light, steady rain, and determined not to lose our sleep, have laid a coil of rigging down so as to keep us out of the water which was washing about decks, and stowed ourselves away upon it, covering a jacket over us, and slept as soundly as a Dutchman between two featherbeds.

For a week or ten days after crossing the line, we had the usual variety of calms, squalls, head winds, and fair winds—at one time braced sharp upon the wind, with a taut bowline, and in an hour after, slipping quietly along, with a light breeze over the taffrail, and studding sails set out on both sides—until we fell in with the northeast trade winds; which we did on the afternoon of—

*Sunday, August 28th,* in lat. 12° N. The trade-wind clouds had been in sight for a day or two previously, and we expected to take the trades every hour. The light southerly breeze, which had been breathing languidly during the first part of the day, died away toward noon, and in its place came puffs from the northeast, which caused us to take in our studding sails and brace up; and, in a couple of hours more, we were bowling gloriously along, dashing the spray far ahead

and to leeward, with the cool, steady northeast trades freshening up the sea, and giving us as much as we could carry
our royals to. These winds blew strong and steady, keeping
us generally upon a bowline, as our course was about north-
northwest; and, sometimes, as they veered a little to the eastward, giving us a chance at a main-topgallant studding sail,
and sending us well to the northward, until—

Sunday, September 4th, when they left us in lat. 22° N.,
lon. 51° W., directly under the Tropic of Cancer.

For several days we lay "humbugging about" in the horse
latitudes, with all sorts of winds and weather, and occasionally, as we were in the latitude of the West Indies, a thunderstorm. It was hurricane month, too, and we were just in
the track of the tremendous hurricane of 1830, which swept
the North Atlantic, destroying almost everything before it.

The first night after the trade winds left us, while we were
in the latitude of the island of Cuba, we had a specimen of
a true tropical thunderstorm. A light breeze had been blowing
from aft during the first part of the night, which gradually
died away, and before midnight it was dead calm, and a
heavy black cloud had shrouded the whole sky. When our
watch came on deck at twelve o'clock, it was as black as
Erebus; the studding sails were all taken in, and the royals
furled; not a breath was stirring; the sails hung heavy and
motionless from the yards; and the stillness and the darkness,
which was almost palpable, were truly appalling. Not a word
was spoken, but everyone stood as though waiting for something to happen. In a few minutes the mate came forward,
and in a low tone, which was almost a whisper, told us to
haul down the jib. The fore and mizzen topgallant sails were
taken in in the same silent manner; and we lay motionless
upon the water, with an uneasy expectation, which, from the
long suspense, became actually painful. We could hear the
captain walking the deck, but it was too dark to see anything
more than one's hand before the face. Soon the mate came
forward again, and gave an order, in a low tone, to clew up
the main-topgallant sail; and so infectious was the awe and
silence that the clew lines and buntlines were hauled up without any singing out at the ropes. An English lad and myself
went up to furl it; and we had just got the bunt up, when the
mate called out to us something, we did not hear what; but,
supposing it to be an order to bear a hand, we hurried and

made all fast, and came down, feeling our way among the rigging. When we got down we found all hands looking aloft, and there, directly over where we had been standing, upon the main-topgallant masthead, was a ball of light, which the sailors call a corposant (*corpus sancti*), and which the mate had called out to us to look at. They were all watching it carefully, for sailors have a notion that if the corposant rises in the rigging it is a sign of fair weather, but if it comes lower down there will be a storm. Unfortunately, as an omen, it came down, and showed itself on the topgallant yardarm. We were off the yard in good season, for it is held a fatal sign to have the pale light of the corposant thrown upon one's face. As it was, the English lad did not feel comfortably at having had it so near him, and directly over his head. In a few minutes it disappeared, and showed itself again on the fore-topgallant yard; and, after playing about for some time, disappeared once more, when the man on the forecastle pointed to it upon the flying-jib boom end. But our attention was drawn from watching this, by the falling of some drops of rain, and by a perceptible increase of the darkness, which seemed suddenly to add a new shade of blackness to the night. In a few minutes, low, grumbling thunder was heard, and some random flashes of lightning came from the southwest. Every sail was taken in but the topsails; still, no squall appeared to be coming. A few puffs lifted the topsails, but they fell again to the mast, and all was as still as ever. A moment more, and a terrific flash and peal broke simultaneously upon us, and a cloud appeared to open directly over our heads, and let down the water in one body, like a falling ocean. We stood motionless, and almost stupefied; yet nothing had been struck. Peal after peal rattled over our heads, with a sound which seemed actually to stop the breath in the body, and the "speedy gleams" kept the whole ocean in a glare of light. The violent fall of rain lasted but a few minutes, and was followed by occasional drops and showers; but the lightning continued incessant for several hours, breaking the midnight darkness with irregular and blinding flashes. During all this time there was not a breath stirring, and we lay motionless, like a mark to be shot at, probably the only object on the surface of the ocean for miles and miles. We stood hour after hour, until our watch was out, and we were relieved, at four o'clock. During all this time hardly a word was spoken; no bells were struck, and the wheel was silently relieved. The rain fell at intervals in heavy showers, and we stood drenched through and blinded by the flashes, which broke the Egyptian darkness with a brightness that seemed almost malignant; while the thunder rolled in peals, the concussion of which appeared to shake the very ocean. A ship is not often injured by lightning, for the electricity is separated by the great number of points she presents, and the quantity of iron which she has scattered in various parts. The electric fluid ran over our anchors, topsail sheets and ties; yet no harm was done to us. We went below at four o'clock, leaving things in the same state. It is not easy to sleep when the very next flash may tear the ship in two, or set her on fire; or where the deathlike calm may be broken by the blast of a hurricane, taking the masts out of the ship. But a man is no sailor if he cannot sleep when he turns in, and turn out when he's called. And when, at seven bells, the customary "All the larboard watch, ahoy!" brought us on deck, it was a fine, clear, sunny morning, the ship going leisurely along, with a soft breeze and all sail set.

# CHAPTER XXXV

From the latitude of the West Indies, until we got inside the Bermudas, where we took the westerly and southwesterly winds, which blow steadily off the coast of the United States early in the autumn, we had every variety of weather, and two or three moderate gales, or, as sailors call them, double-reef-topsail breezes, which came on in the usual manner, and of which one is a specimen of all. A fine afternoon; all hands at work, some in the rigging, and others on deck; a stiff breeze, and ship close upon the wind, and skysails brailed down.

Latter part of the afternoon, breeze increases, ship lies over
to it, and clouds look windy. Spray begins to fly over the
forecastle, and wets the yarns the boys are knotting; ball them
up and put them below. Mate knocks off work and clears up
decks earlier than usual, and orders a man who has been
employed aloft to send the royal halyards over to windward,
as he comes down. Breast backstays hauled taut, and a tackle
got upon the martingale backrope. One of the boys furls the
mizzen royal. Cook thinks there is going to be "nasty work,"
and has supper ready early. Mate gives orders to get supper
by the watch, instead of all hands, as usual. While eating
supper, hear the watch on deck taking in the royals. Coming
on deck, find it is blowing harder, and an ugly head sea running. Instead of having all hands on the forecastle in the dog
watch, smoking, singing, and telling yarns, one watch goes
below and turns in, saying that it's going to be an ugly
night, and two hours' sleep is not to be lost. Clouds look
black and wild; wind rising, and ship working hard against
a heavy head sea, which breaks over the forecastle, and
washes aft through the scuppers. Still, no more sail is taken
in, for the captain is a driver, and, like all drivers, very
partial to his topgallant sails. A topgallant sail, too, makes
the difference between a breeze and a gale. When a topgallant
sail is on a ship, it is only a breeze, though I have seen ours
set over a reefed topsail, when half the bowsprit was under
water, and it was up to a man's knees in the lee scuppers.
At eight bells, nothing is said about reefing the topsails, and
the watch go below, with orders to "stand by for a call." We
turn in, growling at the "old man" for not reefing the topsails when the watch was changed, but putting it off so as to
call all hands, and break up a whole watch below. Turn in "all
standing," and keep ourselves awake, saying there is no use
in going to sleep to be waked up again. Wind whistles on
deck, and ship works hard, groaning and creaking, and pitching into a heavy head sea, which strikes against the bows,
with a noise like knocking upon a rock. The dim lamp in the
forecastle swings to and fro, and things "fetch away" and go
over to leeward. "Doesn't that booby of a second mate ever
mean to take in his topgallant sails? He'll have the sticks
out of her soon," says Old Bill, who was always growling,
and, like most old sailors, did not like to see a ship abused.
By and by, an order is given; "Aye, aye, sir!" from the

forecastle; rigging is thrown down on deck; the noise of a
sail is heard fluttering aloft, and the short, quick cry which
sailors make when hauling upon clew lines. "Here comes
his fore-topgallant sail in!" We are wide awake, and know
all that's going on as well as if we were on deck. A well-
known voice is heard from the masthead singing out to the
officer of the watch to haul taut the weather brace. "Hallo!
There's Ben Stimson aloft to furl the sail!" Next thing, rigging
is thrown down directly over our heads, and a long-drawn
cry and a rattling of hanks announce that the flying jib has
come in. The second mate holds onto the main-topgallant sail
until a heavy sea is shipped, and washes over the forecastle
as though the whole ocean had come aboard; when a noise
further aft shows that that sail, too, is taking in. After this
the ship is more easy for a time; two bells are struck, and
we try to get a little sleep. By and by, *bang, bang, bang* on
the scuttle—"All ha-a-ands, a-ho-o-y!" We spring out of our
berths, clap on a monkey jacket and southwester, and
tumble up the ladder. Mate up before us, and on the forecastle, singing out like a roaring bull; the captain singing
out on the quarterdeck, and the second mate yelling, like a
hyena, in the waist. The ship is lying over half upon her
beam ends; lee scuppers under water, and forecastle all in
a smother of foam. Rigging all let go, and washing about
decks; topsail yards down upon the caps, and sails flapping
and beating against the masts; and starboard watch hauling
out the reef tackles of the main topsail. Our watch haul out
the fore, and lay aloft and put two reefs into it, and reef
the foresail, and race with the starboard watch to see which
will masthead its topsail first. All hands tally on to the main
tack, and while some are furling the jib and hoisting the
staysail, we mizzentopmen double-reef the mizzen topsail
and hoist it up. All being made fast, "Go below, the watch!"
and we turn in to sleep out the rest of the time, which is
perhaps an hour and a half. During all the middle, and
for the first part of the morning watch, it blows as hard as
ever, but toward daybreak it moderates considerably, and we
shake a reef out of each topsail, and set the topgallant sails
over them; and when the watch come up, at seven bells, for
breakfast, shake the other reefs out, turn all hands to upon
the halyards, get the watch tackle upon the topgallant sheets
and halyards, set the flying jib, and crack on to her again.

Our captain had been married only a few weeks before he left Boston, and, after an absence of over two years, it may be supposed he was not slow in carrying sail. The mate, too, was not to be beaten by anybody; and the second mate, though he was afraid to press sail, was still more afraid of the captain, and, being between two fears, sometimes carried on longer than any of them. We snapped off three flying-jib booms in twenty-four hours, as fast as they could be fitted and rigged out; sprung the spritsail yard, and made nothing of studding-sail booms. Beside the natural desire to get home, we had another reason for urging the ship on. The scurvy had begun to show itself on board. One man had it so badly as to be disabled and off duty, and the English lad, Ben, was in a dreadful state, and was daily growing worse. His legs swelled and pained him so that he could not walk; his flesh lost its elasticity, so that if pressed in it would not return to its shape; and his gums swelled until he could not open his mouth. His breath, too, became very offensive; he lost all strength and spirit; could eat nothing; grew worse every day; and, in fact, unless something was done for him, would be a dead man in a week, at the rate at which he was sinking. The medicines were all, or nearly all, gone, and if we had had a chestful they would have been of no use, for nothing but fresh provisions and *terra firma* has any effect upon the scurvy. This disease is not so common now as formerly, and is attributed generally to salt provisions, want of cleanliness, the free use of grease and fat (which is the reason of its prevalence among whalemen), and, last of all, to laziness. It never could have been from the last cause on board our ship; nor from the second, for we were a very cleanly crew, kept our forecastle in neat order, and were more particular about washing and changing clothes than many better-dressed people on shore. It was probably from having none but salt provisions, and possibly from our having run very rapidly into hot weather, after our having been so long in the extremest cold.

Depending upon the westerly winds which prevail off the coast in the autumn, the captain stood well to the westward, to run inside of the Bermudas, and in the hope of falling in with some vessel bound to the West Indies or the southern states. The scurvy had spread no further among the crew, but there was danger that it might; and these cases were bad ones.

*Sunday, September 11th.* Lat. 30° 04′ N., lon. 63° 23′ W.; the Bermudas bearing north-northwest, distant one hundred and fifty miles. The next morning about ten o'clock, "Sail ho!" was cried on deck; and all hands turned up to see the stranger. As she drew nearer, she proved to be an ordinary-looking hermaphrodite brig, standing south-southeast, and probably bound out from the northern states to the West Indies, and was just the thing we wished to see. She hove to for us, seeing that we wished to speak her, and we ran down to her, boom-ended our studding sails, backed our main topsail, and hailed her: "Brig ahoy!" "Hallo!" "Where are you from, pray?" "From New York, bound to Curaçao." "Have you any fresh provisions to spare?" "Aye, aye! Plenty of them!" We lowered away the quarter boat instantly, and the captain and four hands sprang in, and were soon dancing over the water and alongside the brig. In about half an hour they returned with half a boatload of potatoes and onions, and each vessel filled away and kept on her course. She proved to be the brig *Solon*, of Plymouth, from the Connecticut River, and last from New York, bound to the Spanish Main, with a cargo of fresh provisions, mules, tin bake pans, and other "notions." The onions were fresh; and the mate of the brig told the men in the boat, as he passed the bunches over the side, that the girls had strung them on purpose for us the day he sailed. We had made the mistake, on board, of supposing that a new President had been chosen the last winter, and, as we filled away, the captain hailed and asked who was President of the United States. They answered, Andrew Jackson; but, thinking that the old General could not have been elected for a third time, we hailed again, and they answered, Jack Downing, and left us to correct the mistake at our leisure.

Our boat's crew had a laugh upon one of our number, Joe, who was vain and made the best show of everything. The style and gentility of a ship and her crew depend upon the length and character of the voyage. An India or China voyage always is "the thing," and a voyage to the Northwest Coast (the Columbia River or Russian America) for furs is romantic and mysterious, and if it takes the ship round the world, by way of the Islands and China, it outranks them all. The grave, slab-sided mate of the schooner leaned over the rail, and spoke to the men in our boat: "Where are you from?" Joe answered up quick, "From the Nor'west Coast." "What's your cargo?" This was a poser; but Joe was ready with an equivoke. "Skins," said he. "Here and there a *horn?*" asked the mate, in the dryest manner. The boat's crew laughed out, and Joe's glory faded. Apropos of this, a man named Sam, on board the *Pilgrim*, used to tell a story of a mean little captain in a mean little brig, in which he sailed from Liverpool to New York, who insisted on speaking a great, homeward-bound Indiaman, with her studding sails out on both sides, sunburned men in wide-brimmed hats on her decks, and a monkey and paroquet in her rigging, "rolling down from St. Helena." There was no need of his stopping her to speak her, but his vanity led him to do it, and then his meanness made him so awestruck that he seemed to quail. He called out, in a small, lisping voice, "What ship is that, pray?" A deep-toned voice roared through the trumpet, "The *Bashaw*, from Canton, bound to Boston. Hundred and ten days out! Where are you from?" "*Only* from Liverpool, *sir*," he lisped, in the most apologetic and subservient voice. But the humor will be felt by those only who know the ritual of hailing at sea. No one says "sir," and the "only" was wonderfully expressive.

It was just dinnertime when we filled away, and the steward, taking a few bunches of onions for the cabin, gave the rest to us, with a bottle of vinegar. We carried them forward, stowed them away in the forecastle, refusing to have them cooked, and ate them raw, with our beef and bread. And a glorious treat they were. The freshness and crispness of the raw onion, with the earthy taste, give it a great relish to one who has been a long time on salt provisions. We were ravenous after them. It was like a scent of blood to a hound. We ate them at every meal, by the dozen, and filled our pockets with them, to eat in our watch on deck; and the bunches, rising in the form of a cone, from the largest at the bottom, to the smallest, no larger than a strawberry, at the top, soon disappeared. The chief use, however, of the fresh provisions was for the men with the scurvy. One of them was able to eat, and he soon brought himself to, by gnawing upon raw potatoes and onions; but the other, by this time, was hardly able to open his mouth, and the cook took the potatoes raw, pounded them in a mortar, and gave him the juice to drink. This he swallowed, by the teaspoonful at a time, and rinsed it about his gums and throat. The strong earthy taste and smell of this extract of the raw potato at first produced a shuddering through his whole frame, and, after drinking it, an acute pain, which ran through all parts of his body; but knowing by this that it was taking strong hold, he persevered, drinking a spoonful every hour or so, and holding it a long time in his mouth, until, by the effect of this drink, and of his own restored hope (for he had nearly given up in despair), he became so well as to be able to move about, and open his mouth enough to eat the raw potatoes and onions pounded into a soft pulp. This course soon restored his appetite and strength, and in ten days after we spoke the *Solon,* so rapid was his recovery that, from lying helpless and almost hopeless in his berth, he was at the masthead, furling a royal.

With a fine southwest wind we passed inside of the Bermudas, and, notwithstanding the old couplet, which was quoted again and again by those who thought we should have one more touch of a storm before our voyage was up—

> "If the Bermudas let you pass,
>   You must beware of Hatteras"—

we were to the northward of Hatteras, with good weather, and beginning to count, not the days, but the hours, to the time when we should be at anchor in Boston harbor.

Our ship was in fine order, all hands having been hard at work upon her, from daylight to dark, every day but Sunday from the time we got into warm weather on this side the Cape.

It is a common notion with landsmen that a ship is in her finest condition when she leaves port to enter upon her voyage, and that she comes home, after a long absence—

> "With overweathered ribs and ragged sails;
>   Lean, rent, and beggared by the strumpet wind."

But so far from that, unless a ship meets with some accident, or comes upon the coast in the dead of winter, when work cannot be done upon the rigging, she is in her finest order at the end of the voyage. When she sails from port, her rigging

is generally slack; the masts need staying; the decks and sides
are black and dirty from taking in cargo; riggers' seizings and
overhand knots in place of nice seamanlike work; and everything, to a sailor's eye, adrift. But on the passage home, the
fine weather between the tropics is spent in putting the ship
in the neatest order. No merchant vessel looks better than an
Indiaman, or a Cape Horner, after a long voyage, and
captains and mates stake their reputation for seamanship
upon the appearance of their ships when they haul into the
dock. All our standing rigging, fore and aft, was set up and
tarred, the masts stayed, the lower and topmast rigging rattled
down (or up, as the fashion now is); and so careful were
our officers to keep the ratlines taut and straight, that we
were obliged to go aloft upon the ropes and sheer poles with
which the rigging was swifted in; and these were used as
jury ratlines until we got close upon the coast. After this
the ship was scraped, inside and out, decks, masts, booms,
and all; a stage being rigged outside, upon which we scraped
her down to the waterline, pounding the rust off the chains,
bolts, and fastenings. Then, taking two days of calm under
the line, we painted her on the outside, giving her open
ports in her strake, and finishing off the nice work upon
the stern, where sat Neptune in his car, holding his trident,
drawn by sea horses; and retouched the gilding and coloring
of the cornucopia which ornamented her billethead. The
inside was then painted, from the skysail truck to the waterways: the yards, black; mastheads and tops, white; monkey
rail, black, white, and yellow; bulwarks, green; plank-sheer,
white; waterways, lead color; &c., &c. The anchors and ringbolts, and other iron work, were blackened with coal tar;
and the steward was kept at work, polishing the brass of the
wheel, bell, capstan, &c. The cabin, too, was scraped, varnished, and painted; and the forecastle scraped and scrubbed,
there being no need of paint and varnish for Jack's quarters.
The decks were then scraped and varnished, and everything
useless thrown overboard; among which, the empty tar barrels
were set on fire and thrown overboard, of a dark night, and
left blazing astern, lighting up the ocean for miles. Add to all
this labor the neat work upon the rigging—the knots, Flemish
eyes, splices, seizings, coverings, pointings, and graffings which
show a ship in crack order. The last preparation, and which
looked still more like coming into port, was getting the

anchors over the bows, bending the cables, rousing the hawsers up from between decks, and overhauling the deep-sea lead line.

*Thursday, September 15th.* This morning the temperature and peculiar appearance of the water, the quantities of gulf-weed floating about, and a bank of clouds lying directly before us, showed that we were on the border of the Gulf Stream. This remarkable current, running northeast, nearly across the ocean, is almost constantly shrouded in clouds and is the region of storms and heavy seas. Vessels often run from a clear sky and light wind, with all sail, at once into a heavy sea and cloudy sky, with double-reefed topsails. A sailor told me that, on a passage from Gibraltar to Boston, his vessel neared the Gulf Stream with a light breeze, clear sky, and studding sails out, alow and aloft; while before it was a long line of heavy, black clouds, lying like a bank upon the water, and a vessel coming out of it, under double-reefed topsails, and with royal yards sent down. As they drew near, they began to take in sail after sail, until they were reduced to the same condition; and, after twelve or fourteen hours of rolling and pitching in a heavy sea, before a smart gale, they ran out of the bank on the other side, and were in fine weather again, and under their royals and skysails. As we drew into it, the sky became cloudy, the sea high, and everything had the appearance of the going off, or the coming on, of a storm. It was blowing no more than a stiff breeze; yet the wind, being northeast, which is directly against the course of the current, made an ugly, chopping sea, which heaved and pitched the vessel about, so that we were obliged to send down the royal yards, and to take in our light sails. At noon, the thermometer, which had been repeatedly lowered into the water, showed the temperature to be seventy; which was considerably above that of the air, as is always the case in the center of the Stream. A lad who had been at work at the royal masthead came down upon deck, and took a turn round the longboat; and, looking pale, said he was so sick that he could stay aloft no longer, but was ashamed to acknowledge it to the officer. He went up again, but soon gave out and came down, and leaned over the rail, "as sick as a lady passenger." He had been to sea several years, and had, he said, never been sick before. He was made so by the irregular pitching motion of the vessel, increased by the height to which he had been above the hull, which is like the fulcrum of the lever. An old sailor, who was at work on the topgallant yard, said he felt disagreeably all the time, and was glad, when his job was done, to get down into the top, or upon deck. Another hand was sent to the royal masthead, who stayed nearly an hour, but gave up. The work must be done, and the mate sent me. I did very well for some time, but began at length to feel very unpleasantly, though I never had been sick since the first two days from Boston, and had been in all sorts of weather and situations. Still, I kept my place, and did not come down, until I had got through my work, which was more than two hours. The ship certainly never acted so before. She was pitched and jerked about in all manner of ways; the sails seeming to have no steadying power over her. The tapering points of the masts made various curves against the sky overhead, and sometimes, in one sweep of an instant, described an arc of more than forty-five degrees, bringing up with a sudden jerk, which made it necessary to hold on with both hands, and then sweeping off in another long, irregular curve. I was not positively sick, and came down with a look of indifference, yet was not unwilling to get upon the comparative *terra firma* of the deck. A few hours more carried us through, and when we saw the sun go down, upon our larboard beam, in the direction of the continent of North America, we had left the bank of dark, stormy clouds astern, in the twilight.

# CHAPTER XXXVI

*Friday, September 16th.* Lat. 38° N., lon. 69° 00′ W. A fine southwest wind; every hour carrying us nearer in toward the land. All hands on deck at the dog watch, and nothing talked about but our getting in; where we should make the land; whether we should arrive before Sunday; going to church; how Boston would look; friends; wages paid; and the like. Everyone was in the best spirits; and, the voyage being nearly at an end, the strictness of discipline was relaxed, for it was not necessary to order in a cross tone what all were ready to do with a will. The differences and quarrels which a long voyage breeds on board a ship were forgotten, and everyone was friendly; and two men, who had been on the eve of a fight half the voyage, were laying out a plan together for a cruise on shore. When the mate came forward, he talked to the men, and said we should be on George's Banks before tomorrow noon; and joked with the boys, promising to go and see them, and to take them down to Marblehead in a coach.

*Saturday, 17th.* The wind was light all day, which kept us back somewhat; but a fine breeze springing up at nightfall, we were running fast in toward the land. At six o'clock we expected to have the ship hove to for soundings, as a thick fog, coming up, showed we were near them; but no order was given, and we kept on our way. Eight o'clock came, and the watch went below, and, for the whole of the first hour, the ship was driving on, with studding sails out, alow and aloft, and the night as dark as a pocket. At two bells the captain came on deck, and said a word to the mate, when the studding sails were hauled into the tops, or boom-ended, the after yards backed, the deep-sea lead carried forward, and everything got ready for sounding. A man on the spritsail yard with the lead, another on the cathead with a handful of the line coiled up, another in the fore chains, another in the waist, and another in the main chains, each with a quantity of the line coiled away in his hand. "All ready there, forward?" "Aye, aye, sir!" "He-e-ave!" "Watch, ho! Watch!" sings the man on the spritsail yard, and the heavy lead drops into the water. "Watch, ho! Watch!" bawls the man on the cathead, as the last fake of the coil drops from his hand, and "Watch, ho! Watch!" is shouted by each one as the line falls from his hold, until it comes to the mate, who tends the lead, and has the line in coils on the quarterdeck. Eighty fathoms and no bottom! A depth as great as the height of St. Peter's! The line is snatched in a block upon the swifter, and three or four men haul it in and coil it away. The after yards are braced full, the studding sails hauled out again, and in a few minutes more, the ship had her whole way upon her. At four bells backed again, hove the lead, and—soundings! At sixty fathoms! Hurrah for Yankee land! Hand over hand we hauled the lead in, and the captain, taking it to the light, found black mud on the bottom. Studding sails taken in; after yards filled, and ship kept on under easy sail all night, the wind dying away.

The soundings on the American coast are so regular that a navigator knows as well where he has made land by the soundings, as he would by seeing the land. Black mud is the soundings of Block Island. As you go toward Nantucket, it changes to a dark sand; then, sand and white shells; and on George's Banks, white sand; and so on. As our soundings showed us to be off Block Island, our course was due east, to Nantucket Shoals and the South Channel; but the wind died away and left us becalmed in a thick fog, in which we lay the whole of Sunday. At noon of—

*Sunday, 18th,* Block Island bore, by calculation, NW. ¼ W. fifteen miles; but the fog was so thick all day that we could see nothing.

Having got through the ship's duty, and washed and changed our clothes, we went below, and had a fine time overhauling our chests, laying aside the clothes we meant to go ashore in, and throwing overboard all that were worn out and good for nothing. Away went the woolen caps in which we had carried hides upon our heads, for sixteen months, on the coast of California; the duck frocks for tarring down rigging; and the worn-out and darned mittens and patched woolen trousers which had stood the tug of Cape Horn. We hove them overboard with a good will; for there is nothing like being quit of the very last appendages, remnants, and mementos of our hard fortune. We got our chests all ready for going ashore; ate the last "duff" we expected to have on board the ship *Alert;* and talked as confidently about matters on shore as though our anchor were on the bottom.

"Who'll go to church with me a week from today?"

"I will," says Jack; who said aye to everything.

"Go away, salt water!" says Tom. "As soon as I get both legs ashore, I'm going to shoe my heels, and button my ears behind me, and start off into the bush, a straight course, and not stop till I'm out of the sight of salt water!"

"Oh, belay that! If you get once moored, stem and stern, in old Barnes's grogshop, with a coal fire ahead and the bar under your lee, you won't see daylight for three weeks!"

"No!" says Tom. "I'm going to knock off grog and go and board at the Home, and see if they won't ship me for a deacon!"

"And I," says Bill, "am going to buy a quadrant and ship for navigator of a Hingham packet!"

Harry White swore he would take rooms at the Tremont House and set up for a gentleman; he knew his wages would hold out for two weeks or so.

These and the like served to pass the time while we were lying waiting for a breeze to clear up the fog and send us on our way.

Toward night a moderate breeze sprang up, the fog, however, continuing as thick as before; and we kept on to the eastward. About the middle of the first watch, a man on the forecastle sang out, in a tone which showed that there was not a moment to be lost, "Hard up the helm!" and a great ship loomed up out of the fog, coming directly down upon us. She luffed at the same moment, and we just passed each other, our spanker boom grazing over her quarter. The officer of the deck had only time to hail, and she answered, as she went into the fog again, something about Bristol. Probably a whaleman from Bristol, Rhode Island, bound out. The fog continued through the night, with a very light breeze, before which we ran to the eastward, literally feeling our way along. The lead was heaved every two hours, and the gradual change from black mud to sand showed that we were approaching Nantucket South Shoals. On Monday morning, the increased depth and dark-blue color of the water, and the mixture of shells and white sand which we brought up, upon sounding, showed that we were in the channel, and nearing George's; accordingly, the ship's head was put directly to the northward, and we stood on, with perfect confidence in the soundings, though we had not taken an observation for two days, nor seen land; and the difference of an eighth of a mile out of the way might put us ashore. Throughout the day a provokingly light wind prevailed, and at eight o'clock, a small fishing schooner, which we passed, told us we were nearly abreast of Chatham lights. Just before midnight, a light land breeze sprang up, which carried us well along; and at four o'clock, thinking ourselves to the northward of Race Point, we hauled upon the wind and stood into the bay, west-northwest, for Boston light, and began firing guns for a pilot. Our watch went below at four o'clock, but could not sleep, for the watch on deck were banging away at the guns every few minutes. And indeed, we cared very little about it, for we were in Boston Bay; and if fortune favored us, we could all "sleep in" the next night, with nobody to call the watch every four hours.

We turned out, of our own will, at daybreak, to get a sight of land. In the gray of the morning, one or two small fishing smacks peered out of the mist; and when the broad day broke upon us, there lay the low sand hills of Cape Cod over our larboard quarter, and before us the wide waters of Massachusetts Bay, with here and there a sail gliding over its smooth surface. As we drew in toward the mouth of the harbor, as toward a focus, the vessels began to multiply, until the bay seemed alive with sails gliding about in all directions; some on the wind, and others before it, as they were bound to or from the emporium of trade and center of the bay. It was a stirring sight for us, who had been months on the ocean without seeing anything but two solitary sails; and over two years without seeing more than the three or four traders on an almost desolate coast. There were the little coasters, bound to and from the various towns along the south shore, down in the bight of the bay, and to the eastward; here and there a square-rigged vessel standing out to seaward; and, far in the distance, beyond Cape Ann, was the smoke of a steamer, stretching along in a narrow black cloud upon the water. Every sight was full of beauty and interest. We were coming back to our homes; and the signs of civilization and prosperity and happiness, from which we had been so long banished, were multiplying about us. The high land of Cape Ann and the rocks and shore of Cohasset were full in sight, and lighthouses standing like sentries in white before the harbors; and even the smoke from the chimneys on the plains of Hingham was seen rising slowly in the morning air. One of our boys was the son of a bucket-maker; and his face lighted up as he saw the tops of the

well-known hills which surround his native place. About ten
o'clock a little boat came bobbing over the water, and put
a pilot on board, and sheered off in pursuit of other vessels
bound in. Being now within the scope of the telegraph stations,
our signals were run up at the fore; and in half an hour
afterward, the owner on 'Change, or in his counting room,
knew that his ship was below; and the landlords, runners,
and sharks in Ann Street learned that there was a rich prize
for them down in the bay—a ship from round the Horn,
with a crew to be paid off with two years' wages.

The wind continuing very light, all hands were sent aloft
to strip off the chafing gear; and battens, parcelings, roundings, hoops, mats, and leathers came flying from aloft, and
left the rigging neat and clean, stripped of all its sea bandag-
ing. The last touch was put to the vessel by painting the
skysail poles; and I was sent up to the fore, with a bucket of
white paint and a brush, and touched her off, from the
truck to the eyes of the royal rigging. At noon we lay
becalmed off the lower lighthouse; and, it being about slack
water, we made little progress. A firing was heard in the
direction of Hingham, and the pilot said there was a review
there. The Hingham boy got wind of this, and said if the
ship had been twelve hours sooner he should have been down
among the soldiers, and in the booths, and having a grand
time. As it was, we had little prospect of getting in before
night. About two o'clock a breeze sprang up ahead, from
the westward, and we began beating up against it. A full-
rigged brig was beating in at the same time, and we passed
each other in our tacks, sometimes one and sometimes the
other working to windward, as the wind and tide favored
or opposed. It was my trick at the wheel from two till four;
and I stood my last helm, making between nine hundred and
a thousand hours which I had spent at the helms of our
two vessels. The tide beginning to set against us, we made
slow work; and the afternoon was nearly spent before we
got abreast of the inner light. In the meanwhile, several
vessels were coming down, outward bound; among which, a
fine, large ship, with yards squared, fair wind and fair tide,
passed us like a race horse, the men running out upon her
yards to rig out the studding-sail booms. Toward sundown
the wind came off in flaws, sometimes blowing very stiff, so
that the pilot took in the royals, and then it died away; when,

in order to get us in before the tide became too strong, the royals were set again. As this kept us running up and down the rigging, one hand was sent aloft at each masthead, to stand by to loose and furl the sails at the moment of the order. I took my place at the fore, and loosed and furled the royal five times between Rainsford Island and the Castle. At one tack we ran so near to Rainsford Island that, looking down from the royal yard, the island, with its hospital buildings, nice graveled walks, and green plats, seemed to lie directly under our yardarms. So close is the channel to some of these islands, that we ran the end of our flying-jib boom over one of the outworks of the fortifications on George's Island; and had an opportunity of seeing the advantages of that point as a fortified place; for, in working up the channel, we presented a fair stem and stern, for raking, from the batteries, three or four times. One gun might have knocked us to pieces.

We had all set our hearts upon getting up to town before night and going ashore, but the tide beginning to run strong against us, and the wind, what there was of it, being ahead, we made but little by weather-bowing the tide, and the pilot gave orders to cockbill the anchor and overhaul the chain. Making two long stretches, which brought us into the roads, under the lee of the Castle, he clewed up the topsails, and let go the anchor; and for the first time since leaving San Diego—one hundred and thirty-five days—our anchor was upon bottom. In half an hour more, we were lying snugly, with all sails furled, safe in Boston harbor; our long voyage ended; the well-known scene about us; the dome of the State House fading in the western sky; the lights of the city starting into sight, as the darkness came on; and at nine o'clock the clangor of the bells, ringing their accustomed peals; among which the Boston boys tried to distinguish the well-known tone of the Old South.

We had just done furling the sails, when a beautiful little pleasure boat luffed up into the wind, under our quarter, and the junior partner of the firm to which our ship belonged, Mr. Hooper, jumped on board. I saw him from the mizzen-topsail yard, and knew him well. He shook the captain by the hand, and went down into the cabin, and in a few minutes came up and inquired of the mate for me. The last time I had seen him I was in the uniform of an undergraduate of Harvard College, and now, to his astonishment, there came down from aloft a "rough alley" looking fellow, with duck trousers and red shirt, long hair, and face burned as dark as an Indian's. We shook hands, and he congratulated me upon my return and my appearance of health and strength, and said that my friends were all well. He had seen some of my family a few days before. I thanked him for telling me what I should not have dared to ask; and if—

> "The first bringer of unwelcome news
> Hath but a losing office; and his tongue
> Sounds ever after like a sullen bell"—

certainly I ought ever to remember this gentleman and his words with pleasure.

The captain went up to town in the boat with Mr. Hooper, and left us to pass another night on board ship, and to come up with the morning's tide under command of the pilot.

So much did we feel ourselves to be already at home, in anticipation, that our plain supper of hard bread and salt beef was barely touched; and many on board, to whom this was the first voyage, could scarcely sleep. As for myself, by one of those anomalous changes of feeling of which we are all the subjects, I found that I was in a state of indifference for which I could by no means account. A year before, while carrying hides on the coast, the assurance that in a twelvemonth we should see Boston made me half wild; but now that I was actually there, and in sight of home, the emotions which I had so long anticipated feeling I did not find, and in their place was a state of very nearly entire apathy. Something of the same experience was related to me by a sailor whose first voyage was one of five years upon the Northwest Coast. He had left home a lad, and when, after so many years of hard and trying experience, he found himself homeward bound, such was the excitement of his feelings that, during the whole passage, he could talk and think of nothing else but his arrival, and how and when he should jump from the vessel and take his way directly home. Yet, when the vessel was made fast to the wharf and the crew dismissed, he seemed suddenly to lose all feeling about the matter. He told me that he went below and changed his dress; took some water from the scuttle butt and washed himself leisurely; overhauled his chest, and put his clothes all in order; took his pipe from its place, filled it, and, sitting down upon his chest, smoked it slowly for the last time. Here he looked round upon the forecastle in which he had spent so many years, and being alone and his shipmates scattered, began to feel actually unhappy. Home became almost a dream; and it was not until his brother (who had heard of the ship's arrival) came down into the forecastle and told him of things at home, and who were waiting there to see him, that he could realize where he was, and feel interest enough to put him in motion toward that place for which he had longed, and of which he had dreamed, for years. There is probably so much of excitement in prolonged expectation that the quiet realizing of it produces a momentary stagnation of feeling as well as of effort. It was a good deal so with me. The activity of preparation, the rapid progress of the ship, the first making land, the coming up the harbor, and old scenes breaking upon the view, produced a mental as well as bodily activity, from which the change to a perfect stillness, when both expectation and the necessity of labor failed, left a calmness, almost an indifference, from which I must be roused by some new excitement. And the next morning, when all hands were called, and we were busily at work, clearing the decks, and getting everything in readiness for going up to the wharves—loading the guns for a salute, loosing the sails, and manning the windlass—mind and body seemed to wake together.

About ten o'clock a sea breeze sprang up, and the pilot gave orders to get the ship under way. All hands manned the windlass, and the long-drawn "Yo, heave, ho!" which we had last heard dying away among the desolate hills of San Diego, soon brought the anchor to the bows; and, with a fair wind and tide, a bright sunny morning, royals and skysails set, ensign, streamer, signals, and pennant flying, and with our guns firing, we came swiftly and handsomely up to the city. Off the end of the wharf we rounded to, and let go our anchor; and no sooner was it on the bottom than the decks were filled with people: customhouse officers; Topliff's agent, to inquire for news; others, inquiring for friends on board, or left upon the coast; dealers in grease, besieging the galley to make a bargain with the cook for his slush; "loafers" in general; and, last and chief, boardinghouse runners, to secure their men. Nothing can exceed the obliging disposition of these runners, and the interest they take in a sailor returned from a long voyage with aplenty of money. Two or three of them, at different times, took me by the hand; pretended to remember me perfectly; were quite sure I had boarded with them before I sailed; were delighted to see me back; gave me their cards; had a handcart waiting on the wharf, on purpose to take my things up; would lend me a hand to get my chest ashore; bring a bottle of grog on board if we did not haul in immediately; and the like. In fact, we could hardly get clear of them to go aloft and furl the sails. Sail after sail, for the hundredth time, in fair weather and in foul, we furled now for the last time together, and came down and took the warp ashore, manned the capstan, and with a chorus which waked up half North End, and rang among the buildings in the dock, we hauled her in to the wharf. The city bells were just ringing one when the last turn was made fast and the crew dismissed; and in five minutes more not a soul was left on board the good ship *Alert* but the old shipkeeper, who had come down from the countinghouse to take charge of her.

# TWENTY-FOUR YEARS AFTER

It was in the winter of 1835–6 that the ship *Alert*, in the prosecution of her voyage for hides on the remote and almost unknown coast of California, floated into the vast solitude of the bay of San Francisco. All around was the stillness of nature. One vessel, a Russian, lay at anchor there, but during our whole stay not a sail came or went. Our trade was with remote missions, which sent hides to us in launches manned by their Indians. Our anchorage was between a small island, called Yerba Buena, and a gravel beach in a little bight or cove of the same name, formed by two small, projecting points. Beyond, to the westward of the landing place, were dreary sand hills, with little grass to be seen, and few trees, and beyond them higher hills, steep and barren, their sides gullied by the rains. Some five or six miles beyond the landing place, to the right, was a ruinous presidio, and some three or four miles to the left was the mission of Dolores, as ruinous as the presidio, almost deserted, with but few Indians attached to it, and but little property in cattle. Over a region far beyond our sight there were no other human habitations, except that an enterprising Yankee, years in advance of his time, had put up, on the rising ground above the landing, a shanty of rough boards, where he carried on a very small retail trade between the hide ships and the Indians. Vast banks of fog, invading us from the North Pacific, drove in through the entrance, and covered the whole bay; and when they disappeared, we saw a few well-wooded islands, the sand hills on the west, the grassy and wooded slopes on the east, and the vast stretch of the bay to the southward, where we were told lay the missions of Santa Clara and San José, and still longer stretches to the northward and northeastward, where we understood smaller bays spread out, and large rivers poured in their tributes of waters. There were no settlements on these bays or rivers, and the few ranchos and missions were remote and widely separated. Not only the neighborhood of our anchorage, but the entire region of the great bay, was a solitude. On the whole coast of California there was not a lighthouse, a beacon, or a buoy, and the charts were made up from old and disconnected surveys by British, Russian, and Mexican voyagers. Birds of prey and passage swooped and dived about us, wild beasts ranged through the oak groves, and as we slowly floated out of the harbor with the tide, herds of deer came to the water's edge, on the northerly side of the entrance, to gaze at the strange spectacle.

On the evening of Saturday, the thirteenth of August, 1859, the superb steamship *Golden Gate*, gay with crowds of passengers, and lighting the sea for miles around with the glare of her signal lights of red, green, and white, and brilliant with lighted saloons and staterooms, bound up from the Isthmus of Panama, neared the entrance to San Francisco, the great center of a worldwide commerce. Miles out at sea, on the desolate rocks of the Farallones, gleamed the powerful rays of one of the most costly and effective lighthouses in the world. As we drew in through the Golden Gate, another lighthouse met our eyes, and in the clear moonlight of the unbroken California summer we saw, on the right, a large fortification protecting the narrow entrance, and just before us the little island of Alcatraz confronted us—one entire fortress. We bore round the point toward the old anchoring ground of the hide ships, and there, covering the sand hills and the valleys, stretching from the water's edge to the base of the great hills, and from the old presidio to the Mission, flickering all over with the lamps of its streets and houses, lay a city of one hundred thousand inhabitants. Clocks tolled the hour of midnight from its steeples, but the city was alive from the salute of our guns, spreading the news that the fortnightly steamer had come, bringing mails and passengers from the Atlantic world. Clipper ships of the largest size lay at anchor in the stream, or were girt to the wharves; and capacious high-pressure steamers, as large and showy as those of the Hudson or Mississippi, bodies of dazzling light, awaited the delivery of our mails to take their courses up the bay, stopping at Benicia and the United States Naval Station, and then up the great tributaries—the Sacramento, San Joaquin, and Feather rivers—to the far inland cities of Sacramento, Stockton, and Marysville.

The dock into which we drew, and the streets about it, were densely crowded with express wagons and handcarts to take luggage, coaches and cabs for passengers, and with men —some looking out for friends among our hundreds of passengers—agents of the press, and a greater multitude eager for newspapers and verbal intelligence from the great Atlantic and European world. Through this crowd I made my way, along the well-built and well-lighted streets, as alive as by day, where boys in high-keyed voices were already crying the latest New York papers; and between one and two o'clock in the morning found myself comfortably abed in a commodious room, in the Oriental Hotel, which stood, as well as I could learn, on the filled-up cove, and not far from the spot where we used to beach our boats from the *Alert*.

*Sunday, August 14th*. When I awoke in the morning, and looked from my windows over the city of San Francisco, with its storehouses, towers, and steeples; its courthouses, theaters, and hospitals; its daily journals; its well-filled learned professions; its fortresses and lighthouses; its wharves and harbor, with their thousand-ton clipper ships, more in number than London or Liverpool sheltered that day, itself one of the capitals of the American Republic, and the sole emporium of a new world, the awakened Pacific; when I looked across the bay to the eastward, and beheld a beautiful town on the fertile, wooded shores of the Contra Costa, and steamers, large and small, the ferryboats to the Contra Costa, and capacious freighters and passenger carriers to all parts of the great bay and its tributaries, with lines of their smoke in the horizon— when I saw all these things, and reflected on what I once was and saw here, and what now surrounded me, I could scarcely keep my hold on reality at all, or the genuineness of anything, and seemed to myself like one who had moved in "worlds not realized."

I could not complain that I had not a choice of places of worship. The Roman Catholics have an archbishop, a cathedral, and five or six smaller churches, French, German, Spanish, and English; and the Episcopalians a bishop, a cathedral, and three other churches; the Methodists and Presbyterians have three or four each, and there are Congregationalists, Baptists, a Unitarian, and other societies. On my way to church, I met two classmates of mine at Harvard standing in a doorway, one a lawyer and the other a teacher, and made appointments for a future meeting. A little farther on I came upon another Harvard man, a fine scholar and wit, and full of cleverness and good humor, who invited me to go to breakfast with him at the French house—he was a bachelor, and a late riser on Sundays. I asked him to show me the way to Bishop Kip's church. He hesitated, looked a little confused, and admitted that he was not as well up in certain classes of knowledge as in others, but, by a desperate guess, pointed out a wooden building at the foot of the street, which anyone might have seen could not be right, and which turned out to be an African Baptist meetinghouse. But my friend had many capital points of character, and I owed much of the pleasure of my visit to his attentions.

The congregation at the Bishop's church was precisely like one you would meet in New York, Philadelphia, or Boston. To be sure, the identity of the service makes one feel at once at home, but the people were alike, nearly all of the English race, though from all parts of the Union. The latest French bonnets were at the head of the chief pews, and businessmen at the foot. The music was without character, but there was an instructive sermon, and the church was full.

I found that there were no services at any of the Protestant churches in the afternoon. They have two services on Sunday; at 11 A.M., and after dark. The afternoon is spent at home, or in friendly visiting, or teaching of Sunday schools, or other humane and social duties.

This is as much the practice with what at home are called the strictest denominations as with any others. Indeed, I found individuals, as well as public bodies, affected in a marked degree by a change of oceans and by California life. One Sunday afternoon I was surprised at receiving the card of a man whom I had last known, some fifteen years ago, as a strict and formal deacon of a Congregational Society in New England. He was a deacon still, in San Francisco, a leader in all pious works, devoted to his denomination and to total abstinence; the same internally, but externally—what a change! Gone was the downcast eye, the bated breath, the solemn, non-natural voice, the watchful gait, stepping as if he felt responsible for the balance of the moral universe! He walked with a stride, an uplifted open countenance, his face covered with beard, whiskers, and mustache, his voice strong and natural—and, in short, he had put off the New England deacon and become a human being. In a visit of an hour I learned much from him about the religious societies, the moral reforms, the "Dashaways"—total-abstinence societies, which had taken strong hold on the young and wilder parts of society—and then of the Vigilance Committee, of which he was a member, and of more secular points of interest.

In one of the parlors of the hotel, I saw a man of about sixty years of age, with his feet bandaged and resting in a chair, whom somebody addressed by the name of Lies.* Lies! thought I. That must be the man who came across the country from Kentucky to Monterey while we lay there in the *Pilgrim* in 1835, and made a passage in the *Alert*, when he used to shoot with his rifle bottles hung from the topgallant-studding-sail boom ends. He married the beautiful Doña Rosalía Vallejo, sister of Don Guadalupe. There were the old high features and sandy hair. I put my chair beside him, and began conversation, as anyone may do in California. Yes, he was the

* Pronounced *Leese*.

Mr. Lies; and when I gave my name he professed at once to remember me, and spoke of my book. I found that almost— I might perhaps say quite—every American in California had read it; for when California "broke out," as the phrase is, in 1848, and so large a portion of the Anglo-Saxon race flocked to it, there was no book upon California but mine. Many who were on the coast at the time the book refers to, and afterward read it, and remembered the *Pilgrim* and *Alert,* thought they also remembered me. But perhaps more did remember me than I was inclined at first to believe, for the novelty of a collegian coming out before the mast had drawn more attention to me than I was aware of at the time.

Late in the afternoon, as there were vespers at the Roman Catholic churches, I went to that of Notre Dame des Victoires. The congregation was French, and a sermon in French was preached by an abbé; the music was excellent, all things airy and tasteful, and making one feel as if in one of the chapels in Paris. The Cathedral of St. Mary, which I afterward visited, where the Irish attend, was a contrast indeed, and more like one of our stifling Irish Catholic churches in Boston or New York, with intelligence in so small a proportion to the number of faces. During the three Sundays I was in San Francisco, I visited three of the Episcopal churches, and the Congregational, a Chinese Mission Chapel, and on the Sabbath (Saturday) a Jewish synagogue. The Jews are a wealthy and powerful class here. The Chinese, too, are numerous, and do a great part of the manual labor and small shopkeeping, and have some wealthy mercantile houses.

It is noticeable that European Continental fashions prevail generally in this city—French cooking, lunch at noon, and dinner at the end of the day, with *café noir* after meals, and to a great extent the European Sunday—to all which emigrants from the United States and Great Britain seem to adapt themselves. Some dinners which were given to me at French restaurants were, it seemed to me—a poor judge of such matters, to be sure—as sumptuous and as good, in dishes and wines, as I have found in Paris. But I had a relish-maker which my friends at table did not suspect—the remembrance of the forecastle dinners I ate here twenty-four years before.

*August 17th.* The customs of California are free; and any person who knows about my book speaks to me. The newspapers have announced the arrival of the veteran pioneer of all. I hardly walk out without meeting or making acquaintances. I have already been invited to deliver the anniversary oration before the Pioneer Society, to celebrate the settlement of San Francisco. Any man is qualified for election into this society who came to California before 1853. What moderns they are! I tell them of the time when Richardson's shanty of 1835—not his adobe house of 1836—was the only human habitation between the Mission and the presidio, and when the vast bay, with all its tributaries and recesses, was a solitude—and yet I am but little past forty years of age. They point out the place where Richardson's adobe house stood, and tell me that the first court and first town council were convened in it, the first Protestant worship performed in it, and in it the first capital trial by the Vigilance Committee held. I am taken down to the wharves, by antiquaries of a ten or twelve years' range, to identify the two points, now known as Clark's and Rincon, which formed the little cove of Yerba Buena, where we used to beach our boats—now filled up and built upon. The island we called Wood Island, where we spent the cold days and nights of December, in our launch, getting wood for one year's supply, is clean shorn of trees; and the bare rocks of Alcatraz Island, an entire fortress. I have looked at the city from the water, and at the water and islands from the city, but I can see nothing that recalls the times gone by, except the venerable Mission, the ruinous presidio, the high hills in the rear of the town, and the great stretches of the bay in all directions.

Today I took a California horse of the old style—the run, the loping gait—and visited the presidio. The walls stand as they did, with some changes made to accommodate a small garrison of United States troops. It has a noble situation, and I saw from it a clipper ship of the very largest class, coming through the Gate, under her fore-and-aft sails. Thence I rode to the fort, now nearly finished, on the southern shore of the Gate, and made an inspection of it. It is very expensive and of the latest style. One of the engineers here is Custis Lee, who has just left West Point at the head of his class—a son of Colonel Robert E. Lee, who distinguished himself in the Mexican War.

Another morning I ride to the Mission Dolores. It has a strangely solitary aspect, enhanced by its surroundings of the most uncongenial, rapidly growing modernisms; the hoar of ages surrounded by the brightest, slightest, and rapidest of modern growths. Its old belfries still clanged with the discordant bells, and Mass was saying within, for it is used as a place of worship for the extreme south part of the city.

In one of my walks about the wharves, I found a pile of dry hides lying by the side of a vessel. Here was something to feelingly persuade me what I had been, to recall a past scarce credible to myself. I stood lost in reflection. What were these hides—what were they not—to us, to me, a boy, twenty-four years ago? These were our constant labor, our chief object, our almost habitual thought. They brought us out here, they kept us here, and it was only by getting them that we could escape from the coast and return to home and civilized life. If it had not been that I might be seen, I should have seized one, slung it over my head, walked off with it, and thrown it by the old toss—I do not believe yet a lost art—to the ground. How they called up to my mind the months of curing at San Diego, the year and more of beach and surf work, and the steeving of the ship for home! I was in a dream of San Diego, San Pedro—with its hill so steep for taking up goods, and its stones so hard to our bare feet—and the cliffs of San Juan! All this, too, is no more! The entire hide business is of the past, and to the present inhabitants of California a dim tradition. The gold discoveries drew off all men from the gathering or cure of hides, the inflowing population made an end of the great droves of cattle; and now not a vessel pursues the—I was about to say dear—the dreary, once hated business of gathering hides upon the coast, and the beach of San Diego is abandoned and its hide houses have disappeared. Meeting a respectable-looking citizen on the wharf, I inquired of him how the hide trade was carried on. "Oh," said he, "there is very little of it, and that is all here. The few that are brought in are placed under sheds in winter, or left out on the wharf in summer, and are loaded from the wharves into the vessels alongside. They form parts of cargoes of other materials." I really felt too much, at the instant, to express to him the cause of my interest in the subject, and only added, "Then the old business of trading up and down the coast and curing hides for cargoes is all over?" "Oh, yes, sir," said he, "those old times of the *Pilgrim* and *Alert* and *California*, that we read about, are gone by."

*Saturday, August 20th.* The steamer *Senator* makes regular trips up and down the coast, between San Francisco and San Diego, calling at intermediate ports. This is my opportunity to revisit the old scenes. She sails today, and I am off, steaming among the great clippers anchored in the harbor, and gliding rapidly round the point, past Alcatraz Island, the lighthouse, and through the fortified Golden Gate, and bending to the southward—all done in two or three hours, which, in the *Alert*, under canvas, with head tides, variable winds, and sweeping currents to deal with, took us full two days.

Among the passengers I noticed an elderly gentleman, thin, with sandy hair and a face that seemed familiar. He took off his glove and showed one shriveled hand. It must be he! I went to him and said, "Captain Wilson, I believe." Yes, that was his name. "I knew you, sir, when you commanded the *Ayacucho* on this coast, in old hide-droghing times, in 1835–6." He was quickened by this, and at once inquiries were made on each side, and we were in full talk about the *Pilgrim* and *Alert*, *Ayacucho* and *Loriotte*, the *California* and *Lagoda*. I found he had been very much flattered by the praise I had bestowed in my book on his seamanship, especially in bringing the *Pilgrim* to her berth in San Diego harbor, after she had drifted successively into the *Lagoda* and *Loriotte*, and was coming into him. I had made a pet of his brig, the *Ayacucho*, which pleased him almost as much as my remembrance of his bride and their wedding, which I saw at Santa Barbara in 1836. Doña Ramona was now the mother of a large family, and Wilson assured me that if I would visit him at his rancho, near San Luis Obispo, I should find her still a handsome woman, and very glad to see me. How we walked the deck together, hour after hour, talking over the old times —the ships, the captains, the crews, the traders on shore, the ladies, the missions, the southeasters! Indeed, where could we stop? He had sold the *Ayacucho* in Chile for a vessel of war, and had given up the sea, and had been for years a ranchero. (I learned from others that he had become one of the most wealthy and respectable farmers in the state, and that his rancho was well worth visiting.) Thompson, he said, hadn't the sailor in him; and he never could laugh enough at his *fiasco* in San Diego, and his reception by Bradshaw. Faucon was a sailor and a navigator. He did not know what had become of George March (*ante*, pp. 191, 240), except that he left him in Callao; nor could he tell me anything of handsome Bill Jackson (*ante*, p. 83), nor of Captain Nye of the *Loriotte*. I told him all I then knew of the ships, the masters, and the officers. I found he had kept some run of my history, and needed little information. Old Señor Noriego of Santa Barbara, he told me, was dead, and Don Carlos and Don Santiago, but I should find their children there, now in middle life. Doña Angustia, he said, I had made famous by my praises of her beauty and dancing, and I should have from her a royal reception. She had been a widow, and remarried since, and had a daughter as handsome as herself. The descendants of Noriego had taken the ancestral name of De la Guerra, as they were nobles of Old Spain by birth; and the boy Pablo, who used to make passages in the *Alert*, was now Don Pablo de la Guerra, a senator in the state legislature for Santa Barbara County.

The points in the country, too, we noticed, as we passed them—Santa Cruz, San Luis Obispo, Point Año Nuevo, the opening to Monterey, which to my disappointment we did not visit. No; Monterey, the prettiest town on the coast, and its capital and seat of customs, had got no advantage from the great changes, was out of the way of commerce and of the travel to the mines and great rivers, and was not worth stopping at. Point Conception we passed in the night, a cheery light gleaming over the waters from its tall lighthouse, standing on its outermost peak. Point Conception! That word was enough to recall all our experiences and dreads of gales, swept decks, topmast carried away, and the hardships of a coast service in the winter. But Captain Wilson tells me that the climate has altered; that the southeasters are no longer the bane of the coast they once were, and that vessels now anchor inside the kelp at Santa Barbara and San Pedro all the year round. I should have thought this owing to his spending his winters on a rancho instead of the deck of the *Ayacucho*, had not the same thing been told me by others.

Passing round Point Conception, and steering easterly, we opened the islands that form, with the mainland, the canal of Santa Barbara. There they are, Santa Cruz and Santa Rosa; and there is the beautiful point, Santa Buenaventura; and there lies Santa Barbara on its plain, with its amphitheater of high hills and distant mountains. There is the old white mission with its belfries, and there the town, with its one-story adobe houses, with here and there a two-story wooden house of later build; yet little is it altered—the same repose in the golden sunlight and glorious climate, sheltered by its hills; and then, more remindful than anything else, there roars and tumbles upon the beach the same grand surf of the great Pacific as on the beautiful day when the *Pilgrim*, after her five months' voyage, dropped her weary anchors here; the same bright-blue ocean, and the surf making just the same monotonous, melancholy roar, and the same dreamy town, and gleaming white mission, as when we beached our boats for the first time, riding over the breakers with shouting Kanakas, the three small hide traders lying at anchor in the offing. But now we are the only vessel, and that an unromantic, sail-less, spar-less, engine-driven hulk!

I landed in the surf, in the old style, but it was not high enough to excite us, the only change being that I was somehow unaccountably a passenger, and did not have to jump overboard and steady the boat, and run her up by the gunwales.

Santa Barbara has gained but little. I should not know, from anything I saw, that she was now a seaport of the United States, a part of the enterprising Yankee nation, and not still a lifeless Mexican town. At the same old house where Señor Noriego lived, on the piazza in front of the courtyard, where was the gay scene of the marriage of our agent, Mr. Robinson, to Doña Anita, where Don Juan Bandini and Doña Angustia danced, Don Pablo de la Guerra received me in a courtly fashion. I passed the day with the family, and in walking about the place; and ate the old dinner with its accompaniments of frijoles, native olives and grapes, and native wines. In due time I paid my respects to Doña Angustia, and, notwithstanding what Wilson told me, I could hardly believe that after twenty-four years there would still be so much of the enchanting woman about her. She thanked me for the kind and, as she called them, greatly exaggerated compliments I had paid her; and her daughter told me that all travelers who came to Santa Barbara called to see her mother, and that she herself never expected to live long enough to be a belle.

Mr. Alfred Robinson, our agent in 1835-6, was here, with a part of his family. I did not know how he would receive me, remembering what I had printed to the world about him at a time when I took little thought that the world was going to read it; but there was no sign of offense, only a cordiality which gave him, as between us, rather the advantage in status.

The people of this region are giving attention to sheep raising, winemaking, and the raising of olives, just enough to keep the town from going backwards.

But evening is drawing on, and our boat sails tonight. So, refusing a horse or carriage, I walk down, not unwilling to be a little early, that I may pace up and down the beach, looking off to the islands and the points, and watching the roaring, tumbling billows. How softening is the effect of time! It touches us through the affections. I almost feel as if I were lamenting the passing away of something loved and dear—the boats, the Kanakas, the hides, my old shipmates! Death, change, distance, lend them a character which makes them quite another thing from the vulgar, wearisome toil of uninteresting, forced manual labor.

The breeze freshened as we stood out to sea, and the wild waves rolled over the red sun, on the broad horizon of the Pacific; but it is summer, and in summer there can be no bad weather in California. Every day is pleasant. Nature forbids a drop of rain to fall by day or night, or a wind to excite itself beyond a fresh summer breeze.

The next morning we found ourselves at anchor in the bay of San Pedro. Here was this hated, this thoroughly detested spot. Although we lay near, I could scarce recognize the hill up which we rolled and dragged and pushed and carried our heavy loads, and down which we pitched the hides, to carry them barefooted over the rocks to the floating longboat. It was no longer the landing place. One had been made at the head of the creek, and boats discharged and took off cargoes from a mole or wharf, in a quiet place, safe from southeasters. A tug ran to take off passengers from the steamer to the wharf, for the trade of Los Angeles is sufficient to support such a vessel. I got the captain to land me privately, in a small boat, at the old place by the hill. I dismissed the boat, and, alone, found my way to the high ground. I say found my way, for neglect and weather had left but few traces of the steep road the hide vessels had built to the top. The cliff off which we used to throw the hides, and where I spent nights watching them, was more easily found. The population was doubled—that is to say, there were two houses, instead of one, on the hill. I stood on the brow and looked out toward the offing, the Santa Catalina Island, and, nearer, the melancholy Dead Man's Island, with its painful tradition, and recalled the gloomy days that followed the flogging, and fancied the *Pilgrim* at anchor in the offing. But the tug is going toward our steamer, and I must awake and be off. I walked along the shore to the new landing place, where were two or three storehouses and other buildings, forming a small depot; and a stagecoach, I found, went daily between this place and the Pueblo. I got a seat on the top of the coach, to which were tackled six little less than wild California horses. Each horse had a man at his head, and when the driver had got his reins in hand, he gave the word, all the horses were let go at once, and away they went on a spring, tearing over the ground, the driver only keeping them from going the wrong way, for they had a wide, level *pampa* to run over the whole thirty miles to the Pueblo. This plain is almost tree-less, with no grass, at least none now in the drought of mid-summer, and is filled with squirrel holes, and alive with squir-rels. As we changed horses twice, we did not slacken our speed until we turned into the streets of the Pueblo.

The Pueblo de los Angeles I found a large and flourishing town of about twenty thousand inhabitants, with brick side-walks, and blocks of stone or brick houses. The three prin-cipal traders when we were here for hides in the *Pilgrim* and *Alert* are still among the chief traders of the place—Stearns, Temple, and Warner, the two former being reputed very rich. I dined with Mr. Stearns, now a very old man, and met there Don Juan Bandini, to whom I had given a good deal of notice in my book. From him, as indeed from everyone in this town, I met with the kindest attentions. The wife of Don Juan, who was a beautiful young girl when we were on the coast, Doña Refugio, daughter of Don Santiago Argüello, the *comandante* of San Diego, was with him, and still handsome. This is one of several instances I have noticed of the preserving quality of the California climate. Here, too, was Henry Mellus, who came out with me before the mast in the *Pilgrim*, and left the brig to be agent's clerk on shore. He had experienced varying fortunes here, and was now married to a Mexican lady, and had a family. I dined with him, and in the afternoon he drove me round to see the vineyards, the chief objects in this region. The vintage of last year was estimated at half a million of gallons. Every year new square miles of ground are laid down to vineyards, and the Pueblo promises to be the center of one of the largest wine-producing regions in the world. Grapes are a drug here, and I found a great abundance of figs, olives, peaches, pears, and melons. The climate is well suited to these fruits, but is too hot and dry for successful wheat crops.

Toward evening, we started off in the stagecoach, with again our relays of six mad horses, and reached the creek before dark, though it was late at night before we got on board the steamer, which was slowly moving her wheels, under way for San Diego.

As we skirted along the coast, Wilson and I recognized, or thought we did, in the clear moonlight, the rude white Mission of San Juan Capistrano, and its cliff, from which I had swung down by a pair of halyards to save a few hides—a boy who could not be prudential, and who caught at every chance for adventure.

As we made the high point off San Diego, Point Loma, we were greeted by the cheering presence of a lighthouse. As we swept round it in the early morning, there, before us, lay the little harbor of San Diego, its low spit of sand, where the water runs so deep; the opposite flats, where the *Alert* grounded in starting for home; the low hills, without trees, and almost without brush; the quiet little beach; but the chief objects, the hide houses, my eye looked for in vain. They were gone, all, and left no mark behind.

I wished to be alone, so I let the other passengers go up to the town, and was quietly pulled ashore in a boat, and left to myself. The recollections and the emotions all were sad, and only sad. "*Fugit, interea fugit irreparabile tempus.*" The past was real. The present, all about me, was unreal, unnatural, repellent. I saw the big ships lying in the stream, the *Alert*, the *California*, the *Rosa*, with her Italians; then the handsome *Ayacucho*, my favorite; the poor dear old *Pilgrim*, the home of hardship and hopelessness; the boats passing to and fro; the cries of the sailors at the capstan or falls; the peopled beach; the large hide houses, with their gangs of men; and the Kanakas interspersed everywhere. All, all were gone! Not a vestige to mark where one hide house stood. The oven, too, was gone. I searched for its site, and found, where I thought it should be, a few broken bricks and bits of mortar. I alone was left of all, and how strangely was I here! What changes to me! Where were they all? Why should I care for them—poor Kanakas and sailors, the refuse of civilization, the outlaws and beachcombers of the Pacific! Time and death seemed to transfigure them. Doubtless nearly all were dead; but how had they died, and where? In hospitals, in fever climes, in dens of vice, or falling from the mast, or dropping exhausted from the wreck—

> "When for a moment, like a drop of rain,
> He sinks into thy depths with bubbling groan,
> Without a grave, unknelled, uncoffined, and unknown."

The lighthearted boys are now hardened middle-aged men, if the seas, rocks, fevers, and the deadlier enemies that beset a sailor's life on shore have spared them; and the then strong men have bowed themselves, and the earth or sea has covered them.

Even the animals are gone—the colony of dogs, the broods of poultry, the useful horses; but the coyotes bark still in the woods, for they belong not to man, and are not touched by his changes.

I walked slowly up the hill, finding my way among the few bushes, for the path was long grown over, and sat down where we used to rest in carrying our burdens of wood, and to look out for vessels that might, though so seldom, be coming down from the windward.

To rally myself by calling to mind my own better fortune and nobler lot, and cherished surroundings at home, was impossible. Borne down by depression, the day being yet at its noon, and the sun over the old point (it is four miles to the town, the presidio—I have walked it often, and can do it once more), I passed the familiar objects, and it seemed to me that I remembered them better than those of any other place I had ever been in: the opening to the little cave; the low hills where we cut wood and killed rattlesnakes, and where our dogs chased the coyotes; and the black ground where so many of the ship's crew and beachcombers used to bring up on their return at the end of a liberty day, and spend the night *sub Jove.*

The little town of San Diego has undergone no change whatever that I can see. It certainly has not grown. It is still, like Santa Barbara, a Mexican town. The four principal houses

of the *gente de razón*—of the Bandinis, Estudillos, Argüellos,
and Picos—are the chief houses now; but all the gentlemen—
and their families, too, I believe—are gone. The big, vulgar
shopkeeper and trader, Fitch, is long since dead; Tom Wright-
ington, who kept the rival *pulpería*, fell from his horse when
drunk, and was found nearly eaten up by coyotes; and I can
scarce find a person whom I remember. I went into a familiar
one-story adobe house, with its piazza and earthen floor, inhabited by a respectable lower-class family by the name of
Muchado, and inquired if any of the family remained, when
a bright-eyed middle-aged woman recognized me, for she had
heard I was on board the steamer, and told me she had married a shipmate of mine, Jack Stewart, who went out as second mate the next voyage, but left the ship and married and
settled here. She said he wished very much to see me. In a
few minutes he came in, and his sincere pleasure in meeting
me was extremely grateful. We talked over old times as long
as I could afford to. I was glad to hear that he was sober and
doing well. Doña Tomasa Pico I found and talked with. She
was the only person of the old upper class that remained on
the spot, if I rightly recollect. I found an American family
here, with whom I dined—Doyle and his wife, nice young
people, Doyle agent for the great line of coaches to run to
the frontier of the old States.

I must complete my acts of pious remembrance, so I take
a horse and make a run out to the old mission, where Ben
Stimson and I went the first liberty day we had after we left
Boston (*ante*, p. 111). All has gone to decay. The buildings
are unused and ruinous, and the large gardens show now only
wild cactuses, willows, and a few olive trees. A fast run brings
me back in time to take leave of the few I knew and who
knew me, and to reach the steamer before she sails. A last
look—yes, last for life—to the beach, the hills, the low point,
the distant town, as we round Point Loma and the first beams
of the lighthouse strike out toward the setting sun.

*Wednesday, August 24th.* At anchor at San Pedro by daylight. But instead of being roused out of the forecastle to row
the longboat ashore and bring off a load of hides before breakfast, we were served with breakfast in the cabin, and again
took our drive with the wild horses to the Pueblo and spent
the day; seeing nearly the same persons as before, and again
getting back by dark. We steamed again for Santa Barbara,

where we only lay an hour, and passed through its canal and round Point Conception, stopping at San Luis Obispo to land my friend—as I may truly call him after this long passage together—Captain Wilson, whose most earnest invitation to stop here and visit him at his rancho I was obliged to decline.

*Friday evening, August 26th,* we entered the Golden Gate, passed the lighthouses and forts, and clipper ships at anchor, and came to our dock, with this great city, on its high hills and rising surfaces, brilliant before us, and full of eager life.

Making San Francisco my headquarters, I paid visits to various parts of the state: down the bay to Santa Clara, with its live oaks and sycamores, and its Jesuit College for boys; and San José, where is the best girls' school in the state, kept by the Sisters of Notre Dame—a town now famous for a year's session of the "legislature of a thousand drinks"—and thence to the rich Almaden quicksilver mines, returning on the Contra Costa side through the rich agricultural country, with its ranchos and the vast grants of the Castro and Soto families, where farming and fruit-raising are done on so large a scale. Another excursion was up the San Joaquin to Stockton, a town of some ten thousand inhabitants, a hundred miles from San Francisco, and crossing the Tuolumne and Stanislaus and Merced, by the little Spanish town of Hornitos, and Snelling's Tavern, at the ford of the Merced, where so many fatal fights are had. Thence I went to Mariposa County, and Colonel Frémont's mines, and made an interesting visit to *"the* Colonel," as he is called all over the country, and Mrs. Frémont, a heroine equal to either fortune—the salons of Paris and the drawing rooms of New York and Washington, or the roughest life of the remote and wild mining regions of Mariposa—with their fine family of spirited, clever children. After a rest there, we went on to Clark's Camp and the Big Trees, where I measured one tree ninety-seven feet in circumference without its bark, and the bark is usually eighteen inches thick; and rode through another which lay on the ground, a shell, with all the insides out, rode through it mounted, and sitting at full height in the saddle; then to the wonderful Yosemite Valley, itself a stupendous miracle of nature, with its Dome, its Capitan, its walls of three thousand feet of perpendicular height—but a valley of streams, of waterfalls, from the torrent to the mere shimmer of a bridal veil, only enough to reflect a rainbow, with their plunges of twenty-five hundred feet, or their smaller falls of eight hundred, with nothing at the base but thick mists, which form and trickle, and then run and at last plunge into the blue Merced that flows through the center of the valley. Back by the Coulterville trail, the peaks of Sierra Nevada in sight, across the North Fork of the Merced, by Gentry's Gulch, over hills and through cañóns, to Frémont's again, and thence to Stockton and San Francisco—all this at the end of August, when there has been no rain for four months, and the air is clear and very hot, and the ground perfectly dry; windmills, to raise water for artificial irrigation of small patches, seen all over the landscape, while we travel through square miles of hot dust, where they tell us, and truly, that in winter and early spring we should be up to our knees in flowers; a country, too, where surface gold-digging is so common and unnoticed that the large, six-horse stagecoach, in which I traveled from Stockton to Hornitos, turned off in the highroad for a Chinaman, who, with his pan and washer, was working up a hole which an American had abandoned, but where the minute and patient industry of the Chinaman averaged a few dollars a day.

These visits were so full of interest, with grandeurs and humors of all sorts, that I am strongly tempted to describe them. But I remember that I am not to write a journal of a visit over the new California, but to sketch briefly the contrasts with the old spots of 1835–6, and I forbear.

How strange and eventful has been the brief history of this marvelous city, San Francisco! In 1835 there was one board shanty. In 1836, one adobe house on the same spot. In 1847, a population of four hundred and fifty persons, who organized a town government. Then came the *auri sacra fames*, the flocking together of many of the worst spirits of Christendom; a sudden birth of a city of canvas and boards, entirely destroyed by fire five times in eighteen months, with a loss of sixteen millions of dollars, and as often rebuilt, until it became a solid city of brick and stone, of nearly one hundred thousand inhabitants, with all the accompaniments of wealth and culture, and now (in 1859) the most quiet and well-governed city of its size in the United States. But it has been through its season of Heaven-defying crime, violence, and blood, from which it was rescued and handed back to soberness, morality, and good government, by that peculiar invention of Anglo-Saxon Republican America, the solemn, awe-inspiring Vigilance Committee of the most grave and responsible citizens, the last resort of the thinking and the good, taken to only when vice, fraud, and ruffianism have entrenched themselves behind the forms of law, suffrage, and ballot, and there is no hope but in organized force, whose action must be instant and thorough, or its state will be worse than before. A history of the passage of this city through those ordeals, and through its almost incredible financial extremes, should be written by a pen which not only accuracy shall govern, but imagination shall inspire.

I cannot pause for the civility of referring to the many kind attentions I received, and the society of educated men and women from all parts of the Union I met with; where New England, the Carolinas, Virginia, and the new West sat side by side with English, French, and German civilization.

My stay in California was interrupted by an absence of nearly four months, when I sailed for the Sandwich Islands in the noble Boston clipper ship *Mastiff*, which was burned at sea to the water's edge; we escaping in boats, and carried by a friendly British bark into Honolulu, whence, after a deeply interesting visit of three months in that most fascinating group of islands, with its natural and its moral wonders, I returned to San Francisco in an American whaler, and found myself again in my quarters on the morning of Sunday, December 11th, 1859.

My first visit after my return was to Sacramento, a city of about forty thousand inhabitants, more than a hundred miles inland from San Francisco, on the Sacramento, where was the capital of the state, and where were fleets of river steamers, and a large inland commerce. Here I saw the inauguration of a governor, Mr. Latham, a young man from Massachusetts, much my junior; and met a member of the state senate, a man who, as a carpenter, repaired my father's house at home some ten years before; and two more senators from southern California, relics of another age—Don Andrés Pico, from San Diego, and Don Pablo de la Guerra, whom I have mentioned as meeting at Santa Barbara. I had a good deal of conversation with these gentlemen, who stood alone in an assembly of Americans, who had conquered their country, spared pillars of the past. Don Andrés had fought us at San Pazqual and Sepulveda's rancho, in 1846, and as he fought bravely, not a common thing among the Mexicans, and, indeed, repulsed Kearny, is always treated with respect. He had the satisfaction, dear to the proud Spanish heart, of making a speech before a senate of Americans, in favor of the retention in office of an officer of our army who was wounded at San Pazqual, and whom some wretched caucus was going to displace to carry out a political job. Don Andrés's magnanimity and indignation carried the day.

My last visit in this part of the country was to a new and rich farming region, the Napa Valley, the United States Navy Yard at Mare Island, the river gold workings, and the Geysers, and old Mr. John Yount's rancho. On board the steamer, found Mr. Edward Stanley, formerly member of Congress from North Carolina, who became my companion for the greater part of my trip. I also met—a revival on the spot of an acquaintance of twenty years ago—Don Guadalupe Vallejo; I may say acquaintance, for although I was then before the mast, he knew my story, and, as he spoke English well, used to hold many conversations with me, when in the boat or on shore. He received me with true earnestnesss, and would not hear of my passing his estate without visiting him. He reminded me of a remark I made to him once, when pulling him ashore in the boat, when he was *comandante* at the presidio. I learned that the two Vallejos, Guadalupe and Salvador, owned, at an early time, nearly all Napa and Sonoma, having princely estates. But they have not much left. They were nearly ruined by their bargain with the state, that they would put up the public buildings if the capital should be placed at Vallejo, then a town of some promise. They spent $100,000, the capital was moved there, and in two years removed to San José on another contract. The town fell to pieces, and the houses, chiefly wooden, were taken down and removed. I accepted the old gentleman's invitation so far as to stop at Vallejo to breakfast.

The United States Navy Yard, at Mare Island, near Vallejo, is large and well placed, with deep fresh water. The old *Independence*, and the sloop *Decatur*, and two steamers were there, and they were experimenting on building a dispatch boat, the *Saginaw*, of California timber.

I have no excuse for attempting to describe my visit through the fertile and beautiful Napa Valley, nor even, what exceeded that in interest, my visit to old John Yount at his rancho, where I heard from his own lips some of his most interesting stories of hunting and trapping and Indian fighting, during an adventurous life of forty years of such work, between our back settlements in Missouri and Arkansas, and the mountains of California, trapping the Colorado and Gila, and his celebrated dream, thrice repeated, which led him to organize a party to go out over the mountains, that did actually rescue from death by starvation the wretched remnants of the Donner party.

I must not pause for the dreary country of the Geysers, the screaming escapes of steam, the sulphur, the boiling caldrons of black and yellow and green, and the region of Gehenna, through which runs a quiet stream of pure water; nor for the park scenery, and captivating ranchos of the Napa Valley, where farming is done on so grand a scale, where I have seen a man plow a furrow by little red flags on sticks, to keep his range by, until nearly out of sight, and where, the wits tell us, he returns the next day on the back furrow; a region where, at Christmas time, I have seen old strawberries still on the vines, by the side of vines in full blossom for the next crop, and grapes in the same stages, and open windows, and yet a grateful wood fire on the hearth in early morning; nor for the titanic operations of hydraulic surface mining, where large mountain streams are diverted from their ancient beds, and made to do the work, beyond the reach of all other agents, of washing out valleys and carrying away hills, and changing the whole surface of the country, to expose the stores of gold hidden for centuries in the darkness of their earthy depths.

*January 10th, 1860.* I am again in San Francisco, and my revisit to California is closed. I have touched too lightly and rapidly for much impression upon the reader on my last visit into the interior; but, as I have said, in a mere continuation to a narrative of a seafaring life on the coast, I am only to carry the reader with me on a revisit to those scenes in which the public has long manifested so gratifying an interest. But it seemed to me that slight notices of these entirely new parts of the country would not be out of place, for they serve to put in strong contrast with the solitudes of 1835-6 the developed interior, with its mines, and agricultural wealth, and rapidly filling population, and its large cities, so far from the coast, with their education, religion, arts, and trade.

On the morning of January 11th, 1860, I passed, for the eighth time, through the Golden Gate, on my way across the delightful Pacific to the Oriental world, with its civilization three thousand years older than that I was leaving behind. As the shores of California faded in the distance, and the summits of the Coast Range sank under the blue horizon, I bade farewell—yes, I do not doubt, forever—to those scenes which, however changed or unchanged, must always possess an ineffable interest for me.

It is time my fellow-travelers and I should part company. But I have been requested by a great many persons to give some account of the subsequent history of the vessels and their crews with which I had made them acquainted. I attempt the following sketches in deference to these suggestions, and not, I trust, with any undue estimate of the general interest my narrative may have created.

Something less than a year after my return in the *Alert*, and when, my eyes having recovered, I was again in college life, I found one morning in the newspapers, among the arrivals of the day before, "The brig *Pilgrim*, Faucon, from San Diego, California." In a few hours I was down in Ann Street, and on my way to Hackstadt's boardinghouse, where I knew Tom Harris and others would lodge. Entering the front room, I heard my name called from amid a group of bluejackets, and several sunburned, tar-colored men came forward to speak to me. They were, at first, a little embarrassed by the dress and style in which they had never seen me, and one of them was calling me *Mr*. Dana; but I soon stopped that, and we were shipmates once more. First, there was Tom Harris, in a characteristic occupation. I had made him promise to come and see me when we parted in San Diego; he had got a directory of Boston, found the street and number of my father's house, and, by a study of the plan of the city, had laid out his course, and was committing it to memory. He said he could go straight to the house without asking a question. And so he could, for I took the book from him, and he gave his course, naming each street and turn to right or left, directly to the door.

Tom had been second mate of the *Pilgrim*, and had laid up no mean sum of money. True to his resolution, he was going to England to find his mother, and he entered into the

comparative advantages of taking his money home in gold
or in bills—a matter of some moment, as this was in the dis-
astrous financial year of 1837. He seemed to have his ideas
well arranged, but I took him to a leading banker, whose
advice he followed; and, declining my invitation to go up and
show himself to my friends, he was off for New York that
afternoon, to sail the next day for Liverpool. The last I ever
saw of Tom Harris was as he passed down Tremont Street on
the sidewalk, a man dragging a handcart in the street by his
side, on which were his voyage-worn chest, his mattress, and
a box of nautical instruments.

Sam seemed to have got funny again, and he and John the
Swede learned that Captain Thompson had several months before sailed in command of a ship for the coast of Sumatra,
and that their chance of proceedings against him at law was
hopeless. Sam was afterward lost in a brig off the coast of
Brazil, when all hands went down. Of John and the rest of
the men I have never heard. The Marblehead boy, Sam,
turned out badly; and, although he had influential friends,
never allowed them to improve his condition. The old carpenter, the Finn, of whom the cook stood in such awe (*ante*,
p. 41), had fallen sick and died in Santa Barbara, and was
buried ashore. Jim Hall, from the Kennebec, who sailed with
us before the mast, and was made second made in Foster's
place, came home chief mate of the *Pilgrim*. I have often
seen him since. His lot has been prosperous, as he well de-
served it should be. He has commanded the largest ships, and,
when I last saw him, was going to the Pacific coast of South
America, to take charge of a line of mail steamers. Poor,
luckless Foster I have twice seen. He came into my rooms in
Boston, after I had become a barrister and my narrative had
been published, and told me he was chief mate of a big ship;
that he had heard I had said some things unfavorable of him
in my book; that he had just bought it, and was going to read
it that night, and if I had said anything unfair of him, he
would punish me if he found me in State Street. I surveyed
him from head to foot, and said to him, "Foster, you were
not a formidable man when I last knew you, and I don't believe you are now." Either he was of my opinion, or thought
I had spoken of him well enough, for the next (and last)
time I met him he was civil and pleasant.

I believe I omitted to state that Mr. Andrew B. Amerzene,

the chief mate of the *Pilgrim*, an estimable, kind, and trust-worthy man, had a difficulty with Captain Faucon, who thought him slack, was turned off duty, and sent home with us in the *Alert*. Captain Thompson, instead of giving him the place of a mate off duty, put him into the narrow between decks, where a space, not over four feet high, had been left out among the hides, and there compelled him to live the whole wearisome voyage, through trades and tropics, and round Cape Horn, with nothing to do—not allowed to con-verse or walk with the officers, and obliged to get his grub himself from the galley, in the tin pot and kid of a common sailor. I used to talk with him as much as I had opportunity to, but his lot was wretched, and in every way wounding to his feelings. After our arrival, Captain Thompson was obliged to make him compensation for this treatment. It happens that I have never heard of him since.

Henry Mellus, who had been in a countinghouse in Boston, and left the forecastle, on the coast, to be agent's clerk, and whom I met, a married man, at Los Angeles in 1859, died at that place a few years ago, not having been successful in com-mercial life. Ben Stimson left the sea for the fresh water and prairies, settled in Detroit as a merchant, and when I visited that city, in 1863, I was rejoiced to find him a prosperous and respected man, and the same generous-hearted shipmate as ever.

This ends the catalogue of the *Pilgrim*'s original crew, ex-cept her first master, Captain Thompson. He was not em-ployed by the same firm again, and got up a voyage to the coast of Sumatra for pepper. A cousin and classmate of mine, Mr. Channing, went as supercargo, not having con-sulted me as to the captain. First, Captain Thompson got into difficulties with another American vessel on the coast, which charged him with having taken some advantage of her in get-ting pepper; and then with the natives, who accused him of having obtained too much pepper for his weights. The natives seized him, one afternoon, as he landed in his boat, and de-manded of him to sign an order on the supercargo for the Spanish dollars that they said were due them, on pain of being imprisoned on shore. He never failed in pluck, and now ordered his boat aboard, leaving him ashore, the officer to tell the supercargo to obey no direction except under his hand. For several successive days and nights, his ship, the

*Alciope,* lay in the burning sun, with rain squalls and thunder-clouds coming over the high mountains, waiting for a word from him. Toward evening of the fourth or fifth day he was seen on the beach, hailing for the boat. The natives, finding they could not force more money from him, were afraid to hold him longer, and had let him go. He sprang into the boat, urged her off with the utmost eagerness, leaped on board the ship like a tiger, his eyes flashing and his face full of blood, ordered the anchor aweigh, and the topsails set, the four guns, two on a side, loaded with all sorts of devilish stuff, and wore her round, and, keeping as close into the bamboo village as he could, gave them both broadsides, slam-bang into the midst of the houses and people, and stood out to sea! As his excitement passed off, headache, languor, fever set in—the deadly coast fever, contracted from the water and night dews on shore and his maddened temper. He ordered the ship to Penang, and never saw the deck again. He died on the passage, and was buried at sea. Mr. Channing, who took care of him in his sickness and delirium, caught the fever from him, but, as we gratefully remember, did not die until the ship made port, and he was under the kindly roof of a hospitable family in Penang. The chief mate, also, took the fever, and the second mate and crew deserted; and, although the chief mate recovered and took the ship to Europe and home, the voyage was a melancholy disaster. In a tour I made round the world in 1859-60, of which my revisit to California was the beginning, I went to Penang. In that fairy-like scene of sea and sky and shore, as beautiful as material earth can be, with its fruits and flowers of a perpetual summer—somewhere in which still lurks the deadly fever—I found the tomb of my kinsman, classmate, and friend. Standing beside his grave, I tried not to think that his life had been sacrificed to the faults and violence of another; I tried not to think too hardly of that other, who at least had suffered in death.

The dear old *Pilgrim* herself! She was sold, at the end of this voyage, to a merchant in New Hampshire, who employed her on short voyages, and, after a few years, I read of her total loss at sea, by fire, off the coast of North Carolina.

Captain Faucon, who took out the *Alert,* and brought home the *Pilgrim,* spent many years in command of vessels in the Indian and Chinese seas, and was in our volunteer navy during the late war, commanding several large vessels in succession, on the blockade of the Carolinas, with the rank of lieutenant. He has now given up the sea, but still keeps it under his eye, from the piazza of his house on the most beautiful hill in the environs of Boston. I have the pleasure of meeting him often. Once, in speaking of the *Alert's* crew, in a company of gentlemen, I heard him say that that crew was exceptional; that he had passed all his life at sea, but whether before the mast or abaft, whether officer or master, he had never met such a crew, and never should expect to; and that the two officers of the *Alert*, long ago shipmasters, agreed with him that, for intelligence, knowledge of duty and willingness to perform it, pride in the ship, her appearance and sailing, and in absolute reliableness, they never had seen their equal. Especially he spoke of his favorite seaman, French John. John, after a few more years at sea, became a boatman, and kept his neat boat at the end of Granite Wharf, and was ready to take all, but delighted to take any of us of the old *Alert's* crew, to sail down the harbor. One day Captain Faucon went to the end of the wharf to board a vessel in the stream, and hailed for John. There was no response, and his boat was not there. He inquired, of a boatman near, where John was. The time had come that comes to all! There was no loyal voice to respond to the familiar call, the hatches had closed over him, his boat was sold to another, and he had left not a trace behind. We could not find out even where he was buried.

Mr. Richard Brown, of Marblehead, our chief mate in the *Alert*, commanded many of our noblest ships in the European trade, a general favorite. A few years ago, while stepping on board his ship from the wharf, he fell from the plank into the hold and was killed. If he did not actually die at sea, at least he died as a sailor—he died on board ship.

Our second mate, Evans, no one liked or cared for, and I know nothing of him, except that I once saw him in court, on trial for some alleged petty tyranny toward his men—still a subaltern officer.

The third mate, Mr. Hatch, a nephew of one of the owners, though only a lad on board the ship, went out chief mate the next voyage, and rose soon to command some of the finest clippers in the California and India trade, under the new order of things—a man of character, good judgment, and no little cultivation.

Of the other men before the mast in the *Alert*, I know nothing of peculiar interest. When visiting, with a party of ladies and gentlemen, one of our largest line-of-battle ships, we were escorted about the decks by a midshipman, who was explaining various matters on board, when one of the party came to me and told me that there was an old sailor there with a whistle round his neck, who looked at me and said of the officer, "*He* can't show *him* anything aboard a ship." I found him out, and, looking into his sunburned face, covered with hair, and his little eyes drawn up into the smallest passages for light—like a man who had peered into hundreds of northeasters—there was old "Sails" of the *Alert*, clothed in all the honors of boatswain's mate. We stood aside, out of the "cun" of the officers, and had a good talk over old times. I remember the contempt with which he turned on his heel to conceal his face, when the midshipman (who was a grown youth) could not tell the ladies the length of a fathom, and said it depended on circumstances. Notwithstanding his advice and consolation to "Chips," in the steerage of the *Alert*, and his story of his runaway wife and the flag-bottomed chairs (*ante*, p. 238), he confessed to me that he had tried marriage again, and had a little tenement just outside the gate of the yard.

Harry Bennett, the man who had the palsy, and was unfeelingly left on shore when the *Alert* sailed, came home in the *Pilgrim*, and I had the pleasure of helping to get him into the Massachusetts General Hospital. When he had been there about a week, I went to see him in his ward, and asked him how he got along. "Oh! First-rate usage, sir; not a hand's turn to do, and all your grub brought to you, sir." This is a sailor's paradise—not a hand's turn to do, and all your grub brought to you. But an earthly paradise may pall. Bennett got tired of indoors and stillness, and was soon out again, and set up a stall, covered with canvas, at the end of one of the bridges, where he could see all the passers-by, and turn a penny by cakes and ale. The stall in time disappeared, and I could learn nothing of his last end, if it has come.

Of the lads who, beside myself, composed the gig's crew, I know something of all but one. Our bright-eyed, quick-witted little cockswain, from the Boston public schools, Harry May, or Harry Bluff, as he was called, with all his songs and gibes, went the road to ruin as fast as the usual means could carry him. Nat, the "bucketmaker," grave and sober, left the seas, and, I believe, is a hack driver in his native town, although I have not had the luck to see him since the *Alert* hauled into her berth at the North End.

One cold winter evening, a pull at the bell, and a woman in distress wished to see me. Her poor son George—George Somerby—"you remember him, sir; he was a boy in the *Alert;* he always talks of you; he is dying in my poor house." I went with her, and in a small room, with the most scanty furniture, upon a mattress on the floor—emaciated, ashy pale, with hollow voice and sunken eyes—lay the boy George, whom we took out a small, bright boy of fourteen from a Boston public school, who fought himself into a position on board ship (*ante*, p. 221), and whom we brought home a tall, athletic youth, that might have been the pride and support of his widowed mother. There he lay, not over nineteen years of age, ruined by every vice a sailor's life absorbs. He took my hand in his wasted, feeble fingers, and talked a little with his hollow, death-smitten voice. I was to leave town the next day for a fortnight's absence, and whom had they to see to them? The mother named her landlord; she knew no one else able to do much for them. It was the name of a physician of wealth and high social position, well known in the city as the owner of many small tenements, and of whom hard things had been said as to his strictness in collecting what he thought his dues. Be that as it may, my memory associates him only with ready and active beneficence. His name has since been known the civilized world over, from his having been the victim of one of the most painful tragedies in the records of the criminal law. I tried the experiment of calling upon him; and, having drawn him away from the cheerful fire, sofa, and curtains of a luxurious parlor, I told him this simple tale of woe, of one of his tenants, unknown to him even by name. He did not hesitate; and I well remember how, in that biting, eager air, and at a late hour, he drew his cloak about his thin and bent form, and walked off with me across the Common, and to the South End, nearly two miles of an exposed walk, to the scene of misery. He gave his full share, and more, of kindness and material aid; and, as George's mother told me, on my return, had with medical aid and stores, and a clergyman, made the boy's end as comfortable and hopeful as possible.

The *Alert* made two more voyages to the coast of California, successful, and without a mishap, as usual, and was sold by Messrs. Bryant and Sturgis, in 1843, to Mr. Thomas W. Williams, a merchant of New London, Connecticut, who employed her in the whale trade in the Pacific. She was as lucky and prosperous there as in the merchant service. When I was at the Sandwich Islands in 1860, a man was introduced to me as having commanded the *Alert* on two cruises, and his friends told me that he was as proud of it as if he had commanded a frigate.

I am permitted to publish the following letter from the owner of the *Alert,* giving her later record and her historic end, captured and burned by the rebel *Alabama:*

NEW LONDON, March 17, 1868

RICHARD H. DANA, ESQ.

Dear Sir—I am happy to acknowledge the receipt of your favor of the 14th inst., and to answer your inquiries about the good ship *Alert.* I bought her of Messrs. Bryant and Sturgis, in the year 1843, for my firm of Williams and Haven, for a whaler, in which business she was successful until captured by the rebel steamer *Alabama,* September, 1862, making a period of more than nineteen years, during which she took and delivered at New London upwards of twenty-five thousand barrels of whale and sperm oil. She sailed last from this port, August 30, 1862, for Hurd's Island (the newly discovered land south of Kerguelen's), commanded by Edwin Church, and was captured and burned on the 9th of September following, only ten days out, near or close to the Azores, with thirty barrels of sperm oil on board, and while her boats were off in pursuit of whales.

The *Alert* was a favorite ship with all owners, officers, and men who had anything to do with her; and I may add almost all who heard her name asked if that was the ship the man went in who wrote the book called *Two Years Before the Mast;* and thus we feel, with you, no doubt, a sort of sympathy at her loss, and that, too, in such a manner, and by wicked acts of our own countrymen.

My partner, Mr. Haven, sends me a note from the office this P.M., saying that he had just found the last logbook, and would send up this evening a copy of the last entry on it; and if there should be anything of importance I will enclose it to you, and if you have any further inquiries to put, I will, with great pleasure, endeavor to answer them.

Remaining very respectfully and truly yours,

Thomas W. Williams

P.S. Since writing the above I have received the extract from the logbook, and enclose the same.

### The Last Entry in the Logbook of the Alert

September 9, 1862

Shortly after the ship came to the wind, with the main yard aback, we went alongside and were hoisted up, when we found we were prisoners of war, and our ship a prize to the Confederate steamer *Alabama*. We were then ordered to give up all nautical instruments and letters appertaining to any of us. Afterward we were offered the privilege, as they called it, of joining the steamer or signing a parole of honor not to serve in the army or navy of the United States. Thank God no one accepted the former of these offers. We were all then ordered to get our things ready in haste, to go on shore— the ship running off shore all the time. We were allowed four boats to go on shore in, and when we had got what things we could take in them, were ordered to get into the boats and pull for the shore—the nearest land being about fourteen miles off—which we reached in safety, and, shortly after, saw the ship in flames.

So end all our bright prospects, blasted by a gang of miscreants, who certainly can have no regard for humanity so long as they continue to foster their so-called peculiar institution, which is now destroying our country.

I love to think that our noble ship, with her long record of good service and uniform success, attractive and beloved in her life, should have passed, at her death, into the lofty regions of international jurisprudence and debate, forming a part of the body of the "Alabama Claims"; that, like a true ship, committed to her element once for all at her launching, she perished at sea, and, without an extreme use of language, we may say, a victim in the cause of her country.

R. H. D., JR.

BOSTON, May 6, 1869

SHIP

BARK

FULL-RIGGED BRIG

HERMAPHRODITE BRIG

SHIP. — A ship is square-rigged throughout; that is, she has tops, and carries square sails on all three of her masts.

BARK. — A bark is square-rigged at her fore and mainmasts, and differs from a ship in having no top, and carrying only fore-and-aft sails at her mizzenmast.

BRIG. — A full-rigged brig is square-rigged at both her masts.

HERMAPHRODITE BRIG. — An hermaphrodite brig is square-rigged at her foremast; but has no top, and only fore-and-aft sails at her mainmast.

HERMAPHRODITE BRIGS sometimes carry small square sails aloft at the main; in which case they are called BRIGANTINES, and differ from a FULL-RIGGED BRIG in that they have no top at the main-mast, and carry a fore-and-aft mainsail instead of a square mainsail and trysail.

## A SHIP'S SAILS

1 Fore topmast staysail.
2 Jib.
3 Flying jib.
4 Fore spencer.
5 Main spencer.
6 Spanker.
7 Foresail.
8 Fore topsail.
9 Fore topgallant sail.
10 Fore royal.
11 Fore skysail.
12 Mainsail.
13 Main topsail.
14 Main topgallant sail.
15 Main royal.
16 Main skysail.
17 Mizzen topsail.
18 Mizzen topgallant sail.
19 Mizzen royal.
20 Mizzen skysail.
21 Lower studdingsail.
21a Lee ditto.
22 Fore topmast studdingsail.
22a Lee ditto.
23 Fore topgallant studdingsail.
23a Lee ditto.
24 Fore royal studdingsail.
24a Lee ditto.
25 Main topmast studdingsail.
25a Lee ditto.
26 Main topgallant studdingsail.
26a Lee ditto.
27 Main royal studdingsail.
27a Lee ditto.

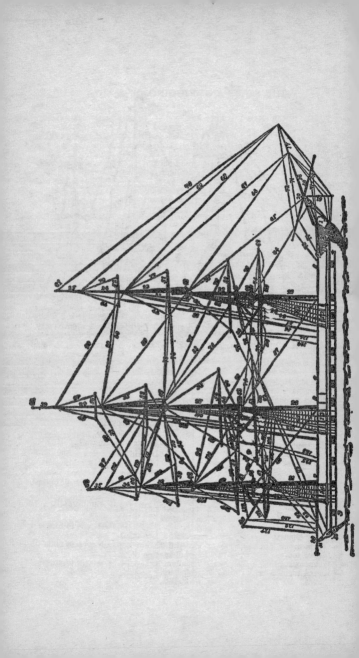

# THE SPARS AND RIGGING OF A SHIP

1 Head.
2 Head-boards.
3 Stem.
4 Bows.
5 Forecastle.
6 Waist.
7 Quarterdeck.
8 Gangway.
9 Counter.
10 Stern.
11 Tafferel.
12 Fore chains.
13 Main chains.
14 Mizzen chains.
15 Bowsprit.
16 Jib-boom.
17 Flying jib-boom.
18 Spritsail yard.
19 Martingale.
20 Bowsprit cap.
21 Foremast.
22 Fore topmast.
23 Fore topgallant mast.
24 Fore royal mast.
25 Fore skysail mast.
26 Mainmast.
27 Main topmast.
28 Main topgallant mast.
29 Main royal mast.
30 Main skysail mast.
31 Mizzenmast.
32 Mizzen topmast.
33 Mizzen topgallant mast.
34 Mizzen royal mast.
35 Mizzen skysail mast.
36 Fore spencer gaff.
37 Main spencer gaff.
38 Spanker gaff.
39 Spanker boom.
40 Fore top.
41 Foremost cap.
42 Fore topmast crosstrees.
43 Main top.
44 Mainmast cap.
45 Main topmast crossbraces.
46 Mizzen top.
47 Mizzenmast cap.
48 Mizzen topmast crosstrees.

49 Fore yard.
50 Fore topsail yard.
51 Fore topgallant yard.
52 Fore royal yard.
53 Main yard.
54 Main topsail yard.
55 Main topgallant yard.
56 Main royal yard.
57 Cross-jack yard.
58 Mizzen topsail yard.
59 Mizzen topgallant yard.
60 Mizzen royal yard.
61 Fore truck.
62 Main truck.
63 Mizzen truck.
64 Fore stay.
65 Mizzen royal yard.
66 Jib stay.
67 Fore topgallant stay.
68 Flying-jib stay.
69 Fore royal stay.
70 Fore skysail stay.
71 Jib guys.
72 Flying-jib guys.
73 Fore lifts.
74 Fore braces.
75 Fore topsail lifts.
76 Fore topsail braces.
77 Fore topgallant lifts.
78 Fore topgallant braces.
79 Fore royal lifts.
80 Fore royal braces.
81 Fore rigging.
82 Fore topmast rigging.
83 Fore topgallant shrouds.
84 Fore topmast backstays.
85 Fore topgallant backstays.
86 Fore royal backstays.
87 Main stay.
88 Main topmast stay.
89 Main topgallant stay.
90 Main royal stay.
91 Main lifts.
92 Main braces.
93 Main topsail lifts.
94 Main topsail braces.
95 Main topgallant lifts.
96 Main topgallant.
97 Main royal lifts.

98 Main royal braces.
99 Main rigging.
100 Main topmast rigging.
101 Main topgallant rigging.
102 Main topmast backstays.
103 Main topgallant backstays.
104 Main royal backstays.
105 Cross-jack lifts.
106 Cross-jack braces.
107 Mizzen topsail lifts.
108 Mizzen topsail braces.
109 Mizzen topgallant lifts.
110 Mizzen topgallant braces.
111 Mizzen royal lifts.
112 Mizzen royal braces.
113 Mizzen stay.
114 Mizzen topmast stay.
115 Mizzen topgallant stay.
116 Mizzen royal stay.
117 Mizzen skysail stay.
118 Mizzen rigging.
119 Mizzen topmast rigging.
120 Mizzen topgallant shrouds.
121 Mizzen topmast backstays.
122 Mizzen topgallant backstays.
123 Mizzen royal backstays.
124 Fore spencer vangs.
125 Main spencer vangs.
126 Spanker vangs.
127 Ensign halyards.
128 Spanker peak halyards.
129 Foot-rope to fore yard.
130 Foot-rope to main yard.
131 Foot-rope to crossjack yard.

# AFTERWORD

Van Wyck Brooks reminds us that no Massachusetts mind was ever far from the sea. At one of Margaret Fuller's conversations James Freeman Clark spoke of the beauty of American ships. Essays, he said, should be written about them, as people wrote of the art of the Greeks, for the ship was the loveliest object in the world. As he gazed at a clipper ship, Horatio Greenough exclaimed, "There is something I should not be ashamed to show Phidias!" This remark, like the age itself, looks forward and backward at the same moment: a standard of excellence from the past and a homemade example for the future. Few things could symbolize the transcendental world of longing so well as a ship.

In 1839 Herman Melville, twenty years of age, sailed as a hand for Liverpool on the *St. Lawrence*, turning on the sea eyes that henceforth seldom averted their gaze. He was home in time for publication of a book written—we might say— with him in mind: a manual for the seafarer, *Two Years Before the Mast* was also a book of sea poetry.

It seems hard, more than a century later to think of *Two Years Before the Mast* as one of the first books of its kind: a book that opened the sea to the landlocked seafaring mind. Until Dana this mind had been free to sail, but not actually to inhabit the ship in question: a difference akin to that between the covered wagon and the clouds on the horizon. Dana puts the oakum in the reader's soft hands, the sailor's lingo in his mouth.

Reasons of health—that durable prod to adventure, as valid today as when the first escapist coined it—prompted both Dana and Melville to take to the high seas. In Dana's case it was his eyes, a bookish strain from his studies at Harvard. In

376

writing his book Dana was motivated by practical concerns, rather than romantic ones—his sense of outrage and injustice at the lot of the common seaman in the Merchant Marine. As so often happens, a book hammered out for one purpose better serves another: few modern readers, finishing Dana's report, will bear in mind the injustice rather than the high adventure. The contrary is likely—the injustice will appear to be a part of it: one of the necessary hazards of the voyage, one of the trials and risks of high adventure.

In writing better than he knew, Dana did a good deal for the life of the common seaman, but we cannot adequately assess what he did for the uncommon writer and dreamer. Richard Halliburton's *Royal Road to Romance* and books that every season contribute countless detours are in the direct line of descent from Dana's *Two Years Before the Mast*. The spirit of the age speaks out in certain men who find nothing unusual in what they are saying, and in that modest estimate they are both right and wrong. Thoreau observes this when he says:

> . . . and I felt this was the heroic age itself, though we know it not, for the hero is commonly the simplest and obscurest of men.

Richard Henry Dana, Jr., one of Emerson's pupils and the son of a poet, was neither simple nor obscure, but what he made articulate was part of the age itself, and felt by the simplest men. He returned from this voyage with his eyes restored, finished his legal training at Harvard, and with concrete, practical results in mind wrote and published his manual of a seaman's life. Herman Melville, exactly four years his junior, was one of the countless young men to read, and respond, to it.

A book of real adventure has a quality distinct from what we assume to be fiction. It is easily sensed but often difficult to define. The esthetic of this distinction is perhaps summed up in Whitman's line

> I am the man, I suffer'd, I was there.

Until our experience and our sentiments are closely examined, that seems to be a basic distinction. But we are soon in trouble, since it is good fiction that leaves the most profound impression upon us. We all live, but our lives leave upon us

very blurred and inadequate impressions. To reassure ourselves that we are alive, we turn from the facts of life to fiction. If, on the other hand, we have too much of books, that
too palls and we must turn to life. Without the other, one is
always lacking: in this polarity we have the ivory tower and
the marketplace. The writer, with his eyes strained, turns to
the sea, and the sailor, with his wits dull, turns to the book:
both seek a more life-enhancing reality.

On various levels of sophistication, however, we know that
facts are not fiction: and that the *true* story is something
more, and something less, than the one that is imagined. A
different level of consciousness seems to be involved. The
reader of Defoe's *Journal of the Plague Year* feels cheated
and deceived when he learns it is fiction. He did not primarily
seek the realistic impression, or even the experience, but es-
sentially the *facts*. There are abundant facts in the fiction of
Conrad and Melville, and there is something more than facts
in Dana. Otherwise his book would go unread. The reader
of Dana will be spared, however, the increasing burden of
ponderable meaning that is currently a greater menace to the
*Pequod* than the white whale. All of that he is spared: what
he seeks and finds is what it is like to sail before the mast.
If there are depths to fathom, they are in the reader, rather
than the book.

The facts of Dana's voyage could be summed up, as they
often have been, on the flap of the jacket. Other facts, let us
say like those in *Walden*, are no more than data if taken out
of their context. When Thoreau lists the materials that went
into his house, and then those on which he lived, and what
these things cost him

| | | |
|---|---|---|
| House | $28 | 12½ |
| Farm, one year | 14 | 72½ |
| Food, eight months | 8 | 74 |
| Clothing, etc., eight months | 8 | 40¾ |

few poetical passages in literature will compare with the elo-
quence of these simple figures. But taken out of the context
of his experience they are nothing but signs on a piece of
shelf paper, notes that we daily jot down on a telephone pad.

Nor is it an accident that Dana and Thoreau were neighbors and contemporaries. If one half of the New England
mind was transcendental, the other half was acutely fact-

conscious. The poetry inherent in commonplace things was about to find its voice in Whitman, but it is already fully conscious in Thoreau.

When Dana writes:

> . . . . Tarring the stays is more difficult, and is done by an operation which the sailors call "riding down." A long piece of rope—topgallant-studding-sail halyards, or something of the kind—is taken up to the masthead from which the stay leads, and rove through a block for a girtline, or, as the sailors usually call it, a gantline; with the end of this a bowline is taken round the stay, into which a man gets with his bucket of tar and bunch of oakum, and the other end being fast on deck, with someone to tend it, he is lowered down gradually, and tars the stay carefully as he goes. . . . In this manner I tarred down all the head stays, but found the rigging about the jib booms, martingale, and spritsail yard, upon which I was afterward put, the hardest. Here you have to "hang on with your eyelids" and tar with your hands.

he is not self-aware, as a poet, might be, that he is giving us more than accurate information, but neither would he detail such artifacts if he were not aware of their import to the reader. I have no conception what a *martingale* is, but there is spray in my face when the word is sounded. I too hang on with my eyelids and tar with my hands.

A skillful, novelistic use of detail occurs where he reports as in a diary . . .

> *Monday, November 10th.* During a part of this day we were hove to, but the rest of the time were driving on, under close-reefed sails, with a heavy sea, a strong gale, and frequent squalls of hail and snow.
> *Tuesday, November 11th.* The same.
> *Wednesday.* The same.
> *Thursday.* The same.

The laconic repetition of the word "same" conveys not only information, data, but experience. This is the way the man at sea—or the man on the plains—apprehends *time*.

It is perhaps to our advantage as readers that a tragedy occurred on the voyage out, while Dana's senses were alert to the resonance of this experience, a death at sea.

> Death is at all times solemn, but never so much as at sea. A man dies on shore; his body remains with his friends, and "the mourners go about the streets"; but when a man falls

overboard at sea and is lost, there is a suddenness in the
event, and a difficulty in realizing it, which give to it an air
of awful mystery. A man dies on shore—you follow his body
to the grave, and a stone marks the spot. You are often prepared for the event. There is always something which helps
you to realize it when it happens, and to recall it when it
has passed. A man is shot down by your side in battle, and
the mangled body remains an object, and a real evidence;
but at sea, the man is near you—at your side—you hear his
voice, and in an instant he is gone, and nothing but a vacancy
shows his loss. Then, too, at sea—to use a homely but expressive phrase—you miss a man so much.

This passage has something of the power, as well as the
style and manner, of Donne's celebrated *Devotions*. It gives
rise to the feeling that Dana is something more of a poet than
either he or his contemporaries were aware: and that his ignorance of this gift was both a loss to him as well as to us.

Here he describes an iceberg, sighted near the Horn:

. . . And there lay, floating in the ocean, several miles off,
an immense, irregular mass, its top and points covered with
snow, and its center of a deep indigo color. . . . As far as
the eye could reach, the sea in every direction was of a deep
blue color, the waves running high and fresh, and sparkling
in the light, and in the midst lay this immense mountain island, its cavities and valleys thrown into deep shade, and its
points and pinnacles glittering in the sun. . . . But no description can give any idea of the strangeness, splendor, and,
really, the sublimity, of the sight. Its great size . . . its slow
motion, as its base rose and sank in the water, and its high
points nodded against the clouds; the dashing of the waves
upon it, which, breaking high with foam, lined its base with
a white crust; and the thundering sound of the cracking of
the mass, and the breaking and tumbling down of huge pieces;
together with its nearness and approach, which added a slight
element of fear—all combined to give to it the character of
sublimity.

If this reminds us of Melville, other passages seem to anticipate him.

. . . but one of the finest sights that I have ever seen was an
albatross asleep upon the water, during a calm, off Cape
Horn, when a heavy sea was running. There being no breeze,
the surface of the water was unbroken, but a long, heavy
swell was rolling, and we saw the fellow, all white, directly

ahead of us, asleep upon the waves, with his head under his wing; now rising on the top of one of the big billows, and then falling slowly until he was lost in the hollow between. He was undisturbed for some time, until the noise of our bows, gradually approaching, roused him, when, lifting his head, he stared upon us for a moment, and then spread his wide wings and took his flight.

Vivid and suggestive as these passages are, one can also sense in what manner a writer like Melville would have improved upon them, but this very *want* of polish contributes to the reality of the impression. It has immediacy, some of the phases read like notes: we are not led to feel that he has improved on the experience by recollecting it too well in tranquillity. It gains in being closer to what we might have felt ourselves, had we been there.

The extent to which young Dana spoke to Melville, a young man with his eyes and ears wide open, is superficially apparent everywhere, but has, as well, its profound reaches. Of special interest is the English sailor, Bill Jackson. Dana describes him in this manner:

. . . He was tall; but you only perceived it when he was standing by the side of others, for the great breadth of his shoulders and chest made him appear but little above the middle height. His chest was as deep as it was wide, his arm like that of Hercules, and his hand "the fist of a tar—every hair a rope yarn." With all this, he had one of the pleasantest smiles I ever saw. His cheeks were of a handsome brown, his teeth brilliantly white, and his hair, of a raven black, waved in loose curls all over his head and fine, open forehead; and his eyes he might have sold to a duchess at the price of diamonds, for their brilliancy. . . . Take him with his well-varnished black tarpaulin, stuck upon the back of his head, his long locks coming down almost into his eyes, his white duck trousers and shirt, blue jacket, and black kerchief, tied loosely round his neck, and he was a fine specimen of manly beauty. . . . His strength must have been great, and he had the sight of a vulture. It is strange that one should be so minute in the description of an unknown, outcast sailor, whom one may never see again, and whom no one may care to hear about; yet so it is. Some persons we see under no remarkable circumstances, but whom, for some reason or other, we never forget. He called himself Bill Jackson. . . .

If we think—and if we know him, we can't help it—of Melville's Billy Budd, this is a strange and memorable passage indeed. Can we doubt the impression it made on the twenty-year-old Herman Melville? Almost fifty years later, Melville evokes Billy Budd, a fine specimen of manly beauty, in this manner:

> . . . As little did he observe that something about him pro-voked an ambiguous smile in one or two harder faces among the bluejackets. Nor less unaware was he of the peculiar favorable effect his person and demeanor had upon the more intelligent gentlemen of the quarter-deck. Nor could this well have been otherwise. Cast in a mold peculiar to the finest physical examples of those Englishmen in whom the Saxon strain would seem not at all to partake of any Norman or other admixture, he showed in face that humane look of re-poseful good nature which the Greek sculptor in some in-stances gave to his heroic strong man, Hercules. But this again was subtly modified by another and pervasive quality. The ear, small and shapely, the arch of the foot, the curve in mouth and nostril, even the indurated hand dyed to the orange-tawny of the toucan's bill, a hand telling of the hal-yards and tar-buckets. But, above all, something in the mo-bile expression, and every chance attitude and movement, something suggestive of a mother eminently favored by Love and the Graces. . . .

Just as it is Art that makes upon the artist an impression superior to that made by nature, I am persuaded that the manly sailor of Dana made upon the young Melville an ever-lasting impression of the "Handsome Sailor," an image upon which he could graft the nuances and complexities of his own intentions. A further and still more persuasive point, in my opinion, is that both men seem more open to manly beauty than to feminine. One might think that after months at sea the sight of Spanish señoritas, at a dance in California, would rouse in Dana some dream of feminine beauty: but on this subject he is not merely restrained, but indifferent. It is Bill Jackson, the manly sailor, who stirs him, as it does Melville, to a concept of ideal beauty.

It will be easy for some readers, as it was for me, to forget that this book was conceived as a protest and written to im-prove the lot of the common sailor. The protest is there, but it blends with the experience, and we feel such hardships are necessary to two years before the mast. Other readers might feel that too much space is given to Dana's landlocked stay in California, where for months on end no mast of any sort is in sight. But to the reader of 1840 these descriptions would have been welcome. California was a new word as well as a new place. In ten years it would spring into panic and prominence. Long trips around the Horn would soon bring gold-seekers who preferred death by water to the ordeal by covered wagon. The armchair traveler learns of this new world through Dana's eyes. On the natives he speaks with a distinctly fastidious accent:

> The Californians are an idle, thriftless people, and can make nothing for themselves. The country abounds in grapes, yet they buy, at a great price, bad wine made in Boston and brought round by us. . . .

The note on grapes is of interest, and may have been remarked by many a prospective vintner.

Although Dana describes life on board simply and clearly, certain details, of interest to the modern reader, go unmentioned. Neither his temperament, nor the times, were appropriate. The life of men without women would receive a different emphasis today. It is the very absence of this emphasis, on which the modern reader is sated, that gives to his report, strange as it should seem, a manliness and a sanity that the sex-ridden adventure curiously lacks, where men are too often reduced to the state of sick animals. Seeing how much can be said without it, would many modern readers wish it inserted? I doubt it. It is one of the obsessions that the modern mind seeks to escape. In Dana's civilized, well-bred mind, a concept of what a *man* is is always present; this unspoken assurance gives the book its character. Boys soon to be men have long found in it much food for thought. If masts are not so high as they once seemed, the sea still takes and gives a man's measure, and the depth of the sea may prove to be more profound than space. From it life once emerged, and if necessary it will emerge again.

WRIGHT MORRIS

# SELECTED BIBLIOGRAPHY

### OTHER WORKS BY RICHARD HENRY DANA, JR.

*The Seaman's Friend* (1841)
*To Cuba and Back; A Vacation Voyage* (1859)
*Speeches in Stirring Times and Letters to a Son* (1910)
Metzdorf, R. F. (ed.) *Autobiographical Sketch (1815–1842)*. Hamden, Connecticut; Shoe String Press Inc., 1953.

### BIBLIOGRAPHY & CRITICISM

Johnson, J. S. *On Richard Henry Dana and Two Years Before the Mast*. San Francisco: Windsor Press, 1936.
Shapiro, S. *Richard Henry Dana, Jr. 1815–1882*. East Lansing, Michigan: Michigan State University Press, 1961.

# A NOTE ON THE TEXT

*Two Years Before the Mast* was first published in 1840. This Signet Classic is a reprint of the "New Edition, with Subsequent Matter by the Author," which was published by Houghton, Mifflin and Company in 1869. The spelling and punctuation have been brought into conformity with modern American style.